D0560096

COCAINE

COCAINE
A CLINICIAN'S HANDBOOK

edited by

ARNOLD M. WASHTON
The Washton Institute

MARK S. GOLD
Fair Oaks Hospital

THE GUILFORD PRESS
New York London

© 1987 The Guilford Press
A Division of Guilford Publications, Inc.
200 Park Avenue South, New York, New York 10003

All rights reserved

No part of this book may be reproduced, stored in a retrieval system, or transmitted, in any form or by any means, electronic, mechanical, photocopying, microfilming, recording, or otherwise, without written permission from the Publisher.

Printed in the United States of America

Last digit is print number: 9 8 7 6 5 4 3 2 1

Library of Congress Cataloging-in-Publication Data

Cocaine : a clinician's handbook.

  Includes bibliographies and index.
  1. Cocaine habit.   I. Washton, Arnold M.   II. Gold,
Mark S.   [DNLM: 1. Cocaine. 2. Substance Dependence.
WM 280 C6588]
RC568.C6C625   1987   616.86′3   87–12015
ISBN 0-89862-725-7

616. 8647
C659 w
238420

Contributors

CAROL ATKINSON, PhD, Addiction Research and Treatment Service, Department of Psychiatry, University of Colorado School of Medicine, Denver, Colorado.

SHEILA B. BLUME, MD, Alcoholism and Compulsive Gambling Programs, South Oaks Hospital, Amityville, New York; Department of Psychiatry, State University of New York at Stony Brook, Stony Brook, New York.

IRA J. CHASNOFF, MD, Departments of Pediatrics and Psychiatry, Northwestern University Medical School, Chicago, Illinois.

SIDNEY COHEN, MD, Neuropsychiatric Institute, School of Medicine, University of California at Los Angeles, Los Angeles, California.

THOMAS J. CROWLEY, MD, Addiction Research and Treatment Service, Department of Psychiatry, University of Colorado School of Medicine, Denver, Colorado.

CHARLES A. DACKIS, MD, Hampton Hospital, Mount Holly, New Jersey.

ROBERT L. DUPONT, MD, Bensinger, DuPont & Associates, Inc., Rockville, Maryland; Center for Behavioral Medicine, Rockville, Maryland; Department of Psychiatry, Georgetown University Medical School, Washington, DC.

TODD WILK ESTROFF, MD, Research Facilities, Fair Oaks Hospital, Summit, New Jersey; Gulf Coast Hospital, Fort Walton Beach, Florida.

IRL EXTEIN, MD, Fair Oaks Hospital at Boca/Delray, Delray Beach, Florida.

FRANK GAWIN, MD, Yale University School of Medicine, New Haven, Connecticut; Cocaine Abuse Treatment Program, APT Foundation, New Haven, Connecticut.

MARK S. GOLD, MD, Fair Oaks Hospital, Summit, New Jersey.

REESE T. JONES, MD, Department of Psychiatry and Langley Porter Neuropsychiatric Institute, University of California, San Francisco, San Francisco, California.

E. J. KHANTZIAN, MD, Department of Psychiatry, Harvard Medical School at The Cambridge Hospital, Cambridge, Massachusetts.

LAWRENCE S. KIRSTEIN, MD, Regent Hospital, New York, New York.

HERBERT KLEBER, MD, Yale University School of Medicine, New

Haven, Connecticut; Substance Abuse Treatment Unit, Connecticut Mental Health Center and APT Foundation, New Haven Connecticut.

SUSAN KRILL-SMITH, MSW, Private practice, Denver, Colorado.

HENRY R. LESIEUR, PhD, Department of Sociology and Anthropology, St. John's University, Jamaica, New York; Consultant, South Oaks Foundation, Amityville, New York.

ROBERT B. MILLMAN, MD, Department of Psychiatry and Public Health, Payne Whitney Clinic, New York Hospital–Cornell Medical Center, New York, New York.

ELLEN R. MOREHOUSE, ACSW, CAC, Student Assistance Services, White Plains, New York.

ROBERT SBRIGLIO, MD, Liberation Programs, Inc., Stamford, Connecticut.

SIDNEY H. SCHNOLL, MD, PhD, Departments of Medicine and Psychiatry, Medical College of Virginia, Richmond, Virginia.

BRAD SELGESTAD, JD, MD, Private practice, Denver, Colorado.

RONALD K. SIEGEL, PhD, Department of Psychiatry and Biobehavioral Sciences, School of Medicine, University of California at Los Angeles, Los Angeles, California.

KARL VEREBEY, PhD, New York State Division of Substance Abuse Services Testing and Research Laboratory, Brooklyn, New York; Department of Psychiatry, SUNY Health Science Center at Brooklyn, Brooklyn, New York.

ARNOLD M. WASHTON, PhD, The Washton Institute, New York, New York, and Ardsley, New York.

CHARLES V. WETLI, MD, Metropolitan Dade County Medical Examiner Department, Miami, Florida; Department of Pathology, University of Miami School of Medicine, Miami, Florida.

Contents

Preface   **xiii**

Introduction   **xv**
ARNOLD M. WASHTON

PART ONE   BASIC AND BIOMEDICAL ISSUES   1

1   Causes of the Cocaine Outbreak   3
SIDNEY COHEN

Supply Factors   3
External Factors   4
Internal Factors   5
Intrinsic Drug Factors   6
Discussion   7
Summary   8

2   Recent Trends in Cocaine Abuse as Seen from the "800-Cocaine" Hotline   10
ARNOLD M. WASHTON AND MARK S. GOLD

The First Cocaine Hotline   10
National Survey: 1983   12
A Comparison of National Surveys   15
Adolescent Cocaine Use   17
Cocaine Use in the Workplace   19
Comment   19

3   Medical and Biological Consequences of Cocaine Abuse   23
TODD WILK ESTROFF

Cocaine-Induced Sudden Death   23
Delayed Deaths   24
Nonfatal Acute Medical Complications   25
Tanking Up   25
Chronic Medical Complications   26
Chronic Problems Common to All Routes   26
Intranasal Cocaine Use   27

Intravenous Cocaine Use   27
Crack—Free-Base Cocaine   28
Coca Paste Smokers   28
Psychiatric Complications   29
Self-Medicating with Cocaine   30
Chemical Brain Changes   30
Summary   31

4   **Fatal Reactions to Cocaine**   33
CHARLES V. WETLI

Historical Perspective   33
Introduction   34
Fatal Cocaine Overdose from Recreational Use   35
Medical Complications and Sudden Death from
   Intravenous Cocaine Abuse   38
Deaths from the Nasal Use of Cocaine   42
Deaths from the Use of Cocaine During Sexual Activity   42
Smoking Cocaine   43
The Body Packer Syndrome   44
Cardiovascular Deaths Due to Cocaine   45
Cocaine Psychosis and Sudden Death   47
Infectious Complications of Cocaine Abuse   49
Profile of Cocaine Fatalities   50

5   **Psychopharmacology of Cocaine**   55
REESE T. JONES

Historical Notes   55
Chemistry   56
Routes of Administration   56
Cocaine Effects on Brain Function   58
Mechanisms of Action   59
Metabolism   61
Absorption   62
Tolerance   65
Dependence   67
Interactions with Other Drugs   67

6   **Brain Mechanisms in Cocaine Dependency**   73
IRL EXTEIN AND CHARLES A. DACKIS

Neuropharmacology of Cocaine   73
Cocaine Dependency   74
Brain Pleasure Systems, Cocaine, and Dopamine   76

Effects of Cocaine on Specific Neurotransmitters   77
Catecholamine Depletion Hypothesis of Cocaine
    Dependency and Withdrawal   79
Hormonal Changes in Cocaine Dependency   80
Pharmacological Treatments in Cocaine Dependency   81
Summary and Conclusions   82

PART TWO   TREATMENT APPROACHES   85

7   **Emergency Treatment of Acute Cocaine Reactions   87**
    ROBERT SBRIGLIO AND ROBERT B. MILLMAN

    Cocaine Preparations   88
    Adverse Effects   88
    Acute Cocaine Reactions   90
    Summary   93

8   **Inpatient Cocaine Abuse Treatment   96**
    LAWRENCE S. KIRSTEIN

    Evaluation   98
    Rehabilitation   101
    Discharge Planning   104
    Summary   105

9   **Outpatient Treatment Techniques   106**
    ARNOLD M. WASHTON

    Contraindications for Outpatient Treatment   107
    Treatment Goals   108
    Urine Testing   108
    Phases of Treatment   109
    Cocaine Recovery Groups   114
    Other Interventions   115
    Psychiatric Issues   116
    Success Rates   117

10 **Pharmacological Treatments of Cocaine Abuse   118**
    HERBERT D. KLEBER AND FRANK H. GAWIN

    If Cocaine Is Being Used for Self-Medication,
        What Is It Treating?   119
    General Treatments   121
    Comparisons to Psychotherapeutic Interventions   131
    Conclusions   131

11 Treating Adolescent Cocaine Abusers   135
ELLEN R. MOREHOUSE

Extent of the Problem   135
Assessment   137
Treatment Planning   138
Issues in Adolescent Treatment   138
The Beginning Phase of Treatment   141
Preparing for Abstinence   142
Scheduling Outpatient Sessions   142
Value of Groups   143
Contacts with Parents   144
Finding Alternatives   145
Other Issues   148
Conclusion   150

12 A Treatment for Cocaine-Abusing Health Care Professionals   152
THOMAS J. CROWLEY, SUSAN KRILL-SMITH, CAROL ATKINSON,
AND BRAD SELGESTAD

Description of the Sample   153
Procedures in Evaluation and Treatment   156
Problems of Outcome Research   168
Confidentiality and Contingency Contracting among
      Health Care Professionals   169
Conclusions   170

PART THREE   SPECIAL TOPICS   173

**13 Cocaine Smoking: Nature and Extent of Coca Paste and Cocaine
     Free-Base Abuse   175**
RONALD K. SIEGEL

Definitions   175
History   176
Epidemiology   178
Problems of Preparing and Smoking Cocaine Free Base   181
Clinical Features of Cocaine Smoking   183
Overview   188

14 Cocaine in the Workplace: The Ticking Time Bomb   192
ROBERT L. DuPONT

15 Alcohol Problems in Cocaine Abusers   202
SHEILA B. BLUME

Drinking Patterns in Cocaine Abusers   202
Treatment Considerations   203
Adjuncts to Treatment for the Dual Abusers   204
Family Alcoholism   205
A Note on the Cocaine Abuser Who Enrolls in
    an Alcoholism Program   205
Summary   205

Appendix 15A: Information for Those Taking Antabuse   206

16 Pathological Gambling in Cocaine Abusers   208
SHEILA B. BLUME AND HENRY R. LESIEUR

Pathological Gambling in Cocaine Abusers:
    Why Be Concerned?   208
Pathological Gambling: An Addiction without a Drug   209
Characteristics of Cocaine Abusers with Problems Related
    to Gambling   209
Diagnosis of Pathological Gambling   210
Prevention of Pathological Gambling in Cocaine Abusers   211
Identification of Pathological Gamblers   212
Treatment Considerations   212
Summary   213

17 Cocaine Abuse Detection by Laboratory Methods   214
KARL VEREBEY

Cocaine Disposition   217
The Metabolic Products of Cocaine   218
Methods of Analysis, Sensitivity, and Cost   219
Correlation between Behavioral Effects and Concentration
    of Cocaine and BE   220
Concentration of Cocaine and BE in Blood and Urine   221
The Time Frame of Detection of Cocaine and BE   222
Choice of Body Fluid, Collection, and Specimen Handling   224
The Reliability of Testing: Interpretation of Test Results   225
Conclusion   226

**18 Psychiatric and Psychodynamic Factors in Cocaine
Dependence   229**
E. J. KHANTZIAN

Recent Findings in Addicts: General   230
Cocaine Dependence   234
Comments and Conclusion   237

19 Consequences of Cocaine and Other Drug Use in Pregnancy   241
IRA J. CHASNOFF AND SIDNEY H. SCHNOLL

Neonatal Assessment   245
Infant Assessment   246

Index   253

Preface

This book is written primarily for health care professionals—psychologists, psychiatrists, physicians, social workers, nurses, drug and alcohol abuse counselors, and other medical or mental health clinicians. It is intended to provide clinically useful information on a wide range of topics relevant to the treatment of cocaine dependence and other cocaine-related problems.

As much as we would like to take credit for conceiving the idea of this book, it rightfully belongs to many of the colleagues we encountered from 1983 through 1985 during the course of a heavy schedule of professional conferences and other speaking engagements all across the United States. We each received countless requests for written information about cocaine and the treatment of cocaine dependence from clinicians of many different disciplines who attended our presentations and lectures. When we originally presented the idea for this book to Seymour Weingarten, editor-in-chief of Guilford Press, he responded enthusiastically and almost without hesitation, readily seeing that there was a pressing need for a professional book on cocaine written specifically for clinicians. Similarly, when we originally contacted the contributors to this volume, all of whom are recognized authorities on their respective topics, they were enthusiastic about the project and readily made the commitment to submit a chapter despite numerous other obligations.

Although this book focuses on the singular topic of cocaine, it is not based on a single treatment approach or theoretical orientation. As an edited volume, it represents a collection of chapters by authors who come from a variety of professional orientations and backgrounds. We have attempted here to bring together in a single volume the collective wisdom and experience of some of the leading authorities in the chemical dependency field. To a large extent, the topics that we chose to cover in this book were determined by the availability of experts on specific topics, rather than by a preconceived master plan of the book's contents.

This book is by no means exhaustive on the subject of cocaine. Because of unforeseen and unavoidable circumstances, three additional chapters that were scheduled to appear could not be completed in time to meet the publication deadline. Their topics were family treatment approaches, special issues in the treatment of female cocaine abusers, and the role of self-help groups in recovery from cocaine. Already running far behind schedule, we were faced with the extremely difficult choice of either further postponing publication of the book or publishing it without these three chapters. Although we have no doubt that these chapters would have significantly broadened and enhanced this volume, we had to yield to the pressures of time on us and on our publisher.

This book does not profess to be a compendium of scientific facts about cocaine, nor does it offer the final word on each topic that is covered. The treatment of cocaine problems must be considered a relatively new field, one in which effective treatment approaches are just starting to be developed. Therefore, we specifically asked all contributors to share with our readers the benefits of their *experience* rather than giving an exhaustive review of their topic. In this connection, it is important for our readers to be aware of the instructions and guidelines we gave to the authors. We asked each author: (1) to focus very specifically on clinically relevant material; (2) to convey to the reader practical, useful information based on the author's direct clinical experience, and not to withhold clinical impressions, opinions, and suggestions—even if not yet scientifically validated; (3) to avoid lengthy literature reviews and extensive presentations of research data; (4) to write in a style acceptable to clinicians from a variety of disciplines, both medical and nonmedical; and (5) to be brief and to the point on the designated topic. It appears that all were successful in this task.

We are grateful to our contributors for taking time out of their hectic, overbooked schedules to share their knowledge and experience. We are grateful to Seymour Weingarten, Rennie Childress, and the others at Guilford Press for helping to make this book a reality. We are especially grateful to our concerned and dedicated colleagues who made us aware of the need for this book. Perhaps most of all, we are grateful to the many victims of cocaine dependence who have taught us almost everything we know about the problem.

Arnold M. Washton
Mark S. Gold

Introduction

ARNOLD M. WASHTON

The treatment of cocaine dependence and cocaine-related problems is one of the most critical issues in the substance abuse field today. The escalation of cocaine use across most areas of the United States and the dramatic increase in the number of cocaine users seeking treatment have placed new and unanticipated demands on the existing treatment system. Most alcohol and drug abuse treatment programs were established before the recent demand for cocaine-specific treatment, and are now finding it necessary to adapt their treatment strategies in order to accommodate the needs of this new clientele.

The escalation of cocaine use is affecting other segments of the health care system as well. Cocaine users are appearing with increasing frequency at hospital emergency rooms, health clinics, mental health facilities, and private clinicians' offices seeking help for many different types of drug-related medical and psychiatric problems. Often the patient's presenting complaint is something other than cocaine. Often the clinician is not especially familiar with alcohol or drug problems. Often, then, there is a failure to properly identify, diagnose, and treat the patient's cocaine problem. The result for the patient can be devastating, or even fatal.

The Clinical Challenge

The cocaine problem in the United States has posed new challenges to the field of substance abuse treatment. It has forced a reevaluation of traditional definitions of *addiction* and *addictive drugs*. It has helped to reduce some of the long-standing barriers between alcohol and drug abuse treatment. And it has forced the existing treatment system to expand and alter its services, the better to accommodate the needs of the middle-class addict.

Redefining Addiction

Until recently, cocaine was viewed as a relatively safe drug that did not lead to addiction. Even those who were willing to concede that cocaine might be

Arnold M. Washton, The Washton Institute, New York, New York, and Ardsley, New York.

somewhat more habit-forming than alcohol or marijuana were likely to describe it as having the potential to cause only *psychological* dependence, not the more ominous problem of *physical* addiction like that produced by heroin or other so-called physically addicting drugs.

The word *addiction* has serious implications for most people. The possibility of becoming an "addict" is disconcerting, and most people are inclined to avoid using a drug that is considered "addictive." Unfortunately, the absence of a dramatic withdrawal syndrome following cocaine use creates artificial confidence in occasional and regular users alike. Most assume they are not exposing themselves to the potential danger of developing an addiction and that their use of the drug can be controlled by willpower alone, whenever they might choose to exert it.

Cocaine has shown us that it is probably better to define *addiction* in terms of certain behaviors associated with a drug rather than by the presence or absence of a withdrawal syndrome following its use. It is not withdrawal symptoms that lock a person into compulsive cocaine use but, rather, the reinforcing effects of the drug, both positive and negative, in conjunction with drug-induced chemical changes in brain activity. Many clinicians have now opted for defining addiction as a loss of control over intake of a drug that leads to its compulsive use despite adverse effects to the person's health or psychosocial functioning. The presence of a physical withdrawal syndrome with certain drugs may be only one factor (and not always the most significant one) that contributes to compulsive use. The compulsion to use cocaine seems to develop from a combination of at least several factors, including the extreme but short-lived euphoria, the unpleasant rebound dysphoria, and lingering feelings of anhedonia and depression that may persist for several days or weeks after stopping cocaine use. In addition, recent evidence indicates that cocaine causes significant biochemical changes in the brain that give rise to the repeated cravings and urges for the drug that drive compulsive use. In this way, cocaine may indeed be physically addicting although it causes no dramatic withdrawal syndrome. Chemical changes in brain activity caused by cocaine are certainly no less physical than some of the classic withdrawal symptoms associated with other drugs. Thus, cocaine has broadened our view of addiction and has prompted further scientific inquiry into the effects of mood-altering drugs on the brain.

Drugs versus Alcohol: Bridging the Gap

Another by-product of the cocaine problem in the United States has been a reduction in some of the traditional barriers between alcohol and drug abuse treatment. One reason is that very few cocaine users are involved only with cocaine. The use of alcohol among cocaine users is extremely common.

In addition, many cocaine users become involved with tranquillizers, sleeping pills, marijuana, or opiates in order to self-medicate the unpleasant side effects of cocaine. In the process, some become multiply addicted. Similarly, in recent years an increasing number of alcoholics have become involved with cocaine. These developments have begun to break down the long-standing stereotypes held by drug addicts and alcoholics about each other and by the respective groups of clinicians who treat them. The so-called pure alcoholic or drug addict is rapidly becoming extinct. Not only are more chemical abusers combining drugs and alcohol, but, moreover, alcohol has become recognized as a major factor in relapse to drugs just as drugs have become recognized as a major factor in relapse to alcohol. In an increasing number of cases, the two problems have become inseparable or synonymous. Self-help groups for drug addicts such as Cocaine Anonymous (CA) and Narcotics Anonymous (NA), based on the same Twelve Step program as the original Alcoholics Anonymous (AA), have begun to flourish in many parts of the country. Despite earlier biases, an increasing number of AA meetings have become receptive to including drug addicts, and vice versa.

All these developments have lent further acceptance and usefulness to the generic concepts of chemical dependency and addictive disease, regardless of the particular substances involved. They have also underscored the importance of total abstinence from all mood-altering chemicals as a desirable treatment goal for drug addicts and alcoholics alike. It is not surprising that clinicians who treat alcoholism are finding it necessary to understand drug problems in order to be effective with their patients. Likewise, clinicians who treat drug addicts are finding it equally necessary to understand alcohol problems. It has become essential that these areas of professional training overlap. Interaction between these two professional groups and their respective regulatory and funding bureaucracies has begun to develop.

The Middle-Class Addict

The middle-class cocaine abuser has presented new challenges to the treatment system. There is a subgroup among these users with a markedly different demographic and clinical profile from that of the majority who have appeared for drug abuse treatment in the past. Typically, they are employed (often in highly skilled or professional jobs), are well educated, earn substantial incomes, have no criminal history, have good family support systems, have no history of drug addiction before cocaine, and have no current or past psychiatric illness. Among the changes that have been prompted by this subgroup are: (1) a proliferation of private facilities offering a high level of confidentiality, privacy, and professional care required to attract such clients into treatment, and (2) an increasing emphasis on outpatient treatment and shorter length of residential stays to minimize disruption to the patient's employment.

Crack

The recent appearance of "crack" has presented additional challenges to the treatment system. If nothing else, it has led to an increased demand for treatment. Smoking cocaine free base or crack (the name given to preprepared chunks of free base sold on the street) often leads to a pattern of rapidly escalating, compulsive use and a tenacious addiction. In contrast to snorting cocaine powder, smoking free base is usually not associated with a prolonged period of occasional use before the user becomes addicted. Moreover, crack users who appear for treatment are often experiencing severe psychiatric symptoms, including paranoid delusions, severe depression, volatility, and suicidal or homicidal ideation. Crack users pose a special challenge for the development of effective treatment techniques.

Aim and Scope of This Book

The aim of this book is to give clinicians information that is directly relevant to the treatment of cocaine abusers. The length and style of the book is tailored to the practicing clinician interested in the subject matter but short on time. A wide range of topics are covered, but every chapter addresses clinically relevant issues. Each chapter is intentionally succinct and focused.

The book is divided into three major sections: Part One, Basic and Biomedical Issues; Part Two, Treatment Approaches; and Part Three, Special Topics.

Part One addresses a variety of basic issues: the causes of the cocaine epidemic; the profile of cocaine users and their associated problems; the medical consequences of cocaine; death from cocaine; the psychopharmacology of cocaine; and brain mechanisms underlying cocaine dependency.

Part Two focuses on treatment issues: acute reactions and medical emergencies associated with cocaine use; inpatient treatment approaches; outpatient treatment approaches; pharmacological treatments for cocaine dependence; and special treatment techniques for two subgroups of cocaine abusers—adolescents and health care professionals.

Part Three deals with special clinical problems associated with smoking cocaine free base or crack, with the combined use of cocaine and alcohol, and with the use of cocaine during pregnancy. The interesting association between cocaine use and pathological gambling is also explored.

COCAINE

PART ONE

BASIC AND BIOMEDICAL ISSUES

1

Causes of the Cocaine Outbreak

SIDNEY COHEN

Thirty years after its isolation from coca leaves in 1885, cocaine was being misused by uncritical physicians who mistook its powerful stimulant properties as cures for depression, morphine addiction, chronic tuberculosis, and a long list of other disorders. In retrospect, it is easy to say that it was simply mood elevation that they were observing, not actual cures. Then, as the disheartening adverse effects of high-dose or consistent cocaine use were identified, this first outbreak of cocainism subsided about a decade after its onset.

The extravagant claims of the prescribers and their patients left a more sustaining effect. A large number of patent medicines containing cocaine, especially those touted for asthma and hay fever, were almost pure cocaine. The tonics, elixirs, and fluid-extracts containing cocaine or coca kept the use of the substance alive until 1906 when the Pure Food and Drug Act required the proper labeling of cocaine "and other narcotics" on proprietary medicines. The Harrison Act of 1914 dealt the final blow to the cocaine-containing patent medicines by forbidding their manufacture and sale.

But this was by no means the end of the story. As early as 1911 an international conference on the illicit trafficking of cocaine was held. There were to be many others. The point is that, on the periphery of society, microcultures of cocaine snorters, swallowers, and shooters still existed. Cocaine use hit a low point during the 1930s when the advent of the amphetamines almost eradicated demand. But it persisted, with fluctuations, until the 1970s when the current epidemic became evident.

What can be said about the causes of the present upsurge in cocaine use? The many contributing factors to the current outbreak of cocainism are the subject of this chapter.

Supply Factors

The infrastructure was in place. Despite the low-level activity on the illegal cocaine market before 1970, supply channels from South America, at least

Sidney Cohen. Neuropsychiatric Institute, School of Medicine, University of California at Los Angeles, Los Angeles, California.

to the larger cities, were established. As the demand grew, the basic supply net could be expanded, and later enormously extended to every city in the country.

It is believed that demand for the drug drove supplies, although later on easy availability probably fostered demand. The question, therefore, is why demand grew so significantly. As demand increased, the need for coca leaves was met by vast increases in the planting of coca bushes both in the countries that traditionally grew them, Bolivia and Peru, and in other lands like Colombia and Ecuador, and more recently Brazil, Argentina, Venezuela, and others (Cohen, 1985). Efforts to control this crop have been only partially successful. It is believed that more coca leaves are harvested now than during any previous period.

Traditionally, the coca leaves were first harvested after 2 or 3 years. Using the *epadu* variety, the leaves can be gathered in 6 months, speeding up the processing of cocaine significantly.

Availability. Availability is defined here to mean the presence of the drug in sufficient quantities to satisfy users' needs at a cost that is not prohibitive. In the recent past, the price of cocaine ($3,000 per ounce of adulterated material) was so high that it served as a deterrent to frequent use for most people. In recent years costs have decreased, the quality has improved, and supplies remain abundant. In many northwestern South American cities, the price of coca paste is so low that even the indigent can afford it. This has resulted in an enormous problem with very large numbers of cocaine-dependent people in countries like Peru, Bolivia, and Columbia (Jeri, 1984). In the United States recent flooding of the marketplace with crack—ready-to-use free base in $10 or $20 packages—has resulted in an upsurge of new consumers.

Affluence. During the past 5 years disposable income has increased and the price of cocaine has come down. This encourages new consumer groups to try this prestigious drug. Wealth is a negative prognostic factor in cocaine users because it provides unlimited access to the drug.

External Factors

Peer pressure. Peer persuasion and peer cocaine use are potent factors in initiating and perpetuating cocaine indulgence. Parties where cocaine is available cause the non-user to assume that snorting is an acceptable habit. If the cocaine habit were not spread by the friendship group, few people would become involved. The donor's motives may be either to share the pleasures of the drug or to recruit more people to buy his or her cocaine.

Media encouragement. During the first years of cocaine's ascendancy it was not unusual to see television and films either remarking on the drug favorably or at least showing casual cocaine use. Even the identification of stars who had overdone cocaine and were in rehabilitation helped to glamorize the drug. The audiovisual media are potent in shaping of values and behaviors, especially for young people. More recently, permissive media attitudes about cocaine have essentially disappeared.

The prevailing cocaine mythology. As the cultural proscriptions against the use of illicit and licit drugs for "recreational" purposes were broached during the 1960s, cocaine use became a part of the drug scene. Snorting was the initial mode, and most experimenters were occasional consumers. They experienced the cocaine euphoria and nothing untoward happened. Of course, since these intrepid chemical explorers were ignorant of the cocaine disasters of the late 1880s (Jones, 1961), the fictitious notion arose that cocaine was harmless, an opinion that has persisted to this day in some circles. The immediate pleasurable reaction and costliness (because demand exceeded supplies) made cocaine the champagne of drugs, attracting the wealthy, their hangers-on, and the famous, which in turn gave it added glamor. Cocaine was "in." Consumers believed the worst that could happen was a hole in the nose, whereas we now know that that is the least of the cocaine abuser's problems (Cohen, 1984). At any rate, intelligent people were sucked into the cocaine trap out of ignorance. What kept them in was the initial experience of euphoria and cocaine-induced feelings of competency.

Internal Factors

Susceptibility and predisposition. Inevitably, people with certain personality and character disorders will be overrepresented among all drug abusers. This is apparently true of cocainists.

On the other hand, it is undeniable that persons whose history and behavioral patterns could hardly merit a psychiatric diagnosis have also become locked into compulsive cocaine use. The first exposure may have been induced by curiosity or a willingness to accept the enthusiastic descriptions of friends. Over months or years the infrequent sniffing may gradually become incessant and out of control. The person who started using cocaine, not to treat psychological pain but just for fun, now attempts to quit or cut down. Success is infrequent, however, because now the psychological pain can be extreme as a result of reward-center dysfunctions. Kleber and Gawin (1984) report a high percentage of diagnoses from the *Diagnostic and Statistical Manual of Mental Disorders*, 3rd edition (DSM-III) (American Psychiatric Association, 1980) diagnoses in chronic cocaine users, but other clinicians indicate that most of their cocaine abusers could not be given a psychiatric diagnosis prior to their involvement.

It is difficult to agree with the statement that "those individuals who characteristically deal with stress with active confrontation with their environment choose stimulant drugs" (Milkman & Shaffer, 1985). This hypothesis has never been demonstrated by research or clinical experience. Cocaine dependency is characterized by multiple drug use with depressants such as alcohol representing a frequent second abused drug. What is the character structure of those who also use sedatives, stimulants, hallucinogens, and so forth?

Those people who have low thresholds for ambiguity and dissonance or have high levels of anxiety or hopelessness obtain sufficient relief of their noxious feelings to become consistent users of a drug like cocaine. In effect they are prescribing cocaine for their emotional disorders. Without supervision, however, psychoactive drugs, especially cocaine, can be precarious.

Hedonism and sociopathy.   It is said that we live in a time of "pleasure now, pay later." If so, cocaine is the perfect chemical for our times. The pleasure is *now*, instantly if a rapid delivery method is used. About one-quarter of all users will pay later at an exorbitant price.

The hedonistic philosophy is often associated with societal decadence, which might be defined as a widespread loss of goals, values, and feelings of personal and community responsibility. Under such conditions the option to use pleasure-giving or frustration-removing drugs is readily exercised.

Those with an antisocial personality disorder seem particularly liable to have a substance abuse problem, and cocaine is particularly attractive to them. They are apt to become low-level distributors of the chemical and may be seen more frequently in treatment situations than in the criminal justice system.

Depression.   It can also be said that we are living in an age of depression, one filled (like many others), with forebodings and menacing threats. Cocaine may be an apt drug for depressives in search of relief. It cannot resolve the depression, but may provide some transient surcease—which keeps the depressed customer coming back.

Life stress.   Disabling stress is considered a strong feature of this era, because of the rate of social and technological change, the depersonalization of society, and the lack of acceptable goals and values. It is difficult to believe that these pressures exceed the stresses felt by previous generations. Nevertheless, many athletes, performing artists, and executives believe they need the boost in self-esteem and the racing mental function that cocaine can produce.

Intrinsic Drug Factors

The pharmacologic imperative.   If some sinister master chemist wanted to design a drug that would predictably entrap large numbers of its users, it would resemble cocaine. Cocaine scores a "10" on the euphoria scale, and the reward is immediate. Its brief period of activity necessitates frequent refills, and that means more intense conditioning to continue the drug-seeking behavior. Over time, with recurrent use, tolerance develops so that more of the drug is needed to achieve the earlier elation. As tolerance to the euphoriant effect evolves, the point will be reached when the doses no longer elicit pleasure, but, in fact, displeasure is experienced. Contrary to common sense, the compulsion to continue use persists, partly because of the intense conditioning, partly because the dysphoria demands the hope of relief.

If our master chemist really wanted to control large populations, he or she would have to make the drug affordable to all. This poses no problem for cocaine because, without interference, a dose can be made as inexpensive as a cigarette.

Discussion

This assortment of causes contributing to cocaine use requires reanalysis to extract those of primary importance. Although any one of the contributory factors may be sufficient to initiate and perpetuate use, some are more powerful inducers than others.

Availability is a potent element—a necessary, though not sufficient, factor in the genesis of cocaine use. Attempts to decrease availability as a preventive measure are appropriate, because making any drug more difficult to obtain has been shown to result in a somewhat reduced prevalence. On the other hand, with cocaine around at a low cost, it would seem impossible to contain the epidemic. Therefore, efforts to reduce both supply and demand must be made simultaneously.

Suggestions to legalize all drugs have been made in the press out of frustration over the apparent inability to deal with our drug problem. From what we know of cocaine's reinforcing properties, this approach would be an unmitigated disaster.

Peer persuasion is a significant contributor to the induction of cocaine use and sometimes to its perpetuation. As used here, *peers* would include spouse, parents, children, and siblings. For some, refusing a proffered line or two of cocaine is exceedingly difficult. In some circles, not using cocaine makes it difficult to participate in most conversations.

Ignorance about cocaine and its consequences ranks high in any listing of causes. Many people would never become involved with cocaine if they had an accurate perception of its problems. This does not mean that reciting the possible outcomes will induce any user to desist, but non-users may benefit from accurate information by not becoming involved. What can alter cocaine-using behavior is seeing one's acquaintances lose life, the liberty of choice, and the pursuit of happiness because of cocaine.

If our present outbreak is one day contained, this does not mean that future cocaine crazes will not appear. The lessons of the past are never learned or are soon forgotten. Cocaine, at first, is a very seductive drug. The fact that it can lead to an unhappy ending is never considered until the unhappiness begins.

Cocaine's pharmacology keeps the user using. The euphoria is so brief that it resembles an incomplete orgasm. The mainliner, the free baser, and the coca paste smoker are driven to keep trying to get back to that momentary high. As their reward areas are bathed in an oversupply of dopamine, they become tolerant of stimulation, even refractory to it. They reach a point where nothing is rewarding, neither cocaine nor life's pleasures. In an effort to get out of this emotional black hole, they take more cocaine—and more again—without effect. Thus the snow freak—the cocaine abuser—is in an intolerable bind.

The pursuit of happiness, the search for a "high," is a pervasive human drive. Does this mean that periodic escalations of chemical euphoriant use are inevitable? As we scan the past, the answer would seem to be "yes." Our species has not yet achieved the ability to deal successfully with stress and dysphoria. Neither have we quite succeeded in living life gladly. We seem to be incomplete creatures: *Homo sapiens* is not yet sapient. Therefore, many people are likely to seek positive mood-changing substances for some time to come. This does not mean that the large numbers of people who survive without intoxicants are less content, less happy. On the contrary, the nature of chemical consciousness change is such that the pleasures of drugs do not seem to be sustaining. Unlike memories of an actual pleasure-giving experience, they cannot be relished in retrospect.

It is too much to expect that all of us will someday be wise enough to enjoy the "sober certainty of waking bliss." But it is not impossible to assume that many or most of us will be able to look beyond the immediate pleasures of a drug like cocaine to the longer-term consequences and then make an informed decision about benefits and costs.

Summary

Cocaine is accessible to increasing consumer markets, and is now pandemic rather than epidemic in its spread, having invaded North America, much of South America, western Europe, and cities in the Far East. Induction into cocaine use occurs primarily when groups of friends push the drug onto the novice. The novice's ignorance and misinformation about cocaine's effects over time makes his or her entry into a cocaine user's career easy. Finally, the pharmacologic action of the drug makes extrication problematic even after everything has been lost.

Stimulant epidemics tend to be short. For example, the first cocaine flare-up subsided with a few years, and the speed outburst of the 1970s was over in about 3 or 4 years. For some of the reasons already stated, our current problem may be an exception, and it is difficult to discern an end at this time.

REFERENCES

American Psychiatric Association. (1980). *Diagnostic and statistical manual of mental disorders* (3rd ed.). Washington, DC: Author.

Cohen, S. (1984). Recent developments in the abuse of cocaine. *Bulletin on Narcotics, 36,* 3-14.

Cohen, S. (1985). *Cocaine: The bottom line.* Rockville, MD: American Council on Drug Education.

Jeri, F. R. (1984). Coca paste smoking in some Latin American countries: A severe and unabated form of addiction. *Bulletin on Narcotics, 36,* 15-32.

Jones, E. (1961). *The life and work of Sigmund Freud.* New York: Basic Books.

Kleber, H. D., & Gawin, F. H. (1984). A review of current and experimental treatments. In J. Grabowski (Ed.), *Cocaine: Pharmacology, effects and treatment of abuse,* NIDA Research Monograph No. 50 (pp. 111-129). Washington, DC: U.S. Government Printing Office.

Milkman, H. B., & Shaffer, H. J. (Eds.). (1985). *The addictions: Multidisciplinary perspectives and treatments.* Lexington, MA: Lexington Books.

2

Recent Trends in Cocaine Abuse as Seen from the "800-Cocaine" Hotline

ARNOLD M. WASHTON AND MARK S. GOLD

In this chapter we describe recent trends in cocaine use in the United States as seen from surveying a large number of callers to the "800-COCAINE" hotline over the past three years. We begin by briefly recounting how the hotline was first established. We then summarize a succession of hotline surveys. Finally, we compare our hotline findings with other sources of information on cocaine use.

The First Cocaine Hotline

In January 1983 the first telephone hotline specifically for cocaine users was established by the first author (AMW) to serve the New York metropolitan area. The idea for the hotline emerged from a series of clinical experiences and observations by the author in late 1982 while working in a publicly funded research and treatment program for heroin addicts in the East Harlem section of New York City. Despite the fact that this clinic was located in a high-crime ghetto area and was devoted almost exclusively to treating intravenous (IV) heroin addicts, the author started to receive an increasing number of calls from employed, middle-class cocaine users who had been trying unsuccessfully to find help for their drug problem.

The complaints from most of these people were roughly the same:

1. They knew they had become "addicted" to cocaine in the sense of being unable to stop using the drug despite the onset of serious drug-related problems.

2. While attempting to seek help for their problem, they had been told by others that cocaine was nonaddictive and, therefore, formal treatment was neither necessary nor available.

3. They knew of many other people who also were having similar problems.

Arnold M. Washton. The Washton Institute, New York, New York, and Ardsley, New York.

Mark S. Gold. Fair Oaks Hospital, Summit, New Jersey.

At that time not a single drug abuse treatment clinic in New York was offering a specific program for cocaine abusers. The author proceeded to establish the first program of this type in December 1982 and asked several local radio stations to play a public service announcement stating that anyone wanting help for a "cocaine problem" could call a special hotline telephone number. Callers were assured complete anonymity and confidentiality. The response was astounding. Beginning on the very first day of these announcements, the hotline started to receive hundreds of calls from cocaine abusers and from others who were concerned about someone with a cocaine problem.

In addition to exposing a large area of unmet need for information and treatment, the New York hotline presented a unique opportunity to conduct pioneering research. From among the hundreds of callers to the hotline each day, a random sample of 55 was selected to participate in an anonymous telephone research interview lasting about 30–40 minutes. The interview was based on an extensive research questionnaire that was designed to collect information on the demographics of the callers, their history and current patterns of cocaine use, their use of other drugs, the effects and side effects of cocaine, and a wide range of possible drug-related medical, psychiatric, and social problems.

The results of this survey (Washton & Tatarsky, 1984) not only provided one of the first profiles of cocaine users, but also supplied dramatic evidence of severe, compulsive patterns of cocaine use associated with numerous adverse effects to the user's health and functioning. The typical respondent in this random sample was a white, middle-class male, 25–35 years old, with no prior history of drug addiction or psychiatric illness. Nearly all said they felt addicted to cocaine and unable to stop using the drug despite the many problems it was causing.

These early hotline experiences caught the attention of both local and national media, and before long many people from places far outside New York were calling the hotline for help. It was becoming increasingly clear that cocaine problems were prevalent not only in New York, but in many other parts of the United States as well.

In May 1983, the "800-COCAINE" line (Gold, 1984), a national toll-free hotline, was established to serve the entire country. This 24-hour service quickly attracted nationwide publicity and within the first 3 months of its operation received calls from more than 37 different states across the United States. The hotline received an average of at least 1,400 calls per day and logged over 1.5 million calls in its first 3 years.

The national hotline also provided a unique opportunity for research. Surveys on the hotline have included over 4,000 cocaine users who have cooperated in efforts to study different aspects of the phenomenon. These studies provide one of the few available sources of information about changes in the cocaine epidemic, such as trends or shifts in patterns of cocaine use in the United States. Comparing the reuslts of hotline surveys taken at different points in time has helped to detect some of the major trends in cocaine abuse over the past 3 years. The details of these surveys have been published in at least several reports (Washton & Gold, 1984; Washton, Gold, & Pottash, 1983; Washton, Gold, Pottash, & Semlitz, 1984), but in this chapter we will focus on the major findings with particular emphasis on changing patterns and trends. Our discussion will begin with the first national survey conducted in 1983 and its comparison with a subsequent survey in 1985. Surveys of adolescent cocaine users and of cocaine use in the workplace will also be presented.

Before presenting the survey results, it is important to acknowledge that certain inherent methodological limitations influence the interpretation of the hotline data. For one, hotline callers must be considered to be a skewed sample of respondents, since they include many individuals whose problem with cocaine is likely to be more severe than that of other users who might not seek any form of assistance. There is no doubt that hotline callers do not represent all cocaine users, and, indeed, may selectively exclude those in earlier stages of drug use as well as those who have not yet experienced significant drug-related problems. (This problem also applies to studies of treatment populations.) Second, the geographic distribution of respondents is distinctly unrepresentative of a true cross-section of cocaine users in the United States. The volume of calls from a particular geographic area of the country is influenced to a significant degree by the amount of media attention the hotline receives in that area at a given point in time and by the temporal relationship between this publicity and the data collection process. Finally, one must take into account that our data were collected entirely by telephone from anonymous callers. Whereas on the other hand the freedom to report anonymously is exactly what has made the surveys possible, the accuracy of the callers' responses and their tendency either to exaggerate or to downplay the extent of their drug problem can be questioned. With these caveats in mind, perhaps the hotline surveys should be viewed as no more than rough indicators of emerging patterns and trends.

National Survey: 1983

The first national survey (Washton et al., 1983) was based on a random sample of 500 callers to the hotline during its initial 3 months of operation, May–July 1983. The sample included callers from 37 different states across the United States, with the majority being from New York, New Jersey, California, and Florida, which collectively represented 63% of the entire sample. Each caller voluntarily consented to an anonymous 30–40 minute telephone interview in which the research questionnaire was administered.

This study amplified and extended the earlier New York hotline survey by Washton & Tatarsky (1984). It provided the first multistate demographic profile of cocaine users in the United States and more fully described the phenomenon of cocaine dependency and its consequences.

The average age of the 500 respondents was 30, with most being between 25 and 40 years old at the time of their call to the hotline. The youngest callers were 16, the oldest 78. Sixty-seven percent were male, 33% female. The overwhelming majority (85%) were white; 15% were black or Hispanic. Many were well educated, on average having completed just over 14 years of schooling. The sample included many college graduates, degreed professionals, and highly skilled business executives and technicians. Forty percent had incomes over $25,000 per year.

The respondents had begun their use of cocaine an average of 4.9 years before calling the hotline, and over 90% had started with intranasal use (snorting). At the time of their call, 61% were taking the drug intranasally, 21% were free-base smoking, and 18% were intravenous users. About half the sample were using cocaine daily, at a street cost of $75–$150 per gram. Many reported binge patterns of use in which they used the drug continuously for 2 or 3 days at a time until their supply of the drug, money, or physical energy was totally exhausted. Some said they used the drug only on weekends. On average they were using about 6 grams per week, although this ranged from 1 to 32 grams per week. They said they had been spending an average of $637 per week for cocaine during the week before they called the hotline, with a range from about $100 to $3,200. The vast majority of callers (80%) said that when the cocaine high wore off, they felt depressed, irritable, restless, and drained of energy—a rebound dysphoric reaction commonly referred to as the cocaine "crash." The importance of the crash lies in the fact that 68% of the respondents said that in order to alleviate the unpleasant aftereffects of cocaine they were led to abuse other drugs such as alcohol, sleeping pills, tranquilizers, or opiates. This finding revealed that cocaine abuse is likely to promote polydrug abuse and dependence. Many of the callers had become multiply dependent on a combination of cocaine, alcohol, and tranquilizers.

The questionnaire included a series of items to probe the issue of drug dependency and addiction. Callers were asked to indicate which, if any, of the items characterized their involvement with cocaine. Their replies provide clear evidence of the dependence-producing capacity of the drug and its ability to dominate the user even in the face of extreme negative consequences. Overall, 61% said they felt addicted to cocaine; 83% said they could not turn down the drug when it was available; 73% said they had lost control and could not limit their cocaine use; 67% said they had been unable to stop using cocaine except for brief periods lasting no longer than a month. Over half the respondents said that cocaine had become more important to them than food, sex, recreational activities, social relationships, and job or career. Although it had become clear that cocaine use was impairing their functioning, most said that they feared feeling distressed and unable to function properly without the drug.

Their compulsion to continue using cocaine despite serious adverse effects became even more clearly evident from the questionnaire items on drug-related consequences to health and functioning. This section of the questionnaire included a total of 59 items on physical, psychological, and social problems associated with cocaine use.

Over 90% of the respondents reported five or more adverse effects that they attributed to their cocaine use. The five leading physical problems were chronic insomnia (82%), chronic fatigue (76%), severe headaches (60%), nasal and sinus infections (56%), and disrupted sexual functioning (55%). Other serious physical problems included cocaine-induced brain seizures with loss of consciousness (reported by 14% of the sample) and nausea and vomiting (reported by 39%). The leading psychological problems were depression, anxiety, and irritability, each reported by more than 80% of the sample. Paranoia, loss of interest in non-drug-related activities, difficulty concentrating, and loss of non-drug-using friends were each reported by more than 60%. Nine percent reported a cocaine-induced suicide attempt.

Numerous personal and social problems were also reported. For example, 45% said they had stolen money from their employers and from family or friends to support their cocaine habit. Most were in debt, having spent all their monetary assets on cocaine. Some had mortgaged their home, lost their business or profession, squandered their inheritance or trust fund, or sold their valuables for cocaine. Thirty-six percent said they had dealt drugs to support their cocaine habit; 26% reported marital or relationship problems ending in separation or divorce; 17% had lost a job because of cocaine; 12% had been arrested for a drug-related crime (dealing or possession of cocaine), and 11% reported a cocaine-related automobile accident.

It is commonly believed that people who use cocaine only by snorting it are immune to becoming dependent on the drug or from suffering serious adverse consequences. Our earlier clinical experience, however, did not support this view nor did the large numbers of intranasal users who called the hotline to report serious problems (Washton et al., 1983). We therefore made a special effort to examine our survey data for a comparison between the different routes of drug administration (Washton & Gold, 1984). We found that intranasal users reported patterns and consequences of cocaine use similar to those of free-base and IV users. The incidence and types of consequences reported by each group of users were comparable to one another, with one major difference: The free-base and IV users tended to show greater disruption of psychosocial functioning and were more likely to report nearly all of the most serious ill effects. For example, free-base and IV users reported higher rates of cocaine-related brain seizures, automobile accidents, job loss, and extreme paranoia. This finding may have been at least partly due to the higher dosages of cocaine used by the free-base and IV groups. Intranasal users who reported comparably high levels of use also reported comparably serious adverse effects. The data suggested that possibly another important difference between the different methods of using cocaine is the speed at which the user becomes addicted. Intranasal users typically reported a rather long period of occasional nonproblematic use, sometimes 2–4 years, before becoming dependent on the drug. Those who started out with free-base or IV use or who later switched to these methods after an initial period of snorting cocaine said that their drug use had reached problematic levels almost immediately—relatively few described their free-base or IV use, even in its beginning stages, as "recreational" or nonproblematic. Most felt they were overcome almost immediately by irresistible drug cravings.

A Comparison of National Surveys

Table 2-1 compares selected results of the 1983 survey with a similar survey conducted almost 2 years later in 1985 (unpublished). These data reveal a number of significant shifts in patterns of cocaine use, as outlined in this section.

The proportion of hotline calls from the southern and midwestern regions of the United States has increased significantly, although the absolute number of calls remain highest from the northeastern and western regions of the country. This finding indicates that cocaine use has spread to virtually all areas of the United States, including many small towns and rural areas that in 1983 were thought to be largely exempt from the cocaine epidemic. The hotline continues to receive calls from many sparsely populated areas of the country, including small towns in Wyoming, Montana, Mississippi, New Mexico, Alabama, and other states. Large cities and adjoining suburbs in the Northeast, California, and Florida continue to show the highest absolute volume of calls.

The profile of hotline callers has changed substantially since 1983 when most callers were white middle- and upper-class employed males between the ages of 25 and 35. With the continuing spread of cocaine use over the past 2 years, it appears that a broader cross-section of the American population has become involved in this phenomenon. As a result, no single demographic profile accurately describes the majority of cocaine users: There is no longer a "typical" user. The data in Table 2-1 indicate increasing cocaine use among women, minority groups, lower income groups, and adolescents. The major demographic shifts can be summarized as follows:

1. *Women.* In 1983 female cocaine abusers made up about one-third of

TABLE 2-1. Comparison of Two "Hotline" Surveys: 1983 and 1985[a]

	1983	1985
Origin of calls		
Northeast	47%	32%
Midwest	11%	23%
West	33%	22%
South	9%	23%
Demographics		
Males	67%	58%
Females	33%	42%
Whites	85%	64%
Blacks/Hispanics	15%	36%
Average age	30 yr	27 yr
Adolescents	1%	7%
Yearly income:		
$0–$25,000	60%	73%
Over $25,000	40%	27%
Cocaine Use		
Consumption	6.5 gm/wk	7.2 gm/wk
Expenditure	$637	$535
Intranasal	61%	52%
Free base	21%	30%
Intravenous	18%	18%
Use of other drugs to alleviate cocaine side effects	68%	87%
Auto accident on cocaine	11%	19%
Use of cocaine at work	42%	74%

[a]Each survey is based on a random sample of 500 callers during a 3-month time period: May–July 1983 and January–March 1985.

the randomly sampled callers to the hotline. In 1985 they make up nearly half of the callers. Our more detailed surveys of female callers reveal that the vast majority (87%) are introduced to cocaine by a male companion and often receive "gifts" of cocaine from men, indicative of how the drug has become incorporated into social relationships. On average, women report using less cocaine than men and are less likely to resort to drug dealing as a way to support their use. However, women are more likely than men to report extreme depression due to chronic cocaine use and to exchange sexual favors for the drug.

2. *Minority and Lower Income Groups.* The proportion of black and Hispanic callers has more than doubled since 1983. Similarly, more callers now report earning less than $25,000 per year.

3. *Adolescents.* The average age of callers has decreased, reflecting the spreading use of cocaine among younger users, including adolescents, college students, and other young adults. For adolescents aged 13–19 there has been a sevenfold increase in the percentage of hotline calls since 1983. A specific survey of adolescent cocaine users is presented later in this chapter.

The surveys indicate that levels of cocaine use have increased, as shown by the callers' self-reported estimates of weekly consumption. There has also been an increasing tendency for users to shift from snorting cocaine to free-base smoking. The data further indicate that the price of cocaine on the illicit market has dropped considerably, from an average of approximately $98 per gram (gm) in 1983 to about $75/gm in 1985.

Our surveys show an increasing problem of polydrug abuse among current cocaine abusers. With increasing levels of cocaine consumption, users say they are more likely to resort to other drugs and alcohol in order to relieve the unpleasant side effects of cocaine. Abuse of alcohol and sedative–hypnotic drugs appears to be the rule rather than the exception among current cocaine abusers.

Cocaine-related automobile accidents reported by hotline callers have nearly doubled since 1983. In 1985 nearly one-fifth of all callers said they had had at least one automobile accident resulting in personal injury or property damage while under the influence of cocaine or a combination of cocaine and other drugs. The opposing effects of stimulants and depressants that differ with regard to the onset and duration of their actions appear to create an especially dangerous situation. Because cocaine's short-term stimulant effects temporarily mask the depressant effects of alcohol, cocaine users are able to consume a large quantity of alcohol without initially feeling the intoxicating effects of the alcohol, which might otherwise lead them to refrain from driving. When the cocaine wears off in only 20–30 minutes, the driver may suddenly become severely intoxicated or even stuporous from the alcohol, with resulting gross and unexpected impairment of driving ability.

The percentage of callers who say they use cocaine at work increased sharply from 42% in 1983 to 74% in 1985. A more detailed survey of cocaine use in the workplace is presented later in this chapter.

Adolescent Cocaine Use

Our surveys show dramatic increases in cocaine use by adolescents. In a specific survey of adolescent cocaine users (Washton et al., 1984), we interviewed 100 randomly selected hotline callers who were between the ages of 13 and 19. The interview included a structured research questionnaire requiring a 30–40 minute telephone interview.

Survey Results. A descriptive profile of the adolescent sample is shown in Table 2-2. Most were white male high school students in the 11th or 12th grade, with many from urban and suburban middle-class families. The time lag between snorting their first line of cocaine and evidence of cocaine-related disruption of functioning that led them to call the hotline averaged 1.5 years, as contrasted with over 4 years in adult survey samples. Most were snorting cocaine, although 12% had switched to more intensified

TABLE 2-2. Adolescent Cocaine Abusers ($N = 100$)

Demographics		Current Use	
Males	65%	Consumption	1.4 gm/wk
Whites	83%	Expenditure	$95/wk
Average age	16.2 yr	Intranasal	88%
Average education	11.4 yr	Free base	10%
		Intravenous	2%
First use			
Time before call	1.5 yr	*Use of Other Drugs to*	
Intranasal	100%	*Relieve Cocaine Side Effects*:	
		Marijuana	92%
		Alcohol	85%
		Sedatives	64%
		Heroin	4%

methods of use. Nearly every subject reported multiple, combination drug use. Cocaine was often combined with or followed immediately by use of marijuana, alcohol, and sedative–hypnotic drugs, usually to counteract cocaine's unpleasant side effects. Most said that they were purchasing drugs from schoolmates and older users or dealers, often in or around school premises.

A wide range of cocaine-related medical, social, psychiatric, and school problems were reported by the adolescent respondents. School performance was reported to have suffered considerably because of the continuing cocaine use and its resulting problems. Seventy-five percent had missed days of school, 69% said their grades had dropped significantly, 48% had experienced disciplinary problems due to drug-related disruption of mood and behavior, and 31% had been expelled for cocaine-related difficulties. To support their escalating drug use, 44% had been selling drugs; 31% were stealing from family, friends, or employer; and 62% were using lunch or travel money or income from a part-time job to buy drugs. Among the most serious drug-related consequences were cocaine-induced brain seizures with loss of consciousness (19%), automobile accidents (13%), suicide attempts (14%), and violent behavior (27%). As with adult users, common complaints included insomnia, fatigue, depression, irritability, shortness of temper, paranoia, headaches, nasal and sinus problems, poor appetite, weight loss, memory and concentration problems, and heart palpitations. In most cases, loss of interest in non-drug-using friends, family activities, and sports or hobbies was also reported. Nearly all the subjects said that the only limit on their cocaine use was money: If they had more money, they would use more cocaine. The results of this survey show that adolescents do indeed have sufficient access to cocaine to become serious abusers and that their vulnerability to the dependence-producing properties of the drug and to disruption of functioning may be greater than that of adults.

Cocaine Use in the Workplace

The problem of drug use in the workplace is a matter of rapidly escalating concern, not only to employers but also to society at large. The scope of this problem in terms of cocaine's negative impact on individual health and safety and on the nation's economy is just beginning to be recognized. It seemed to us that if most cocaine users are employed, then there must be a great deal of cocaine and other drug use occurring in the workplace. To our knowledge, no previous attempts had been made to study this phenomenon by actually interviewing drug-using employees. A random sample of 227 employed cocaine abusers who called the hotline were interviewed about their drug use on the job.

Survey Results. The demographic profile of these drug-using employees was as follows: 70% were male; 61% were white; 53% were 20–29 years old, 40% were 30–39 years old, and 7% were 40 years old or over; 67% earned under $25,000 per year; 32% earned $26,000–50,000, and 1% earned over $50,000. Their occupations included the following: automobile mechanic, attorney, stockbroker, legal secretary, salesperson, real estate agent, airline flight attendant, dentist, nurse, optician, pharmacist, physician, laboratory technician, bank executive, prison guard, carpenter, electrician, office clerk, postal employee, public utility worker, security guard, computer programmer, retail store owner, pipe fitter, bus driver, and railway switchman.

Seventy-four percent said they used drugs at work. This includes respondents who said that they had self-administered drugs during working hours (or breaks), as well as those who had come to work while already under the influence of drugs. The types of drugs used at work were cocaine (83%), alcohol (39%), marijuana (33%), sedative–hypnotics (13%), and opiates (10%). (The total of these percentages exceeds 100% because most subjects reported multiple drug use.) Sixty-four percent said that drugs were readily obtainable at their place of work, and 44% said they had dealt drugs to fellow employees. Twenty-six percent reported being fired from at least one previous job because of drug-related problems; 39% feared that a raise in salary would lead to further escalation of their drug use. Eighteen percent said they had stolen money from co-workers in order to buy drugs, and 20% reported having been involved in at least one drug-related accident on the job.

Comment

Clearly, cocaine abuse has grown from what appeared to be a relatively minor problem in the 1960s and 1970s to a major public health problem today. Government reports issued in 1973 (National Commission on Marijuana and Drug Abuse, 1973; Strategy Council on Drug Abuse, 1973) concluded that problems associated with cocaine use did not appear to be significant and that few who used the drug actually sought professional help in drug abuse treatment programs or elsewhere. It was further stated that there had been no confirmed cases of cocaine overdose deaths. Unfortunately, these reports and others in the medical literature (e.g., Van Dyke & Byck, 1982) have served to legitimize and fuel the myth that cocaine is harmless and nonaddictive. The apparent low rates of problematic cocaine use in the early 1970s were probably more the result of the drug's high price and limited availability, rather than its presumed low potential for abuse.

As seen from our hotline surveys and other sources, the situation today has changed dramatically. There is now clear-cut evidence that cocaine use can lead to addiction and to severe drug-related consequences. The academic debates about whether or not cocaine is truly addictive will probably continue, but the behavioral evidence is indisputable.

Consistent with our hotline experience, government surveys in the past few years, as reviewed by Adams and Durell (1984), show that the prevalence of cocaine use in the United States has increased significantly since the late 1970s. Similarly, there have been significant increases in the occurrence of medical consequences related to cocaine use, as documented by government statistics on cocaine-related emergency room episodes, deaths, and admissions to government-sponsored treatment programs (Kozel, Crider, & Adams, 1982).

In addition to an overall increase in the prevalence òf cocaine abuse and its health consequences, the hotline surveys have identified other noteworthy trends. Here, too, the major findings are consistent with government surveys (Adams & Durrel, 1984). The hotline data show major demographic shifts in user profiles indicating increased cocaine use among women, minority groups, lower income groups, and adolescents. It has become abundantly clear that cocaine use is no longer restricted primarily to white middle- and upper-class adult males. A major contributor to this spreading use has been the increasing availability of cocaine at reduced prices, which has made the drug more accessible to a much larger segment of the population. On average, a gram of cocaine is now cheaper than an ounce of marijuana in many places across the United States. The greater accessibility to cocaine has no doubt also contributed to more intensified use among current users, as reflected in the higher dosages reported by hotline callers and the increasing popularity of free-base smoking—a method of administration that almost invariably leads to more compulsive, higher-dose use. A 1982 government report (Kozel et al., 1982) indicated a dramatic increase in cocaine free basing, from 1% of treatment admissions in 1979 to almost 7% in 1982. The recent appearance of "crack" has further intensified this problem, as discussed in Chapter 13 in this book.

The greater tendency toward polydrug abuse reported by hotline callers is also supported by the 1982 government report (Kozel *et al.*, 1982) which stated that 82% of all primary cocaine abusers admitted to government treatment programs said they were experiencing at least one other concurrent drug problem. This phenomenon could be explained by the fact that as an individual's cocaine abuse intensifies so do the negative aftereffects of the cocaine, thus creating a greater need to alleviate these aftereffects with other substances.

The presumed safety of intranasal cocaine use has been challenged consistently in all of the hotline surveys. Intranasal users continue to account for over 50% of callers to the hotline and for the majority of treatment admissions for cocaine problems in our own programs and elsewhere. Consistent with the survey findings, other observations (Adams, 1982) indicate that both free-base smoking and IV use of cocaine are more likely to engender daily, compulsive use patterns than does intranasal use. Nonetheless, the potential dangers of snorting cocaine should not be underestimated. In addition to problems of addiction and drug-related dysfunction, there have been instances of death from intranasal cocaine verified by coroner's reports (Wetli & Wright, 1979).

One might hope that the current upsurge in cocaine use would be a short-lived, temporary phenomenon—a passing fad that would dissipate as quickly as it seemed to appear. Unfortunately, this seems highly unlikely. The current cocaine epidemic has already become too pervasive, and indications are that it is still growing at a rate that would make rapid resolution of the problem all but impossible. The enormous profits of the illicit cocaine industry have resulted in increased production and supplies of the drug and a powerful motivation to continue making the drug available to as large a segment of the U.S. population as possible. Since there is often a time lag of several years between the onset of cocaine use and its escalation to the point where the user is driven to seek help, the peak effects of the current epidemic in the United States may not be seen for several years to come. Although public education and other prevention efforts may help to discourage future experimentation, at present it appears that if supplies of the drug continue to increase while prices continue to decline, the current epidemic is likely to become even more widespread and intensified.

REFERENCES

Adams, E. H. (1982). *Abuse/availability trends of cocaine in the United States: Drug surveillance reports, 1982* (Volume 2). Rockville, MD: NIDA Division of Epidemiology and Statistical Reports.

Adams, E. H., & Durell, J. (1984). Cocaine: A growing public health problem. In J. Grabowski (Ed.), *Cocaine: Pharmacology, effects, and treatment of abuse*, NIDA Research Monograph No. 50 (DHHS Publication No. ADM 84-1326, pp. 9-14). Washington, DC: U.S. Government Printing Office.

Gold, M. S. (1984). *800-Cocaine*. New York: Bantam Books.

Kozel, N. J., Crider, P. A., Adams, E. H. (1982). *National surveillance of cocaine use and related health consequences* (DHHS Publication No. CDC 82-8017). Atlanta, GA: Centers for Disease Control. Also published in *Morbidity and Mortality Weekly Report, 20,* No. 31, 265-273.

National Commission on Marihuana and Drug Abuse. (1973, March). *Drug use in America: Problem in perspective.* Second report of the National Commission on Marijuana and Drug Abuse. Washington, DC: National Institute on Drug Abuse.

Strategy Council on Drug Abuse. (1973). *Federal strategy for drug abuse and drug traffic prevention, 1973.* Washington, DC: U.S. Government Printing Office.

Van Dyke, C., & Byck, R. (1982). Cocaine. *Scientific American, 246,* 128-141.

Washton, A. M., & Gold, M. S. (1984). Chronic cocaine abuse: Evidence for adverse effects on health and functioning. *Psychiatric Annals, 14,* 773-743.

Washton, A. M., Gold, M. S., & Pottash, A. C. (1983). Intranasal cocaine addiction. *Lancet,* p. 1378 (letter).

Washton, A. M., Gold, M. S., Pottash, A. C., & Semlitz, L. (1984). Adolescent cocaine abusers. *Lancet, 2* (letter).

Washton, A. M., & Tatarsky, A. (1984). Adverse effects of cocaine abuse. In L. S. Harris (Ed.), *Problems of drug dependence, 1983,* NIDA Research Monograph No. 44 (pp. 247-254). Washington, DC: U.S. Government Printing Office.

Wetli, C. V., & Wright, R. K. (1979). Death caused by recreational cocaine use. *Journal of the American Medical Association, 241,* 2519-2522.

3

Medical and Biological Consequences of Cocaine Abuse

TODD WILK ESTROFF

When Erlenmeyer accused Sigmund Freud of unleashing the third scourge of humankind (after opiates and alcohol) in 1887, he correctly perceived that cocaine was both addicting and deadly and not the innocent lark that Freud had thought it was. Almost from the moment that purified cocaine became available for medical use as the first local anesthetic it was also rapidly recognized as potentially dangerous by many medical sources of the day. Because that knowledge was lost for many years, it is interesting and informative to reexamine what was common knowledge a hundred years ago.

Cocaine-Induced Sudden Death

In 1891, J. B. Mattison, in the *Medical and Surgical Reporter*, reviewed over 200 severe life-threatening reactions and 6 deaths. His conclusions, though quaint in language, are as relevant and devastating today as they were then:

> 1) cocaine may be toxic; 2) this effect is not rare; 3) there is a lethal dose of cocaine; 4) the lethal dose is uncertain; 5) dangerous or deadly results may follow doses usually deemed safe; 6) toxic effects may be the result of a sequence of doses large or small, in patients young or old, the feeble or the strong; 7) the danger, near and remote, is the greatest when given under the skin; 8) cardiac or renal weaknesses increase this risk; 9) purity of the drug will not exempt from ill result; 10) caution is needful under all conditions; 11) Reclus' method, Corning's device, or Esmarchs' bandage should be used when injecting; 12) nitrate of amyl, hypodermic morphia, hypodermic ether, alcohol, ammonia, and caffeine should be at command. (p. 650)

Todd Wilk Estroff. Research Facilities, Fair Oaks Hospital, Summit, New Jersey; Gulf Coast Hospital, Fort Walton Beach, Florida.

Another reference, from 1892, states:

> At a recent meeting of the Société de Chirurgie of Paris, a letter from Professor
> Germain See was read in which he stated that he had collected particulars of
> two hundred and sixty accidents with hypodermic injections of cocaine, of
> which twenty-one terminated fatally. The professor considers the drug to be
> dangerous, and pronounces himself opposed to its employment. [Anonymous,
> 1892]

An official American Medical Association (AMA) study of local-anesthetic
deaths in 1925 (Maier, 1925) reported that "cocain [sic] alone or in combination with epinephrine caused the greatest number of deaths" in a series of
41 local-anesthetic-related deaths and "procain [sic] is certainly far safer
than any of the other local anesthetics in common use." It was also suggested that cocaine not be injected into the submucosa or used subcutaneously.

Unfortunately, all this information was lost through lack of familiarity
with the drug as cocaine fell from use in medicine. It was replaced by newer
and safer local anesthetics and by longer acting stimulants, in the form of
amphetamine and methamphetamine, which were released and came into
use in the 1930s. An alternative explanation is that this crucial information
was intentionally suppressed in order to make cocaine a chic, acceptable
drug of abuse. In the late 1960s and early 1970s, after amphetamines were
recognized as dangerous, the search was on for drugs to replace them.
Cocaine became known as the champagne of abusable drugs. It was touted
as completely safe, harmless, and nonaddicting. Cocaine use took off,
addicting completely new segments of the population who had never before
been involved in substance abuse to any appreciable extent.

Dramatic rises in cocaine-related deaths were reported by a number of
investigators starting in the late 1970s (Dimaio & Garriott, 1978; Finkle &
McCloskey, 1977; Nakamura & Noguchi, 1981; Wetli & Wright, 1979). This
corresponds exactly to the rapid rise in the abuse of cocaine and is, of
course, causally related.

Delayed Deaths

New evidence that prolonged administration of cocaine was dangerous came
when Deneau, Yanagita, & Seevers (1969), experimenting with rhesus monkeys, gave them unlimited access to intravenous (IV) cocaine for a 30-day
period. The experiment could not be completed because the monkeys used
such enormous quantities of cocaine that they all died. Other monkeys
exposed to unlimited amounts of morphine, codeine, amphetamine, pento-
barbital, ethanol, and caffeine became addicted but did not die.

More recent studies indicate that cocaine is much more deadly than heroin when abused in unlimited quantities. Bozarth & Wise (1985) reported 90% deaths in rats using unlimited quantities of cocaine for 30 days, as compared to only 36% deaths in a control population given unlimited access to heroin. Another factor that increases cocaine's inherent toxicity is the severe weight loss that accompanies unlimited cocaine abuse in both monkeys and rats.

Death, sudden or delayed, when it occurs, is usually the result of uncontrolled seizures, paralysis of breathing muscles, irregularities of heartbeat, or cardiac arrest. It can occur so quickly that the victim never receives medical attention other than from the coroner. Severe reactions can occur with an amount of cocaine as small as that contained in one or two lines of cocaine.

Nonfatal Acute Medical Complications

Immediate toxic side effects can include seizures, elevated blood pressure severe enough to cause strokes (Lichtenfeld, Rubin, & Feldman, 1984), and heart attacks (Coleman, Ross, & Naughton, 1982; Young & Glauber, 1947), and severe elevations of body temperature. When a cocaine abuser is seen in an acute toxic state in an emergency room, it is a true medical emergency. The patient, if not constantly monitored, can suffer a sudden cardiovascular or respiratory collapse and die. Specific medical complications, such as seizures, arrhythmias, or severe hypertension, are treated symptomatically when they occur because no specific antidote for cocaine overdose is known (Gay, 1982).

Cocaine can also affect judgment and timing, leading to increased job-related accidents and motor vehicle injuries. Those cocaine addicts who finance their habits through dealing and stealing often place themselves in dangerous situations where they can be beaten, shot, or stabbed by other dealers or the police.

Tanking Up

Tanking up refers to the phenomenon of ingesting excessive amounts of cocaine and any other abusable drug or alcohol immediately prior to entering an inpatient treatment facility. It is based on abusers' unreasonable fears that they are going to be made as uncomfortable as possible as a form of punishment for their drug abuse. They are convinced that no treatment will be available if they need it. Unfortunately, tanking up is extremely dangerous. It often results in severe overdoses and dramatically increases the risk of the sudden severe side effects already mentioned, especially respiratory arrest.

Chronic Medical Complications

Medical Risk Factors. Cocaine abusers who have diseases such as heart, liver, or kidney disease; or epilepsy, hypertension, or a vulnerability to stroke, are, of course, more susceptible to becoming medically ill while abusing cocaine. They are playing an unusual form of Russian roulette with cocaine because they are often unaware of the existence of these illnesses until a severe reaction occurs.

Street Cocaine Risk Factors. Street cocaine causes problems that increase side effects because it is neither pure nor sterile. It averages around 50%–60% cocaine with the rest made up of almost any white powder, which can include local anesthetics, stimulants like amphetamine, sugars, even talc or baby powder. In addition, neither the cocaine nor the impurities are sterile; in fact, they often contain a variety of bacteria, fungi, and viruses that can cause severe infections.

Chronic Problems Common to All Routes

The most frequent medical complication common to all routes of cocaine abuse is dental. This is partially related to the local anesthetic effects and partly to the severity of the addiction in which the abuser neglects every external personal need in the pursuit of more cocaine. Severe addicts ignore food, clothing, shelter, and sexual needs so it is not surprising that dental care is only undertaken when tooth pain from cavities or severe abscesses becomes unbearable. Cocaine suppresses appetite so much that thin, often emaciated, patients, suffering from vitamin deficiencies, are the rule (Estroff & Gold, 1986).

Tendency to Multiple Addictions. Another, often overlooked, complication of cocaine addiction is a marked tendency to develop addiction to other substances (Estroff & Gold, 1986). This occurs in response to the severe case of "jittery nerves" that occurs in cocaine addicts who are coming down from the cocaine high and ingest another drug to help smooth things out. The classical combination is the *speedball,* a combination of cocaine and an opiate, usually heroin. Other drugs that can substitute for the heroin include Valium, Librium, barbiturates, Quaaludes, and especially alcohol. When a cocaine addict is also addicted to these substances, a more prolonged, complicated detoxification is often necessary. If this important diagnosis is missed, as it often is, a severe, prolonged, uncontrolled withdrawal may result. At the very least, the patient becomes extremely uncomfortable; at the worst, patients can develop potentially life-threatening delirium tremens–like symptoms. Multiple addictions and multiple withdrawals are not rare—they are the rule among heavy cocaine abusers.

Other long-term medical complications of cocaine abuse are specifically related to the route of abuse.

Intranasal Cocaine Use

Intense blood vessel constriction is another property of cocaine (Ritchie & Green, 1980). It can be very useful to reduce bleeding during an operation, but it is harmful when cocaine is snorted directly onto the mucous membranes for prolonged periods of time. The constriction is so severe that the tissues are starved for food and oxygen brought by the blood. If this continues for an extended period of time, the mucous membrane dies at the surface, a scab or an ulcer forms, and the dead tissue falls away. When this process is repeated often enough, the tissue loss becomes so severe that a hole in the nasal septum—a nasal septal perforation—is created. Further use at this point can lead to collapse of the major supporting structures of the nose itself. Some authors have stated that nasal septal perforation is not common (Grinspoon & Bakalar, 1981), but this is incorrect.

If the vasoconstriction does not last too long, the starvation can be relieved by the delivery of extra blood to the mucous membranes. So much blood is delivered that the blood vessels become leaky and produce a runny nose and sniffles resembling the symptoms of a cold. Some addicts block this crucial healing process by self-medication with nasal sprays, which prolong the vasoconstriction and dramatically increase the likelihood of nasal septal perforation. Severe infections and inflammation of the lungs and the sinuses of the head can result when particles of cocaine contaminants and bacteria lodge there as the cocaine is snorted. The vocal chords and gag reflex can be paralyzed, resulting in hoarse voice and aspiration pneumonia.

Intravenous Cocaine Use

Lack of sterility can lead to the development of severe bacterial and fungal infections in many diverse organ systems (Estroff & Gold, 1986). IV cocaine is neither sterile nor pure. This includes the cocaine itself and the water with which it is mixed. Most cocaine addicts know nothing about sterile technique and, as a result, do not disinfect their needles or their skin before injection. The skin, naturally, is the organ most often infected, with cellulitis and abscesses occurring at the local site of injection. Distant spread can also occur, however, as septic material is carried throughout the right side of the heart, lodging in the lungs. This can cause right-sided endocarditis and pneumonia. Occasionally metastatic infections occur, causing brain abscesses and endophthalmitis (Masi, 1978). Most of these infections are caused by unusual organisms such as fungi or fastidious bacteria. Multiple bacterial infections are also common.

Granuloma formation has been reported in lungs, liver, brain, and eyes (Michelson, Whitcher, Wilson, & O'Connor, 1979) due to talc and silica adulterating the cocaine. These granulomas can become so severe that pulmonary hypertension develops (Robertson, Reynolds, & Wilson, 1976).

IV cocaine addicts often share dirty needles, thereby exposing themselves to a variety of severe virally transmitted diseases (Estroff & Gold, 1986). Hepatitis A, hepatitis B, non-A non-B hepatitis, delta agent hepatitis (an RNA virus), Epstein–Barr virus and most important and deadly of all, HTLV-III virus (Human T Lymphocyte Virus III, another RNA retrovirus) are all spread by these means of blood-to-blood contact. HTLV-III has been implicated as the cause of AIDS (acquired immunodeficiency syndrome). Earlier, this disease was limited to homosexual men, IV drug abusers, and hemophiliacs, but it has started to spread to their children and into other populations. IV cocaine abuse is one of the major ways in which AIDS has entered the middle-class heterosexual population. IV cocaine addicts can present with any of the unusual AIDS-related infections. Viruses cause disseminated herpes simplex and cytomegalovirus infections, while intracellular protozoa such as pneumocystis carinii and toxoplasmosis can cause pneumonia and central nervous system (CNS) infections. Cryptococcal meningitis and disseminated candidiasis of the mouth, pharynx, and large and small intestine are caused by fungi, and disseminated tuberculosis can be caused by either typical or atypical mycobacteria. Generalized lymphadenopathy and unusual cancers such as Kaposi sarcoma or diffuse undifferentiated non-Hodgkin lymphoma are also part of the disease complex.

IV cocaine addicts who develop persistent hepatitis B viremia are also susceptible to a disease indistinguishable from polyarteritis nodosa (Sergent, Lockshin, & Christian, 1976).

Crack—Free-Base Cocaine

Users of free-base cocaine and crack have been reported to have damage to the diffusing surface of the lungs, as evidenced by decreased carbon monoxide diffusing capacity (Weiss, Goldenheim, Mirin, Hales, & Mendelson, 1981). Free base has also been suggested as a cause of a syndrome closely resembling pseudomembraneous colitis, presenting with abdominal pain and diarrhea immediately following the cocaine smoking (Fishel, Hamamoto, Barbul, Jiji, & Efron, 1985).

Coca Paste Smokers

Coca paste, a mixture of about equal thirds of cocaine hydrochloride, cocaine sulfate, and cocaine free base, is one of the most frequently abused forms of cocaine in South American countries, especially Peru. It is smoked in a fashion similar to free basing. As is true with free basers, there is evidence on pathological specimens that smoking coca paste causes damage to the alveoli when the substance is abused in massive amounts. Among these abusers, very low white blood cell (WBC) counts, on the order of 2,000 WBC/cc, have been noted, with a marked drop in the absolute lymphocyte count. This possible alteration in the cocaine abuser's immune system leads to severe chronic tuberculosis and to fungal infections that do not respond well to conventional therapies. This may be caused or exacerbated by infectious diseases or malnutrition, which are endemic to the region (Jeri, personal communication, 1985).

Psychiatric Complications

Cocaine-Induced. Cocaine can induce psychiatric symptoms in healthy individuals if enough of it is ingested. The symptoms occur and progress in four overlapping stages as the dose rises, and they disappear in reverse order as blood levels fall (Estroff & Gold, 1986; Jeri, Sanchez, Del Pozo, Fernandez, & Carbajar, 1980; Post, 1975; Siegal, 1982). The first stage, *cocaine euphoria*, is quite pleasurable, with increased sexual arousal, feelings of remarkable pleasure, and increased intellectual functioning and energy. In addition, abusers may be affectively labile, hyperactive, anorexic, insomniac, and prone to violence. All these symptoms are remarkably similar to those of a manic or hypomanic episode.

This first stage occurs only while blood levels are rising. As soon as they start to level off or fall, the second stage, *cocaine dysphoria*, sets in, with symptoms similar to those of major depression. Anxiety, sadness, apathy, anorexia, insomnia, and aggressiveness begin and increase in intensity as time goes on. Most insidious of all is the development of an intense, irresistible craving to use more cocaine.

Symptoms can progress further at higher blood levels to *cocaine hallucinosis*, in which signs of psychosis begin to occur. The cocaine addict has sufficient reality testing left to realize that the perceptions are not correct, despite the experience of paranoid thoughts bordering on delusions and auditory, visual, olfactory, and tactile hallucinations. Knowing that their symptoms are not real, they have enough self-control not to act on their psychotic symptoms, but this does not keep them from constantly checking their environment. They remain hypervigilant, often staring out of a window for hours watching for the police or the FBI, believing they are "out to get me." They are so paranoid that they often arm themselves at this point and may later use the weapon if they progress into the last stage, *cocaine psychosis*.

When a patient reaches the stage of cocaine psychosis, reality testing is absent. Abusers are convinced that all their hallucinations and delusions are real, and they may act on paranoid delusions to the extent of harming others or themselves in a desperate attempt to escape nonexistent persecutors.

Tactile hallucinations can be especially prominent, to the point where the abusers injure themselves in vain attempts to rid their bodies of "bugs" and "worms" crawling under their skin.

All these psychiatric symptoms depend on the dose of cocaine abused, the frequency of use, and the individual abuser's underlying predisposition to psychiatric illness. There is some evidence of a kindling effect whereby multiple small doses of cocaine can, over time, produce psychiatric symptoms or seizures that only a large dose could previously have produced (Post & Kopanda, 1976).

Cocaine-Exacerbated Psychopathology. Cocaine can be the key to a Pandora's box of severe psychopathology in unsuspecting but vulnerable individuals. Prolonged, new symptoms of panic disorder, major depression, bipolar disorder, or schizophrenia may be precipitated by cocaine abuse and persist long after the cocaine has disappeared from the body. These disorders may not clear up spontaneously but may require additional treatment with psychiatric medications.

Self-Medicating with Cocaine

Psychiatric patients with primary major depression, bipolar disorder, cyclothymic disorder, or attention deficit disorder (ADD) occasionally start on the road to addiction by using cocaine to self-medicate their disorder. Cocaine can produce significant but brief relief from severe depression, or it can be used as a pharmacological switch to produce a manic blast in a bipolar or cyclothymic patient. Doses tend to escalate rapidly, often worsening the psychiatric disorder and leading to addiction.

Because of the plethora of cocaine-induced psychiatric and behavioral symptoms that can occur, it is a mistake to make any diagnosis of a primary psychiatric disorder unless the patient has been fully detoxified and observed drug free over a period of several weeks.

Chemical Brain Changes

It is also probable that cocaine causes changes in brain biochemistry that may be responsible for the production of drug-induced euphoria, drug craving, and some of the behavioral changes seen while patients are withdrawing from cocaine. Elevated prolactin levels (Dackis, Gold, Estroff, & Sweeney, 1984; Estroff, Dackis, Sweeney, & Pottash, 1985) and blunted thyroid-stimulating hormone (TSH) responses to thyrotropin-releasing hormone (TRH) stimulation (Dackis & Gold, 1985) may be mediated through dopaminergic pathways, causing chronic dopamine depletion, thus suggesting possible treatment of cocaine craving and withdrawal symptoms using dopamine agonists such as bromocriptine (Dackis & Gold, in press).

Summary

Clearly, cocaine abuse is both medically and psychiatrically dangerous. It can cause sudden death even in small doses, as well as producing a wide range of acute and chronic medical disorders. Psychiatric and behavioral symptoms can be mistaken for a wide variety of psychiatric disorders if the cocaine abuse remains undetected. The spectrum of medical and psychiatric disorders encountered is markedly influenced by amount of cocaine ingested and the route of administration. Careful, complete evaluation of these complicated, difficult patients is a must before *any* definitive treatment is begun.

REFERENCES

Anonymous. (1892). Cocaine fatalities. *New York Medical Journal, 55*, 457.

Bozarth, M. A., & Wise, R. A. (1985). Toxicity associated with long term intravenous heroin and cocaine self administration in the rat. *Journal of the American Medical Association, 254*, 81–83.

Coleman, D. L., Ross, T. F., & Naughton, J. L. (1982). Myocardial ischemia and infarction related to recreational cocaine use. *The Western Journal of Medicine, 136*, 444–446.

Dackis, C. A., & Gold, M. S. (1985). Bromocriptine as a treatment for cocaine abuse. *Lancet, 1*(8438), 1151–1152.

Dackis, C. A., & Gold, M. S. (in press). Bromocriptine treatment for cocaine abuse: The dopamine depletion hypothesis. *American Academy of Clinical Psychiatrists.*

Dackis, C. A., Gold, M. S., Estroff, T. W., & Sweeney, D. R. (1984). Hyperprolactinemia in cocaine abuse. *Society for Neuroscience, 321*(9), 1099.

Deneau, G., Yanagita, I., & Seevers, M. H. (1969). Self administration of psychoactive substances by the monkey: A measure of psychological dependence. *Psychopharmacologia* (Berlin), *16*, 30–48.

Dimaio, V. J. M., & Garriott, J. C. (1978). Four deaths due to intravenous injection of cocaine. *Forensic Science International, 12*, 119–125.

Estroff, T. W., Dackis, C. A., Sweeney, D. R., & Pottash, A. L. C. (1985). Neurochemical changes in cocaine and opiate abuse. *American Psychiatric Association Abstract,* NR180, p. 97.

Estroff, T. W., & Gold, M. S. (1984). Psychiatric misdiagnosis. In M. S. Gold, R. B. Lydiard, & J. S. Carman (Eds.), *Advances in psychopharmacology: Predicting and improving treatment response* (pp. 34–66). Boca Raton, FL: CRC Press.

Estroff, T. W., & Gold, M. S. (1986). Medical and psychiatric complications of cocaine abuse and possible points of pharmacological treatment. In B. Stimmel (Ed.), *Advances in alcohol and substance abuse* (Vol. 5, Nos. 1–2, pp. 61–76). New York: Haworth Press.

Finkle, B. S., & McCloskey, K. L. (1977). The forensic toxicology of cocaine. In *Cocaine: 1977* (U.S. Department of Health, Education and Welfare Publication No. AIM 77-432, pp. 153–192). Washington, DC: U.S. Government Printing Office.

Fishel, R., Hamamoto, G., Barbul, A., Jiji, V., & Efron, G. (1985). Cocaine colitis: Is this a new syndrome? *Diseases of the Colon and Rectum, 28*, 264–266.

Gay, G. R. (1982). Clinical management of acute and chronic cocaine poisoning. *Annals of Emergency Medicine, 11*, 562–572.

Grinspoon, L., & Bakalar, J. B. (1981). Adverse effects of cocaine: Selected issues. *Annals of the New York Academy of Science, 362*, 125–131.

Jeri, F. R., Sanchez, C. C., Del Pozo, T., Fernandez, M., & Carbajal, C. (1980). Further experience with the syndromes produced by coca paste smoking. In F. R. Jeri (Ed.), *Cocaine 1980: Proceedings of the Interamerican Seminar on Medical and Sociological Aspects of Coca and Cocaine* (Lima, Peru, July 1-6) (pp. 76-85). Lima: Pacific Press.

Lichtenfeld, P. J., Rubin, D. B., & Feldman, R. S. (1984). Subarachnoid hemorrhage precipitated by cocaine snorting. *Archives of Neurology, 41,* 223-224.

Maier, H. W. (1925). Central action of cocain [*sic*]. *Journal of the American Medical Association, 84,* 712.

Masi, R. J. (1978). Endogenous endophthalmitis associated with bacillus cereus bacteremia in a cocaine addict. *Annals of Ophthalmology, 10,* 1367-1370.

Mattison, J. B. (1891). Cocaine poisoning. *Medical and Surgical Reporter, 65,* 645-650.

Michelson, J. B., Whelcher, J. P., Wilson, S., & D. O'Connor, G. R. (1979). Possible foreign body granuloma of the retina associated with intravenous cocaine addiction. *American Journal of Ophthalmology, 87,* 278-280.

Nakamura, G. R., & Noguchi, T. T. (1981). Fatalities from cocaine overdoses in Los Angeles County. *Clinical Toxicology, 18,* 895-905.

Post, R. M. (1975). Cocaine psychoses: A continuum model. *American Journal of Psychiatry, 132,* 225-231.

Post, R. M., & Kopanda, R. T. (1976). Cocaine, kindling and psychosis. *American Journal of Psychiatry, 133,* 627-634.

Ritchie, J. M., & Greene, N. M. (1980). Local anesthetics. In L. S. Goodman & A. Gilman (Eds.), *The pharmacological basis of therapeutics.* New York: Macmillan.

Robertson, C. H., Reynolds, R. D., & Wilson, J. E. (1976). Pulmonary hypertension and foreign body granulomas in intravenous drug abusers. *American Journal of Medicine, 61,* 657-664.

Sergent, J. S., Lockshin, M. D., & Christian, C. L. (1976). Vasculitis with heptatitis B antigenemia. *Medicine, 55,* 1-18.

Siegal, R. K. (1982). Cocaine freebase use. *Journal of Psychoactive Drugs, 14,* 311-320.

Weiss, R. D., Goldenheim, P. D., Mirin, S. M., Hales, C. A., & Mendelson, J. H. (1981). Pulmonary dysfunction in cocaine smokers. *American Journal of Psychiatry, 138,* 1110-1112.

Wetli, C. V., & Wright, R. D. (1979). Death caused by recreational cocaine use. *Journal of the American Medical Association, 241,* 2519-2522.

Young, D., & Glauber, J. J. (1947). Electrocardiographic changes resulting from acute cocaine intoxication. *American Heart Journal, 34,* 272-279.

4

Fatal Reactions to Cocaine

CHARLES V. WETLI

Historical Perspective

Reports of death from both the medical and nonmedical use of cocaine appeared as early as 1891 (Peterson, 1977; Verlander & Johns, 1981) and continued into the early part of this century (McLaughlin, 1973; Sears, 1980; Webster, 1930). Many of those reports are anecdotal accounts, and the cases were certainly not substantiated by systematic medicolegal death investigation or confirmed by toxicologic testing. Consequently, many of the adverse reactions attributed to the unregulated and unrestrained use of cocaine have been seriously questioned (McLaughlin, 1973; Sears, 1980; Courtwright, 1982). Despite inadequate documentation, the public of the early 20th century perceived cocaine as a pernicious and addictive drug, which inexorably led to a deterioration of life-style, debilitation, and eventual death (Ageyev, 1984; McLaughlin, 1973; Webster, 1930). This perception remained long after the availability and use of cocaine were restricted by the Harrison Narcotics Act of 1914.

When cocaine again became popular as a recreational drug in the 1970s, it was claimed that there was little proof to substantiate any adverse effects of cocaine. Earlier perceptions were attributed to misinterpretation, hysteria, and unfounded assumptions. It was even claimed that nobody ever died from snorting cocaine unless harmful substances (cutting agents) were added to the drug by unscrupulous dealers (Gottlieb, 1976). This assertion was lent some credence by the lack of any reports of fatal cocaine overdoses in the more current medical literature. The few articles that did discuss cocaine and its toxic reactions usually stated only that death from cocaine was possible but rare (Cohen, 1975; Grinspoon, Bakalar, 1979; Pearman, 1979; Peterson, 1979). This impression was based on the lack of current data as well as on the usage patterns of the times. However, reports of fatal reactions to cocaine, with toxicologic confirmation, began to appear in the forensic science literature as case reports (DiMaio & Garriott, 1978; Lundberg et al., 1977; Price, 1974) between 1974 and 1978. Subsequently, sur-

Charles V. Wetli. Metropolitan Dade County Medical Examiner Department, Miami, Florida; Department of Pathology, University of Miami School of Medicine, Miami, Florida.

veys, case reports, and systematic studies (Bednarczyk, 1980; Bost, 1985; Drug Abuse Warning Network, 1984; Finkle & McCloskey, 1978; Mittleman & Wetli, 1984; Sander, Ryser, Lamoreaux, & Raleigh, 1985; Wetli & Wright, 1979) of cocaine-related deaths are increasing, and it is now evident that cocaine may cause sudden death by a variety of mechanisms, regardless of the route of ingestion.

Introduction

The investigation of the potentially fatal consequences of a drug widely used for its mood-altering effects rquires careful evaluation of several factors (Hankes, 1984; Wetli, 1984). These include the potential for a fatal overdose, life-threatening toxic manifestations, the physical and mental effects of chronic consumption, and behavioral alterations that may threaten the life of the user or others' lives. Each recreational drug provides a different profile of fatal and potentially fatal consequences. Methaqualone (Quaaludes), for example, had a high potential for fatal overdose when the drug was cheap and easily available. Subsequently, expense and relative unavailability changed the profile to one of traumatic death (mostly vehicular crashes) due to behavioral modification (Wetli, 1983). Life-threatening toxic reactions or complications from chronic consumption were not apparent with methaqualone.

The profile for cocaine-related fatalities must be regarded as incomplete and changing. This is largely the result of limited scientific data, regional variations in availability, the purity of street cocaine, and changing patterns of use. The current profile is that cocaine kills predominantly by overdose and by acute toxic reaction. Chronic consumption may lead to fatal medical complications, such as certain infections. So far, deaths from behavioral modifications are less evident in that cocaine is not directly associated with vehicular crashes or other traumatic deaths (Finkle & McCloskey, 1978; Mittleman & Wetli, 1984; Wetli & Wright, 1979). This area, however, has not been much explored and may be more significant than currently realized. Thus, in one series of 240 cocaine-related fatalities (Mittleman & Wetli, 1984), 175 were due to trauma: 123 were homicide victims, 27 were traumatic suicides, and the rest were accidental traumatic deaths (mostly vehicular crashes). In particular, it has been suggested that cocaine intoxication or postcocaine depression may lead to suicide ("Adverse Effects of Cocaine Abuse," 1984; Cohen, 1984; Hankes, 1984). However, the extent of completed suicides stemming from the expense, life-style, or mental health consequences of cocaine addiction is unknown.

The following sections discuss cocaine-induced fatalities from overdose, acute toxic reactions, and medical complications.

Fatal Cocaine Overdose from Recreational Use

From the outset it must be emphasized that nationwide statistics grossly underestimate the true incidence of cocaine overdose deaths. Not only are there wide variations in the jurisdiction and investigative capabilities of medical examiner–coroner systems, but toxicologic testing is not always available because of the sophisticated equipment and procedures needed to test for cocaine. The rapid metabolism of cocaine during life and its rapid deterioration in the postmortem state further compound the difficulties involved in identifying cocaine overdose deaths. Thus, a person who takes a lethal dose of cocaine yet survives in a hospital emergency room for a few hours may well have a negative test for cocaine in the blood, and the death may therefore be attributed to natural causes (e.g., an epileptic seizure). Likewise, an individual who dies from a cocaine overdose and is not found until the next day may have no cocaine remaining in the blood because of continued hydrolysis and the action of enzymes in the blood such as cholinesterase. Since the rapid breakdown of cocaine continues in the test tube, the blood sample must be preserved with sodium fluoride to inhibit this deterioration (Basett, 1983; Liu, Budd, & Griesmer, 1982).

The increasing frequency with which cocaine overdose deaths are being reported (Bost, 1985; Drug Abuse Warning Network, 1984; Mittleman & Wetli, 1984; Sander et al., 1985) is partly the result of greater awareness and improved death investigation. More important, however, is the increased availability and continued popularity of cocaine (Mittleman & Wetli, 1984), as well as the emergence of more intense and destructive patterns of use (Pollin, 1985).

For a case to be reported as an overdose of cocaine, the toxicologic analysis must not reveal substantial amounts of other drugs (or poisons). If the analysis reveals high levels of both cocaine and morphine, for example, the case would be classified as a polydrug overdose. It is not known how many deaths have resulted from the purchase of street cocaine that also contained other potentially lethal substances. This apparently has occurred in New Orleans, where samples of cocaine were found to contain phencyclidine (PCP), which culminated in the deaths of several people (Dr. Richard Garey, personal communication, June 1985). Despite the intention to ingest cocaine, these deaths would be attributed to polydrug intoxication or to intoxication with phencyclidine, depending on the toxicologic analysis. Hence, by definition, a cocaine-induced fatality is due solely to the cocaine.

In Dade County, Florida (which includes the city of Miami and has a total population of about 1.7 million people), the frequency of fatal cocaine intoxication has risen dramatically over the past 15 years (Figure 4-1). In the early 1970s only 1 or 2 cocaine overdose deaths per year were identified.

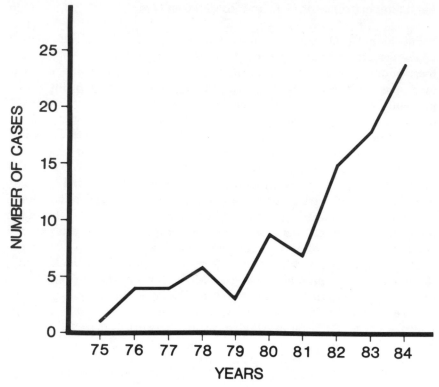

FIGURE 4-1. Deaths attributed to cocaine intoxication have risen from one or two per year in the early 1970s to two per month in 1984 in Dade County, Florida. The graph does not include cases of heart attack, intracranial hemorrhage, or other medical catastrophes induced by cocaine.

Since then the incidence has risen to a current rate of 2 per month. This rapid escalation of cocaine overdose deaths is primarily attributed to the appearance of a cocaine glut beginning in the summer of 1983. This resulted in a greater availability and reduced prices for illicit cocaine of much greater purity (Drug Enforcement Administration, Miami Field Division, personal communication, April 1984). This in turn led to a predictable increase in the incidence of fatal cocaine intoxication. The trend continues in 1986, with street samples usually being 85–90% pure and cheaper and more widely available than ever before. This, plus the popularity and affordability of so-called crack or rock cocaine, is reflected in another increase in cocaine-induced fatalities: As of mid-1986, the death rate from cocaine in Dade County, Florida, has gone from two per month to nearly two per week.

Prior to mid-1978, the typical cocaine overdose victim was a 26-year-old white male (Wetli & Wright, 1979). Although blacks made up about 29% of the cocaine overdose victims, they had a much greater tendency to use cocaine in association with heroin (but not necessarily by speedballing, where heroin and cocaine are injected simultaneously). Since mid-1978, the average age of cocaine overdose fatalities increased to 29 years, and blacks made up 39% of the victims (Mittleman & Wetli, 1984). Since the black population of Dade County is about 17%, it is obvious that blacks are demographically overrepresented in the population of fatal cocaine intoxications. A similar increase in the number of women dying from cocaine overdoses was also demonstrated (from 29% to 42%) in these studies.

Reviews concerning the medical uses of cocaine indicate a "safe maximum dose" for topical application on the mucous membranes in an adult of about 1 mg/kg of body weight, to between 100 mg and 200 mg (Pearman, 1979; Sears, 1980; Verlander & Johns, 1981). The median lethal dose (LD50) for oral ingestion in humans is said to be 500 mg (Gay & Inaba, 1976). However, death from cocaine toxicity has occurred with doses below 200 mg (Sears, 1980), whereas others have survived after ingesting 1,000 mg or more (Gay & Inaba, 1976; Van Dyke & Byck, 1976; Wetli & Mittleman, 1981). This wide variation in susceptibility to the effects of cocaine precludes any definitive statement of what constitutes a "safe" dose, especially in the recreational user. Besides variations in tolerance, stimulants (particularly adrenaline and amphetamines), antihypertensive agents, and antidepressants may potentiate the action of cocaine and thereby increase its toxicity (Pearman, 1979; Sears, 1980; Verlander & Johns, 1981). The toxicity may also be enhanced in individuals who have deficiencies in the enzymes in the blood necessary to detoxify cocaine (cholinesterase). For comparison, the average line of street cocaine is said to contain between 12 mg and 25 mg of cocaine (Price, 1974; Siegel, 1974).

In surgical patients, the average peak concentration of cocaine in the blood is 0.31 mg/l (Basett, 1982). The average blood concentration in those who have died from the recreational use of cocaine is about 6 mg/l (Mittleman & Wetli, 1984). However, the range of blood cocaine concentration seen in overdose fatalities is extremely wide, from less than 1 mg/l to greater than 20 mg/l (Bednarczyk, Grossman, & Wymer, 1980; DiMaio & Garriott, 1978; Finkle & McCloskey, 1978; Mittleman & Wetli, 1984; Wetli & Wright, 1979). Although this wide range is somewhat artifactual because of the postmortem deterioration of cocaine, it also emphasizes the marked variability in susceptibility to the lethal effects of the drug. Indeed, some individuals who died from causes totally unrelated to cocaine (e.g., gunshot wounds) had higher blood concentrations than some of those who died from a cocaine overdose (Mittleman & Wetli, 1984; Wetli & Wright, 1979). Thus cocaine differs from most other drugs in that the blood concentration by itself is of limited help in determining whether or not the death was in fact due to cocaine. It is therefore apparent that other factors also play a significant role in determining a fatal reaction. These factors could be a deficiency in the enzyme cholinesterase, a release of adrenaline, the presence of certain other drugs, or a still unidentified aberration of brain chemistry. Although an increase in the purity of street cocaine is reflected in an increased rate of death from its nonmedical use, it is not certain that purity alone accounts for all cocaine-induced fatalities. For many of the deaths it is evident that the pattern of cocaine use was no different from the individual's accustomed pattern (Mittleman & Wetli, 1984; Wetli & Wright, 1979): It was usually (but not always) the frequent, experienced user of the drug who died after ingesting a usual amount of cocaine. This phenomenon of a sudden unexpected sensitivity to cocaine has been termed "kindling" (Caldwell, 1976; Dougherty, 1984; Stripling & Ellinwood, 1976) or reverse tolerance.

The exact chemical mechanism by which cocaine causes death is still in question. Some (Verlander & Johns, 1981) contend that cocaine is not truly a stimulant drug but that it selectively depresses inhibitory areas of the brain, which then leave the stimulation circuits unopposed. Also, cocaine has a direct toxic action on the cardiovascular system (Mule, 1984; Pearman, 1979; Sears, 1980; Verlander & Johns, 1981). In most reported cases where the terminal event was witnessed (Bednarczyk, 1980; DiMaio & Garriott, 1978; Finkle & McCloskey, 1978; Lundberg et al., 1977; Mittleman & Wetli, 1984; Price, 1974; Wetli & Wright, 1979), the victim went into violent convulsions followed rapidly by respiratory collapse and death. The seizures often occurred suddenly and without warning, sometimes preceded by body temperatures of 105°F or more (hyperthermia). Except for bite marks of the tongue or lower lip from the convulsions, autopsy findings are generally nonspecific but typical for a respiratory mechanism of death (Finkle & McCloskey, 1978; Mittleman & Wetli, 1984; Wetli & Wright, 1979). This is consistent with cocaine's interference with the respiratory centers of the brain, either directly, or by the terminal convulsions, or both. In other instances, the victim simply collapsed without preterminal convulsions, suggesting the mechanism of death in these cases was the toxic action of cocaine on the cardiovascular system. Deaths have occurred following all routes of ingestion, including nasal application (snorting).

Medical Complications and Sudden Death from Intravenous Cocaine Abuse

Intravenous (IV) administration of any drug results very rapidly in high blood levels, and leads to enhanced effects on the brain, the cardiovascular system, or any other target organ. It is therefore not surprising that most reports of fatalities involving the nonmedical use of cocaine are due to IV injection (Bednarczyk, 1980; Finkle & McCloskey, 1978; Mittleman &

Wetli, 1984; Wetli & Wright, 1979). Aside from bite marks (induced by preterminal convulsions) and hyperthermia, the postmortem examination of these victims is usually unremarkable except for their skin lesions (Mittleman & Wetli, 1984). Fresh injection sites (Figure 4-2), which are usually multiple and on the upper extremities, are typically large, salmon-colored ecchymoses (bruises), often with a central clear zone about the needle puncture itself (Mittleman & Wetli, 1984; Wetli & Wright, 1979). Older lesions take on various hues of blue and yellow and apparently disappear without leaving any sequelae or scars. Some chronic users, however, develop shallow cutaneous ulcers averaging about 1 cm in diameter and exhibiting signs of slow healing (Figure 4-3). The base of the ulcer is usually red to gray and with rolled pearly white to gray margins (indicative of chronic epidermal overgrowth). Eventually these ulcers heal, leaving round or oval atrophic (soft and wrinkled) scars (Mittleman & Wetli, 1984; Yaffee, 1968). The large bruises of fresh injection sites, the ulcers, and the scars have been induced experimentally by injecting cocaine subcutaneously into laboratory rats (Bruckner, Berg, & Levy, 1982). In the IV cocaine abuser, the drug gets into the subcutaneous tissues from leakage around the vein, from missing the vein altogether, or from "skin popping." Initially the blood

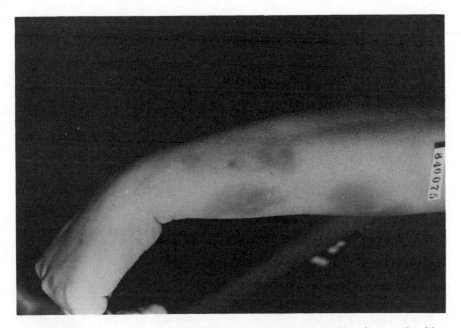

FIGURE 4-2. Fresh injection sites are characterized by large bruises, frequently with a central clear zone.

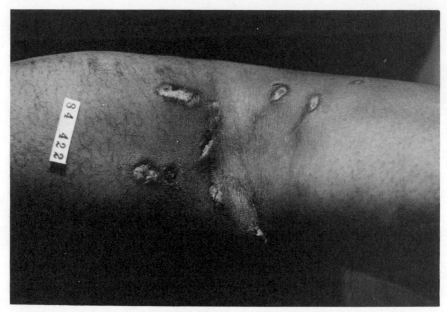

FIGURE 4-3. Skin ulcers from IV cocaine abuse. These are probably focal areas of cutaneous gangrene. They may heal very slowly, leaving a soft round or oval scar.

vessels in the skin become severely constricted, and this is followed by a pronounced engorgement of the vessels, which rupture and leave blood beneath the skin. The constriction of the vessels leads to focal ischemia (diminished blood and oxygen to the area). Also, cocaine appears to be directly toxic to the capillary endothelial cells (Bruckner *et al.*, 1982). These combined effects of ischemia and direct toxicity to the local blood vessels result in a focal area of cutaneous gangrene, and hence the skin ulcer. The healing process is slow because of the blood vessel damage. This mechanism would also account for the perforation of the nasal septum in chronic nasal users of cocaine.

Another cutaneous complication of IV cocaine abuse is necrotizing fasciitis, where large areas of skin are sloughed. The process may or may not be complicated by infection of the area. As the process becomes chronic, fibrosis or scarring lead to obstruction of the lymphatic system, resulting in a pronounced swelling of the involved extremity (brawny edema) similar to elephantiasis (Figure 4-4). This swelling further compromises the circulation of blood in the extremity, thereby inhibiting the healing process and, in fact, promoting further deterioration. Although most reported cases of necrotizing fasciitis also have a history of IV heroin abuse, the phenomenon appears to be more specifically related to the IV or subcutaneous injection

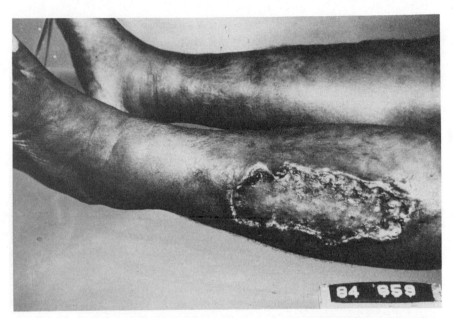

FIGURE 4-4. A large area of sloughed skin and elephantiasis (brawny edema) in a chronic IV user of cocaine.

of cocaine (Fellner & Weinstein, 1979; Jacobson & Hirschman, 1982), and may be seen in the absence of any history of heroin use.

It should be noted that the cutaneous stigmata and autopsy findings of the IV cocaine user are significantly different from those of IV narcotics abusers (Mittleman & Wetli, 1984; Wetli, Davis, & Blackbourne, 1972; Wetli & Wright, 1979). The IV narcotics addict frequently injects excipients (e.g., talc, starch) used as fillers in medications intended for oral consumption. These excipients are not soluble and therefore act like microscopic splinters of foreign particles in the skin and the lungs. The body's defenses cannot destroy these materials, and hence a chronic inflammatory reaction ensues. In the lungs, microscopic granulomas with foreign particles are observable. In the skin, the chronic inflammation and granulomas lead to extensive scarring—the "tracks" so characteristic of narcotic addicts. In contrast, the IV cocaine user injects soluble materials, thereby greatly diminishing the likelihood of peripheral scarring or tracks. Consequently, the peripheral extremity scars of IV cocaine users are relatively small and inconspicuous, and are a result of the repeated mechanical trauma of injection. The other cutaneous stigmata (bleeding beneath the skin, ulcers, round atrophic scars, and necrotizing fasciitis) are therefore predominantly the effect of the local toxicity of cocaine on the cutaneous blood vessels.

Deaths from the Nasal Use of Cocaine

It has frequently been remarked that it would be difficult, if not impossible, to snort enough cocaine to result in death. That this is simply not true, however, has been amply documented in both medical and surgical situations (Pearman, 1979; Sears, 1980; Verlander & Johns, 1981), as well as in recreational users of cocaine (Finkle & McCloskey, 1978; Mittleman & Wetli, 1984; Wetli & Wright, 1979). Also, interviews with over 300 intranasal cocaine addicts revealed an 8% incidence of cocaine-related seizures (Washton, Gold, & Pottash, 1983). Considering that seizures are a frequent precursor to respiratory collapse and death in cocaine overdose, it is perhaps surprising that the incidence of death from the intranasal use of cocaine is not even higher. Because of the vasoconstrictive effect of cocaine, not all of the drug is absorbed immediately after nasal application. In fact, cocaine may remain in the nasal passages for as long as 3 hours after ingesetion (Van Dyke, Barash, Jatlow, & Byck, 1976). Postmortem examinations in our facility have revealed that cocaine may persist for even longer periods in the nasal passages. In actual practice, the cocaine user will snort the drug many times within a few hours. Although some of the drug is absorbed, much remains as a blanket along the nasal mucosa since the blood vessels are constricted. Eventually these blood vessels will become patent and absorb the remaining cocaine. If this happens rapidly enough, one could, theoretically, have an unexpected surge of cocaine into the bloodstream, triggering convulsions possibly leading to respiratory collapse and death. This conjecture appears plausible since there is frequently a delay of 30–60 minutes between the nasal ingestion of cocaine and the onset of the convulsions, and because the average postmortem blood levels of cocaine are the same as for those who die after IV injection of the drug (Mittleman & Wetli, 1984).

Deaths from the Use of Cocaine During Sexual Activity

A century ago, cocaine-soaked lint was unsuccessfully applied to the genitals of boys and girls as a deterrent to masturbation (Hammond, 1886). Today, however, cocaine is regarded by many as an aphrodisiac, because it relaxes inhibitions (DuPont, 1982), is a central nervous system stimulant and provides local anesthesia to the genital mucous membranes (Daugherty, 1982) to prolong sexual activity. The drug may be applied to the head of the penis or into the vagina (DuPont, 1982). However, cocaine is highly soluble and rapidly absorbed from any mucosal surface, including the vagina, which is a highly vascular structure. When sexually stimulated, the numerous blood vessels beneath the mucosa become engorged and will readily absorb a soluble drug like cocaine into the bloodstream. Death from this route of administration is therefore quite likely, especially in a population of sexually active individuals who believe in its aphrodisiac properties. The actual incidence of death under these circumstances is unknown, and the number of deaths actually identified from the use of cocaine during sexual activity is quite small. In large part, this probably reflects the reluctance of people to admit that the death of an associate occurred during sexual activity (as is true also with heart attack victims who die during sexual intercourse). This reluctance is further intensified when illicit drugs are used during the sexual activity and when the activity itself may be regarded as "kinky" (e.g., putting cocaine mixed with a lubricant into the vagina).

Smoking Cocaine

At present, deaths from smoking cocaine hydrochloride or free-base cocaine are relatively infrequent, but they do occur. This does not suggest any inherent safety in smoking cocaine. The expense of free-base cocaine smoking and the fact that the route of ingestion is not known in many cocaine fatalities probably accounts for the relatively low incidence of actually identified cases. Indeed, blood levels achieved from smoking cocaine are almost instantaneous and simulate the effect of IV injection (Van Dyke & Byck, 1982). Smoking cocaine has engendered real concern in that toxic reactions are far more commonplace than with intranasal use (Siegel, 1979). The psychological reactions have been so frightening that even lay publications have had articles warning against free-base cocaine smoking even while failing to condemn the use of cocaine in general (Perry, 1980). In 1986 the smoking of cocaine has become more widespread and popular because of the introduction of crack or rock cocaine. This material has been analyzed to be 35–100% pure, and is immediately and completely absorbed when smoked. The intensified usage patterns and addictiveness of this form of cocaine are now regarded as major factors contributing to the rising death rate from cocaine intoxication.

Besides death from cocaine toxicity alone, free-base cocaine has certain indirect lethal ramifications, not the least of which is the burn and explosion hazard stemming from the use of ether during preparation. This potential problem has now been largely eliminated with the introduction of crack, where the cocaine base is made by mixing the hydrochloride salt with baking soda and water. Most of the medical complications are respiratory in nature and are potentially life threatening (Adrouny, 1985; Bush et al., 1984; Dougherty, 1984; Shesser, Davis, & Edelstein, 1981; Weiss et al., 1981). These include hemoptysis (coughing up blood) and leakage of air into the soft tissues of the chest (pneumomediastinum), the chest cavity (pneumothorax), and around the heart (pneumopericardium).

The Body Packer Syndrome

"Body packers" are individuals who swallow packets of cocaine or insert them into body orifices (rectum or vagina), in a smuggling attempt (Wetli & Mittleman, 1981). Typically, the person swallows 100 or more packages, each containing between 1 gm and 7 gm of about 90% pure cocaine. Sometimes they will also take a constipating agent to prevent the premature elimination of the packets while aboard the airplane (Caruana *et al.*, 1984; Siegel, 1979). Having reached their destination and cleared customs, they proceed to take laxatives and enemas to expel the packets and thereby retrieve the cocaine. The time required to pass all the packets by this method is about 27 hours (Caruana *et al.*, 1984). The packaging material has varied over the past several years. Before 1980, the condoms were popular (Suarez, Arango, & Lester, 1979); later, food-wrapping plastic or balloons were used (Wetli & Mittleman, 1981). These wrappings were subsequently replaced by heavy latex of the type used for surgical gloves or finger cots (latex splints to treat sprained fingers). Sometimes the cocaine was first wrapped in cellophane or aluminum foil (Caruana *et al.*, 1984; McCarron & Wood, 1983). Most recently the packets appear to have been machine packaged (McCarron & Wood, 1983). The more recent fatal cases observed in our facility and the nonfatal cases observed in a local emergency room (Dr. Richard Beerman, personal communication, June 1985) have had packets of cocaine that were compressed into a rock-hard oblong mass, wrapped with a thin layer of hard clear plastic, and wrapped again (three or more times) with the tips of surgical gloves (Figure 4-5). Each packet was approximately 1.5 inches long and 0.5 inch in diameter.

Although many individuals have succeeded with this method of smuggling, serious hazards exist. The most commonly reported complications (besides police arrest and incarceration) are intestinal obstruction and acute cocaine toxicity, which have been seen with all the various types of packaging materials. Some have ruptured, others have leaked, and in others the cocaine simply leached out of the intact package (Wetli & Mittleman, 1981). Because the latex or cellophane coverings are semipermeable membranes, water in the stomach or intestines may eventually pass through the wrapping material and dissolve the cocaine. The dissolved cocaine, in turn, may then pass through the membrane and into the gastrointestinal tract, from where it is immediately absorbed into the blood. Signs of acute cocaine toxicity (or bowel obstruction) in a body packer require immediate surgical intervention to remove the packets. Deaths have occurred in flight, in the customs areas of the airport, in hotel rooms near the airport, and in hospital emergency rooms.

The hotel room death scene of a body packer is fairly typical. The victim is usually a white male found dead in bed. The body temperature is

FIGURE 4-5. Thirty-three packets of cocaine are in the stomach of this body packer. Each was 1.5 inches long and 0.5 inch in diameter. Despite wrapping in plastic and latex, one broke open to kill the victim.

quite high (104° F or more), and he has bite marks on the tongue and lower lip from preterminal convulsions. Wet towels and ice buckets may be scattered about the room, evidence of futile attempts to lower the body temperature. A passport or airline ticket usually indicates recent arrival from a South American country. The presence of laxatives and enemas (something most international travelers don't need) completes the picture.

Cardiovascular Deaths Due to Cocaine

Cocaine has a stimulant effect on the cardiovascular system similar to that observed with d-amphetamine and adrenaline (Bettinger, 1980; Fischman et al., 1976; Sears, 1980; Van Dyke & Byck, 1982; Verlander & Johns, 1981). The major dose-related effects are statistically significant increases in both heart rate and blood pressure (Bettinger, 1980; Fischman et al., 1976; Fischman & Schuster, 1982) brought about primarily by the stimulation of the sympathetic nervous system (Van Dyke & Byck, 1982). Toxic reactions include a marked increase in heart rate (atrial and ventricular tachycardia), disturbances of heart rhythm (ectopy), and hypertensive crisis (Benowitz, Rosenberg, & Becker, 1979; Mittleman, Mittleman, & Elser, 1984; Pearman,

1979; Sears, 1980; Verlander & Johns, 1981). Consequently, individuals with any form of cardiovascular disease (particularly involving the coronary arteries) or with hypertension would be at risk for aggravating their underlying disease by ingesting cocaine (especially in the amounts taken by recreational users of the drug). Expected fatal complications would be sudden death from an abnormal cardiac rhythm, heart attack (myocardial infarction), and intracerebral hemorrhage (rupture of an intracerebral "berry" aneurysm or bleeding into the brain substance itself as may be seen with a hypertensive crisis). It is thought that drug-induced hypertension occurs rapidly and is potentially more acutely injurious than chronic hypertension, since the cardiovascular system is not conditioned to these pressures (Benowitz et al., 1979). It should also be noted that cocaine has a direct toxic action on the heart (Mule, 1984), and there is a growing suspicion that it may also directly constrict the coronary arteries (Cohen, 1984; Howard, Hueter, & Davis, 1985; Schachne, Roberts, & Thompson, 1984), resulting in heart attacks in otherwise healthy individuals with normal coronary arteries.

The number of deaths related to the cardiovascular toxicity of cocaine is unknown, but the incidence is even more underestimated than that of cocaine overdose deaths. In most instances, the death would be attributed to the underlying disease process as determined clinically or to the morphologic abnormality as demonstrated at autopsy (e.g., intracerebral hemorrhage or coronary arteriosclerosis). The manner of death would be regarded as natural, since sudden death often occurs from these processes. Consequently, since the cause of death was demonstrated clinically or at the autopsy, toxicologic testing would not be ordered. If the testing was ordered and cocaine was detected, problems would arise in interpreting the results. Thus, in one reported case, a man died of the spontaneous rupture of an intracerebral aneurysm after 2 hours of snorting cocaine (Lundberg et al., 1977). The drug was detected at autopsy in the nose, blood, and tissues. However, since these aneurysms may rupture spontaneously without necessarily an identifiable precipitating factor, the presence of cocaine would most likely be interpreted as "possibly contributory" or simply "incidental to death." The same dilemma occurs in those who die suddenly from coronary artery disease where cocaine was detected incidentally (Mittleman & Wetli, 1984). To complicate matters even further, the sudden death of a person with no morphological abnormalities seen at autopsy, but with cocaine in the blood, may well be regarded as a cocaine overdose without further delineation of the mechanism of death (i.e., whether the death was from the effect of cocaine on the brain or on the heart). Therefore, deaths from the cardiovascular effects of recreational cocaine use have long been suspected but have lacked the requisite proof and documentation needed for scientific certainty. In recent years, however, a number of clinical reports

have appeared documenting both fatal and near-fatal instances of cardiovascular toxicity related to cocaine abuse (Benchimol, Bartall, & Desser,
1978; Coleman, Ross, & Naughton, 1982; Howard, Hueter, & Davis, 1985;
Kossowsky & Lyon, 1984; Mittleman, Mittleman, & Elser, 1984; Nanji &
Filipenko, 1984; Pasternak, Colvin, & Bauman, 1985; Schachne, Roberts, &
Thompson, 1984). These include hypertensive crisis, disturbances of heart
rhythm, and heart attacks. Many of the reported victims were under
40 years of age, and some had had normal coronary arteries (as demonstrated by angiography or at autopsy). The mechanism of cocaine in producing these abnormalities has been attributed to the overall stimulant
effect of increasing heart rate and blood pressure, a direct toxic action on
the heart muscle, and spasm of the coronary arteries. Also, reports have
recently appeared documenting spontaneous intracerebral hemorrhage following the snorting of cocaine (Caplan, Hier, & Banks, 1982; Lichtenfeld,
Rubin, & Feldman, 1984; Schwartz & Cohen, 1984). Most of those victims
were in their 20s, and the hemorrhage was attributed to the transient
hypertension induced by cocaine. This growing amount of clinical evidence
is now leading to a more accurate assessment and reevaluation of the fatal
cardiovascular reactions to cocaine (Mittleman & Wetli, 1987), including
recent evidence that the chronic use of cocaine may directly cause or
accelerate the development of coronary artery disease (Simpson & Edwards,
1986).

Cocaine Psychosis and Sudden Death

Cocaine may produce a variety of psychiatric syndromes (Post, 1975; Resnick & Resnick, 1984). These range from dysphoria (with symptoms of
depression, anxiety, and tearfulness) to delusional states and behavior indistinguishable from acute paranoid schizophrenia. Cocaine-induced paranoia
and hallucinations may lead to violent behavior (Post, 1975) and therefore
indirectly lead to the death of the cocaine user or another person.

More recently, cases of cocaine-induced excited delirium resulting in
sudden death by an unknown mechanism have been reported (Fishbain &
Wetli, 1981; Wetli & Fishbain, 1985). Excited delirium is not a primary
psychiatric problem but a mental aberration secondary to a drug or a
disease process. Its features include illusions, disturbed attention, disturbed
perceptions, and impaired thinking (Lipowsky, 1979). When induced by
cocaine, the excited delirium is frequently accompanied by high body
temperatures (hyperthermia) and dilated pupils (mydriasis), both of which
are frequent signs of cocaine toxicity.

Typically, the victim suddenly becomes paranoid shortly after ingesting
cocaine by any route. This is followed by hyperexcitability, frequently
accompanied by bizarre behavior (such as rushing into automobile traffic,

attempting to jump out of a moving automobile, or taking off all one's clothing). Violent behavior is frequently manifested by smashing a variety of objects, especially furniture and glass. The disturbance is characteristically bizarre and intense, and invariably leads to a request for police assistance. When the police arrive, they usually find the victim has unexpected strength, to the extent that several people are needed to subdue and restrain the individual. After being restrained, the victim typically continues to thrash about for some time and then, usually within an hour, suddenly dies. The death generally occurs while the victim is still in police custody, or shortly after arriving at a hospital emergency room.

The mechanism of death in these people is unknown. However, none of these deaths were preceded by convulsions, which are typical in the usual cocaine overdose. Postmortem examination usually discloses only superficial injuries incurred during the disturbance (and from fighting against the restraints). Blood concentrations of cocaine are generally less than 1 mg/l, or about 6 times less than those seen with a typical cocaine overdose. Since cocaine may sensitize the heart to the effects of adrenaline and related hormones, it is quite possible that these deaths are the result of cocaine-induced cardiac toxicity leading to a fatal disturbance of heart rhythm (ventricular fibrillation).

What triggers the excited delirium in some people and not in others is unknown. Speculations about increased purity or reverse tolerance (an accentuated reaction without an increase in the amount ingested) have been proffered (Post, 1975; Wetli & Fishbain, 1985). Some cases of this syndrome have been associated with combined cocaine and alcohol intoxication (Dr. R. H. Cravey and Dr. V. Spiehler, personal communication, February 1985), but this has not been a constant finding.

The fickle and unpredictable nature of cocaine was further demonstrated by a man who ingested about 800 mg (his estimate) of the same sample of cocaine which induced a fatal excited delirium in his brother (Wetli & Fishbain, 1985, case 6). He had no psychotic or other disturbed reaction, and merely commented to the author that "It was real good cocaine!"

The intensity of the cocaine-induced excited delirium resembles that seen with a toxic reaction to phencyclidine (Nakamura & Noguchi, 1979), including an apparent increase in strength, diminished pain perception, and the potential for violent death. This is illustrated in the following case:

Early one afternoon a woman went outside her house to investigate sounds of breaking glass and shouting. Her next door neighbor, a 23-year-old white male, had smashed several windows of his house and was slumped over the broken-out window of his bathroom. She immediately returned to her house to notify the police. Her neighbor, who was completely naked, followed her into the house and proceeded to use her shower while she called the police. The man then went on to smash windows and a glass patio door of the woman's house before running away. Police and rescue personnel found him slumped in a corner of his garage. A large amount of blood was on the floor, and he had sustained numerous deep lacerations of his upper extremities. Resuscitative attempts at the scene and in a local hospital emergency room were futile. It was subsequently learned that the victim was a known IV user of cocaine, and that he had injected himself with the drug shortly before his psychotic episode. The body temperature was not recorded in the emergency room. The postmortem examination revealed multiple deep lacerations of the upper extremities which severed some major blood vessels and resulted in his death. Analysis of a blood sample (taken upon admission to the emergency room) revealed a concentration of 0.40 mg/l cocaine and 4.2 mg/l lidocaine. No other drugs, including phencyclidine, were detected.

Infectious Complications of Cocaine Abuse

Local and systemic infections arising from the abuse of cocaine are primarily related to the IV injection of the drug. Some infections are common to the IV abuse of any drug, and are primarily the result of unhygienic practices. These complications include peripheral cellulitis and abscesses, viral hepatitis, infection of the heart valves (endocarditis), pneumonia, lung abscesses, tetanus, and malaria. Occasionally there are isolated reports of unusual infections associated with intravenous cocaine abuse ("Case Records of the Massachusetts General Hospital," 1984; "Wound Botulism Associated with Parenteral Cocaine Abuse," 1982), but it is not certain whether this is due to the cocaine itself or to unhygienic IV drug abuse. As with IV drug abusers in general, there is also the possibility of contracting acquired immunodeficiency syndrome (AIDS) (Cohen, 1984; "Update on AIDS," 1982).

Recently, reports have surfaced specifically linking primary fungus infections of the brain to the intravenous abuse of stimulant drugs, namely amphetamines and cocaine (Micozzi & Wetli, 1985; Wetli, Weiss, Cleary, & Gyori, 1984). These cases are of interest because fungus infections of the brain are very rare unless there is some predisposing factor (such as a fungal pneumonia) or severe debilitation due to some other disease process (e.g., cancer). The cases described in these reports, however, were free of any other associated disease. All had a long history of IV amphetamine and/or cocaine abuse. The initial symptoms were neurological (slurred speech, weakness, double vision, etc.) and were rapidly progressive. Coma usually developed within a day or two of the onset of symptoms, and death occurred within a week. One individual survived but remains with severe neurologic deficits (paralyzed, unable to speak, and able to follow only simple commands).

It has been speculated that these unique cases may represent a variant of AIDS brought on by the IV abuse of stimulant drugs. Also, it is possible that these drugs specifically damaged the cerebral blood vessels, thereby providing a substrate for fungi that have a propensity to invade blood vessel walls. This latter contention is supported by the observation that IV injection of amphetamines into laboratory animals results in damage to the cerebral blood vessels (Rumbaugh, Fang, & Higgins, 1976).

Profile of Cocaine Fatalities

"When the complications of prolonged, compulsive use are forgotten, a drug like cocaine is rediscovered" (Cohen, 1984). Along with this rediscovery comes the realization that cocaine kills in a variety of ways regardless of the route of administration. Most frequently documented are cases of sudden death following IV injection or nasal application (snorting). These deaths are typically preceded by violent convulsions, which may occur without warning. Prodromal symptoms of hyperthermia, dysphoria, or other signs of cocaine toxicity may or may not have been present. Potentially lethal and fatal toxic reactions are now being documented as well. These include hypertensive crisis (with deleterious effects on the heart and the potential for intracerebral hemorrhage) as well as direct cardiovascular toxicity leading to an abnormal heart rhythm and heart attacks. Cocaine-induced psychotic reactions have been associated with both violent death and sudden cardiovascular collapse. IV users of cocaine are additionally subject to a variety of common and unique infections, including primary fungal infections of the brain. The potential for suicide and other types of violent death among cocaine users has not yet been thoroughly studied. Only recently has there emerged scientific evidence linking an increased fetal mortality to the use of cocaine during pregnancy (Chasnoff et al., 1985). Long-term effects on surviving children of mothers who use cocaine during pregnancy is not known, but the data suggest an increased risk for congenital anomalies and sudden death. And the profile for cocaine fatalities will continue to develop until there is a widespread realization that cocaine is not a harmless drug—it kills.

REFERENCES

Adrouny, A., & Magnusson, P. (1985). Pneumopericardium from cocaine inhalation. *New England Journal of Medicine, 313*, 48–49.

Adverse effects of cocaine abuse. (1984). In M. Abromowitz (Ed.), *Medical letter on drugs and therapeutics* (Vol. 26, Issue 662, pp. 51–52).

Ageyev, M. (1984). *Novel with cocaine.* New York: Dutton.

Baselt, R. C. (1982). Cocaine. In *Disposition of toxic drugs and chemicals in man* (2nd ed., pp. 193–198). Davis, CA: Biomedical Publications.

Baselt, R. C. (1983). Stability of cocaine in biological fluids. *Journal of Chromatography, 268,* 502–505.

Benchimol, A., Bartall, H., & Desser, K. B. (1978). Accelerated ventricular rhythm and cocaine abuse. *Annals of Internal Medicine, 88,* 519–520.

Bednarczyk, L. R., Gressmann, E. A., & Wymer, R. L. (1980). Two cocaine-induced fatalities. *Journal of Analytical Toxicology, 4,* 263–265.

Benowitz, N. L., Rosenberg, J., & Becker, C. E. (1979). Cardiopulmonary catastrophes in drug-overdosed patients. *Medical Clinics of North America, 63,* 267 297.

Bettinger, J. (1980). Cocaine intoxication: Massive oral overdose. *Annals of Emergency Medicine, 9,* 429–430.

Bost, R. O. (1985). Deaths involving cocaine. *Forensic Science Gazette* (New Series), *2,* 1–2.

Bruckner, J. V., Beng, W. D. J., & Levy, B. M. (1982). Histopathological evaluation of cocaine induced skin lesion in the rat. *Journal of Cutaneous Pathology, 9,* 83–95.

Bush, M. N., Rubenstein, R., Hoffman, I., & Bruno, M. S. (1984). Spontaneous pneumediastinum as a consequence of cocaine use. *New York State Journal of Medicine, 84,* 618–619.

Caldwell, J. (1976). Physiological aspects of cocaine usage. In S. J. Mulé (Ed.), *Cocaine: Chemical, biological, clinical, social and treatment aspects* (pp. 189–199). Cleveland: CRC Press.

Caplan, L. R., Hier, D. B., & Banks, G. (1982). Stroke and drug abuse. *Current Concepts of Cardiovascular Disease—Stroke, 13,* 869–872.

Caruana, D. S., Weinbach, B., Goerg, D., & Gardner, L. B. (1984). Cocaine packet ingestion—Diagnosis, management and natural history. *Annals of Internal Medicine, 100,* 73–74.

Case records of the Massachusetts General Hospital. (1984). *New England Journal of Medicine, 311,* 1365–1370.

Chasnoff, I. J., Burns, W. J., Schnoll, S. H., & Burns, K. A. (1985). Cocaine use in pregnancy. *New England Journal of Medicine, 313,* 666–669.

Cohen, S. (1975). Cocaine. *Journal of the American Medical Association, 231,* 74–75.

Cohen, S. (1984). Recent developments in the abuse of cocaine. *Bulletin on Narcotics, 36,* 3–13.

Coleman, D. L., Ross, T. F., & Naughton, J. L. (1982). Myocardial ischemia and infarction related to recreational cocaine use. *Western Journal of Medicine, 136,* 444–446.

Courtwright, D. T. (1982). *Dark paradise: Opiate addiction in America before 1940.* Cambridge, MA: Harvard University Press (pp. 96–99, 197–199).

DiMaio, V. J., & Garriott, J. C. (1978). Four deaths due to intravenous injection of cocaine. *Forensic Science International, 12,* 119–125.

Dougherty, R. J. (1982). Pharmacological/psychological aspects. In *Proceedings of the Symposium on Cocaine, May 3 and 4, 1982* (p. 51). New York: New York State Division of Substance Abuse Services and Narcotic and Drug Research, Inc.

Dougherty, R. J. (1984). Status of cocaine abuse 1984. *Journal of Substance Abuse Treatment, 1,* 157–161.

Drug Abuse Warning Network (DAWN). (1984). *Trend data through January–June 1984,* NIDA Statistical Series G, No. 14. Washington, DC: U.S. Government Printing Office.

DuPont, R. L. (1982). Problem of using cocaine as an aphrodisiac. *Medical Aspects of Human Sexuality, 16,* 14.

Fellner, M. J., & Weinstein, L. H. (1979). Cutaneous stigmata of drug addiction. *International Journal of Dermatology, 18,* 305–306.

Finkle, B. S., & McCloskey, R. L. (1978). The forensic toxicology of cocaine (1971–1976). *Journal of Forensic Science, 23*, 173–189.

Fischman, M. W., & Schuster, C. R. (1982). Cocaine self-administration in humans. *Federation Proceedings, 41*, 241–246.

Fischman, M. W., Schuster, C. R., Resnekov, L., Schick, F. E., Krasnegor, N. A., Fennell, W., & Freedman, D. X. (1976). Cardiovascular and subjective effects of intravenous cocaine administration in humans. *Archives of General Psychiatry, 33*, 983–989.

Fishbain, D. L., & Wetli, C. V. (1981). Cocaine intoxication, delirium and death in a body packer. *Annals of Emergency Medicine, 10*, 531–532.

Gay, G. R., & Inaba, D. S. (1976). Acute and chronic toxicology of cocaine abuse: Current sociology, treatment and rehabilitation. In S. J. Mulé (Ed.), *Cocaine: Chemical, biological, clinical and treatment aspects* (pp. 245–252). Cleveland: CRC Press.

Gottleib, A. (1976). *The pleasures of cocaine.* Berkeley, CA: And/Or Press (pp. 55, 62).

Grinspoon, L., & Bakalar, J. B. (1979). Cocaine. In R. I. DuPont, A. Goldstein, & J. O'Donnel (Eds.), *Handbook on drug abuse* (Chapter 22, pp. 241–247). Washington, DC: NIDA and Office of Drug Abuse Policy.

Hammond, W. A. (1886). Remarks on cocaine and the so-called cocaine habit. *Journal of Nervous and Mental Disorders, 13*, 754–759.

Hankes, L. (1984). Cocaine: Today's drug. *Journal of the Florida Medical Association, 71*, 235–239.

Howard, R. E., Hueter, D. C., & Davis, G. J. (1985). Acute myocardial infarction following cocaine abuse in a young woman with normal coronary arteries. *Journal of the American Medical Association, 254*, 95–96.

Jacobson, J. M., & Hirschman, S. Z. (1982). Necrotizing fasciitis complicating intravenous drug abuse. *Archives of Internal Medicine, 142*, 634–635.

Kossowsky, W. A., & Lyon, A. F. (1984). Cocaine and acute myocardial infarction: A probable connection. *Chest, 86*, 729–731.

Lichtenfeld, P. J., Rubin, D. B., & Feldman, R. B. (1984). Subarachnoid hemorrhage precipitated by cocaine snorting. *Archives of Neurology, 41*, 223–224.

Lipowsky, Z. J. (1979). Organic mental disorders: Introduction and review of syndromes. In H. F. Kaplan, A. M. Freedman, & B. M. Sodock (Eds.), *Comprehensive textbook of psychiatry* (3rd ed.) (Vol. III, pp. 1359–1392). Baltimore: Williams and Wilkins.

Liu, Y., Budd, R. D., & Griesmer, E. C. (1982). Study of the stability of cocaine and benzoylecgonine, its major metabolite, in blood samples. *Journal of Chromatography, 248*, 318–320.

Lundberg, G. D., Garriott, J. C., Reynolds, P. C., Cravey, R. H., & Shaw, R. F. (1977). Cocaine-related death. *Journal of Forensic Science, 22*, 402–408.

McCarron, M. M., & Wood, J. D. (1983). The cocaine "body packer" syndrome—Diagnosis and treatment. *Journal of the American Medical Association, 250*, 1417–1420.

McLaughlin, G. T. (1973). Cocaine: The history and regulation of a dangerous drug. *Cornell Law Review, 58*, 537–573.

Micozzi, M. S., & Wetli, C. V. (1985). Intravenous amphetamine abuse, primary cerebral mucormycosis and acquired immunodeficiency. *Journal of Forensic Science, 30*, 504–510.

Mittleman, H. W., Mittleman, R. E., & Elser, B. (1984). Cocaine. *American Journal of Nursing, 84*, 1092–1095.

Mittleman, R. E., & Wetli, C. V. (1984). Death caused by recreational cocaine use. *Journal of the American Medical Association, 252*, 1889–1893.

Mittleman, R. E., & Wetli, C. V. (1987). Cocaine and sudden "natural" death. *Journal of Forensic Science, 32*(1), 11–19.

Mulé, S. J. (1984). The pharmacodynamics of cocaine abuse. *Psychiatric Annals, 14*, 724–727.

Nakamura, G. R., & Noguchi, T. T. (1979). PCP: A drug of violence and death. *Journal of Police Science and Administration, 7*, 459–466.

Nanji, A. A., & Filipenko, J. D. (1984). Asystole and ventricular fibrillation associated with cocaine intoxication. *Chest, 85*, 132–133.

Pasternak, P. F., Colvin, S. B., & Bauman, F. B. (1985). Cocaine-induced angina pectoris and acute myocardial infarction in patients younger than 40 years. *American Journal of Cardiology, 55*, 847–848.

Pearman, K. (1979). Cocaine: A review. *Journal of Laryngology and Otology, 93*, 1191–1199.

Perry, C. (1980). Freebase—A treacherous obsession. *Rolling Stone*, May 1.

Peterson, R. C. (1977). NIDA Research Monograph Series, No. 13 (pp. 12, 154). Washington, DC: U.S. Government Printing Office.

Peterson, R. C. (1979). *Statement before the Select Committee on Narcotics Abuse and Control.* U.S. Congress, House of Representatives, July 24.

Pollin, W. (1985). The danger of cocaine. *Journal of the American Medical Association, 254*, 98.

Post, R. M. (1975). Cocaine psychoses: A continuum model. *American Journal of Psychiatry, 132*, 225–231.

Price, K. R. (1974). Fatal cocaine poisoning. *Journal of the Forensic Science Society, 14*, 329–333.

Resnick, R. B., & Resnick, E. B. (1984). Cocaine abuse and its treatment. *Psychiatric Clinics of North America, 7*, 713–728.

Rumbaugh, C. L., Fang, H. C. H., Higgins, R.E., Bergeron, R. T., Segall, H. D., & Teal, J. S. (1976). Cerebral microvascular injury in experimental drug abuse. *Investigations in Radiology, 11*, 282–294.

Sander, R., Ryser, M. A., Lamoreaux, T. C., & Raleigh, K. (1985). An epidemic of cocaine associated deaths in Utah. *Journal of Forensic Science, 30*, 478–484.

Schachne, J. S., Roberts, B. H., & Thompson, P. D. (1984). Coronary artery spasm and myocardial infarction associated with cocaine use. *New England Journal of Medicine, 310*, 1665–1666.

Schwartz, K. A., & Cohen, J. A. (1984). Subarachnoid hemorrhage precipitated by cocaine snorting. *Archives of Neurology, 41*, 705 (letter).

Sears, B. E. (1980). Potential hazards of the medical administration of cocaine. *Oklahoma State Medical Association Journal, 73*, 97–100.

Shesser, R., Davis, C., & Edelstein, S. (1981). Pneumomediastinum and pneumothorax after inhaling alkaloidal cocaine. *Annals of Emergency Medicine, 10*, 213–215.

Siegel, R. M. (1979a). Cocaine: Recreational use and intoxication. In R. C. Peterson & R. C. Stillman (Eds.), *Cocaine: 1977.* NIDA Research Monograph No. 13 (p. 139). Washington, DC: U.S. Government Printing Office.

Siegel, R. K. (1979b). Cocaine smoking. *New England Journal of Medicine, 300*, 373.

Simpson, R. W., & Edwards, W. D. (1986). Pathogenesis of cocaine-induced ischemic heart disease. *Archives of Pathology and Laboratory Medicine, 110*, 479–484.

Stripling, J. S., & Ellinwood, E. H. (1976). Cocaine: Physiological and behavioral effects of acute and chronic administration. In S. J. Mulé (Ed.), *Cocaine: Chemical, biological, clinical, social and treatment aspects* (pp. 167–185). Cleveland: CRC Press.

Suarez, C., Arango, A., & Lester, L. (1977). Cocaine condom ingestion. *Journal of the American Medical Association, 238*, 1391–1392.

Update on acquired immunodeficiency syndrome (AIDS)—United States. (1982). *Morbidity and Mortality Weekly Report, 31*, 507 ff.

Van Dyke, C., Barash, P. G., Jatlow, P., & Byck, R. (1976). Cocaine: Plasma concentrations after intranasal application in man. *Science, 191*, 859–861.

Van Dyke, C., & Byck, R. (1976). Cocaine 1884–1974. In E. H. Ellinwood & M. M. Kilbey (Eds.), *Cocaine and other stimulants* (pp. 1–30). New York: Plenum Press.

Van Dyke, C., & Byck, R. (1982). Cocaine. *Scientific American, 246*, 128–141.

Verlander, J. M., & Johns, M. E. (1981). The clinical use of cocaine. *Otolaryngology Clinics, 14*, 521–531.

Washton, A. M., Gold, M. S., & Pottash, A. C. (1983). Intranasal cocaine addiction. *Lancet, 2*, 1374.

Webster, R. W. (1930). *Legal medicine and toxicology.* Philadelphia: Saunders (pp. 640–644).

Weiss, R. D., Goldenheim, P. D., Mirin, S. M., Hales, C. A., & Mendelson, J. H. (1981). Pulmonary dysfunction in cocaine smokers. *American Journal of Psychiatry, 138*, 1110–1112.

Wetli, C. V. (1983). Changing patterns of methaqualone abuse: A survey of 246 fatalities. *Journal of the American Medical Association, 249*, 621–626.

Wetli, C. V. (1984). The investigation of drug-related deaths—An overview. *American Journal of Forensic Medicine and Pathology, 5*, 111–120.

Wetli, C. V., Davis, J. M., & Blackbourne, B. D. (1972). Narcotic addiction in Dade County, Florida: An analysis of 100 consecutive autopsies. *Archives of Pathology, 93*, 330–343.

Wetli, C. V., & Fishbain, D. L. (1985). Cocaine-induced psychosis and sudden death in recreational cocaine users. *Journal of Forensic Science, 30*, 873–880.

Wetli, C. V., & Mittleman, R. E. (1981). The body packer syndrome: Toxicity following ingestion of illicit drugs packaged for transportation. *Journal of Forensic Science, 26*, 492–500.

Wetli, C. V., Weiss, S. D., Cleary, T. J., & Gyori, E. (1984). Fungal cerebritis from intravenous drug abuse. *Journal of Forensic Science, 29*–260–268.

Wetli, C. V., & Wright, R. K. (1979). Death caused by recreational cocaine use. *Journal of the American Medical Association, 241*, 2519–2522.

Wound botulism associated with parenteral cocaine abuse. (1982). *Morbidity and Mortality Weekly Report, 31*, 87–88.

Yaffee, H. S. (1968). Dermatologic manifestation of cocaine addiction. *Cutis, 4*, 286–287.

5

Psychopharmacology of Cocaine

REESE T. JONES

Historical Notes

Cocaine has been used in medical practice for almost a century. The pharmacology of such an old drug should be well understood. It is not. Cocaine's local anesthetic properties, its central nervous system stimulant actions, and its cardiovascular effects after ingestion by a variety of routes—oral, snuffing, smoking, chewing, and by injection—and its addictive properties were first described before 1900 began (Freud, 1974).

For hundreds of years before its first use in a medical setting, cocaine was regularly consumed in large areas of South America by coca leaf chewing (Allen, 1981; Holmstedt & Fredga, 1981). Plants containing psychoactive alkaloids have had so long an association with humans that coca, coffee, tobacco, and opium-producing plants no longer exist in the wild state, but exist only as cultigens (Holmstedt & Fredga, 1981). The pharmacology of coca leaf and other alkaloid-containing plants like tobacco or coffee is not necessarily identical with the pharmacology of the pure alkaloid (Bedford, Turner, & Elsohly, 1982). The pharmacology of the three major stimulant alkaloids—caffeine, nicotine, and cocaine—has much in common, to the extent that for a period it appeared that coca might join tobacco and coffee as a favored psychoactive drug (Freud, 1974).

Much of cocaine psychopharmacology as we now understand it was described in general terms but then largely forgotten until a renaissance in cocaine psychopharmacology occurred about 1975, when, in response to public concern over increased use, the National Institute on Drug Abuse (NIDA) funded research projects to study the psychopharmacology of cocaine in humans.

Publications describing those studies and others since then provide better documented information on relationships between cocaine dose, route of administration, tissue levels of cocaine, and some of its metabolites, and characterize a limited range of physiologic and psychologic effects (Chow et al., 1985; Fischman et al., 1976; Inaba, Stewart, & Kalow, 1978;

Reese T. Jones. Department of Psychiatry and Langley Porter Neuropsychiatric Institute, University of California, San Francisco, San Francisco, California.

Javaid, Fischman, Schuster, Dekirmenjian, & Davis, 1978; Post, Kotin, & Goodwin, 1974; Resnick, Kestenbaum, & Schwartz, 1977). However, gaps remain concerning the psychopharmacology of cocaine. For example, mechanisms and sites of action, and reasons for individual differences in vulnerability to toxic effects, remain uncertain; although patients describe and behave as if cognition is impaired, no human studies have systematically examined this. Information from clinical observations and therapeutic trials that may help explain mechanisms of action and better define the nature of the cognitive disturbances is described elsewhere in this book.

There is still only a relatively small literature on the human psychopharmacology of cocaine. The more extensive literature describing research in animals is sometimes difficult to compare directly to the human experience because of species differences in drug metabolism; use of different doses or routes of administration; and a tendency to focus on acute, single-dose studies, whereas many cocaine-induced problems in humans follow repetitive administration.

Chemistry

Cocaine chemistry constrains certain aspects of its psychopharmacology, although, as with other social phenomena and social drugs, mode and pattern of cocaine use are determined by fad, fashion, and media as well. Cocaine occurs in the leaves of the bush *Erythroxylon coca*, in the amount of about 1% or less, along with many other alkaloids (Lindgren, 1981). As with any plant, cocaine content varies with growing and harvesting conditions and plant genetics. The cocaine in the plant exists as a base and, hence, is relatively insoluble in water. Through a relatively simple extraction using organic solvents, separation, and recrystallization, the cocaine in its basic form is extracted from the plant and usually converted to a salt (generally the hydrochloride), so that it becomes very soluble in water. In this respect cocaine is like nicotine, also a weak base, in that water or lipid solubility, and hence ability to cross membranes, depends on pH. As with nicotine, cocaine base in an acidic environment crosses nasal or buccal membranes relatively slowly and inefficiently. In contrast, in an alkaline environment or when taken as the salt, cocaine is very rapidly absorbed. When smoked, cocaine is absorbed almost instantly by the 70 m^2 membranes of the capillary vessel network of lung alveoli, and 80–90% of the cocaine in the smoke is absorbed independent of pH. Cocaine smoked in the base form is less likely to be broken down by excess heat than is the salt.

Routes of Administration

Cocaine is consumed by diverse routes and over an extremely wide range of doses, thus making generalizations about its psychopharmacology imprecise. People take cocaine intranasally, intravenously, orally, by chewing, sublingually, and by smoking. Both in theory and in clinical practice, behavioral and physiologic effects and toxicity, and probably dependence liability, vary with route of administration.

Improved assays have led to more information on relationships between dose, route of administration, tissue level, and subsequent effects. These assays document quantitatively what has long been known by cocaine users. Oral ingestion, usually in the form of an elixir, was a common form of cocaine use in the late 19th and early 20th centuries (Freud, 1974). In recent years, snuffing has become a popular route, possibly reflecting the ready availability of the salt, as well as fads determining preferred drug route. Sublingual use is becoming popular and would, of course, deliver a higher dose when the salt is used. If cocaine base is taken sublingually, it must be in an alkaline environment for optimal bioavailability. Either the salt or the base can be injected intravenously (although low solubility in water limits the dose of the base) and, because cocaine exists in a partially dissociated form in blood, would be equally efficacious.

Smoking cocaine is by far the most efficient and fastest way to deliver the drug to the brain in the most concentrated dose. Smoked cocaine reaches brain in 6–7 seconds over the route from lung to left heart to brain, whereas an intravenous (IV) injection takes two to three times as long traversing a far longer route. Cocaine taken nasally or sublingually begins to reach the brain in 2–3 minutes; orally, in 8–10 minutes.

Choice of route is determined partially by chemistry and pharmacokinetic considerations, but also by fashions and fads in drug taking. The choice is sometimes a rational one based on the psychopharmacology of cocaine—for example, the use of smoked material to produce maximum alteration in brain function. In other instances, like the selection of the nasal instead of the sublingual route, the choice is as likely based on current fashions rather than on cocaine pharmacokinetics.

It is unclear whether the demands of the marketplace determine the chemical formulation of cocaine products or whether the market shapes use patterns. Snuffing cocaine is facilitated by the availability of the salt, hence by the availability of cocaine hydrochloride in the illicit market. For smoking cocaine, the base offers advantages. Cocaine base is now more readily available in the illicit market, and smoked use is more common (Jekel et al., 1986). What is cause and what consequence is a matter of conjecture. Cocaine marketing is rarely planned by business consultants using data from consumer surveys, although the market does appear to respond to demand.

Why the nasal route became so popular is unclear. The relative bioavailability (about 30%) and intensity of many cocaine effects are similar after oral or nasal doses (Van Dyke, Jatlow, Barash, & Byck, 1978; Van Dyke, Ungerer, Jatlow, Barash, & Byck, 1982; Wilkinson, Van Dyke, Jatlow, Barash, & Byck, 1980). In extensive comparisons, we find similar intensity and patterns of effects after nasal and oral doses in research subjects given oral, nasal, and intravenous cocaine. The rate of change in mood is slightly faster and begins earlier after snuffing, but only by a few minutes. However, rate of change in plasma (and presumably in brain) drug levels and associated subjective changes may be a very important consideration in determining preferred route of psychoactive administration.

The relationships between plasma concentrations of cocaine, cocaine effects, and brain levels are not simple or predictable ones (Mayersohn & Perrier, 1978). Because of the very rapid metabolism and tissue uptake of cocaine, venous blood levels do not adequately represent entry levels into an organ, particularly an organ like the brain. Regional distribution of cocaine levels in various organs is not well characterized. Brain cocaine levels were surprisingly high in comparison to plasma levels in people dying of overdoses (Chinn, Crouch, Peat, Finkle, & Jennison, 1980). The vasculature of the nasopharynx and sublingual areas makes it likely that cocaine brain levels during the earliest phases of drug absorption may considerably exceed systemic venous plasma levels. Brain levels in rats given radiolabeled cocaine suggest cocaine is taken up very rapidly by brain (Misra, Nayak, Block, & Mulé, 1975, 1976). The best illustration of the importance of rate of brain uptake is the intense but very transient psychological effect of cocaine smoking (Paly, Jatlow, Van Dyke, Jeri, & Byck, 1982; Perez-Reyes, Diguiseppi, Ondrusek, Jeffcoat, & Cook, 1982). The initial effects of smoked cocaine are more intense and rapid in onset than comparable intravenous doses could produce. Presumably, levels fall just as rapidly because of the distribution and the metabolism.

Cocaine Effects on Brain Function

People take cocaine primarily to alter brain function. The desired consequences are all stimulant-induced alterations in brain function—pleasant feelings, euphoria (Fischman et al., 1976), relief of fatigue (Fischman & Schuster, 1980), and boredom—and the other expected consequences of central nervous system (CNS) stimulation. Cocaine's actions on the CNS are complex. In the most general way, effects on brain function are similar to those produced by other CNS stimulants—amphetamines, caffeine, and the like (Leith & Barrett, 1981; Schechter & Glennon, 1985). Other cocaine effects resemble those produced by local anesthetics, particularly its membrane-stabilizing properties.

Over 50 years ago, one of the first descriptions of human electroencephalographic (EEG) activity used cocaine to alter brain electrical activity. A more recent study confirms those early reports that increased beta activity follows modest doses of cocaine (Herning, Jones, Hooker, Mendelson, &

Blackwell, 1985). Late components of auditory event–related potentials thought to reflect the efficiency of information processing are markedly decreased by small doses of cocaine (Herning, Jones, Hooker, & Tulunay, 1985). Other laboratories report that stimulants like methylphenidate increase rather than decrease the amplitude of these P300 components. It is generally assumed that methylphenidate, amphetamine, and related stimulants have pharmacologic actions and many mechanisms in common with cocaine (Angrist & Sudilovsky, 1978). The different pattern of evoked potential changes suggests there may be differences as well. None of the EEG changes are pathognomonic for cocaine and thus cannot confirm recent use.

Among the earliest reported toxic effects of cocaine were convulsions (Myers & Earnest, 1984), generally thought to reflect CNS stimulant effects. Early studies noting that, after high doses of cocaine, convulsive behavior was often followed by death generally associated with respiratory depression assumed that cocaine acted mainly at a cortical level. In recent years, more precise neurophysiologic recording techniques with implanted electrodes indicate that changes in limbic system function precede generalized motor convulsions and even precede measurable changes in cortical electrical activity (Lesse, 1980). Cocaine-induced seizures originating in limbic structures provide a useful model to investigate temporal lobe epilepsy and psychoses associated with psychomotor seizures (Lesse, 1980). An interesting difference between cocaine and amphetamine is cocaine's propensity to induce seizures even after a single dose, whereas amphetamines generally require repeated administration.

The relative lack of interest in the human electrophysiology of cocaine is surprising, since in animals one of the most dramatic consequences of repetitive cocaine administration is a phenomenon referred to as "kindling" (Ellinwood & Kilbey, 1980; Post, Kopanda, & Black, 1976; Russell & Stripling, 1985). Kindling, a term used to describe increased sensitivity and responsivity in a number of neural systems, appears to represent an enhanced propagation of electrical signals. The locus of activity is in limbic system structures, and is possibly of etiologic significance in the mimicking of schizophreniclike mental phenomena by chronic cocaine administration. Evidence of EEG kindling has not been reported in long-term, frequent cocaine users. On the other hand, brain wave changes in such populations have not been studied systematically.

Mechanisms of Action

As with other psychoactive drugs, the mechanisms of cocaine's actions are not understood. Cocaine is a potent local anesthetic blocking the generation and conduction of nerve impulses by effects on cell membranes. Cocaine's

CNS stimulant properties are not necessarily related to those attributes, since other potent local anesthetics have little or no cocainelike effects on mood.

Although there is some evidence of selective binding sites, a good case for specific cocaine receptors has not appeared (Misre et al., 1975; Reith, Sershen, & Lajtha, 1985). Mechanisms related to generalized cocaine effects on membrane stability are more consistent with the data thus far (Matthews & Collins, 1983).

Neurochemical Substrates

A problem in understanding the neurochemical substrates of cocaine's actions is that many animal experiments examine only acute effects after one or very few doses rather than the more clinically relevant consequences of repeated administration. Single doses of cocaine and other stimulants and perhaps all psychoactive drugs may have quite different consequences than chronic, repeated administration (Ellinwood & Kilbey, 1980; Post et al., 1976). Traditionally, it is said that the stimulating effects of cocaine are due to its ability to block the reuptake of norepinephrine. Although a partial explanation, it is not a complete one since many psychoactive drugs (for example, some antidepressants) also block the reuptake of neurotransmitters but are not stimulants and do not produce mood states or behaviors like those associated with cocaine use.

Cocaine facilitates release and inhibits norepinephrine reuptake but also alters neurotransmitter systems involving dopamine and serotonin (Friedman, Gershon, & Rotrosen, 1975; Reith, Sershen, Allen, & Lajtha, 1983). Dopaminergic neurons mediate many cocaine effects (Hunt, Switzman, & Amit, 1985). Dopamine reuptake is decreased, release is facilitated, receptor number and activity are increased, with the net effect being functional dopamine depletion after repeated use (Dackis, Gold, Davies, & Sweeney, 1985). It decreases the uptake of tryptophan and, hence, impairs regulatory processes important in the biosynthesis of serotonin (Knapp & Mandell, 1972). Serotonin depletion may enhance the excitatory effects of dopamine and norepinephrine. Cocaine can interact with the cholinergic system as well (Liang & Quastel, 1969). An acetylcholinesterase inhibitor inhibits cocaine-induced hyperactivity and stereotypy in rats (Post et al., 1976). Thus, under conditions of repeated use, the direct effects of cocaine on various neurochemical systems can interact with the parallel neurochemical correlates of conditioning and learning on those systems. For example, electrophysiologic phenomena, numbers and activity of receptor/binding sites (e.g., dopamine alpha and beta adrenergic receptors), and mechanisms that alter kinetics change with repeated cocaine exposure (Ellinwood & Kilbey, 1980).

Pharmacokinetics

The pharmacokinetics of cocaine and its metabolites, particularly absorption and route-dependent differences in metabolism and excretion, are not yet fully worked out. Great variability, both within groups of subjects in the same laboratory and between laboratories, characterizes published cocaine kinetic values. For example, estimates of terminal elimination half-life after IV doses range from 19 minutes (mean 41.4) (Javaid, Musa, Fischman, Schuster, & Davis, 1983) to 168 minutes (Kogan, Verebey, dePace, Resnick, & Mulé, 1977). Many of the earlier studies describing kinetics did not sample blood levels long enough after cocaine administration to properly characterize the terminal phase of clearance. Numbers of subjects in most published studies are very small. In a large sample ($N = 60$) of infrequent cocaine users, we found terminal half-life to range from a mean of 61 minutes after 0.2 mg/kg of cocaine given intravenously to 80 minutes at a dose of 0.6 mg/kg. At any given dose level, however, there was enormous between-subject variability in half-lives and metabolic clearance and equally great variability when the same subject was tested on more than one occasion a week or two apart. Similar variability appears on kinetic parameters such as plasma level versus time area under the curve, peak plasma levels, and time to peak plasma levels. Possibly, even when given intravenously, cocaine's powerful vasoconstrictive properties tend to alter its uptake, distribution, and metabolism.

Metabolism

Cocaine metabolism differs enough between species so that to understand the clinical pharmacology of cocaine in humans, humans must be investigated (Inaba et al., 1978). Degradation by plasma esterases is an important metabolic path (Jatlow, Barash, Van Dyke, Radding, & Byck, 1979). Humans have 4 to 20 times more esterase activity than animals do (Foldes, 1978). Rats have no cocaine esterase activity in liver or plasma (Stewart, Inaba, Lucassen, & Kalow, 1979). Understanding cocaine metabolism presents challenging analytic problems, since a significant hepatic metabolism as well as a separate metabolic route via blood esterases (and probably a not insignificant nonenzymatic metabolism) coexist (Kloss, Rosen, & Rauckman, 1984). Cocaine is rapidly metabolized to a number of water-soluble metabolites, mainly excreted in urine (Fish & Wilson, 1969). The major metabolites in urine are benzoylecgonine (Foltz, Fentiman, & Foltz, 1980; Kogan et al., 1977) and ecgonine methyl ester (Ambre, 1985; Ambre, Ruo, Smith, Backer, & Smith, 1982). These hydrolysis products are generally assumed to result from the action of esterases in the liver and in the serum, although benzoylecgonine may be formed nonenzymatically *in vivo*. M-

Demethylated metabolites of each of the above can occur. An active metabolite, norcocaine, occurs in animals and in very low levels in humans (Hawks, Kopin, Colburn, & Thoa, 1974; Jindal, Lutz, & Verstergaard, 1978; Just & Moyer, 1977). The effects of norcocaine in humans have not been studied, although it inhibits norepinephrine reuptake, has local anesthetic actions, and alters schedule-controlled behavior (Bedford, Nall, Borne, & Wilson, 1981; Borne et al., 1977). Ecgonine methyl ester in urine or benzoylecgonine in urine or blood are useful as markers of cocaine use. Benzoylecgonine with a 6–9 hour half-life and ecgonine methyl ester with a 3–4 hour terminal half-life provide longer-lasting indicators of time of most recent cocaine use (Ambre, 1985).

Consideration of species differences is important when trying to understand cocaine metabolism. For example, cocaine is a potent hepatotoxin in some strains of mice, possibly because of hepatic tissue binding of a metabolite (Evans, 1982; Freeman & Harbison, 1981; Kloss et al., 1984). However, in humans, most other species and even other strains of mice, liver damage does not seem associated with cocaine use.

Most cocaine studies in animals, particularly behavioral studies, have rarely measured cocaine or cocaine metabolite tissue levels, let alone examined kinetics (Bozarth & Wise, 1985). Thus the extent of metabolic variation between species is not well characterized. Certainly, cholinesterase activity varies greatly across species (Foldes, 1978). Considering the efficient hepatic and nonhepatic metabolism, however, the functional impact of higher or lower than a certain level of cholinesterase activity could well depend on route of administration as well as on species. In addition, rate of administration and total dose interact to determine intensity of effects.

Absorption

Absorption rate and total amount absorbed depend on route of administration. Dose, of course, determines cocaine effects, but rate of absorption is almost as important a determinant of acute effects and toxicity. Under conditions favoring slow absorption, even a large dose may have fewer effects than would a much smaller total dose very rapidly absorbed because metabolism and disposition of cocaine are relatively rapid.

Since cocaine is a potent vasoconstrictor, its rate of absorption is altered by its effects on regional vasculature when it is given subcutaneously or across nasal or sublingual mucous membranes. Acute toxic reactions from cocaine are most often associated with rapid onset of high plasma levels, usually after rapid absorption. Estimates of what constitutes a lethal dose of cocaine vary greatly. The lethal dose depends very much on route of administration. Without question, serious acute and chronic behavioral impairment and fatal toxicity are possible by any route of administration. However, a relatively larger quantity of cocaine taken at a more rapid pace will be required for equal toxicity, depending on the rate of uptake as it might be route dependent.

Nasal and Oral Administration

Cocaine is as readily absorbed orally as nasally. Its bioavailability (20–30%) orally is about the same as by nasal administration (Wilkinson *et al.*, 1980). The widespread use of cocaine in the early 20th century in Europe and the United States was mainly in the form of oral elixirs. Cocaine is still commonly taken by chewing coca leaf or sucking on powdered coca leaves in those cultures where that tradition persists (Allen, 1981; Holmstedt, Lindgren, Rivier, & Plowman, 1979). When coca leaves are chewed, there is a combination of cocaine absorption directly from mucous membranes in the mouth and by swallowing and thus some avoidance of the very high initial first-pass hepatic metabolism. When coca leaves are chewed, measurable levels of cocaine appear in the blood as soon as 5 minutes after chewing (Holmstedt *et al.*, 1979; Paly, Van Dyke, Jatlow, Cabieses, & Byck, 1979). When swallowed, cocaine is readily measured in blood within 10–15 minutes and perhaps even earlier (Van Dyke *et al.*, 1978).

Peak subjective and other effects are slower in onset with oral or nasal use, possibly allowing a certain degree of tolerance to develop as the effects manifest themselves. The chronic toxicity of cocaine appears different and less when the drug is ingested by chewing coca leaves rather than by taking the pure alkaloid (Allen, 1981; Bedford, Turner, & Elsohly, 1982; Negrete, 1978).

Cocaine produces excellent anesthesia with a rapid onset and vasoconstriction of mucous membranes. Thus, it has been extensively used as an anesthetic for nasal surgery. Absorption after nasal administration is more rapid than is oral administration, but only during the initial 5–10 minutes or so. The peak plasma levels of cocaine, time of peak plasma levels, and bioavailability after snuffing are very similar to oral administration.

Plasma levels of cocaine do not necessarily indicate organ levels, for example brain levels (Spiehler & Reed, 1985), nor do they predict time of peak effects. For example, in an instance where cocaine blood levels were being measured in surgical patients, a patient developed restlessness, excitement, and bradycardia within 2 minutes after cotton packs containing 5% cocaine solution were inserted nasally. Even though the packs were immediately removed, peak plasma cocaine levels 75 minutes later were 350 ng/ ml, a level threefold higher than usually seen at that dose. Earlier, 20 minutes after the pack was removed, plasma levels were only 100 ng/ml. For reasons that are not well understood, the systemic uptake, particularly brain uptake, of cocaine after nasal administration can be extremely rapid and not always reflected in peripheral venous blood levels.

Plasma level differences between nasal ingestion of cocaine crystals and ingestion of solution are small. Variations in plasma cocaine levels seem to be more a function of total dose rather than of concentration of cocaine solution used. Some of the relatively rare acute toxic reactions when cocaine spray is used in anesthesic procedures may be due to inhalation of cocaine mist that diffuses into lung alveoli, is quickly absorbed, and produces CNS cocaine levels much higher than could be obtained through slower absorption from nasal or pharyngeal mucosa or trachea (Brodsky & Goldwyn, 1977; Campbell & Adriani, 1958).

When cocaine is instilled into the nasopharynx as either crystalline material or spray, relatively little appears in saliva during the absorptive phase, suggesting relatively complete absorption and/or metabolism from nasopharynx rather than partial swallowing. However, cocaine is very slowly cleared from nasal mucous membranes. Nasal swabs reveal measurable levels as long as 3 hours after inhalation, probably the result of impaired ciliary action on the nasal mucous blanket (Bedford *et al.*, 1981).

Parenteral Administration

Although a once popular route, subcutaneous or intramuscular injection of cocaine is less common among parenteral users. Cocaine-induced vasoconstriction, and thus self-induced slowing of absorption, makes that route less desirable for the user seeking rapid or intense peak effects. The magnitude and range of effects following IV injection are related both to dose and to the rapidity of injection. Subjective and physiologic effects begin within 30 seconds after a rapid IV dose, peak within minutes after the injection, and then decrease relatively rapidly over the next 30 minutes. Dose–effect relationships have not been well characterized under laboratory conditions in humans at dose levels greater than 0.6 mg/kg. That dose of cocaine will produce peak plasma levels of cocaine between 300 and 400 ng/ml. A dose 5 to 6 times that amount but injected slowly over 60 minutes as multiple doses may produce peak cocaine levels of over 1,000 ng/ml with no greater subjective or cardiovascular effects than the rapidly injected but much lower dose. This, of course, is the expected pattern of drug response with a rapidly metabolized, rapidly distributed drug.

Inhaled or Smoked Cocaine

Only a direct injection into the carotid artery or brain could deliver a concentrated bolus of cocaine any more rapidly to the CNS than does inhalation or smoking. IV administration in a peripheral vein can rapidly deliver a large amount of drug systemically; but, particularly in the case of a vasoconstrictive, rapidly distributed, and rapidly metabolized drug like cocaine, injection into a peripheral vein can never quite achieve the initial high blood/brain level ratio that smoking can. An analogy here is the experience with nicotine and tobacco and the obvious advantages of smoked nicotine for producing rapid, intense effects.

The intense and relatively brief mental and physiologic state following a single inhalation or two of cocaine (Siegel, 1982) reflects the effects of a concentrated bolus efficiently delivered to the brain. The pathway from the lung, to the left heart, to the carotid artery, to the brain with an 8-second transit time is far more direct than the path an injection into an arm vein must travel: venous return to right heart, to lungs and then left heart before reaching the brain. The efficiency of smoking, particularly the amount of cocaine delivered to the lung alveoli, varies with the technique used. Most cocaine smoking techniques do not allow for precise temperature regulation, so that small variations from optimal pipe or cigarette temperature may either increase delivery or destroy available cocaine (Perez-Reyes et al., 1982).

The strong reinforcing effects of smoked cocaine can best be understood by considering tobacco use. Although tobacco taken by chewing or snuff will satisfy nicotine craving to some extent, most nicotine addicts would agree that the first few inhalations of the day from a tobacco cigarette are quite different, a very special way of delivering nicotine to the brain. As the day goes on and smoking is repeated, nicotine becomes less reinforcing and pleasurable. So it is for the cocaine smoker. After a relatively few inhaled doses of cocaine, subsequent use is more determined by a need to avoid an unpleasant, dysphoric letdown after smoking than it is to obtain the positive and pleasurable reinforcing effects initially experienced. Increased behavioral toxicity associated with smoked cocaine can best be understood as a consequence of a drug delivery system that produces more intense drug effects on the brain.

Tolerance

If tolerance did not rapidly develop to many of the desirable (e.g., sought-after) CNS effects of cocaine, it would probably be less of a health problem, since users would need less cocaine taken less often. Tolerance develops rapidly to many but not all cocaine effects (Fischman, Schuster, Javaid, Hatano, & Davis, 1985; Wood, Lai, & Emmett-Oglesby, 1984). Discussions of cocaine tolerance often focus on the extensive but not always consistent evidence of increasing sensitivity to some cocaine effects. Data consistent with the development of traditional concepts of acquired tolerance, that of diminished effects with repeated doses, have also long been available (Teeters, Koppanyi, & Cowan, 1963). Decreased intensity or disappearance of some cocaine effects with repeated doses is not inconsistent with the concomitant increased intensity of or new appearance of other effects, for example CNS kindling, indicating a sensitization to cocaine.

As tolerance and dependence become better understood, there is an appreciation that they involve a host of interacting adaptive mechanisms (Gawin & Kleber, 1986). Some of the neuroadaptive responses to the presence of cocaine or its metabolites may appear as increasing or newly appearing effects (for example, the development of attention dysfunction or a paranoid psychotic state), while concurrently the magnitude of other effects (for example, cardiovascular effects) is decreasing. Concurrently decreasing initial, acute effects and increasing newly appearing effects would be inconsistent with neuroadaptation or tolerance only in the relatively uncommon instances where tolerance to a psychoactive drug can be fully accounted for by more rapid drug metabolism or the production of an active metabolite. Cocaine metabolic or dispositional changes are not of sufficient magnitude to account for the very substantial tolerance that follows repeated doses. Although some still unrecognized active metabolite might possibly account for a gradually developing toxic psychosis, it is unlikely. Tolerance to cocaine is by functional mechanisms; that is, there are adaptive CNS changes that account for it. These adaptive mechanisms are complex and not yet fully understood.

Since cocaine is a short-acting drug, relatively frequent dosing should be necessary to produce optimal conditions for tolerance to appear, particularly if the measures of tolerance are not sensitive ones. That is often the case in animal studies that do not find tolerance. Once daily or even two or three times daily doses, as have been used in animal studies, are insufficient to produce tolerance in some species except under conditions of prolonged administration. In contrast, even the very earliest accounts of cocaine use in humans described diminished effects with repeated doses in those instances where high doses were used frequently (Fischman & Schuster, 1981; Freud, 1974).

Increasing irritability, restlessness, hypervigilance, and suspicious and paranoid behaviors associated with repeated cocaine use by humans may be a human analogue of CNS kindling phenomenon observed in some animal experiments under some experimental paradigms (Ellinwood & Kilbey, 1980; Post, 1975; Post, Lockfeld, Squillace, & Contel, 1981). Amphetamine-induced psychoses and the toxic syndrome associated with frequent and repeated cocaine use are similar. Most of the differences are explicable by pharmacokinetic differences between cocaine and the amphetamines. Amphetamine-induced psychoses and, perhaps even more so, cocaine-induced psychoses may be a useful model for certain naturally occurring psychoses like schizophrenia.

Questions remain. Are people with genetic predispositions to schizo-phrenia more at risk for cocaine-induced psychoses? Inconsistencies appear. For example, why are the sustained and relatively high plasma levels of cocaine associated with seemingly behaviorally nontoxic use of coca by the Quechua Indians? Animal studies suggest coca leaf contains constituents other than cocaine that alter its pharmacology (Bedford *et al.*, 1981, 1982). Does the coca leaf contain something that antagonizes certain cocaine effects? Does this protect the Quechua? Or is it simply a matter of different bioavailability?

Dependence

Cocaine researchers and those treating cocaine addicts increasingly describe symptoms and behaviors that follow cessation of cocaine use (Gawin & Kleber, 1985, 1986; Kleber & Gawin, 1984). The charactcristic cocaine abstinence syndrome has both psychological and physiological components. The complex pattern of depression, social withdrawal, craving, cognitive disturbance, tremor, muscle pain, appetite disturbance, EEG changes, and changes in sleep is increasingly more difficult to categorize as a consequence of merely "psychological" dependence, particularly as experience accumu-lates with high-dose, chronic users (Gawin & Kleber, 1986).

Patients resume cocaine use to decrease their withdrawal signs and symptoms, with some temporary success. Resumed cocaine use, however, then produces irritability, paranoia, delusional and confused thinking, and other unpleasant effects—hence the cycling on and off cocaine commonly defined as the *run*. Understanding these cocaine-induced states has theoreti-cal and practical importance when attempting to develop a psychopharma-cologic model for rational treatment (Gawin & Kleber, 1986). The clinical implications of this consistent, fairly predictable set of signs and symptoms following repeated cocaine use are discussed in other chapters in this book.

Interactions with Other Drugs

Cocaine often—in fact usually—is used in combination with alcohol or marijuana or caffeine. Thirty percent of cocaine users report using cocaine in combination with alcohol on almost every occasion of use. Twenty-six percent of cocaine users report concurrent marijuana use every time. Most frequent cocaine users are also tobacco smokers and coffee drinkers. All these drugs share mechanisms and metabolic routes. No controlled labora-tory experiments have been done.

Cocaine, alcohol, and tobacco are individual risk factors for adverse cardiovascular events. Heavy ethanol consumption is associated with in-creased prevalence of hypertension and cardiovascular mortality. Cocaine use is associated with increased cardiovascular mortality. Most victims of sudden cardiac death where cocaine is not involved are cigarette smokers. Such events are often associated with recent ethanol intake. Ethanol, cocaine, and cannabis activate the sympathetic nervous system with increased levels of circulating catecholamines, increased heart rate, and elevated blood pressure; all three are potentially arrhythmogenic. Thus additive or synergistic effects might increase the likelihood of adverse cardiovascular events. Caffeine, by adenosine-mediated mechanisms or otherwise, could alter noradrenergic neuromodulator systems and, thus, the magnitude of cocaine consequences.

Complex behavioral interactions occur during cocaine consumption and the concurrent use of alcohol, tobacco, coffee, marijuana, and probably, in principle, any other psychoactive drugs used repetitively in social situations. For example, people smoke more cigarettes, puff more, or inhale more deeply while drinking alcohol. Cocaine and nicotine may diminish or enhance various psychological effects of alcohol. One obvious mechanism for interactions is that ethanol or cocaine or nicotine may influence the rate of elimination of the drugs used in combination, leading to the need for an increased dose of the second drug in order to maintain a desired body (brain) level.

Opiates, barbiturates, stimulants (amphetamine, etc.), other local anesthetics (lidocaine, procaine, etc.), neuroleptics, antidepressants, and many other drugs are used concurrently with cocaine. The pharmacologic characterization of the interaction between cocaine and other very commonly used therapeutic and illicit drugs is almost unexplored in humans and seldom studied in other species other than in the vast literature on neurochemical or related CNS interactions (Aston-Jones, Aston-Jones, & Koob, 1984; Bagchi, 1985; Thompson & Winsauer, 1985). Much of that animal data suggests that serious or lethal synergistic effects are unlikely. On the other hand, lesser clinically important but probably subtle effects should be expected given the shared mechanisms of action.

REFERENCES

Allen, C. J. (1981). To be Quechua—The symbolism of coca chewing in highland Peru. *American Ethnologist, 8*, 157–162.

Ambre, J. (1985). The urinary excretion of cocaine and metabolites in humans: A kinetic analysis of published data. *Journal of Analytical Toxicology, 9*, 241–245.

Ambre, J., Ruo, J. H., Smith, G. L., Backer, D., & Smith, C. M. (1982). Ecgonine methyl ester, a major metabolite of cocaine. *Journal of Analytical Toxicology, 6*, 26–29.

Angrist, B., & Sudilovsky, A. (1978). In L. L. Iverson, S. D. Iverson, & S. H. Snyder (Eds.), *Handbook of psychopharmacology* (Vol. 11, pp. 99–164). New York: Plenum Press.

Aston-Jones, S., Aston-Jones, G., & Koob, G. F. (1984). Cocaine antagonizes anxiolytic effects of ethanol. *Psychopharmacology, 84*, 28–31.

Bagchi, S. P. (1985). Cocaine and phencyclidine: Heterogeneous dopaminergic interactions with tetrabenazine. *Neuropharmacology, 24*, 37–41.

Bedford, J. A., Nail, G. L., Borne, R. F., & Wilson, M. C. (1981). Discriminative stimulus properties of cocaine, norcocaine, and N-allylnorcocaine. *Pharmacology, Biochemistry and Behavior, 14*, 81–83.

Bedford, J. A., Turner, C. E., & Elsohly, H. N. (1982). Comparative lethality of coca and cocaine. *Pharmacology, Biochemistry and Behavior, 17*, 1087–1088.

Borne, R. F., Bedford, J. A., Buelke, J. L., Craig, C. B., Hardin, T. C., Kibbe, A. H., & Wilson, M. C. (1977). Biological effects of cocaine derivatives: I. Improved synthesis and pharmacological evaluation of norcocaine. *Journal of Pharmaceutical Science, 66*, 119–120.

Bozarth, M. A., & Wise, R. A. (1985). Toxicity associated with long-term intravenous heroin and cocaine self-administration in the rat. *Journal of the American Medical Association, 254, 81*–83.

Brodsky, J. B., & Goldwyn, R. M. (1977). Hemodynamic effects of intranasal and intravenous cocaine. *New England Journal of Medicine, 296*, 1008.

Campbell, D., & Adriani, J. (1958). Absorption of local anesthetics. *Journal of the American Medical Association, 168*, 873–877.

Chinn, D. M., Crouch, D. J., Peat, M. A., Finkle, B. S., & Jennison, T. A. (1980). Gas chromatography–chemical ionization mass spectrometry of cocaine and its metabolites in biological fluids. *Journal of Analytical Toxicology, 4*, 37–42.

Chow, M. J., Ambre, J. J., Ruo, T. I., Atkinson, A. J., Bowsher, D. J., & Fischman, M. W. (1985). Kinetics of cocaine distribution, elimination, and chronotropic effects. *Clinical Pharmacology and Therapeutics, 38*, 318–324.

Dackis, C. A., Gold, M. S., Davies, R. K., & Sweeney, D. R. (1985). Bromocriptine treatment for cocaine abuse: The dopamine depletion hypothesis. *International Journal of Psychiatry in Medicine, 15*, 125–135.

Ellinwood, E. H., & Kilbey, M. M. (1980). Fundamental mechanisms underlying altered behavior following chronic administration of psychomotor stimulants. *Biological Psychiatry, 15*, 749–757.

Evans, M. A. (1982). Role of protein binding in cocaine-induced hepatic necrosis. *Journal of Pharmacology and Experimental Therapeutics, 224*, 73–79.

Fischman, M. W., & Schuster, C. R. (1980). Cocaine effects in sleep-deprived humans. *Psychopharmacology, 72*, 1–8.

Fischman, M. W., & Schuster, C. R. (1981). Acute tolerance to cocaine in humans. In L. S. Harris (Ed.), *Problems of drug dependence, 1980* (Volume 34, pp. 241–242). Rockville, MD: National Institute on Drug Abuse.

Fischman, M. W., Schuster, C. R., Javaid, J., Hatano, Y., & Davis, J. (1985). Acute tolerance development to the cardiovascular and subjective effects of cocaine. *Journal of Pharmacology and Experimental Therapeutics, 235*, 677–682.

Fischman, M. W., Schuster, C. R., Resnekov, L., Schick, J. F. E., Krasnegor, N. A., Fennel, W., & Freedman, D. X. (1976). Cardiovascular and subjective effects of intravenous cocaine administration in humans. *Archives of General Psychiatry, 33*, 983–989.

Fish, F., & Wilson, W. D. C. (1969). Excretion of cocaine and its metabolites in man. *Journal of Pharmacy and Pharmacology, 21*, 1355–1385.

Foldes, F. F. (1978). Enzymes in anesthesiology. In F. F. Foldes (Ed.), *Enzymes in anesthesiology* (pp. 91–168). New York: Springer-Verlag.

Foltz, R. L., Fentiman, A. F., & Foltz, R. B. (Eds.). (1980). Cocaine and its major metabolite, benzoylecgonine. In *GC/MS assays for abused drugs in body fluids*, NIDA Research Monograph No. 32 (pp. 90–109). Washington, DC: U.S. Government Printing Office.

Freeman, R. W., & Harbison, R. D. (1981). Hepatic periportal necrosis induced by chronic administration of cocaine. *Biochemical Pharmacology, 30*, 777–783.

Freud, S. (1974). *Cocaine papers* (R. Byck, Ed.). New York: New American Library. (Original works published 1885–1898.)

Friedman, E., Gershon, S., & Rotrosen, J. (1975). Effects of active cocaine treatment on the turnover of 5-hydroxytryptamine in the rat brain. *British Journal of Pharmacology, 54,* 61–64.

Gawin, F. H., & Kleber, H. D. (1985). Neuroendocrine findings in chronic cocaine abusers: A preliminary report. *British Journal of Psychiatry, 147,* 569–572.

Gawin, F. H., & Kleber, H. D. (1986). Abstinence symptomatology and psychiatric diagnosis in cocaine abusers. *Archives of General Psychiatry, 43,* 107–113.

Hawks, R. L., Kopin, I. J., Colburn, R. W., & Thoa, N. B. (1974). Norcocaine: A pharmacologically active metabolite of cocaine found in brain. *Life Sciences, 15,* 2189–2195.

Herning, R. I., Jones, R. T., Hooker, W. D., Mendelson, J., & Blackwell, L. (1985). Cocaine increases EEG beta: A replication and extension of Hans Berger's historic experiments. *Electroencephalography and Clinical Neurophysiology, 60,* 470–477.

Herning, R. I., Jones, R. T., Hooker, W. D., & Tulunay, F. C. (1985). Information processing components of the event related potential are reduced by cocaine. *Psychopharmacology, 87,* 178–185.

Holmstedt, B., & Fredga, A. (1981). Sundry episodes in the history of coca and cocaine. *Journal of Ethnopharmacology, 3,* 113–147.

Holmstedt, B., Lindgren, J. E., Rivier, L., & Plowman, T. (1979). Cocaine in blood of coca chewers. *Journal of Ethnopharmacology, 1,* 69–78.

Hunt, T., Switzman, L., & Amit, Z. (1985). Involvement of dopamine in the aversive stimulus properties of cocaine in rats. *Pharmacology, Biochemistry and Behavior, 22,* 945–948.

Inaba, T., Stewart, D. J., & Kalow, W. (1978). Metabolism of cocaine in man. *Clinical Pharmacology and Therapeutics, 23,* 547–552.

Jatlow, P., Barash, P. G., Van Dyke, C., Radding, J., & Byck, R. (1979). Cocaine and succinylcholine sensitivity: A new caution. *Anesthesia and Analgesia, 58,* 235–238.

Javaid, J. I., Fischman, M. W., Schuster, C. R., Dekirmenjian, M., & Davis, J. M. (1978). Cocaine plasma concentrations: Relation to physiological and subjective effects in humans. *Science, 200,* 227–228.

Javaid, J. I., Musa, N. M., Fischman, M. W., Schuster, C. R., & Davis, J. M. (1983). Kinetics of cocaine in humans after intravenous and intranasal administration. *Biopharmaceutics and Drug Disposition, 4,* 9–18.

Jekel, J. F., Allen, D. E., Podlewski, M., Clarke, N., Dean-Patterson, S., & Cartwright, P. (1986). Epidemic free-base cocaine abuse. *Lancet, 1*(8479), 459–461.

Jindal, S. P., Lutz, T., & Verstergaard, P. (1978). Mass spectrometric determination of cocaine and its biologically active metabolite, norcocaine, in human urine. *Biomedical Mass Spectrometry, 5,* 658–663.

Just, W. W., & Hoyer, J. (1977). The local anesthetic potency of norcocaine, a metabolite of cocaine. *Experientia, 33,* 70–71.

Kleber, H. D., & Gawin, F. H. (1984). The spectrum of cocaine abuse and its treatment. *Journal of Clinical Psychiatry, 45,* 18–23.

Kloss, M. W., Rosen, G. M., & Rauckman, E. J. (1984). Cocaine-mediated hepatotoxicity: A critical review. *Biochemical Pharmacology, 33,* 169–173.

Knapp, S., & Mandell, A. J. (1972). Narcotic drugs: Effect on the serotonin biosynthetic systems of the brain. *Science, 177,* 1209–1211.

Kogan, M. J., Verebey, K. G., dePace, A. C., Resnick, R. B., & Mulé, S. J. (1977). Quantitative determination of benzoylecgonine and cocaine in human biofluids by gas liquid chromatography. *Analytical Chemistry, 49,* 1965–1969.

Leith, N. J., & Barrett, R. J. (1981). Self-stimulation and amphetamine: Tolerance to d- and l-isomers and cross-tolerance to cocaine and methylphenidate. *Psychopharmacology, 74,* 28–38.

Lesse, H. (1980). Prolonged effects of cocaine on hippocampal activity. *Communications in Psychopharmacology, 4,* 247.

Liang, C. C., & Quastel, J. H. (1969). Effects of drugs on the uptake of acetylcholine in rat brain cortex slices. *Biochemical Pharmacology, 18*, 1187–1194.

Lindgren, J.-E. (1981). Guide to the analysis of cocaine and its metabolites in biological material. *Journal of Ethnopharmacology, 3*, 336–351.

Matthews, J. C., & Collins, A. (1983). Interactions of cocaine with sodium channels. *Biochemical Pharmacology, 32*, 455–460.

Mayersohn, M., & Perrier, D. (1978). Kinetics of pharmacologic response to cocaine. *Research Communications in Chemical Pathology and Pharmacology, 22*, 465–474.

Misra, A. L., Nayak, P. K., Block, R., & Mulé, S. J. (1975). Estimation and disposition of [³H] benzoylecgonine and pharmacological activity of some cocaine metabolites. *Journal of Pharmacy and Pharmacology, 27*, 784–786.

Misra, A. L., Nayak, P. K., Block, R., & Mulé, S. J. (1976). [³H]-Norcocaine and [³H]-pseudococaine: Effect of N-demethylation and C_2-epimerization of cocaine on its pharmacokinetics in rats. *Experientia* (Basel), *32*, 895–897.

Myers, J. A., & Earnest, M. P. (1984). Generalized seizures and cocaine abuse. *Neurology, 34*, 675–676.

Negrete, J. C. (1978). Coca leaf chewing: Public health assessment. *British Journal of Addiction, 73*, 283–290.

Paly, D., Jatlow, P., Van Dyke, C., Jeri, R., & Byck, R. (1982). Plasma cocaine concentrations during cocaine paste smoking. *Life Sciences, 30*, 731–738.

Paly, D., Van Dyke, C. Jatlow, P., Cabieses, F., & Byck, R. (1979). Cocaine plasma concentrations in coca chewers. *Clinical Pharmacology and Therapeutics, 25*, 240.

Perez-Reyes, M., Diguiseppi, S., Ondrusek, G., Jeffcoat, A. R., & Cook, C. E. (1982). Freebase cocaine smoking. *Clinical Pharmacology and Therapeutics, 32*, 459–465.

Post, R. M. (1975). Cocaine psychosis: A continuum model. *American Journal of Psychiatry, 132*, 225–231.

Post, R. M., Kopanda, R. T., & Black, K. E. (1976). Progressive effects of cocaine on behavior and central amine metabolism in rhesus monkeys: Relationship to kindling and psychoses. *Biological Psychiatry, 11*, 403–419.

Post, R. M., Kotin, J., & Goodwin, F. K. (1974). The effects of cocaine on depressed patients. *American Journal of Psychiatry, 131*, 511–517.

Post, R. M., Lockfeld, A., Squillace, K. M., & Contel, N. R. (1981). Drug–environment interaction: Context dependency of cocaine-induced behavioral sensitization. *Life Sciences, 28*, 755–760.

Reith, M. E. A., Sershen, H., Allen, D. L., & Lajtha, A. (1983). A portion of (³H) cocaine binding in brain is associated with serotonergic neurons. *Molecular Pharmacology, 23*, 600–606.

Reith, M. E. A., Sershen, H., & Lajtha, A. (1985). Binding sites for tritiated cocaine in mouse striatum and cerebral cortex had different dissociation kinetics. *Journal of Neurochemistry, 46*, 309–312.

Resnick, R. B., Kestenbaum, R. S., & Schwartz, L. K. (1977). Acute systemic effects of cocaine in man: A controlled study by intranasal and intravenous routes. *Science, 195*, 696–698.

Russell, R. D., & Stripling, J. S. (1985). Monoaminergic and local anesthetic components of cocaine's effects on kindled seizure expression. *Pharmacology, Biochemistry and Behavior, 22*, 427–434.

Schechter, M. D., & Glennon, R. A. (1985). Cathinone, cocaine and methamphetamine: Similarity of behavioral effects. *Pharmacology, Biochemistry and Behavior, 22*, 913–916.

Siegel, R. K. (1982). Cocaine smoking. *Journal of Psychoactive Drugs, 14*, 271–359.

Spiehler, V. R., & Reed, D. (1985). Brain concentrations of cocaine and benzoylecgonine in fatal cases. *Journal of Forensic Sciences, 30*, 1003–1011.

Stewart, D. J., Inaba, T., Lucassen, M., & Kalow, W. (1979). Cocaine metabolism: Cocaine and norcocaine hydrolysis by liver and serum esterases. *Clinical Pharmacology and Therapeutics, 25,* 464–468.

Teeters, W. R., Koppanyi, T., & Cowan, F. F. (1963). Cocaine tachyphylaxis. *Life Sciences, 7,* 509–518.

Thompson, D. M., & Winsauer, P. J. (1985). Cocaine potentiates the disruptive effects of phencyclidine on repeated acquisition in monkeys. *Pharmacology, Biochemistry and Behavior, 23,* 823–830.

Van Dyke, C., Jatlow, P., Barash, P. G., & Byck, R. (1978). Oral cocaine: Plasma concentrations and central effects. *Science, 100,* 211–213.

Van Dyke, C., Ungerer, J., Jatlow, P., Barash, P., & Byck, R. (1982). Intranasal cocaine: Dose relationships of psychological effects and plasma levels. *International Journal of Psychiatry and Medicine, 12,* 1–13.

Wilkinson, P., Van Dyke, C., Jatlow, P., Barash, P., & Byck, R. (1980). Intranasal and oral cocaine kinetics. *Clinical Pharmacology and Therapeutics, 27,* 386–394.

Wood, D. M., Lal, H., & Emmett-Oglesby, M. (1984). Acquisition and recovery of tolerance to the discriminative stimulus properties of cocaine. *Neuropharmacology, 23,* 1419–1423.

6

Brain Mechanisms in Cocaine Dependency

IRL EXTEIN AND CHARLES A. DACKIS

The current epidemic of cocaine abuse has led to an increasing awareness that cocaine is not a benign recreational drug (Gold, 1984). In fact, cocaine is a highly addictive drug. The *Diagnostic and Statistical Manual of Mental Disorders,* 3rd edition (DSM-III) (American Psychiatric Association, 1980) reflects the long-standing uncertainty even among psychiatrists as to whether cocaine is truly addictive. DSM-III lists only "cocaine abuse" and does not include a category of cocaine dependency. Clinical work with cocaine users, however, strongly suggests that genuine addiction to cocaine is becoming a common problem.

Both basic and clinical research have helped us understand how cocaine interacts with the brain's neurochemical reward centers in providing the cocaine high. It is now well established that cocaine reward results from the activation of central dopamine systems in the brain (Wise, 1985). Cocaine euphoria serves as a positive reinforcer, motivating the addict to continue using cocaine. In this regard, cocaine's ability to stimulate endogenous reward centers in the brain is the basis of its addictive potential, suggesting that clinicians and researchers reexamine present criteria for addictive agents. Recent evidence suggests that chronic cocaine use depletes central dopamine systems in the brain (Dackis & Gold, 1985c), and that this effect may lead to abstinence symptoms and craving. Craving constitutes a negative reinforcer of cocaine abuse, which, combined with cocaine euphoria, drives the addiction. Any viable treatment approach must address both craving and euphoria. This chapter will discuss clinical manifestations of cocaine dependency, and the implications of current understanding of brain mechanisms for pharmacological treatment of cocaine withdrawal.

Neuropharmacology of Cocaine

Cocaine is a short-acting (15–30 minute) stimulant of both the central nervous system and the peripheral sympathetic portion of the autonomic

Irl Extein. Fair Oaks Hospital at Boca/Delray, Delray Beach, Florida.
Charles A. Dackis. Hampton Hospital, Mount Holly, New Jersey.

nervous system (Van Dyke & Byck, 1982). Cocaine is absorbed readily into the bloodstream and reaches the brain quickly by the intranasal route (snorting), the inhalation route (free basing or smoking rock or crack), or the intravenous (IV) route (shooting up). The amount and rapidity by which cocaine is delivered to the brain increases from the nasal to the IV to the inhalation routes. A dose of approximately 50 mg can produce intoxication. Peripheral effects of cocaine include increased heart rate, diaphoresis, hyperthermia, and dilated pupils. Central effects of cocaine include euphoria, grandiosity, irritability, hyperactivity, decreased appetite, and sleeplessness. Cocaine overdoses can cause respiratory arrest, myocardial infarction, arrhythmia and seizures as well.

Cocaine has a number of effects on neurotransmitter function that could explain its clinical effects. Many of cocaine's stimulating effects are a function of its potentiation of the catecholamine neurotransmitters norepinephrine (NE) and dopamine (DA) in the brain.

Cells using NE and DA as neurotransmitters occur in discrete locations in the brain stem and project to higher brain areas, including basal ganglia (affecting motor function), limbic system (affecting arousal and basic appetitive drives and aggression), and hypothalamus (affecting hormone function). These diffuse projections of nerve cell axons contribute to the general state of arousal. These neuronal systems exert their effects by releasing packets of DA or NE neurotransmitters into the synapse, the very narrow space between neurons. Once released into the synapse, the neurotransmitter interacts with specific DA or NE receptors on the next neuron to exert central physiological effects. Under normal conditions, DA or NE is rapidly removed from the synapse by a reuptake mechanism, resulting in the neurotransmitter having a brief pulsatile effect on its target receptors.

Cocaine has powerful effects on DA and NE synapses (see Figure 6-1). Cocaine is a potent inhibitor of the DA and NE reuptake pumps (Gold, Washton, & Dackis, 1985). By blocking the normal mechanism of inactivation of NE and DA, the effect of these neurotransmitters is potentiated many times over. Instead of the brief pulse of transmission, there is a tonic neurochemical stimulatory effect, which is the neurophysiological substrate of the state of arousal associated with cocaine intoxication. These neurochemical effects, which are independent of the local anesthetic effects of cocaine, lead to compensatory changes in synthesis of NE and DA and the number and sensitivity of NE and DA receptors that have important implications for cocaine withdrawal, to be discussed later.

Cocaine Dependency

The phenomenon of addiction to or dependency on a drug occurs only for drugs that cause a feeling of elation or euphoria, the so-called drug high. Addicting drugs cause this high by interacting with the brain's naturally

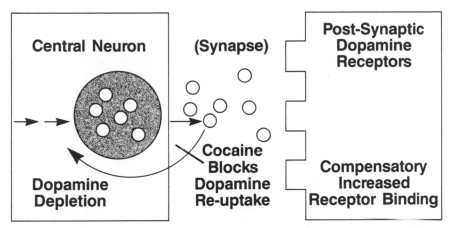

FIGURE 6-1. Effects of chronic cocaine abuse on dopaminergic neurotransmission.

occurring pleasure centers. Chronic use leads to the three classical clinical characteristics that define addiction: psychological dependence, tolerance, and physical withdrawal (Jaffe, 1980).

Psychological dependency may be defined as compulsive drug-seeking behavior despite negative consequences (American Psychiatric Association, 1980). That is, the drug becomes the highest priority in the individual's life, and drug use continues despite mounting financial, legal, marital, occupational, and physical and emotional health problems associated with the drug use. In animal models of this phenomenon, laboratory animals will self-administer cocaine in preference to food until they die (Bozarth & Wise, 1985). In this model, cocaine is more addicting than heroin. The phenomenon of tolerance means that, as time goes on, more and more of the drug is needed to produce the same high. The term *withdrawal* refers to a constellation of signs and symptoms that occur following cessation of drug use. In general, withdrawal symptoms are opposite to those associated with the high or intoxicated state. Withdrawal symptoms represent the clinical manifestation of compensatory brain mechanisms that have developed in response to chronic drug use and are unmasked upon abrupt cessation of drug use.

According to the foregoing definition of drug dependency or addiction, is cocaine an addicting drug? Cocaine certainly causes an intense and usually pleasurable euphoria, although in higher doses and in predisposed individuals the high can give way to feelings of anxiety, panic, and frank paranoia. Cocaine use in a high percentage of users certainly leads to a pattern of compulsive cocaine seeking despite extremely negative medical and psychosocial consequences. The short half-life of cocaine and hence short (15–30 minute) duration of the cocaine high may contribute to the pattern of repetitive cocaine use in an effort to stave off the crash that inevitably follows the high. In addition, intense craving develops after intoxication remits. In fact, the impression of many clinicians who treat cocaine users is that cocaine is one of the most addicting substances known in terms of compulsive drug use. Data from callers to the "800-COCAINE" national hotline substantiate this impression, and cocaine abusers themselves perceive cocaine as addicting. Tolerance has been reported to the effects of cocaine, though sensitization has been reported also.

The question of whether a true physical withdrawal state develops after cessation of cocaine use has aroused controversy. Clearly the cocaine withdrawal is not as florid or distinct as opioid or alcohol withdrawal, but the characteristics of a cocaine withdrawal syndrome are emerging. Cocaine withdrawal is characterized by low energy, depression, irritability, sleep disturbance and craving for cocaine. This syndrome usually lasts for a few days to up to 2 weeks, but does not occur to all patients. The severity of cocaine withdrawal seems related to intensity of use. Regular users of cocaine by the more potent routes of inhalation (smoking free base or rock or crack, or IV injections) tend to have more withdrawal symptoms than do intermittent cocaine snorters. The recent finding that cocaine withdrawal responds to specific pharmacological intervention with the dopamine agonist bromocriptine (Dackis & Gold, 1985d) strongly supports the notion that cessation of chronic cocaine use leads to a distinct, neurochemically determined withdrawal syndrome.

Brain Pleasure Systems, Cocaine, and Dopamine

Classic studies by Olds (1956) showed that electrical stimulation of certain anatomic sites in the brain was reinforcing and led to self-stimulation. These areas were named *pleasure centers*, and evidence implicated the catecholamines NE and DA as having a key role in self-stimulation. Experiments with selective blocking agents helped tease out the relative roles of DA versus NE systems in the reinforcing properties of cocaine. The selective DA receptor blocker pimozide abolished cocaine reinforcement of animal behaviors, but selective NE receptor antagonists phentolamine and phenoxybenzamine did not have this effect (Dewitt & Wise, 1977). The DA receptor agonist apomorphine has reinforcing effects (Baxter, Gluckman, & Scerni, 1976), while NE agonists methoxamine and clonidine do not (Risner & Jones, 1976). Administration of cocaine directly into discrete brain areas of laboratory animals demonstrates that self-administration of cocaine occurs selectively in the medial prefrontal cortex, a structure with DA innervation. Thus the data suggest that DA, not NE, systems mediate the reinforcing or euphoric effects of cocaine. Similar data support the role of DA in the reinforcing effects of amphetamine. Selective DA receptor antagonists have been shown to block the euphoria induced by amphetamines in humans (Angrist, Lee, & Gershon, 1974). This is an important finding supporting the conclusion from animal research that the activation of DA neurons underlies the euphoric effects of central stimulants.

Effects of Cocaine on Specific Neurotransmitters

Dopamine

Many of the effects of cocaine require a fully functional DA system in the brain (Dackis & Gold, 1985c). For instance, if DA neurons are chemically lesioned by the administration of 6-hydroxydopamine, animals will no longer self-administer cocaine. Similarly, cocaine-induced stereotypies and hyperkinesis can be prevented if animals are pretreated with reserpine. Direct DA receptor stimulation by cocaine has long been ruled out as a mechanism of action, and it is now well established that cocaine blocks DA reuptake. This action acutely increases synaptic DA concentrations and therefore leads to increased DA neurotransmission. With chronic exposure to cocaine, however, DA depletion may occur because reuptake blockade prevents the recycling of released DA, which is instead metabolized in the synapse by catechol-0-methyltransferase. In fact, increased levels of the synaptic metabolite 3-methoxy have been measured in animals treated with cocaine (DiGiulio et al., 1978). This suggests that in the presence of cocaine, synaptic DA is metabolized and excreted before there can occur normal reuptake, assimilation in storage vesicles, and recycling for subsequent release. The loss of DA places increased demands on DA synthesis in order to maintain proper neuronal levels of DA. Reuptake blockade can therefore serve as a DA shunt, leading to DA deficiency.

DA synthesis is largely determined by the activity of tyrosine hydroxylase, the rate-limiting enzyme in the conversion from tyrosine. Increased tyrosine hydroxylase activity is found after exposure to cocaine (Dackis & Gold, 1985b), perhaps as a compensatory response to DA depletion resulting from reuptake blockade. In addition, cocaine appears to inhibit DA vesicle binding, exposing it to intracellular metabolism (Dackis & Gold, 1985b). These studies indicate that increased DA neurotransmission after cocaine places demands on the DA synthetic enzymes. As with many homeostatic reactions, increased DA synthesis may fail to compensate totally for cocaine-induced DA depletion. This possibility is suggested by receptor binding studies.

Receptor studies are consistent with DA depletion by cocaine. It has been demonstrated that DA toxins like 6-hydroxydopamine lead to increased postsynaptic DA binding sites (Creese, Burt, & Snyder, 1977). This form of "denervation supersensitivity" appears to represent a compensatory response to the destruction of DA neurons by 6-hydroxydopamine and the subsequent reduction of synaptic DA. The tendency for receptor sensitivity to vary inversely with neurotransmitter availability at the synapse has been previously reviewed as a means of maintaining neuronal homeostasis.

DA binding studies show that after acute cocaine exposure there is increased postsynaptic DA binding. This finding, analogous to that seen after DA neuronal destruction by 6-hydroxydopamine, implies decreased DA availability at the synapse, even though cocaine acutely blocks DA reuptake. After a single dose of cocaine, there is a 37% increase in the number of DA receptor sites (Memo, Pradhan, & Hanbauer, 1981). Postsynaptic DA receptor supersensitivity could explain several cocaine effects in which sensitization has been reported, including psychosis and the phenomenon of kindling (Post, Kopanda, & Black, 1976). DA receptor supersensitivity after cocaine exposure is consistent with DA depletion and decreased DA availability at the synapse.

Direct measurement of brain DA levels after repeated cocaine administrations also reveals decreased levels of DA. These low DA levels were attributed to increased DA turnover. Cocaine elevates brain DA acutely, followed by sharp reductions to normal in a matter of minutes. Neurochemical studies in animals are therefore consistent with acute increases but chronic decreases in DA concentration by cocaine. It is plausible that, over long periods of continued overstimulation by cocaine, DA levels decrease markedly as DA synthesis can no longer keep up with chronic DA loss in the synapse. Reuptake blockade by cocaine prevents the reutilization of DA, maintaining high demands on DA synthesis. It is tempting to speculate that, while cocaine euphoria may result from the acute stimulation of DA neurotransmission, intense cocaine craving and withdrawal states result from the depletion of synaptic DA. Neuroendocrine data in human subjects that will be reviewed later are also consistent with DA depletion.

Norepinephrine

Among the first neuropharmacological effects of cocaine to be reported were adrenergic ones, including not only central activation but increased pulse, blood pressure, tremor, and dilated pupils. As outlined earlier, cocaine blocks the reuptake of NE at NE synapses, as well as facilitating NE release. Furthermore, peripheral and central NE reuptake blockade is seen with cocaine concentrations that are consistent with those found in human cocaine abuse. Thus, whereas cocaine activates postsynaptic NE receptors and their associated target cells, NE neurons themselves may be inhibited by this exogenous agent's activation of inhibitory presynaptic alpha-2 receptors located on NE neurons. This may explain how acute administration of cocaine causes an elevation in NE brain concentrations at 10 minutes, followed by marked reductions below normal levels at 20 minutes. Receptor binding studies demonstrate increased beta receptor populations 12 hours following a single dose of cocaine. Chronic cocaine administration produces even greater increases in beta receptor density as well as increased alpha receptor population. Increased adrenergic receptor sensitivity may explain some of the sensitization effects seen with chronic cocaine use. This would imply that chronic cocaine administration leads to reduced NE turnover and inhibition of NE neurons—the predominant cocaine effect on this system.

Serotonin

Serotonin (5-hydroxytryptamine or 5HT) is a central neurotransmitter in the brain involved in many functions, including arousal, mood, aggression, and endocrine function. Cocaine exerts effects on the 5HT system (Gold, Washton, & Dackis, 1985), although the relationship of these effects to cocaine euphoria and addiction is not clear. Repeated administration of cocaine markedly reduces the concentration of 5HT and its metabolites. Rats pretreated with 5-hydroxytryptophan to reverse 5HT depletion by cocaine fail to manifest behavioral stimulation in response to cocaine. Cocaine has been reported to inhibit the reuptake of 5HT and to inhibit the uptake of tryptophan, as well as the synthetic enzyme tryptophan hydroxylase. The net effect of cocaine on 5HT neurons seems to be reduced turnover, possibly as a compensatory effect from the direct stimulation of 5HT receptors by cocaine.

Catecholamine Depletion Hypothesis of Cocaine Dependency and Withdrawal

As discussed above, evidence suggests that chronic cocaine abuse leads to depletion of neuronal NE and DA with compensatory increased postsynaptic receptor sensitivity (Dackis & Gold, 1985c). Whatever the exact mechanism, one would expect the chronic stimulation from cocaine use to lead to a decrease in the functional activity of both NE and DA neuronal systems. For a long-acting drug, compensatory mechanisms might be constantly overridden by the effects of the drug itself, and become manifest as an abstinence syndrome only after cessation of drug use. For a short-acting drug like cocaine, however, the compensatory decrement in NE and/or DA functional activity may become manifest 30 minutes after a given dose of cocaine and be the neurophysiological substrate of the cocaine crash. The *crash* is the feeling of loss of energy, depression, and cocaine craving that often follows shortly after the high. Thus chronic cocaine effects on NE and/or DA neuronal systems, coupled with the drug's short half-life, may predispose to a pattern of repetitive cocaine use to stave off the crash (a miniepisode of withdrawal). In addition, chronic cocaine use may deplete NE and/or DA stores to the extent that even high doses of cocaine will no longer override the effect. This may explain why the cocaine user often develops an abstinence syndrome in the face of escalating heavy use, or fails to achieve a satisfactory high with chronic use.

Clearly, following cessation of chronic cocaine use, one might expect compensatory deficit states to become manifest as a withdrawal syndrome. The state of anergia and cocaine craving may represent neuroadaptations to chronic use. The more chronic and heavy the cocaine use, the more likely would be the withdrawal syndrome. Weekend intranasal cocaine users often allow enough time between binges for catecholamine turnover and receptor sensitivity to normalize. Patients who smoke crack many times a day, every day, may never attain normal physiology between uses. Our clinical experience is that the daily free-base or IV cocaine user is most likely to have a withdrawal syndrome. Failure to recognize and address this syndrome of cocaine withdrawal can lead to early treatment dropout.

Hormonal Changes in Cocaine Dependency

Prolactin

Cocaine use leads to changes in neuroendocrine functioning that can be measured relatively easily in humans by blood sampling and provide clinical indices of changes in brain neurochemistry secondary to cocaine. Prolactin (PRL) levels in blood have been used as indicators of dopaminergic function, because DA inhibits PRL secretion. For example, antipsychotic medications, which are dopamine receptor blockers, markedly raise prolactin levels. Dackis, Estroff, Gold, and Sweeney (1984) have recently reported that the mean prolactin level in recently admitted cocaine addicts of 35.4 ± 26.9 ng/ml was significantly greater than that of 7.0 ± 5.0 ng/ml in controls. These elevations slowly decreased but did not completely normalize after 2 weeks of abstinence from cocaine. Because decreased dopaminergic activity would be expected to increase prolactin, this finding is consistent with the dopamine depletion theory of cocaine dependency. However, the finding is also consistent with the activation of 5HT neurotransmission by cocaine. The stimulants dextroamphetamine and methylphenidate have been reported to increase prolactin release, presumably by stimulation of 5HT systems. Whatever the mechanism of increased prolactin in cocaine users, this may become a clinically useful marker of active addiction. The effects of chronic elevated prolactin on fertility and sexual function in cocaine addicts needs to be explored.

Thyroid Function

The effects of cocaine on thyroid function are of interest for several reasons. First, NE and DA stimulate the release of thyrotropin-releasing hormone

(TRH) which stimulates the pituitary to release thyroid-stimulating hormone (TSH), which in turn stimulates the thyroid to release thyroxine (T4). Second, the activated state of cocaine intoxication is similar in some respects to a hyperthyroid state, and the energic state of cocaine withdrawal is similar in some respects to a hypothyroid state. Amphetamines have been reported to increase thyroxine (T4) in monkeys and humans (Morley et al., 1980). It may be that some of cocaine's activity properties are mediated through stimulation of the thyroid axis. Dackis, Estroff, Pottash, Sweeney, and Gold (1984) reported that the TSH response to TRH infusion was significantly blunted in cocaine patients. This finding is consistent with the notion that cocaine-induced stimulation of NE and DA systems in brain increases release of TRH from the hypothalamus, leading to down-regulation of pituitary TSH receptors.

Pharmacological Treatments in Cocaine Dependency

Understanding the brain mechanisms of cocaine dependency may lead to pharmacological approaches for blocking the euphoric effects of cocaine and maintaining abstinence. Such understanding may also lead to pharmacological treatment for relieving the symptoms of cocaine withdrawal and facilitating detoxification and entrance into treatment.

If in fact it is cocaine's potentiation of dopaminergic neurotransmission that mediates the powerful euphoric, reinforcing properties of cocaine, then DA antagonists would be expected to block the cocaine high. Neuroleptic medications, which are DA blockers and block cocaine self-stimulation in animals, should prevent cocaine euphoria. However, neuroleptics might also increase cocaine craving. In view of the known side effects of neuroleptics, including tardive dyskinesia, extreme caution should be exercised in considering the possible use of neuroleptics to maintain abstinence from cocaine. Lithium reportedly has some partial cocaine-blocking effects and may have some use in helping maintain abstinence and mood stability during treatment of cocaine addicts (Gawin & Kleber, 1984). It should be emphasized that any pharmacological approach to maintaining abstinence is only part of an overall treatment program that includes urine drug screens, education, family involvement, and participation in peer-oriented recovery groups such as Alcoholics Anonymous (AA), Narcotics Anonymous (NA), and Cocaine Anonymous (CA).

If DA and/or NE depletion or other deficit states mediate the cocaine withdrawal syndrome, the use of nonaddicting pharmacological agents that stimulate or replenish these neurotransmitters may be efficacious in relieving the symptoms of cocaine withdrawal. Ingestion of tyrosine or L-dopa— amino acid precursors of both DA and NE—has been suggested (Gold et al., 1985) and preliminary results suggest some benefit from use of tyrosine. Dopamine receptor agonists such as apomorphine or bromocriptine might be efficacious, as would be amantadine, which facilitates dopaminergic neurotransmission centrally. The efficacy of bromocriptine has been tested directly in cocaine addicts, with exciting preliminary positive results.

Dackis and Gold (1985a) reported that acute single-blind administration of bromocriptine (0.625 mg orally) caused a marked decrease in cocaine craving in patients recently admitted to an inpatient program because of heavy, chronic cocaine use. Preliminary results from open inpatient studies indicate that bromocriptine in doses up to 2.5 mg tid orally can be efficacious for anergy, depression, and craving in the 1–2 week withdrawal period (Extein, Gross, & Gold, 1986). This treatment may prevent premature treatment dropout in some addicts and facilitate entry into other aspects of treatment. Bromocriptine should also normalize DA receptor supersensitivity and elevated prolactin levels. It is noteworthy that bromocriptine is used in neurology to treat Parkinson disease, a dopamine deficiency disease and in endocrinology to treat hyperprolactinemic states associated with infertility and galactorrhea. Neuroleptic treatment during the period of cocaine withdrawal might exacerbate the chemical and clinical changes of withdrawal.

Medications that facilitate noradrenergic neurotransmission have also been reported efficacious in cocaine dependency as well. The tricyclic antidepressants desipramine and imipramine, which block NE reuptake, reportedly relieve some of the symptoms of cocaine withdrawal, including craving (Gawin & Kleber, 1984). These medications also have been reported to have euphoria-blocking properties when used as a part of an abstinence maintenance program. These noradrenergic antidepressants may have efficacy in those cocaine abusers with major depressive syndromes that persist following the several weeks of withdrawal and detoxification (Extein, Dackis, Gold, & Pottash, 1985; Mirin, Weiss, Sollogub, & Michael, 1984). Whether persistent postcocaine depressions are variations of cocaine withdrawal or represent depression as a second illness is an important question for further research.

Summary and Conclusions

1. The euphoric properties of cocaine seem to be the result of blockade of dopamine reuptake, with potentiation of dopaminergic pleasure centers in the brain.

2. Depletion of brain dopamine and/or norepinephrine by chronic cocaine use may be the physiological substrate of the cocaine withdrawal syndrome seen clinically, manifested by anergy, depression, and cocaine craving.

3. The efficacy of the dopamine agonist bromocriptine in relieving

the symptoms of cocaine withdrawal supports the dopamine depletion hypothesis of cocaine addiction, as does the elevated prolactin level reported in cocaine users.

4. Bromocriptine, noradrenergic antidepressants, or other treatments for cocaine withdrawal can be important adjuncts to an overall cocaine addiction treatment program and can help prevent premature dropout.

REFERENCES

American Psychiatric Association. (1980). *Diagnostic and statistical manual of mental disorders* (3rd ed.). Washington, DC: Author.

Angrist, B., Lee, II. K., & Gershon, S. (1974). The antagonism of amphetamine induced symptomatology by a neuroleptic. *American Journal of Psychiatry, 131,* 817.

Baxter, B. L., Gluckman, M. I., & Scerni, R. A. (1976). Apomorphine self-injection is not affected by alpha-methylparatyrosine treatment: Support for dopaminergic reward. *Physiology of Behavior, 4,* 611–612.

Bozarth, M. A., & Wise, R. A. (1985). Toxicity associated with long-term intravenous heroin and cocaine self-administration in the rat. *Journal of the American Medical Association, 254*(1), 81–83.

Creese, I., Burt, D. R., & Snyder, S. H. (1977). Dopamine receptor binding enhancement accompanies lesion-induced behavioral supersensitivity. *Science, 197,* 596–598.

Dackis, C. A., Estroff, T. W., Gold, M. S., & Sweeney, D. R. (1984). Hyperprolactinemia in cocaine abuse. *Social Neuroscience,* Abstract, *10,* 1099.

Dackis, C. A., Estroff, T. W., Pottash, A. L. C., Sweeney, D. R., & Gold, M. S. (1984). *Thyrotropin-releasing hormone testing of cocaine abusers.* Paper presented as new research at the 137th Annual Meeting of the American Psychiatric Association, Los Angeles.

Dackis, C. A., & Gold, M. S. (1985a). Bromocriptine as treatment of cocaine abuse. *Lancet, 1,* 1151–1152.

Dackis, C. A., & Gold, M. S. (1985b). Neurotransmitter and neuroendocrine abnormalities associated with cocaine use. *Psychiatric Medicine,* in press.

Dackis, C. A., & Gold, M. S. (1985c). New concepts in cocaine addiction: The dopamine depletion hypothesis. *Neuroscience and Biobehavioral Reviews, 9,* 469–477.

Dackis, C. A., & Gold, M. S. (1985d). Pharmacological approaches to cocaine addiction. *Journal of Substance Abuse Treatment, 2,* 139–145.

Dewitt, H., & Wise, R. A. (1977). A blockade of cocaine reinforcement in rats with the dopamine receptor blocker pimozide but not with the noradrenergic blockers phentolamine or phenoxybenzamine. *Canadian Journal of Psychology, 31,* 195–203.

DiGiulio, A. M., Groppetti, A., Cattaben, F., Galli, C. L., Maggi, A., Algeri, S., & Ponzio, F. (1978). Significance of dopamine metabolites in the evaluation of drugs acting on dopaminergic neurons. *European Journal of Pharmacology, 52,* 201–207.

Extein, I., Dackis, C. A., Gold, M. S., & Pottash, A. L. C. (1986). Depression in drug addicts and alcoholics. In I. Extein & M. S. Gold (Eds.), *Medical mimics of psychiatric disorders.* Progress in Psychiatry Series. Washington, DC: American Psychiatric Press (pp. 131–162).

Extein, I. L., Gross, D. A., & Gold, M. S. (1986). Cocaine detoxification using bromocriptine. *New Research Program and Abstracts,* 139th Annual Meeting of the American Psychiatric Association, Washington, DC, p. 52.

Gawin, F. H., & Kleber, H. D. (1984). Cocaine abuse treatment: Open pilot trial with desipramine and lithium carbonate. *Archives of General Psychiatry, 41*, 903–909.

Gold, M. S. (1984). *800-COCAINE.* New York: Bantam Books.

Gold, M. S., Washton, A., & Dackis, C. A. (1985). *Cocaine abuse: Neurochemistry, phenomenology, treatments,* NIDA Research Monograph No. 61 (pp. 130–150). Washington, DC: U.S. Government Printing Office.

Jaffe, J. H. (1980). Drug addiction and drug abuse. In A. G. Gilman, L. S. Goodman, & A. Gilman (Eds.), *The pharmacological basis of therapeutics* (6th ed.) (pp. 525–584). New York: Macmillan.

Memo, M., Pradhan, S., & Hanbauer, I. (1981). Cocaine-induced supersensitivity of striatal dopamine receptors: Role of endogenous calmodulin. *Neuropharmacology, 20,* 1145–1150.

Mirin, S M., Weiss, R. D., Sollogub, A., & Michael, J. (1984). Affective illness in substance abusers. In S. M. Mirin (Ed.), *Substance abuse and psychopathology* (pp. 57–77). Clinical Insights Series. Washington, DC: American Psychiatric Press.

Morley, J. E., Shafer, R. B., Elson, M. K., Slag, M. F., Raleigh, M. J., Brammer, G. L., Yuwiler, A., & Hershman, J. M. (1980). Amphetamine-induced hyperthyroxinemia. *Annals of Internal Medicine, 93,* 707.

Olds, J. (1956). Pleasure centers in the brain. *Scientific American, 195,* 105–116.

Post, R. M., Kopanda, R. T., & Black, K. E. (1976). Progressive effects of cocaine on behavior and central amine metabolism in rhesus monkeys: Relationships to kindling and psychosis. *Biological Psychiatry, 11,* 403–419.

Risner, M. E., & Jones, B. E. (1976). Role of noradrenergic and dopaminergic processes in amphetamine self-administration. *Pharmacology, Biochemistry, and Behavior, 5,* 477–482.

Van Dyke, C., & Byck, R. (1982). Cocaine. *Scientific American, 246,* 128–141.

Wise, R. A. (1985). *Neural mechanisms of the reinforcing action of cocaine,* NIDA Research Monograph No. 50 (pp. 15–33). Washington, DC: U.S. Government Printing Office.

TREATMENT APPROACHES

PART TWO

TREATMENT APPROACH

7

Emergency Treatment of Acute Cocaine Reactions

ROBERT SBRIGLIO AND ROBERT B. MILLMAN

Illicit cocaine use has increased dramatically in recent years (Washton & Gold, 1984). The National Household Survey found that the number of people who have tried cocaine at least once increased from 5.4 million in 1974 to 22.2 million in 1985 (NIDA, 1985a); current users rose from 1.6 million in 1977 to 5.8 million 1985 (NIDA, 1985a; Adams & Durell, 1984). In 1975, only 9% of high school seniors in the United States had ever tried cocaine, and 1.9% were current users. By 1985, the percentage of high school seniors having ever tried the drug had increased to 17.3% and current users had increased to 6.7% (NIDA, 1985b).

Whereas previously the morbidity associated with cocaine use was considered to be low, in association with the dramatically increasing prevalence there has been a rising incidence of serious cocaine-related health consequences. Data on adverse health consequences are reflected by hospital emergency room visits and medical examiner cases as collected by the National Institute on Drug Abuse (NIDA) through the Drug Abuse Warning Network (DAWN). Between 1981 and 1985 cocaine-related emergency room admissions increased by 200% (NIDA, 1985c). During the first quarter of 1986 the roughly 3,000 emergency room mentions for cocaine nearly equaled those reported for all of 1981 (NIDA, 1986a).

Over the past several years, the average age of persons admitted to emergency rooms for problems related to cocaine has increased. In 1978, 21% of emergency room admissions were over 30; in 1985, 43% were age 30 or over (NIDA, 1986b). The rate of cocaine-related deaths has also increased in recent years, with more than a threefold increase in medical examiner mentions between 1981 and 1985 (NIDA, 1985c). At the same time there is evidence that more intensive and destructive modes of use, including free basing, the use of crack, intravenous use, and use in combination with other drugs are occurring in existing populations of users (Pollin, 1985).

Robert Sbriglio. Liberation Programs, Inc., Stamford, Connecticut.

Robert B. Millman. Department of Psychiatry and Public Health, Payne Whitney Clinic, New York Hospital–Cornell Medical Center, New York, New York.

Since it may take some time after the initial exposure to cocaine for the individual to require medical attention, it is possible that adverse consequences may continue to rise for some time. Data on adverse health consequences are probably incomplete, however. It is likely that a percentage of the people who experience complications related to their cocaine use are never reported to health authorities. Physicians and hospital personnel may be unaware of the presence of the drug use in the clinical picture. They may not make the correct association, or they may be unwilling to report the drug use in an attempt to protect the confidentiality of their patients.

Cocaine Preparations

Cocaine is available in both licit and illicit preparations. Pharmaceutical cocaine is available as purified cocaine hydrochloride (HCl). Illicit cocaine is available as both cocaine HCl and free base, although the former is usually mixed with a variety of inert or active adulterants (mannitol, lactose, quinine, procaine, or amphetamine). Purity of preparations varies markedly between 10% and 70%. Cocaine HCl is water soluble and therefore is used either intranasally (IN) or intravenously (IV). It has a high melting point, is not readily vaporized, and is not suitable for smoking. Cocaine free base is not water soluble and therefore is not used by either the IN or the IV route. Cocaine free base has a low melting point and is readily smoked (Fishman, 1984).

Often patients will be unable or unwilling to provide a reliable drug history. If possible, a comprehensive history should be obtained from all patients. When necessary, information should also be obtained from family members and friends. A complete physical examination may shed light on the drug-taking pattern, including the mode of administration. Urine and blood specimens should be obtained for immediate toxicology.

Adverse Effects

Adverse effects following cocaine use vary considerably in characteristics and severity depending on a variety of factors. Acute medical and psychiatric complications of cocaine may result from an extension of the pharmacological effects of the drug due to high doses or unusual susceptibility (medical and psychological status of the user) and from the mode of use.

Dose Effects. Cocaine potentiates the effects of the neurotransmitter catecholamines norepinephrine and dopamine. Because of its sympathomimetic properties, cocaine predictably produces pupillary dilatation, tachycardia, increased body temperature, increased serum glucose, increased sphincter tone, decreased gastrointestinal motility, and redistribution of blood flow favoring the brain and skeletal muscles. Cocaine stimulates the central nervous system (CNS), producing elation and euphoria, restlessness, increased perceptual awareness, and cognitive speed (Gold & Verebey, 1984).

In higher doses, cocaine's major serious adverse effects involve the respiratory, cardiovascular, and central nervous systems (Bozarth & Wise, 1985; Jones, 1984; Mittleman & Wetli, 1984). Systemic toxicity to cocaine is characterized by profound sympathetic stimulation of the cardiovascular, respiratory, and central nervous systems, producing a combination of medical and psychological effects also known as the "cocaine reaction" (Gay, 1982). Serious signs and symptoms of cocaine overdose are best treated in a hospital emergency setting where cardiovascular and respiratory functions can be supported and lifesaving measures can be instituted if necessary. The basic equipment required includes an airbag and face mask for ventilation, oxygen, suction, stretcher, electrocardiograph (EKG) monitor and defibrillator, intravenous infusion materials and solutions, and appropriate emergency medications along with qualified medical personnel. Excretion of cocaine can be promoted by acidifying the urine with IV ammonium chloride (Gay, 1982; Mulé, 1984).

User Susceptibility. The medical and psychological status of the user plays a large role in determining the extent and seriousness of cocaine overdose effects. Individuals with compromised neurological, cardiovascular, or respiratory functioning are at higher risk for cocaine-related medical complications. A small number of individuals with an inborn error of metabolism lack the enzyme plasma pseudocholinesterase, the major enzyme involved in the metabolism of cocaine, and can manifest serious intoxication symptoms following exposure to small doses of cocaine (Cohen, 1984). Individuals with a history of psychosis or affective disorder may be at risk for relapse upon exposure to cocaine. Individuals with behavioral problems, poor impulse control, or poor judgment who use cocaine may be at higher risk for causing harm to themselves or others.

Routes of Administration. The usual routes of administration are IN, IV, and free-base smoking (e.g., crack). Overdosage can occur regardless of the route of administration. Cocaine overdose reactions are usually dose related but are not dose *specific* and can vary widely depending on individual characteristics. In an average-sized 70-kg individual, the fatal dose of cocaine is estimated to be about 1,400 mg following intranasal ingestion and 750–800 mg by the subcutaneous, IV, or inhaled route. However, fatalities have been reported after 25 mg of cocaine was applied to mucous membranes (Gay, 1982).

Overdose reactions have been described involving unusual routes of administration. The so-called body packing syndrome is observed in individuals who ingest or conceal multiple small packets of cocaine for smuggling purposes (see Chapter 4). Several fatalities attributed to acute cocaine overdose have been reported in which ruptured or leaking packets were found in the intestine, rectum, or vagina (McCarron & Wood, 1983). These areas are well vascularized and can readily absorb cocaine HCl.

Iatrogenic cocaine overdose reactions (including psychosis, collapse, and death) have been described following application of topical anesthetic solutions of cocaine in hospital patients (Gay, 1982; Jones, 1984; Lesko, Fischman, & Javaid, 1982).

Certain coca leaf herbal teas imported from South America, purported to contain decocainized coca leaves, have been found to contain small amounts of cocaine. Toxic cocaine reactions have been reported in individuals who drink highly concentrated preparations of the tea or chew tea bags with sodium bicarbonate (Seigel, Elsohly, Plowman, Rury, & Jones, 1986).

Acute Cocaine Reactions

Acute cocaine reactions can be classified into two broad general categories: medical and psychological.

Acute Medical Reactions

Hyperthermia. Intense vasoconstriction, increased muscle activity, and consequent reduced heat loss can result in dangerous elevations of body temperature. Treatment is aimed at immediate reduction of body temperature to avoid CNS dysfunction and other tissue damage due to direct thermal injury. A number of deaths have occurred as a result of diffuse intravascular coagulation secondary to intense hyperthermia.

Pulmonary. Cocaine causes an initial increase in the respiratory rate, but with excessive doses the pattern becomes shallow and rapid. Respiratory depression and hypoxia can ensue. Respiratory failure can lead to pulmonary edema, hypoxia, CNS dysfunction, cardiac arrest, and death. A 30° Trendelenberg position will aid venous return and help protect the airway should emesis occur. Respirations should be supported and appropriate emergency measures provided.

Forceful inhalation of cocaine (or any other drug) can produce pneumomediastinum, pneumopericardium, and pneumothorax (Adrouny & Magnusson, 1985; Shesser, Davis, & Edelstein, 1981). These conditions require prompt examination and appropriate radiological studies. Minor cases should be monitored, but they usually resolve spontaneously and are of little consequence. Larger amounts of air in the mediastinum, pericardium, or thorax may require immediate surgical intervention.

Nasal. Chronic intranasal cocaine use can result in rhinitis and episodic epistaxis. The treatment goal of an acute episode of epistaxis is hemostasis, and may require applied pressure, nasal packing, and cautery.

Neurological. Cocaine can produce tremors and convulsive activity in both animals and humans. Overdose victims may complain of confusion and dizziness and may demonstrate hyperreflexia. Clonic–tonic seizure activity may soon follow. Stimulation of the CNS vasomotor and vomiting centers can produce sweating and vomiting.

Signs of excess CNS stimulation may require small IV doses of diazepam (2.5–5.0 mg) or short-acting barbiturates (secobarbital, 50–75 mg) to prevent or treat convulsions (Mulé, 1984). Additional administration of IV succinylcholine has been recommended in certain circumstances to control the airway and eliminate all seizure activity (Gay, 1982). Elevations in blood pressure commonly occur, sometimes leading to CNS hemorrhage and strokes.

Cardiovascular. Cocaine produces tachycardia and cardiac sensitization, which can lead to dangerous cardiac arrhythmias, including a fatal ventricular fibrillation. Rapid heart rate, rhythm disturbances, and increased blood pressure can result in myocardial infarction (Kossowsky & Lyon, 1984) even in young patients with normal coronary arteries and without any cardiac risk factors (Howard, Hueter, & Davis, 1985; Schachne, Roberts, & Thompson, 1984). A careful drug history may identify a drug-related episode, which, after the initial episode is treated, may require targeted treatment.

Hypertension, tachycardia, and some arrhythmias can be treated with IV propranolol (Mulé, 1984). More serious cardiac rhythm disturbances may require antiarrhythmic drugs and more aggressive medical management.

Hematologic. Repeated use of contaminated needles and syringes can lead to bacteremia, septicemia, and a variety of infectious illnesses including hepatitis and acquired immunodeficiency syndrome (AIDS). Even intranasal use of cocaine can produce sepsis in certain vulnerable individuals in whom nasal mucosal erosions extend certain bacterial flora colonization resulting in bacteremia and septicemia (Silverman & Smith, 1985). Septic patients appear acutely ill with fever, chills, and headache and require hospitalization, supportive care, and antibiotics.

Although these conditions are secondary complications of cocaine use, early diagnosis and appropriate treatment can prevent serious sequelae and mortality.

Allergic. True anaphylactic responses or allergies to cocaine are extremely rare (Barash, 1977; Byck & Van Dyke, 1977). A life-threatening anaphylactic reaction to an adulterant of cocaine is possible but unlikely (Finkle & McCloskey, 1977).

Pregnancy. Cocaine can have serious effects on the fetus and neonate of the pregnant drug abuser. Cocaine complicates the outcome of pregnancy and influences neonatal behavior. Cocaine causes placental vasoconstriction, decreasing blood flow to the fetus. A higher incidence of spontaneous abortion, premature labor, and abruptio placentae have been reported in cocaine-using women (Chasnoff, Burns, Schnoll, & Burns, 1985). These obstetric emergencies need to be managed in a hospital setting by trained personnel.

Acute Psychological Reactions

Cocaine abuse can produce a broad range of psychiatric syndromes depending on the premorbid predisposition of the patient, the dose, and the setting. The most common serious psychological effects of cocaine and their appropriate treatments are as follows.

COCAINE INTOXICATION

Cocaine intoxication produces a variety of behavioral, mood, and thought disturbances, which can be subjectively pleasant or unpleasant and which can mimic naturally occurring (non-drug-induced) psychiatric disorders.

Hypomania. Cocaine intoxication can induce increased motor activity, pressured speech, irritability, restlessness, distractibility, elated and grandiose mood, disorganized thinking, and flight of ideas, all resembling hypomanic or manic behavior. A careful history, clinical assessment, and monitoring of clinical course will help resolve differential diagnostic questions. Antipsychotic medication should be used with caution.

Stereotyped Behavior. Individuals may engage in stereotyped behaviors such as pacing or other repetitive activities. Teeth grinding (bruxism) or other tics may develop.

Anxiety. At varying doses, cocaine can produce symptoms of severe generalized anxiety. This may manifest itself as a full-blown panic attack. Treatment of intoxications should be individualized to the patient and the situation but should include verbal reassurance, "talking the patient down," reducing noxious environmental stimuli, and when necessary administering an antianxiety agent such as diazepam (15–20 mg orally every 6–8 hours) (Gay, 1982). Antipsychotic medication should be used with caution.

POST-COCAINE DYSPHORIA

In chronic, heavy users of cocaine, transient euphoria subsequently changes during and between binges to a dysphoric and depressed mood, sometimes accompanied by suicidal ideation. Patients with these symptoms warrant careful psychiatric evaluation and observation and may require hospitalization.

COCAINE PSYCHOSIS

Perceptual distortions and hallucinations can occur with acute cocaine toxicity. Patients may complain of tactile hallucinations, most frequently described as "cocaine bugs"—the sensation that small insects are crawling just beneath the skin (Magnan's sign), particularly in the extremities and the face. Although usually transient, these symptoms may be very disturbing, and patients may resort to scratching, picking, or even purposely burning their own skin in a futile effort to obtain relief. This symptom may assume serious psychotic proportions and may require treatment with antipsychotic medication.

The perceptual disturbances of vision associated with cocaine toxicity are usually described as "snow lights"—glimmers of light in the periphery of the visual field. These fleeting images are of no consequence and do not require any specific treatment.

With higher doses, the initial arousal produced by cocaine can progress to hyperarousal, hypervigilance, paranoid ideation, and finally acute paranoid psychosis with ideas of reference and persecutory delusions. Since this latter condition can lead to assaultiveness with homicidal potential, sensitive psychiatric interviewing and management techniques are needed. Minor tranquilizers should be employed at the outset of treatment. If symptoms persist, major tranquilizers are indicated. The use of antipsychotic medication should be carefully considered in a psychotic individual. Antipsychotics such as the phenothiazines or the butyrophenones are associated with acute side effects and lower seizure threshold; the benefits and risks of each medication group must be carefully weighed.

Summary

An acute cocaine reaction can present as a medical or psychiatric emergency, and in some cases may be life-threatening. An individual may present to an emergency room with a variety of physical or psychological complaints and may or may not give a history of recent cocaine ingestion. If possible, a rapid but comprehensive history should be obtained, including recent ingestion of other drugs, amounts, and routes of administration. A urine and blood drug screen should be obtained to document the presence of cocaine and any other drugs. Recent use of certain drugs other than cocaine may produce signs and symptoms that may complicate assessment and treatment. Treatment of acute cocaine reactions should be instituted on a symptomatic basis while additional data are being obtained.

REFERENCES

Adams, E. H., & Durell, J. (1984). Cocaine: A growing public health problem. In J. Grabowski (Ed.), *Cocaine: Pharmacology, effects, and treatment of abuse*, NIDA Research Monograph No. 50 (pp. 9–14). Washington, DC: U.S. Government Printing Office.
Adrouny, A., & Magnusson, P. (1985). Pneumopericardium from cocaine inhalation. *New England Journal of Medicine, 313*(1), 48–49 (letter).

Barash, P. G. (1977). Cocaine in clinical medicine. In *Cocaine: 1977*, U.S. Department of Health, Education and Welfare Publication No. AIM 77-432 (pp. 193–200). Washington, DC: U.S. Government Printing Office.

Bozarth, M. A., & Wise, R. A. (1985). Toxicity associated with long-term intravenous heroin and cocaine self-administration in the rat. *Journal of the American Medical Association, 254*(1), 81–83.

Byck, R., & Van Dyke, C. (1977). What are the effects of cocaine in man? In *Cocaine: 1977*, U.S. Department of Health, Education and Welfare Publication No. AIM 77-432 (pp. 97–117). Washington, DC: U.S. Government Printing Office.

Chasnoff, I. J., Burns, W. J., Schnoll, S. H., & Burns, K. A. (1985). Cocaine use in pregnancy. *New England Journal of Medicine, 313*(11), 666–669.

Cohen, S. (1984). Cocaine: Acute medical and psychiatric complications. *Psychiatric Annals, 14*(10), 747–749.

Finkle, B. S., & McCloskey, K. L. (1977). The forensic toxicology of cocaine. In *Cocaine: 1977*, U.S. Department of Health, Education and Welfare Publication No. AIM 77-432 (pp. 153–192). Washington, DC: U.S. Government Printing Office.

Fishman, M. W. (1984). The behavioral pharmacology of cocaine in humans. In J. Grabowski (Ed.), *Cocaine: Pharmacology, effects, and treatment of abuse*, NIDA Research Monograph No. 50 (pp. 72–91). Washington, DC: U.S. Government Printing Office.

Gay, G. R. (1982). Clinical management of acute and chronic cocaine poisoning. *Annals of Emergency Medicine, 11*(10), 562–572.

Gold, M. S., & Verebey, K. (1984). The psychopharmacology of cocaine. *Psychiatric Annals, 14*(10), 714–723.

Howard, R. E., Hueter, D. C., & Davis, J. G. (1985). Acute myocardial infarction following cocaine abuse in a young woman with normal coronary arteries. *Journal of the American Medical Association, 254*(1), 95–96.

Jones, R. T. (1984). The pharmacology of cocaine. In J. Grabowski (Ed.), *Cocaine: Pharmacology, effects, and treatment of abuse*, NIDA Research Monograph No. 50 (pp. 34–53). Washington, DC: U.S. Government Printing Office.

Kossowsky, W. A., & Lyon, A. F. (1984). Cocaine and acute myocardial infarction—A probable connection. *Chest, 86*(5), 729–731.

Lesko, L. M., Fischman, M. W., & Javaid, J. I. (1982). Iatrogenic cocaine psychosis. *New England Journal of Medicine, 307*(18), 1153 (letter).

McCarron, M. M., & Wood, J. D. (1983). The cocaine "body packer" syndrome, diagnosis and treatment. *Journal of the American Medical Association, 250*(11), 1417–1420.

Mittleman, R. E., & Wetli, C. V. (1984). Death caused by recreational cocaine use, an update. *Journal of the American Medical Association, 252*(14), 1889–1893.

Mulé, S. J. (1984). The pharmacodynamics of cocaine abuse. *Psychiatric Annals, 14*(10), 724–727.

National Institute on Drug Abuse. (1985a). National household survey on drug abuse. Rockville, MD: Author.

National Institute on Drug Abuse. (1985b). High school senior survey. *Monitoring the Future*. Rockville, MD: Author.

National Institute on Drug Abuse. (1985c). Drug Abuse Warning Network, December data file. Rockville, MD: Author.

National Institute on Drug Abuse. (1986a). Drug Abuse Warning Network, Consistent ER Panel, April file. Rockville, MD: Author.

National Institute on Drug Abuse. (1986b). DAWN Statistical Series Annual Data 1985, Series 1, No. 5, DHHS Publication No (ADM)86-1469.

Pollin, W. (1985). The danger of cocaine. *Journal of the American Medical Association, 254*(1), 98.

Schachne, J. S., Roberts, B. H., & Thompson, P. D. (1984). Coronary artery spasm and myocardial infarction associated with cocaine use. *New England Journal of Medicine, 310*(25), 1665-1666 (letter).

Seigel, R. K., Elsohly, M. A., Plowman, T., Rury, P. M., & Jones, R. T. (1986). Cocaine in herbal tea. *Journal of the American Medical Association, 255*(1), 40 (letter).

Shesser, R., Davis, C., & Edelstein, S. (1981). Pneumomediastinum and pneumothorax after inhaling alkaloidal cocaine. *Annals of Emergency Medicine, 10*, 213-215.

Silverman, H. S., & Smith, A. L. (1985). Staphylococcal sepsis precipitated by cocaine sniffing. *New England Journal of Medicine, 312*(26), 1706.

Washton, A. M., & Gold, M. S. (1984). Chronic cocaine abuse: Evidence for adverse effects on health and functioning. *Psychiatric Annals, 14*(10), 733-743.

8

Inpatient Cocaine Abuse Treatment

LAWRENCE S. KIRSTEIN

The opinions and concepts discussed in this chapter come from the author's direct clinical experience in treating hospitalized cocaine abusers over an 18-month interval in 1984–1985. During this period, more than 150 patients with cocaine abuse problems sought voluntary admission to a private psychiatric hospital. Sociodemographic characteristics of this sample, summarized in Table 8-1, are not significantly different from those described in Washton, Gold, and Pottash (1984). The majority of patients were employed males in their early 30s. The large majority abused marijuana (86%), and a majority were addicted to other drugs (55%).

The inpatient treatment of cocaine abusers plays an integral role in the overall rehabilitation and evaluation of a significant number of patients whose patterns of abuse cannot be successfully arrested in outpatient treatment. Although hospitalization is a more costly and dramatic intervention than an outpatient program, in terms of both finances and the emotional stresses of removing a person from his or her family and job, for patients who meet the criteria in Table 8-2, inpatient treatment is the safest, most likely intervention to help the person achieve abstinence. It is easier for an objective person to recognize that a person who is out of control is in need of inpatient treatment than it is for the cocaine abuser. These patients are engaged in massive denial. They do not believe that others see the behavioral mishaps that are part of the natural evolution of high-dose or chronic cocaine abuse. Convincing an individual that hospitalization is needed requires active confrontation. Often a concentrated effort by a therapist or industrial counselor and family is needed to coerce or convince a reluctant individual. Job jeopardy, pending legal action, and possible marital separation may all be necessary prerequisites for engagement in treatment.

Before describing the phases of a comprehensive inpatient program, certain factors about the setting need to be addressed. Despite the fact that patients may seek voluntary treatment, the setting should be a closed unit. Patients and their belongings should be carefully searched upon admission to prevent drugs or other contraband from coming onto the unit. During the evaluation phase of hospitalization, visiting should be restricted to the

Lawrence S. Kirstein. Regent Hospital, New York, New York.

TABLE 8-1. Demographics

	Number	Percentage
Sex:		
Male	96	63
Female	56	37
Race:		
White	78	51
Black	47	31
Hispanic	27	18
Employed:		
Yes	114	75
No	48	25
Age:		
18–29	58	38
30–39	77	51
40–49	13	9
50+	4	2
Major method of abuse:		
Snorting	61	40
Free base	59	39
Intravenous	32	21
Abusing other drugs:		
Yes	128	84
No	24	16
Addicted:[a]		
None	69	45
Alcohol	41	27
Minor tranquillizers	24	16
Opiates	22	14
Barbiturates	16	11

[a]Some patients were addicted to more than one class of drugs.

TABLE 8-2. Criteria for Hospitalization

Physical dependence on addictive substances
Serious coexisting medical or psychiatric symptoms
Severe impairment of psychosocial functioning
Intermittent but destructive bingeing
Strong resistance to treatment
Failure in outpatient treatment

immediate family (and only if they do not have an active drug history). Vigilance of the staff at all levels, since they do the searches and admit visitors, is a fundamental prerequisite for any drug-free inpatient program. Since the large majority of patients are polydrug users, many of whom require detoxification, it is not necessary to treat cocaine abusers in a program separate from patients with other drug abuse problems.

Since drug toxicity, withdrawal irritability, and drug cravings, among other factors, can precipitate unexpected violent reactions in this patient group, patients must sign a written statement upon admission that they will: (1) submit to requested drug urine or serum tests at any time and (2) agree that violence, sexual acting out, or bringing drugs onto the treatment ward are grounds for immediate discharge. After patients are admitted, sign the drug contract, and are searched, as mentioned before, they are allowed to enter the treatment ward.

The three phases of inpatient treatment are evaluation, rehabilitation, and aftercare planning. The parameters that must be addressed in each phase of treatment are biological–medical, psychological–personality, family–social, legal, and employment.

Evaluation

As soon after admission as possible the cocaine abuser should be seen by both an internist and a psychiatrist. Information in certain areas needs to be obtained immediately; other types of information can be postponed until the patient is medically stable. Table 8-3 addresses those types of information that should be obtained immediately.

One striking fact about cocaine abusers is that they represent a heterogeneous population in terms of length of abuse, route of drug administra-

TABLE 8-3. Screening Areas

---

1. What is the current cocaine abuse pattern?
2. What is the history of all drug abuse/use?
3. What is the current concommitant drug abuse?
4. Does this patient require detoxification?
5. What are the patient's prior treatment experiences?
6. What is the current mental status?
7. What is the likelihood of compliance with treatment?
8. What is the potential for acting out?
9. What factors have motivated the patient to seek treatment at this time?
10. What resources and external factors have influenced the patient to seek hospitalization at this time?

---

tion, social class, and other factors. An inpatient population will include a significant minority of patients who are fairly unsophisticated about drug abuse. It is this subgroup of patients who are at risk to develop withdrawal symptoms, since they underestimate how many other drugs they are using.

The physical examination helps confirm impressions derived from the psychiatric interview. On the basis of the results of a complete physical examination, appropriate action can be undertaken to treat sequelae of drug abuse. This will include the prescription of medications and the ordering of appropriate follow-up laboratory tests. Special tests include pulmonary function studies for free-base or crack users; hepatitis screen for intravenous (IV) abusers; and an ear, nose, and throat (ENT) consultation for some intranasal users. Cohen (1984) and Wetli and Wright (1979) have more thoroughly outlined the medical hazards associated with chronic cocaine use. Routine laboratory testing should include a complete blood count, sequential multiple analysis (CBC, SMA) 12, comprehensive supervised drug screen, and stat serum drug screen when doubts exist about level of toxicity. The results of toxicology screens provide valuable information for fine tuning drug detoxification schedules that are started on the day of admission. One of the more controversial questions that arises is whether any specific treatment needs to be prescribed to diminish the irritability, cravings, and transient depression following cocaine use.

Recently (Dackis & Gold, 1985) reported that bromocriptine may be useful in diminishing cocaine cravings. They suggest that dopaminergic depletion may be the underlying biochemical factor in such cravings. Tennant and Rawson (1983) and Gawin and Kleber (1984) have suggested that tricyclic antidepressants (imipramine and desipramine) may also decrease the cravings.

Thus the initial phase of inpatient cocaine abuse evaluation concerns itself with stabilization of medical problems and treatment of pending withdrawal or intoxicated (toxic) states. Once a patient is stable, the focus broadens. One aspect of the evaluation turns toward establishing a successful individualized rehabilitation effort. The other major thrust of this phase is directed toward determining whether another DSM-III, Axis I, or Axis II diagnosis is present. Depressive disorders, anxiety states, and organic mental syndromes should be ruled out in all cases. This process can be carried out by assessing patients drug free for 1 week while they begin the rehabilitation program. For many patients this is all the workup that is needed. For other patients with residual confusion, an organicity workup may be indicated and can include neuropsychological testing, EEG, CT scan, and neurologic consultation. For patients with underlying mood disorders, medication trials with either anxiolytic or antidepressant medications may be indicated.

This raises a delicate issue, which many patients notice. They have

238420

come to the hospital to get off cocaine, and the idea of taking medication seems antithetical to that goal. They may feel the hospital is simply substituting a legal dependency on pills for an illegal reliance on cocaine. Treatment team members must work through their own feelings about medicating drug abusers. From a medical viewpoint it is malpractice to actively withhold effective treatment for major psychiatric symptoms. However, this does not mean prescribing abusive or addictive medication to treat anxiety, pain, and insomnia.

Helping the patient accept the recommendation to undergo a medication trial is a complicated process. As mentioned before, staff must present a clear message that abusing drugs and taking nonaddictive prescribed medicines are not the same thing. Peer pressure is also an important mechanism to help patients accept medication.

Khantzian & Khantzian (1984) have suggested that there may be a specific psychodynamic predisposition in the cocaine abuse population. They identify four factors that might predispose an individual to become dependent on cocaine: (1) chronic depression, (2) cocaine abstinence depression, (3) cyclothymic or bipolar disorder, and (4) hyperactivity syndrome (attention deficit disorder). Certainly the term *addictive personality* has been in the medical literature for many years. The crucial issue is to distinguish underlying personality traits from behaviors and attitudes that are a consequence of cocaine abuse itself. In our experience, there is tremendous heterogeneity in the personality diagnosis of cocaine abusers. Reviewing diagnosis of 60 completed psychological test batteries (Rorschach and Thematic Apperception Test or TAT) on drug-free cocaine abusers from our inpatient group showed subgroupings of Axis II diagnosis noted in Table 8-4. No specific personality cluster was noted.

Because medical stabilization for cocaine abusers may be accomplished in a few days (with normalization of sleep and eating patterns), the clinical team must be ready to deal with character pathology. This frequently takes the form of patients submitting 72 hours notice to leave the hospital to be treated as outpatients. For cocaine abusers this often occurs within the 4th to 10th day of hospitalization. Breaking through a patient's denial to get

TABLE 8-4. Axis II Psychological Test Results

Diagnostic group	Number	Percentage
Paranoid, schizoid, schizotypal	14	23
Hysteric, borderline, narcissistic	21	35
Antisocial	15	25
Other	10	17

him to stay for treatment requires peer confrontation, staff explanation and interpretation, and family involvement to support the hospital's position. Thus the data derived about personality evaluation from clinical evaluation, history, and psychological testing are very important.

Family evaluation is an essential component of inpatient cocaine abuse treatment. Important information about personality and medical cocaine-related problems, as well as financial, legal, and marital data, can be obtained at the initial family assessment. Relevant data about active drug abuse by family members can usually be obtained at this interview as well. The family contact serves many purposes, only one of which is data gathering. For many of the spouses, cocaine abuse represented the patient's first heavy drug experience. These spouses feel betrayed and angry, and need help in learning how to relate to their cocaine-abusing partners or children. As mentioned earlier, an alliance with the family is crucial in getting patients to accept hospitalization.

Rehabilitation

During the second phase of inpatient treatment, major emphasis is placed on the patient's participation in a highly structured group-oriented program. Patients are assigned to the rehabilitation program when they are medically stable. Prior to that, patients are allowed to attend a limited number of activities, and receive more one-to-one time with nursing staff and the clinical evaluation team. During the evaluation period, patients are restricted to the hospital ward in order to ensure safety and to deter them from leaving. Once patients enter the complete program, they are expected to assume more privileges and responsibilities. In addition to attending all functions on time, they are required to complete a problem and strength list, which they will discuss with their peers and staff. This list provides valuable information that staff bring to the master planning conference on each patient (Table 8-5). Every other week an updated list is presented to both the peer group and staff planning meetings.

Table 8-6 summarizes the various group-oriented meetings that make up the treatment program. Individual and family therapy and medication assessments are also integral parts of the program.

Anonymous groups are integrated into the program from the first week of hospitalization through discharge. Patients should be exposed to all the various types of groups, since it is expected that all patients will begin to take passes to attend an anonymous group in their community prior to discharge. The fit between patient and group cannot be based on cocaine use alone; other variables, including sociodemographic factors, convenience, and concerns about confidentiality may influence attendance at various groups (it may be much more acceptable for a successful businessman

TABLE 8-5. Problem List

Please write down your strengths and weaknesses in each area.

	Strength	Weakness
1. Medical (health)	_____	_____
2. Personal qualities	_____	_____
3. Family relationships	_____	_____
4. Social relationships	_____	_____
5. Work history (include current status)	_____	_____
6. Finances	_____	_____
7. Legal status	_____	_____

to be seen at an Alcoholics Anonymous (AA) meeting than at a Cocaine Anonymous (CA) meeting).

A second type of group is the peer support group, run by a recovered drug addict, which meets daily during the week. The style of this group is confrontational, and the group's task is to talk about addiction, setups, drug behavior, and any other drug-related issues. Strategies to avoid drugs and prevent relapse are addressed. The concept of total abstinence from drugs (including alcohol and marijuana) for a minimum of 6 months is espoused. Two reasons for total abstinence are to prevent a substitute abuse in addition and to prevent lowering one's threshold to experiment with cocaine. The other peer support groups also have clearly defined tasks.

A third type of group is the therapy group. Here, psychodrama addresses feelings and ideas through role playing. Group therapy is an open forum for discussion of ideas and feelings. Multiple family therapy groups

TABLE 8-6. Group Program

Anonymous groups:	*Peer Support:*
Cocaine Anonymous	Drug group
Narcotics Anonymous	Community
Drugs Anonymous	Men's/women's
Alcoholics Anonymous	*Education:*
Therapy groups:	Life skills
Psychodrama	Leisure time
Group	Nutrition
Multifamily	Medication
Other:	
Art	
Dance	
Exercise	
Relaxation	
Music	

have tremendous impact in bringing home the consequences of drug abuse on the family and also helps families learn from each other how to proceed in the future.

A fourth type of group focuses on advocating and improving communication skills. Giving up cocaine may dramatically alter a patient's social life, confidence level, and use of time. Two groups in this category address how patients can fill the time that drug abuse played in their lives.

The medication group is particularly interesting. The hospital pharmacist and a member of the nursing staff lead the group, and patients are asked for topics of interest for upcoming meetings. Information sheets are passed out to the patients. Antabuse and naltrexone are discussed at regular intervals in these groups, as well as in the drug group and in individual sessions with particular patients. For a subgroup of poly abusing patients, the use of antabuse (which blocks alcohol metabolism) or naltrexone (an opiate antagonist), may be an important adjunct in the overall rehabilitation effort.

If a patient is felt to need antabuse and/or naltrexone, it is preferable to start these medications during the rehabilitation phase. In this way signs of liver toxicity and medication tolerance can be evaluated closely. By accepting these medications, patients acknowledge that they are not in control of their addictive tendencies.

The fifth category of groups includes those groups that expose patients to specific skills that they may incorporate into their schedule of free time posthospitalization. As with any other possible aftercare component, patients should attempt to join similar outpatient activities prior to discharge. It is common for patients to become involved in various exercise programs as a result of exposure to the 3 times weekly hospital exercise group. For women this frequently takes the form of aerobics classes or jogging; for men it often takes the form of joining a gymnasium program.

The constant evaluation of the type of progress patients and their families are making in the treatment program occurs in daily staff team meetings. Attendance is mandatory and includes members from the following disciplines: psychiatry, psychology, social work, creative therapies, nursing, dietary therapy, and recreational therapy. At these meetings, patients' problem lists are reviewed and future plans are suggested.

A final component of the rehabilitation phase is random supervised urine monitoring. The importance of maintaining a drug-free unit has previously been mentioned. Once patients are granted passes with nonhospital personnel, they are expected to give urine or serum samples as well as to submit to searches when they return from every pass. This philosophy helps patients abstain from drug use during difficult passes. Repeated drug use on passes is grounds for immediate discharge. For medical–legal reasons it may not be safe to discharge an acutely intoxicated individual. In these instances a significant other must pick up the patient, and alternative treatment arrangements should be furnished to the patient. A physician should see the patient prior to discharge and document current medical status.

Discharge Planning

The third phase of inpatient treatment is discharge planning. This is a time to consolidate the gains made during the protective rehabilitation phase and to extend the new ideas and attitudes to real-life situations. For many cocaine abusers, this final inpatient phase can begin as soon as 3 weeks into their hospitalization. Therapeutic passes are an integral component of discharge planning. Patients should go home and to work in order to confront the scenes of prior cocaine use. Establishing credibility with friends, family, and employer is enhanced by patients' meeting these people in more natural surroundings than the hospital environment. It is not uncommon for patients to note a resurgence of cocaine cravings, and passes must include outpatient anonymous group meetings in preparation for discharge. A surprising number of patients return to the hospital relieved that they have time to organize before going out again or before discharge. Staff at all levels meet with patients to explore aftercare plans. If no unexpected crisis occurs, in either the therapy, the support group, or the patient's psychosocial sphere, then a discharge conference meeting is scheduled. All significant members of the patient's rehabilitation are requested to attend the meeting. From the hospital staff, a drug counselor, individual therapist, social worker, and psychiatrist will be present. From the aftercare support system, an employee assistance contact, therapist, and any other identified outside support person will also be invited.

All the topics on the agenda of the discharge meeting will have already been discussed with the patient by various staff members. Table 8-7 ad-

TABLE 8-7. Discharge Planning Conference

How long is this contract?
What is the frequency of each therapy?
Which type of therapies will be attended?
What is the frequency of anonymous support group meetings?
Will there be urine surveillance and at what frequency?
Will naltrexone or antabuse be used as adjuncts, and for what period of time?
Will psychiatric medications be taken, and how will they be followed?
Who will be responsible for coordinating the aftercare plan?
Who can be contacted if there is any deviation from this plan?
What are the conditions that would necessitate rehospitalization?
Names and phone numbers of contact people

dresses the areas that are discussed in each patient's discharge meeting. After each point is clarified and written down, the patient signs and dates the aftercare contract. The patient also agrees that each member of the aftercare plan may contact the others to express concerns. Anker and Crowley (1982) have highlighted the importance of contingency plans in aftercare treatment of cocaine abusers. The patient then signs and dates his contract and photocopies are made for the chart and for all outpatient personnel.

Summary

An integrated model of inpatient cocaine abuse treatment has been presented. Classical rehabilitation concepts have been combined with general psychiatric treatment principles and recent research findings to meet the needs of a cocaine abuse population. The three phases of the program—evaluation, rehabilitation, and aftercare planning—have been addressed. Treatment philosophy issues, including medications, abstinence, dismissal of patients, and contingency planning, among others, have been discussed. By combining these principles with a diligent follow-up program that is sensitive to both psychosocial and drug abuse problems, cocaine abuse patients can be rehabilitated.

Follow-up data to measure compliance with aftercare and drug abstinence at 6 months and 1 year posthospitalization are needed to compare the relative effectiveness of various treatment programs.

REFERENCES

Anker, A., & Crowley, T. (1982). Use of contingency contracts in specialty clinics for cocaine abuse. In L. S. Harris (Ed.), *Problems of drug dependence, 1981*, NIDA Research Monograph No. 41 (pp. 452–459). Washington, DC: U.S. Government Printing Office.

Cohen, S. (1984). Cocaine: Acute medical and psychiatric complications. *Psychiatric Annals, 14*, 747–749.

Dackis, C., & Gold, M. (1985). Bromocriptine as treatment of cocaine abuse. *Lancet, 1*(8438), 1151–1152.

Gawin, F., & Kleber, M. (1984). Cocaine abuse treatment. *Archives of General Psychiatry, 41*, 903–909.

Khantzian, E., & Khantzian, N. (1984). Cocaine addiction: Is there a psychological predisposition? *Psychiatric Annals, 14*, 753–759.

Tennant, F., & Rawson, R. (1983). Cocaine and amphetamine dependence treated with desipramine. In L. S. Harris (Ed.), *Problems of drug dependence*, NIDA Research Monograph No. 43 (pp. 351–355). Washington, DC: U.S. Government Printing Office.

Washton, A. M., Gold, M. S., & Pottash, A. C. (1984). Survey of 500 callers to a national cocaine helpline. *Psychosomatics, 25*, 771–775.

Wetli, C. V., & Wright, R. (1979). Death caused by recreational cocaine use. *Journal of the American Medical Association, 241*, 2519–2522.

9

Outpatient Treatment Techniques

ARNOLD M. WASHTON

This chapter focuses on techniques for treating cocaine abusers in an outpatient program. The use of an outpatient program as the primary treatment modality for this patient population is of special interest because many (if not most) cocaine abusers who seek professional assistance can be treated effectively on an outpatient basis without hospitalization. The absence of a definitive withdrawal syndrome from cocaine makes the option of outpatient treatment particularly applicable. Unlike the heroin addict or severe alcoholic, the cocaine abuser generally requires no substitute medication and no gradual detoxification regimen. Some patients may experience a generalized dysphoria coupled with sleep and appetite disturbance for several days after stopping cocaine use, but in most cases these symptoms will not be severe enough to warrant inpatient care. Not all cocaine abusers are suitable for outpatient treatment, however, and a number of distinct contraindications to such treatment can be identified, as discussed in the next section of this chapter.

Heightened concerns about cost containment have focused attention on the greater use of outpatient treatment. But the potential advantages of outpatient treatment are not limited to lower dollar costs. From a clinical perspective, this option poses fewer obstacles to the drug abuser who wants professional help. It is less disruptive to work and home life, less stigmatizing, and hence less frightening and objectionable to the prospective patient. Without this option, many drug abusers tend to perpetuate their addiction and its resulting problems in an attempt to avoid hospitalization. The availability of an outpatient program may facilitate earlier treatment entry, thereby avoiding unnecessary suffering and potentially irreversible harm.

The treatment techniques described in this chapter are based largely on my own clinical experience. Although no controlled studies of cocaine abuse treatment have yet appeared in the clinical literature, it is unlikely that any single treatment approach will emerge as the one that is best for every cocaine abuser who seeks professional help (Kleber & Gawin, 1984).

Arnold M. Washton. The Washton Institute, New York, New York, and Ardsley, New York.

This chapter offers some basic clinical guidelines for treating cocaine abusers in a structured outpatient program. Techniques of assessment, diagnosis, and individualized treatment planning have been discussed elsewhere (Washton, Stone, & Hendrickson, in press).

Contraindications for Outpatient Treatment

Despite the numerous advantages of an outpatient program, not all cocaine abusers are suitable for this type of treatment. The patient's appropriateness for outpatient treatment must be carefully assessed. Four basic contraindications to outpatient treatment are as follows:

1. *Cocaine abusers who are physically dependent on other drugs:* Patients who require a carefully supervised medical withdrawal from opiates, alcohol, or sedative–hypnotics should be detoxified on an inpatient basis before entering an outpatient program. Even in those cases where the withdrawal could be safely managed on an outpatient basis, such patients tend to be poor candidates for immediate outpatient treatment for other reasons as well.

2. *Heavy users whose drug compulsion is uncontrollable, especially free-base or IV users:* Most intranasal users can be treated as outpatients, whereas free-base and IV users are more likely to need hospitalization because of their larger drug habits and more severe drug-related dysfunction. It is impossible to specify exactly what amount or frequency of cocaine use would contraindicate treatment as an outpatient. The decision must be based on an assessment of the patient's specific pattern of current drug use, with particular attention to whether the patient will be able, with assistance, to interrupt that pattern in order to achieve initial abstinence. Those who are heavily immersed in dealing cocaine as a primary source of income are usually not suited for primary outpatient treatment.

3. *Patients with severe medical or psychiatric problems:* Outpatient treatment is contraindicated when the patient has serious medical problems (e.g., systemic infection, organ dysfunction, generalized debilitation) requiring hospitalization for proper diagnosis and treatment. Similarly, patients whose poor psychiatric status precludes basic self-care and those who may be at significant risk for suicide or violence should not be treated as outpatients.

4. *Patients who have already failed as outpatients:* Continuing in an outpatient program may be contraindicated when the patient has failed to achieve initial abstinence or has relapsed to uncontrollable drug use. A single such slip is usually not sufficient reason to hospitalize an outpatient, but a pattern of repeated slips should raise greater concern about the patient's ability to benefit from continued outpatient care.

Treatment Goals

An outpatient program must require immediate and complete cessation of cocaine and all other drug use, including use of marijuana and alcohol. A goal of reduced or occasional cocaine use is unrealistic and dangerous for anyone who has become dependent on the drug. Attempts to curtail rather than discontinue cocaine use may be temporarily successful, but inevitably this will set the occasion for another cycle of compulsive use with additional negative consequences.

Requiring complete abstinence from all other mood-altering drugs provides the patient with the widest margin of safety from potential relapse. The long-range goal of treatment must be to develop a reasonably satisfying life-style without drugs. Many cocaine abusers resist the idea of discontinuing marijuana or alcohol use, protesting that they have had no problems with these substances in the past and prefer to continue the practice of "social" or "recreational" use.

The rationale for total abstinence from all drugs is supported by the following observations:

1. While abstaining from cocaine, many patients seek substitute highs and become dependent on other mood-altering substances. This is true even of those who have had no clear-cut history of earlier problems with drugs or alcohol.

2. Drugs that are commonly combined with cocaine, such as marijuana and alcohol, often acquire the capacity to trigger urges for cocaine through associative conditioning.

3. The patient's willpower to resist cocaine can be significantly reduced by the well-known disinhibiting effects of alcohol and other drugs. Even a single glass of wine or beer can render a patient more vulnerable to offers of cocaine.

4. A simultaneous dependency on other drugs or alcohol may not be fully recognized by the patient who has been taking these other substances not to get high but to self-medicate for the unpleasant side effects of cocaine. Attempts to use these other substances occasionally may reinitiate a pattern of abuse.

Urine Testing

Frequent urine testing for all drugs of abuse is a vital and indispensable component of outpatient treatment. Throughout the entire course of treatment, a supervised urine sample should be taken at least two or three times per week and tested for cocaine and other commonly abused drugs such as barbiturates, benzodiazepines, opiates, amphetamines, marijuana, and hallucinogens. Despite mutual trust between patient and clinician, urine testing is necessitated by the reemerging denial and self-deceit characteristic of chemical dependency problems. It must be emphasized that the purpose of urine testing is *not* to catch the patient in a lie. Rather, urine testing is an extremely useful treatment tool that helps to counteract denial, promotes self-control over drug impulses, and provides an objective indicator of treatment progress.

In order to maximize the clinical usefulness of urine testing, any consequences for drug-positive urines should be stipulated at the outset of treatment. Although an occasional slip may be expected during the course of recovery, any emerging pattern of regular or frequent drug use should lead to a revision of the patient's treatment plan. Such revisions might include temporary suspension from a recovery group coupled with more intensive individual contact or, if needed, a mandatory period of hospitalization before returning to the outpatient program. The threat of hospitalization is often an effective deterrent to further drug use.

Phases of Treatment

An outpatient program is best divided into sequential phases that focus on different aspects of the recovery process. The phases should be overlapping and interrelated but should differ somewhat in terms of their major emphasis on certain treatment issues and goals. The phases described here are not rigidly fixed into specific time periods, nor do they focus on a single set of problems to the exclusion of all others. However, these phases do help to structure the flow of the program and to measure treatment progress.

Phase I: Initial Abstinence

The first 30–60 days of treatment should focus intensively on achieving immediate and total abstinence from all mood-altering drugs, including alcohol and marijuana. The initial target should be set as 30 consecutive days of total abstinence. During this early treatment phase, patients should be seen as frequently as needed (often four or five times per week) for emotional support, encouragement, and drug education. Patients must be helped to structure their daily schedules so as to avoid boredom and high-risk situations previously associated with drugs. They should be advised to get rid of any remaining drug supplies and paraphernalia before or on the first day of treatment. They should also be advised to sever immediately any relationships with drug dealers and users. Some of the most important treatment issues that must be addressed during this initial phase include the following:

1. *Resistance and denial:* Usually patients strongly resist giving up all drugs, especially marijuana and alcohol. In addition, there is usually an

unspoken desire to return to using cocaine "occasionally." The patient may see treatment as a way to acquire enough self-control to make occasional cocaine use possible again. The patient may also resist accepting the need to make significant changes in life-style, peer group, and social contacts. There is often strong denial that the chemical dependency problem truly exists and a lack of understanding of how a greater acceptance of the problem can facilitate recovery. To counteract this denial, the clinician must:

1. Take an extensive, detailed inventory of all previous drug-related problems and consequences, with repeated use of this information to counter patients' attempts to minimize their problem.

2. Conduct drug education meetings for patients and family members describing the nature of chemical dependency problems and the stages of recovery.

3. After at least 2–3 weeks of complete abstinence, induct the patient into a cocaine recovery group (to be discussed in more detail later) where the denial and resistance can be most effectively counteracted through contact with recovering peers.

It must be recognized, however, that despite any initial success in breaking through the denial and resistance, these issues will tend to reemerge in various forms throughout treatment.

2. *Urges and cravings:* Patients must be helped to anticipate the occurrence of strong urges and cravings for drugs. Such cravings can occur suddenly and unexpectedly. They are often triggered by specific environmental stimuli (people, places, and things) that have been previously associated with cociane or by certain internal states of feeling such as boredom, depression, and fatigue that have been reliably followed by drug use in the past. Unless properly warned and educated, patients are likely to come to the erroneous conclusion that the occurrence of a strong, unexpected drug urge means that the treatment is not working for them. This may lead to premature, impulsive termination of treatment. It is essential to apprise patients of potential drug cravings and to emphasize that cravings should be expected to occur as a normal, predictable part of the recovery process.

Another common misconception that leads to unnecessary relapse is that once a craving begins it will inevitably build in intensity until drug use becomes an inevitable outcome. It should be pointed out to the patient that cravings and urges are always temporary and tend to reach a peak of intensity within no more than 1–2 hours in most instances. When a craving is first recognized, an immediate change in environment and activities may be helpful. Taking quick action to nullify one's access to drugs, such as seeking out the company of non-using friends or family members, is a useful way to thwart drug-seeking behavior. It is usually easier for patients to devise alternative action plans before experiencing a drug urge rather than trying to do this while the urge is already upon them. Planning ahead and cognitively rehearsing alternative behaviors is crucial.

Another technique that can be useful is to detach oneself from the drug urge in order to examine the feeling from the vantage point of a dispassionate outside observer. Relaxation and other stress reduction techniques may also be helpful. The goal in all these interventions is to block or eliminate the impulse to satisfy the drug urge.

To help patients better understand and cope with potential drug urges, they should be taught the basic principles of conditioning as these apply to addictive behaviors. Discussions should include the mechanics of environmental triggers, how deconditioning can work by reducing the strength of drug urges that are not reinforced by drug use, and how drug-seeking behavior can be thwarted in its earliest stage before a relapse becomes inevitable. Explaining these conditioning phenomena helps to relieve some of the patient's excessive guilt and counterproductive feelings of uniqueness and shame. However, the importance of taking responsibility for one's own behavior, and especially for developing alternative action plans, must be emphasized.

Phase II: Relapse Prevention and Life-Style Change

This phase of recovery should begin after initial abstinence has been achieved and should last for an additional 6–12 months. Treatment should include a twice-weekly cocaine recovery group in conjunction with individual and/or couples therapy at least once per week. The major goals of this phase should be to help patients (1) avoid some of the most common and predictable factors leading to relapse and (2) develop a reasonably comfortable and satisfying life-style that is free of drugs. The following is a discussion of some of the major clinical issues that are relevant to relapse prevention. Additional discussions on the use of relapse prevention techniques can be found in other publications (Marlatt & Gordon, 1985; Zackon, McAuliffe, & Ch'ien, 1985).

1. *Euphoric recall:* Cocaine abusers often have selective memory for the drug-induced euphoria. Although their search for euphoria has ended in dysphoria, depression, and many other drug-related problems, the user's thoughts and associations with cocaine still center primarily on the drug's euphoric effects. The negative experiences are easily forgotten or ignored. It is this selective memory ("euphoric recall") that heightens the patient's ambivalence about giving up cocaine entirely. To the extent that cocaine is still seen as pleasurable and appealing, the potential for relapse is heightened, particularly on occasions when the patient is under stress or emotionally upset.

To counteract euphoric recall, patients must be reminded repeatedly, throughout the course of treatment, of the numerous drug-related consequences that finally compelled them to seek help. The notion that the euphoria can be achieved without undesirable drug-induced consequences must be counteracted whenever patients reminisce nostalgically about the cocaine high. The clinician must take every opportunity to help patients keep the negative associations to cocaine alive. The author has seen evidence that the primary associations to cocaine have been changed from positive to negative in the form of spontaneous reports from patients who have said that resumption of cocaine use after several weeks or months of abstinence actually induced a dysphoric rather than a euphoric reaction. Perhaps as a result of participation in the treatment program, the associations to cocaine become increasingly negative for the patient in such a way that these negative associations eventually override the drug's euphoric effects.

2. *Early warning signs and setups:* It is essential for patients to learn how to attend to the earliest warning signs of potential relapse so that preventive measures can be taken. It is usually impossible to stop an impending relapse once the situation has progressed to a point of no return, so early recognition is crucial. Patients who are headed for a relapse typically engage in a series of telling self-sabotaging acts and setups that precede impending drug use. These include such behaviors as reinitiating contact with drug-using friends, deciding to pass by some of the places formerly associated with buying or using drugs, or allowing stressful circumstances to intensify without taking appropriate action until the point where cocaine use feels justifiable. The clinician must be able to spot potential warning signs and must alert the patient so that each instance can be examined and preventive actions taken.

3. *Testing control:* After a period of initial abstinence, patients often want to see whether they have acquired enough strength to use cocaine in a limited way without losing control. This is usually a dangerous experiment and a clear indication of the patient's continuing denial. For some patients, the desire to test control may well apply to mood-altering substances other than cocaine. Although the patient may fully accept the need to remain completely abstinent from cocaine, he or she may nonetheless want to test control over alcohol or marijuana. As mentioned earlier, use of other drugs impedes the recovery process and may well lead to a cocaine relapse. These control issues may remain hidden and unverbalized by the patient without active prompting from the clinician. These issues cannot be ignored, because the desire to test control is one of the surest and most common precipitants of relapse.

4. *Abstinence violation effect (AVE):* The AVE, as described by Marlatt and Gordon (1985) is one of the most useful concepts in relapse prevention. The AVE refers to the predictable defeatist reaction experienced by an abstaining substance abuser after a slip back to drug use. The slip will

usually set off a complex of intense negative feelings, including feelings of failure; feelings that all progress up to that point has been lost; feelings of guilt, remorse, and self-loathing for having given in to temptation; and feelings of helplessness and victimization. The patient erroneously attributes the slip to personal weakness or a personality defect. If these negative reactions are not prevented or effectively short-circuited, the likelihood that any single slip will escalate into a full-blown destructive relapse is greatly enhanced.

Patients must be educated about the AVE and be prepared with specific plans of action to prevent its potentially devastating effects. For instance, at the very outset of treatment, both patients and family members should be helped to accept the possibility that a slip may occur during the course of recovery and that such an occurrence would not be indicative of treatment failure. No recovering person can be guaranteed a lifetime of total abstinence upon entering a treatment program. Unrealistic expectations will only heighten the patient's sense of failure if any drug use should occur and will also increase the likelihood of premature dropout from treatment. Although it is essential to recognize the possibility of relapse and to know how to minimize its destructive consequences, the patient should not construe this as permission to use drugs occasionally. Total abstinence is still the major treatment goal, but slips and relapses must not be allowed to nullify or derail the recovery process.

5. *Life-style change:* Recovery from cocaine requires more than maintaining abstinence: It requires global changes in life-style and attitude. Priorities and values must be realigned to provide a basic framework for long-lasting recovery. Additional issues that must be addressed include dealing with interpersonal problems, establishing a regular schedule of exercise and recreational activities, making amends with family members and other victims of the drug problem, learning how to have fun without drugs, learning how to reduce stress without drugs, and establishing a reliable peer support network for long-term recovery.

Phase III: Consolidation

This phase should begin after the first year of recovery and continue indefinitely after formal treatment has ended. Treatment during this phase may include individual therapy, participation in a "senior" recovery group, and continuing involvement in Cocaine Anonymous (CA) or another self-help group. The major goals should be to consolidate therapeutic gains and to lay the groundwork for long-term abstinence. Major tasks include coping with flare-up periods; combating overconfidence and renewed denial; addressing issues of arrested development caused by drug use; and achieving greater self-awareness, understanding, and self-acceptance.

Cocaine Recovery Groups

The recovery group is an invaluable component of outpatient treatment. Ideally, each recovery group should consist of 8–12 members, and include both men and women. The group should meet twice weekly and be co-facilitated by a professional therapist and a recovering counselor with several years of abstinence and supervised clinical experience. The group must be part of a comprehensive treatment plan which should also include individual therapy, family therapy, and CA or other self-help group meetings.

Entry of new patients to the group should require at least 30 days of complete abstinence from all drugs and alcohol. Every patient in the group should be required to give a urine sample immediately before or after each group session. The ground rules for group membership should include the following:

1. The identity of all group members is held in strict confidence, without exception.

2. No one is permitted to attend a group session while under the influence of drugs or alcohol.

3. Reliable and punctual attendance at group meetings is required in order to maintain membership.

4. Any group member who offers drugs to another member is permanently expelled from the group immediately.

Each group should include patients who are in different stages of recovery, ranging from those with 1 or 2 months of abstinence to those with 6 or more months of abstinence. This mixture allows new patients the benefit of immediate exposure to positive role models and provides them with living examples that recovery is indeed possible. It also provides the more senior members of the group with a healthy reminder of their own experiences in the early stage of recovery. The groups promote rapid identification among peers and provide a forum for education and experiential learning about a wide variety of recovery issues. The basic themes of the group are those of accepting that one has a chemical dependency problem and learning the ways in which one's behavior, life-style, and attitudes must change in order to achieve long-lasting recovery. Group sessions should focus on specific relapse prevention techniques as these may relate to the immediate and current problems being experienced by one or more members. Many patients find that in the group sessions they are best able to resolve feelings of uniqueness, guilt, and shame. Since many are middle-class individuals with good jobs or careers and no history of previous drug addiction, the opportunity to identify readily with others like themselves seems especially important. Beyond education and role modeling, the group serves a vital role in stimulating and maintaining the patient's motivation to remain drug free. Peer pressure and support are almost always needed to overcome the strong ambivalence about giving up drugs.

At the beginning of treatment, many patients may be strongly resistant to the idea of joining a recovery group because of heightened concerns about confidentiality and the discomfort of sharing personal problems with strangers. Many, however, do adjust to the group situation within the first few sessions and respond very positively to their newly found peer support network. But some individuals may not be clinically appropriate for a recovery group, including those with serious psychiatric disturbance and those who object so strongly to entering the group that attempts to make them do so would undermine the treatment effort.

For patients who have achieved at least 9–12 months of abstinence, a special senior recovery group can be a useful forum in which to keep the recovery process moving forward. At this stage of treatment, the initial recovery group begins to have diminishing usefulness to the more advanced patient. The senior group provides a forum in which to deal more effectively with longer-term recovery issues. The focus of group sessions will often shift from early abstinence issues to topics such as relationship problems, self-esteem problems, sexual problems, and other personal matters that can be discussed more freely when drug urges and the immediate threat of unpredictable relapse have diminished.

Other Interventions

Self-Help Groups. Participation in a self-help group can be a valuable adjunct to outpatient treatment and can also provide a source of ongoing support for the patient after formal treatment has ended. Self-help groups such as Cocaine Anonymous (CA), Alcoholics Anonymous (AA), and Narcotics Anonymous (NA) are based on the traditional Twelve Step program of recovery, which advocates total abstinence from all mood-altering chemicals as the best way to arrest the disease of chemical dependency. Participation in these groups should be strongly encouraged in the vast majority of cases, but need not be made an absolute requirement of outpatient treatment in every single case. Some patients need preliminary help in overcoming their initial fear and hesitation about attending self-help meetings. In general, the more severe a patient's addiction, the more likely he or she is to accept the Twelve Step philosophy and the need to attend self-help meetings.

Family Involvement. Close family members, especially the spouse or parents of the cocaine abuser, should be involved in the treatment for a number of reasons. Family members can provide additional information about the patient's drug use and other behavior. Well-intentioned family members often function as enablers by making excuses for the cocaine abuser, providing money for the drug, or otherwise trying to spare the patient from suffering the consequences of his or her behavior. Family members need instruction and guidance in how to deal with the cocaine abuser and how to provide the necessary support to foster the patient's recovery. They also need an opportunity to deal with their own feelings of anger, blame, guilt, and victimization so as to minimize family stress and confusion, which could themselves lead to the patient's early relapse and treatment failure.

Pharmacologic Treatment. There is no conclusive evidence that antidepressants, lithium, amino acids, or other psychotropic agents block the cocaine euphoria, ameliorate postcocaine symptoms, or eliminate the craving for cocaine. There is no known cocaine antagonist and no medication that has been shown to prevent relapse, despite earlier claims, which have not been replicated. If such medications were found, they might indeed be helpful, especially in extreme or intractable cases where psychological interventions alone have failed. Recent inpatient trials with bromocriptine (Dackis & Gold, 1985), a dopamine agonist, suggest the potential usefulness of this medication in eliminating urges and cravings for cocaine during the immediate post–drug abstinence period, but the clinical efficacy of bromocriptine in treating cocaine abusers remains to be determined by controlled systematic studies.

Psychiatric Issues

Depression is a common side effect of chronic cocaine abuse and a common complaint during initial cocaine abstinence. Symptoms mimicking bipolar disorders, attention deficit disorders, and anxiety disorders may also be generated by cocaine use. Therefore, it is essential to allow a sufficient postcocaine recovery period before making a definitive psychiatric diagnosis or introducing psychotropic medication. In cases where there is a genuine dual diagnosis of psychiatric illness and chemical dependency, both problems must be treated. It is nonetheless imperative that the drug abuse problem be dealt with as a primary disorder and not merely as a symptom of the psychiatric illness. In order to avoid unrealistic or distorted expectations, patients who receive psychotropic medication should be informed that the medication is to treat their psychiatric disorder and not to prevent relapse to drug use. The medication cannot be a substitute for the life-style change and other treatment efforts that are essential to recovery.

In addition to formal treatment interventions, a regular schedule of exercise and planned leisure activities is an important feature of many patients' recovery plan. These activities help not only to reduce stress but also to instill a feeling of greater control over one's life. "Workaholism" and lack of satisfying social or leisure time are often precursors to relapse.

Success Rates

Success rates in an outpatient program depend on a variety of factors, including the severity of abuse, the patient's motivation to be drug free, and the extent to which the program meets the patient's most critical treatment needs. The highest success rates can be expected in those patients who have a strong desire to stop using cocaine, have a history of good functioning before cocaine use, and are able eventually to accept the need for life-style change and total abstinence. In a study of 127 patients who entered an outpatient program, the author found that over 65% of patients completed the 6–12 month program, and over 75% were still drug free at 1–2 year follow-up (Washton, Gold, & Pottash, 1986).

REFERENCES

Dackis, C. A., & Gold, M. S. (1985). Bromocriptine as a treatment for cocaine abuse (letter). *Lancet*, *2*, 1151–1152.

Kleber, H. D., & Gawin, F. H. (1984). The spectrum of cocaine abuse and its treatment. *Journal of Clinical Psychiatry*, *45*, 18–23.

Marlatt, G. A., & Gordon, J. R. (1985). *Relapse prevention.* New York: Guilford Press.

Washton, A. M., Gold, M. S., & Pottash, A. C. (1986). Treatment outcome in cocaine abusers. In L. S. Harris (Ed.), *Problems of drug dependence, 1985*, NIDA Research Monograph No. 67 (pp. 381–384). Washington, DC: U.S. Government Printing Office.

Washton, A. M., Stone, N. S., & Hendrickson, E. H. (in press). Clinical assessment of the chronic cocaine abuser. In G. A. Marlatt & D. M. Donovan (Eds.), *Assessment of addictive behaviors.* New York: Guilford Press.

Zackon, F., McAuliffe, W. E., & Ch'ien, J. M. N. (1985). *Addict aftercare: Recovery, training and self-help,* NIDA Treatment Research Monograph, DHHS Publication No. ADM 85-1341. Washington, DC: U.S. Government Printing Office.

10

Pharmacological Treatments of Cocaine Abuse

HERBERT D. KLEBER AND FRANK H. GAWIN

As recently as 1980 cocaine use was regarded primarily as a psychological rather than a physical problem. Thus, DSM-III lists a category for cocaine abuse, characterized by a pathological pattern of use, impairment in social or occupational functioning, and a duration of at least 1 month, but none for dependence. For that, the presence of tolerance or withdrawal is required, and it was believed that cocaine did not lead to either. Amphetamine dependence is listed, however. As the price of cocaine has dropped, with associated increases in the amount individuals use, and as routes of administration that are less self-limiting than the intranasal (e.g., free basing, the use of crack, and intravenous use) have become more common, the profound seriousness of cocaine dependence has become more evident. Numerous clinical examples exist of inability to cease use in spite of devastating consequences. Tolerance and withdrawal are both known to occur and to be a factor in shaping patterns of use, even though the withdrawal differs from the classic opiate or sedative type. When cocaine use was viewed primarily as psychological habituation, treatment was correspondingly primarily psychological and consisted of behavioral, supportive, or psychodynamic methods to alter addictive behavior. These have recently been reviewed in detail (Kleber & Gawin, 1984).

The perception that a possible neurochemical stratum may account for the persistence of the addiction has prompted a new focus on possible pharmacological interventions. These efforts have produced encouraging preliminary data suggesting two possible roles for some pharmacological agents: 1) for specific diagnostic subpopulations of cocaine abusers who may be using cocaine for self-medication, and (2) as general agents that may reverse cocaine-induced changes, effect craving, or block cocaine euphoria.

Herbert D. Kleber. Yale University School of Medicine, New Haven, Connecticut; Substance Abuse Treatment Unit, Connecticut Mental Health Center and APT Foundation.

Frank H. Gawin. Yale University School of Medicine, New Haven, Connecticut; Cocaine Abuse Treatment Program, APT Foundation.

This chapter describes the possibilities currently suggested by existing clinical research. It is quite likely that even better approaches will be developed in the next decade.

If Cocaine Is Being Used for Self-Medication, What Is It Treating?

Substance abusers have often been observed to be self-regulating painful feelings and psychiatric symptoms via their drug use (Khantzian, 1981; Rounsaville, Weissman, Kleber, & Wilber, 1982). If cocaine use occurs as self-medication, conventional treatments modulating self-medicated symptoms might be indicated. The most important and clearly treatable disorders of this type correspond to DSM-III, Axis 1, categories. Two studies of *Diagnostic and Statistical Manual of Mental Disorders*, 3rd edition (DSM-III) (American Psychiatric Association, 1980) Axis 1 symptomatology in cocaine abusers have recently been presented. Weiss, Mirin, and Michael (1986) presented diagnostic data for 30 hospitalized cocaine abusers, and Gawin and Kleber (1985a, 1985b) reported Axis 1 data on 30 outpatient cocaine abusers. These independent studies both used structured diagnostic interviews and generated very similar results. Depressive disorders (major depression, dysthymic disorder, atypical depression) appeared in approximately 30% and bipolar disorders (including cyclothymic disorder) in approximately 20% of each sample. Also, a smaller but possibly important subgroup of patients (approximately 5%) with attention deficit disorder, residual type (ADD), existed in each sample. Thus a large proportion of cocaine abusers could be self-medicating. Since larger studies have not yet been done, and methodological problems require clarification (Gawin & Kleber, 1985b), the actual prevalence and therapeutic relevance of Axis 1– like psychiatric disorder in cocaine abusers requires further examination.

Accurate psychiatric and behavioral characterization of the cocaine abuser is important because symptoms could provide important guides to both when and what pharmacological adjuncts are indicated (Gawin & Kleber, 1984, 1985b). Two issues confuse the interpretation of symptoms in cocaine abuse. First, definitive diagnoses of psychiatric illness other than substance abuse are difficult to make in the context of active drug abuse because symptoms may arise secondarily from the drug use itself, rather than reflecting psychiatric disorders preceding the drug abuse. Second, distinguishing between the acute depressive symptomatology that occurs immediately after an episode of cocaine use (the postcocaine crash) and more enduring depressive disorder independent of specific use episodes is also difficult. The investigators in the preceding studies attempted to circumvent these issues by gathering extensive historical data as well as corroborating family history data, and by repeated longitudinal evaluations isolated from periods of acute cocaine use and postcocaine symptomatology. However, the diagnostic studies must be considered tentative in the absence of prospective study or more elaborate investigation.

Two groups of pilot efforts that reflect diagnosis in the context of cocaine abuse treatment have been reported. The studies reviewed are all nonblind, nonplacebo preliminary examinations.

Attention Deficit Disorder. Five cocaine abusers with diagnoses of ADD have been reported on by Khantzian and ourselves (1983, 1984) and by Weiss *et al.* (1985). All responded to appropriate stimulant medications, either methylphenidate or pemoline. None of the successfully treated subjects abused methylphenidate or pemoline, and all remained abstinent at least to 6-month follow-up. Patients without ADD tend to abuse the methylphenidate.

Cyclothymic/Bipolar Disorder. In a structured open trial of lithium in subjects who had not responded to psychotherapy-only treatment (Gawin & Kleber, 1984), we found lithium administration was associated with cessation of cocaine abuse and diminished cocaine craving in 9 cyclothymic patients, whereas 5 noncyclothymic cocaine abusers did not appear to benefit from lithium. Six of the responding cyclothymic subjects had first-degree relatives with bipolar disorder, but none of the nonresponders did. The nonresponding subjects also demonstrated more side effects and decreased compliance. Lithium has also been postulated to block cocaine euphoria (explained later), but this was not observed in either subject group.

These data indicate that important subpopulations responsive to specific pharmacotherapies may exist. They also indicate important diagnostic specificity and deleterious consequences of misdiagnosis. However, larger samples and double-blind comparisons are needed to substantiate these findings before we can draw any general clinical conclusions. Our current clinical approach is to adhere strictly to maximal diagnostic criteria for ADD—residual type, requiring both a childhood diagnosis of ADD and a treatment trial with stimulants during childhood before employing stimulant treatment in the context of cocaine abuse. We also require that DSM-III criteria for cyclothymic disorder be fully met before using lithium.

Depressive Disorders. In the same pilot investigation in which lithium was found to be effective for cyclothymic subjects, desipramine was effective for major depressive and dysthymic subjects who had been prior psychotherapy failures. However, nondepressed subjects who had failed in psychotherapy alone and were treated with desipramine also became abstinent, whereas other subjects in our studies without diagnoses who were treated with lithium, methylphenidate, or continued psychotherapy only did not. This is reviewed in more detail later. Consequently it is not clear whether clinically relevant diagnostic specificity exists for cocaine abusers with depressive disorders. Although they do appear to respond to appropriate pharmacotherapy, there is not yet any evidence from pharmacotherapeutic trials that they differ from other difficult-to-treat cocaine abusers.

General Treatments

It is plausible that chronic cocaine abuse could lead to neurophysiological adaptations that require more than psychological intervention. Cocaine exerts its effects neurochemically, and the usual response of the nervous system to such disturbance is compensatory adaptation. It is illogical to assume that this does not occur or is unimportant in cocaine abuse. This does not mean that a classic abstinence syndrome and tolerance uniformly occur; rather, chronic high-dose use may generate sustained neurophysiological modification whose clinical expression is psychological.

Five categories of pharmacological agents have been tried to treat various double-blind, placebo-controlled trials such as to confirm or refute their usefulness. Such trials are underway, however, for some of the agents, and it is expected that more information will thus be available in the next few years. The five categories are: lithium, tricyclic antidepressants, monoamine oxidase inhibitors, stimulants and dopamine agonists, and neurotransmitter precursors. A sixth category of miscellaneous agents will also be discussed.

Lithium Carbonate

Lithium carbonate antagonism of multiple acute stimulant effects, including euphoria, has led to suggestions for its use in treatment of stimulant abuse (e.g., Flemenbaum, 1974; Gold & Byck, 1978; Mandell & Knapp, 1976; Resnick, Washton, La Placa, & Stone-Washton, 1977). Lithium has been found to block behavioral, electrophysiological, and neurochemical effects of acute cocaine and amphetamine. Case studies report blockade of amphetamine euphoria by lithium (Flemenbaum, 1974), as does one double-blind placebo-controlled study of 11 depressed patients (VanKammen & Murphy, 1975). Lithium had more variable results on amphetamine euphoria in 8 patients with personality disorders (Berggren, Tallstedt, & Ahlenius, 1978). In several case studies (Cronson & Flemenbaum, 1978; Gold & Byck, 1978; Mandell & Knapp, 1976), lithium attenuated cocaine-induced euphoria. Decreasing cocaine usage during the lithium treatment was also reported. Lithium did not block IV cocaine euphoria in an experiment done on 6 methadone-treated opiate addicts with significant cocaine abuse (Resnick et al., 1977). Although the latter study was not a direct treatment evaluation, lithium administration was associated with decreases in cocaine abuse, despite lack of euphoria-attenuating effects. Studies of other stimulants (e.g., Jarbe, 1978; Wald, Ebstein, & Belmaker, 1978) report similar results.

In both studies of stimulants reporting no lithium blockade (Resnick *et al.*, 1977; Wald *et al.*, 1978), the agents were administered intravenously in relatively large boluses. Studies using other routes of administration do report blockade. Lithium effects may thus be overridden by large, abrupt increases in stimulant blood levels. Since much street cocaine use is intranasal, the practical impact of this possibility on treatment is unclear and merits examination.

Overall, neurochemical evidence clearly indicates lithium has multiple acute effects that counteract those of cocaine. Clinical evidence further indicates that such properties may be useful in the treatment of stimulant abusers; however, large placebo-controlled studies do not exist. In the study by Gawin and Kleber (1984) cited in the discussion of diagnosis, the responding cyclothymic subjects did not use cocaine to test euphoria-blocking effects, but the nonresponding patients reported cocaine euphoria was unchanged in intensity. Some suggestion of decreased duration of euphoria was noted, but this did not appear to be therapeutically useful.

Although the theoretical focus in lithium treatment of cocaine abuse has been on blockade, another potential mechanism of action exists. Lithium is reported to modulate fluctuations in functional receptor activity (Bunney & Garland, 1983). Lithium's effectiveness in bipolar patients could be due to damping of abnormal oscillations of select neuroreceptor populations (Bunney, Post, Anderson, & Kopanda, 1977). Lithium might thus reverse cocaine-induced neurophysiological changes. Further, bipolar or cyclothymic patients might be more sensitive both to cocaine effects and to opposite lithium effects, which could explain the diagnostic specificity we found in lithium treatment of cocaine abuse. Clearly, lithium's efficacy, diagnostic specificity, and possible mechanisms of action in cocaine abuse treatment all require further study. Table 10-1 sums up the rationale, advantages, and disadvantages of lithium use for this population.

TABLE 10-1. Lithium

Rationale	Advantages	Disadvantages
Pretreatment with lithium blocks numerous behavioral and neurochemical effects of cocaine in animals.	Possible blocking agent May be useful for patients with primary diagnosis of bipolar disorder or cyclothymia	Possible toxicity Several double-blind studies have reported no lithium blockade or stimulants Requires blood monitoring

Stimulants and Dopamine Agonists

METHYLPHENIDATE (MPH)

There is experimental evidence logically supporting possible clinical usefulness of MPH as a general treatment for severe cocaine abuse. Stimulant
high in humans appears to be related both to plasma level prior to an
additive increment and to the characteristics of plasma level changes, rather
than to simple absolute plasma level (VanDyke, Ungerer, Jablow, Barash, &
Byck, 1982). Plasma stimulant level increases in subjects with preexisting
plasma stimulant concentrations may correspond to less euphoric effect
than do identical increases in plasma level in subjects with a baseline of
stimulant-free plasma. Similarly, increases occurring slowly may correspond to less subjective euphoria than do increases occurring more rapidly.
Self-administration data in animals also supports this phenomenon, which
has been called *acute tolerance.*

Since methylphenidate produces euphoria indistinguishable from amphetamine (Brown, Corriveau, & Egert, 1978) and, presumably, from cocaine, MPH could produce consistent tolerance-sustaining effects. Through
such an acute cross-tolerance, a given dose of cocaine would be less eupho-
rogenic and have less abuse liability. This is similar to high-dose methadone
maintenance causing longer term tolerance to opiates and thereby reducing
heroin euphoria and abuse. MPH tolerance would end sooner than methadone tolerance, however, necessitating more frequent readministration, because of its shorter half-life.

Although MPH is an abusible euphorogen, based on actual street use
indices it appears to have less abuse liability than cocaine. This, plus the
aforementioned pharmacological factors, led us to evaluate whether methylphenidate might produce sufficient acute cross-tolerance to cocaine to serve
as a substitute stimulant treatment. However, it was ineffective in five non–
attention deficit disorder (non-ADD) patients treated in an open trial
(Gawin & Kleber, 1985c). The pattern was one of an initial decrease in
craving during the first week that was not sustained with continued treatment. The MPH was discontinued after 5 weeks of treatment failure at
doses of up to 100 mg/day. Methylphenidate actually appeared to increase
both cocaine craving and cocaine use by inducing a mild euphoria that acted
as a conditioned cue for the more intense onset and degree of euphoria
produced by cocaine. Hence, current clinical data indicate substitute stimulant medication may be reasonable only where cocaine is being used as self-
medication for clearly substantiated ADD.

Magnesium pemoline is similar to methylphenidate in that it has been
used successfully to treat ADD in adolescents, in adults with the residual
type, and in cocaine abusers so diagnosed. It differs from MPH in having
less sympathomimetic properties and in being less likely to be self-adminis-

tered in research with primates. Although it can be abused (Polchert & Morse, 1985) the potential seems much less. It appears to act in animals via a dopaminergic mechanism, but the exact mechanism and site of action in humans are unknown. There are no reports in the literature of its use in cocaine abusers without an ADD diagnosis, but, given its lower abuse potential than MPH, it may be worth a cautious trial. Pemoline, however, has been reported to have induced mania, Tourette syndrome, and transient psychosis.

BROMOCRIPTINE

Recently, bromocriptine, a dopamine agonist used to treat conditions such as Parkinsonism and hyperprolactinemia, has been tried to reduce acute cocaine abstinence symptoms and craving (Dackis & Gold, 1985). It was reported successful in 2 cases treated acutely and may warrant a longer term trial to see if the improvement lasts and affects relapse. Like pemoline, bromocriptine should be used cautiously because of reported transient psychotic reactions even in patients without such a history (Turner *et al.*, 1984).

There are two other theoretical problems with dopamine agonists that may or may not prove to be practical issues. The first relates to a possible abuse potential as a way of extending cocaine runs. It has been noted that, at the end of a cocaine binge, cocaine is more likely to be dysphoric than euphoric. This phenomenon likely relates to dopamine depletion and, in theory, could be reversed by a dopamine agonist. The second concern relates to the problem described earlier wtih methylphenidate whereby the drug effect appeared to act as a conditioned cue for desiring the more intense cocaine euphoria. In any event, these issues are researchable ones; until more definitive studies are done, the usefulness of this category of agents is unclear but worthy of further investigation. Table 10-2 summarizes the rationale, advantages, and disadvantages of the group.

Tricyclic Antidepressants (TCAs)

There have been various labels attached to the diminished environmental responsivity displayed by chronic stimulant abusers: anergia and depression (Cohen, 1981); anhedonia (Gawin & Kleber, 1984); or psychasthenia (Ellinwood, 1977). Such symptoms are seldom severe enough or accompanied by sufficient additional symptoms to meet criteria for a DSM-III affective disorder, but they may contribute to an empty subjective existence and thus to increased craving for cocaine-induced euphoria and stimulation.

Intracranial electrical self-stimulation (ICSS) in animals has been used as a model for reward and pleasure in humans. Chronic stimulant administration (cocaine and amphetamine) causes consistent decreases in self-stimu-

TABLE 10-2. Stimulants

Rationale	Advantages	Disadvantages
	Methylphenidate	
Substitution of a stimulant with longer duration of action and less abuse potential than cocaine	Rapid onset of effects Longer acting than cocaine (150 min vs. 90 min) May be useful for patients with primary diagnosis of ADD.	Rapid tolerance to euphoria with subsequent dosage escalation in early clinical trials. Chronic use may increase craving for cocaine via conditioned cues. Patient acceptance diminishes with chronic use. Mild to moderate abuse potential in this population.
	Pemoline	
Substitution of a stimulant with minimal abuse potential Possible dopaminergic mechanism of action	Rapid onset of effects Animal evidence indicates administration is self-limited. May be useful for patients with primary diagnosis of ADD.	Has been reported to induce mania, Tourette syndrome, and transient psychosis. Efficacy and patient compliance in this population unknown. Some limited abuse potential
	Bromocriptine	
Dopamine agonist without abuse potential noted May reduce cocaine withdrawal symptoms and craving if these are related to dopamine depletion	Rapid onset of effects May reduce acute cocaine abstinence symptoms and craving	Has been reported to induce hallucinations and transient psychotic reactions even at low dose. No data yet on length of efficacy or patient compliance. May act as conditioned cue to ultimately increase craving.

lation reward indices and increases in the threshold voltage required to elicit self-stimulation. These stimulant effects have served as a useful animal model for human depression (Willner, 1984) and, more particularly, as a model for the decreased capacity to experience pleasure, or *anhedonia*. Such stimulant-induced changes are reversed by chronic treatment with desipramine (Simpson, 1974), imipramine, or amitriptylene (Kokkinidis, Zacharko, & Predy, 1980).

If human stimulant abusers suffer similar consequences to brain reward capacity, then treatment with *tricyclic antidepressants* (TCAs) may be useful in restoring hedonic capacity and decreasing cocaine craving. There is further evidence from animal research that is consistent with the ICSS data and supports potential usefulness of TCAs for cocaine abuse treatment. Studies of receptor changes in animals have demonstrated increased beta-adrenergic, alpha-adrenergic, and dopaminergic receptor binding. Receptor supersensitivity could be a neurochemical substrate for prolonged postcocaine dysphoria or craving and, consequently, could contribute to failed attempts to end cocaine use. Beta-adrenergic supersensitivity has been hypothesized to be a cause of major depressive illness, and the beta-adrenergic subsensitivity induced by antidepressant treatments may explain their mechanism of action (Charney, Henkes, & Heninger, 1981). Dopaminergic receptor changes following antidepressant treatment are also in the opposite direction from those occurring following long-term administration of cocaine (Koide & Matsushita, 1981; Naber, Wirz-Justwe, Kutka, & Wehr, 1980). These could be even more important than noradrenergic alterations, since dopamine appears to mediate acute cocaine-induced euphoria (Wise, 1984) and anhedonia, craving, or dysphoria after long-term cocaine abuse could be based on homeostatic adaptations to cocaine in dopaminergic systems.

To sum up: The role of the neurotransmitter dopamine in mediating both cocaine effects and postcocaine craving appears to be a crucial one. Cocaine may increase dopaminergic activity *acutely* by any combination of the following: (1) increasing the rate at which it is produced; (2) slowing down the rate at which it is reabsorbed by the nerve cells that manufacture it; (3) slowing the rate at which enzymes in the synapses destroy it; or (4) increasing the number of dopamine receptor sites on the receiving cells at the other side of the synapse.

In *chronic* cocaine abusers, cocaine probably acts by creating more dopamine receptors, a phenomenon called *supersensitivity*. It may be this excess of receptor sites awaiting the dopamine that causes the intense craving that often leads cocaine addicts to give up their attempts to remain abstinent.

Desipramine appears to have the opposite effect from cocaine: It reduces the number or sensitivity of dopamine receptors, and hence perhaps the craving, although evidence is needed that this underlies desipramine's electrophysiological or clinical effects.

Despite the presence of significant suggestive data from the electrophysiological and neurochemical animal literature of the past decade, little systematic evaluation of TCA treatment of cocaine abusers has been done. Tennant and Rawson (1983) reported that desipramine facilitated brief abstinence in 14 cocaine abusers. Their study, however, was based on a rationale involving acute desipramine-induced decreases in noradrenalin reuptake rather than electrophysiological or receptor changes. Consequently 11 of their subjects received desipramine for less than 7 days; the other 3 subjects were not described. One case report indicated that desipramine ameliorated the postcocaine dysphoric and hypersomnolent symptoms that follow binge use (the so-called crash). Recently, Tennant and Tarber (1985) investigated both his initial study and this case report in a controlled double-blind trial of brief desipramine therapy and found no differences from placebo effects.

We have reported on prolonged desipramine treatment in 12 subjects with a history of prior treatment failure in psychotherapy-only treatment (Gawin & Kleber, 1984). Eleven of the 12 demonstrated prolonged abstinence (> 12 weeks). The decreases in cocaine craving followed a delayed time course consistent with desipramine's time course for neuroreceptor changes and its known clinical characteristics in depression. In contrast to Tennant and Rawson's (1982) results, however, half of the patients continued cocaine use throughout the first week and until the third week of treatment. Improvement was unrelated to diagnosis of depression. Although this work shows promise, double-blind substantiation is needed before any extension to routine clinicial use is attempted. Such a study is currently under way at Yale by the authors, and preliminary data suggest the desipramine effect continues to be evident.

Rosecan (1983) has used another tricyclic antidepressant, imipramine, in prolonged open treatment trials in 25 subjects and also describes facilitation of abstinence in over 80% of his sample over a 10-week period. Although neither craving nor cocaine euphoria was measured, the clinical impression from these subjects was that both were substantially reduced. In a clinical challenge with cocaine in 4 imipramine-treated subjects, Rosecan and Klein have reported attenuation of cocaine euphoria (1986). Placebo-treated subjects will need to be contrasted before there is clear evidence that imipramine blocks cocaine effects. We have not observed alterations in cocaine effects in our desipramine-treated subjects. Further, Rosecan's subjects were also treated with tyrosine and tryptophan, and it is not clear, if imipramine is indeed effective as a blocking agent, whether it is so because of serotonergic actions not shared by desipramine, because of the concomitant administration of neurotransmitter precursors, or because of other imipramine effects. Rowbotham, Jones, Benowit, and Jacob (1984) have reported that single doses of trazadone, a presumably serotonergic antidepressant, blocks some physiological effects of cocaine, but not euphoria. All these issues are the subject of current investigations to clarify whether, and by what mechanisms, tricyclic or other antidepressants might be useful in treating chronic cocaine abuse. Table 10-3 summarizes the possible TCA role.

Monoamine Oxidase Inhibitors

Monoamine oxidase inhibitors (MAOIs) have been used to treat depression not responsive to the tricyclic antidepressants as well as patients with a primary diagnosis of atypical depression. Their mild stimulatory effects have the potential to be even more effective than those of the TCAs in treating postcrash anhedonia and anergia. Although no systematic study has yet been done, an open clinical trial (Resnick & Resnick, 1985) of one such agent, phenelzine, suggests such an effect as well as increased dysphoria if cocaine was used. Also, the earlier onset (3–10 days versus 10–21 days for the TCAs) would be an important advantage. Although Resnick has not yet found any adverse interaction if cocaine was used with the phenelzine, the potential for serious, even lethal, toxicity (hypertensive crisis) constitutes a major disadvantage of the agent. There is also the theoretical possibility of auto-oxidation of released dopamine to the neurotoxin, 6-OH dopamine. Table 10-4 summarizes these aspects of the MAOIs.

TABLE 10-3. Tricyclic Antidepressants

Rationale	Advantages	Disadvantages
Animal: Have opposite effects to those of chronic cocaine on dopaminergic system, on catecholamine receptors, and intracranial self-stimulation. *Human*: Clinical data suggests reversal of cocaine associated anhedonia and anergia.	Low incidence of adverse effects Low toxicity potential High patient acceptance May be useful for patients with or without primary diagnosis of depression.	Onset of effects delayed 10–20 days. At times may require monitoring of blood level.

TABLE 10-4. Monoamine Oxidase Inhibitors

Rationale	Advantages	Disadvantages
Similar to that of TCAs	? Broader efficacy than TCAs ? Greater effect on anhedonia and anergia than TCAs ? May be useful for patients with primary diagnosis of atypical depression.	Interaction with cocaine *might* produce lethal toxicity, i.e., hypertensive crisis. Possible auto-oxidation of released dopamine to the neurotoxin 6-OH dopamine. Onset of effects delayed 3–7 days, less than TCAs.

Neurotransmitter Precursors

Since chronic cocaine use is associated with depletion of various neurotransmitters, use of dietary neurotransmitter precursors has been suggested as a way of dealing more rapidly with acute postcocaine dysphoria. They have the advantages of safety and possible rapid onset of effects. Tyrosine, the precursor of dopamine and norepinephrine, was found in an open inpatient clinical trial to ameliorate such symptoms (Gold, Pottash, Annitto, Verebey, & Sweeney, 1983). In a study reported earlier in the chapter (Rosecan, 1983), decreased cocaine craving was reported when tyrosine and tryptophan (the precursor of serotonin) were used along with imipramine to treat cocaine abusers. The contribution of the 3 different agents was not parceled out. As with the other agents already discussed, it is necessary to have double-blind single-agent and longer term studies before the use of these agents can be adequately assessed. Postcocaine dysphoria has been at times considered similar to the withdrawal states from opiate, alcohol, or benzodiazepine dependence. Unlike those conditions, however, cocaine self-administration tends to be episodic and similar to methamphetamine binges described over 15 years ago (Kramer, Fischman, & Littlefield, 1967). Although more cocaine is administered during a binge (or run) to avoid the crash, once the crash is well developed after a prolonged binge, sleep is often more desirable than more cocaine. Thus, to be fully useful, pharmacological agents are more necessary to deal with the predictable postcocaine anhedonia and relapse than with the acute dysphoria (Gawin & Kleber, 1985a). It is even possible that rapid amelioration of the crash could lead to increased ease of using cocaine.

Table 10-5 sums up the characteristics of the neurotransmitter precursor approach.

Miscellaneous Agents

Since cocaine euphoris is presumed to be mediated by dopamine, it is reasonable to assume that *neuroleptics* would block cocaine euphoria. Animal studies have repeatedly demonstrated neuroleptic attenuation of cocaine reward (DeWit & Wise, 1977; Jarbe, 1978) but there is some question whether this is due to motor effects, since some paradigms do not show blockade (Spyraki, Fibiger, & Phillips, 1982). There have been no reported trials of neuroleptic treatment of cocaine abusers. This may be due to the potential difficulty in getting cocaine abusers to comply with a regimen of potentially dysphoric medication, as well as the ethical problems regarding possible tardive dyskinesia. However, since neuroleptics are currently the most plausible potential blocking agents and can be administered in long-acting depot preparations to eliminate compliance problems, they may warrant investigation as possible adjuncts in treatment of *intractable* cocaine abuse. A possible counter to this possibility was the finding that when low-dose haloperidol was given to rhesus monkeys, lever pressing for cocaine increased (Woolverton & Balster, 1981). It may be that partial dopamine blockade translates into dopamine depletion, which is experienced as cocaine craving and leads to desire for *more* drug to surmount the blockade competitively. The situation, obviously a complex one, could be influenced by factors such as neuroleptic dose and degree of blockade.

Other pharmacological treatment possibilities are under investigation or being considered for investigation. These include pyridoxine, a co-enzyme in dopamine synthesis; agonist or antagonist analogues of cholecystokinin (CCK), a brain peptide that modulates dopaminergic function; and arginine vasopressin analogues, possibly active in modulating brain reward responsivity (Fraenkel, Van Beek-Verbeek, Fabriek, & Van Ree, 1983). The

TABLE 10-5. Neurotransmitter Precursors

Rationale	Advantages	Disadvantages
Replacement of depleted neurotransmitters which may ameliorate acute postcocaine dysphoria. (Tyrosine → dopamine and norepinephrine Tryptophan → serotonin)	Safety (no toxicity at dosage level used) Possible immediate effect.	? Efficacy alone. Acute effect of diminished crash symptoms may lead to increased ease of using cocaine.

substantial animal research and early clinical evidence suggest that useful general pharmacological interventions for cocaine abusers may be found. However, much more rigorous clinical and basic research will need to be developed before it is possible to confirm scientifically the most useful of these agents and their target populations.

Comparisons to Psychotherapeutic Interventions

The percentage of patients who stopped cocaine use in pharmacotherapeutic studies reporting positive results (80%) is similar to the percentage in the few reports (Anker & Crowley, 1982; Siegel, 1982; Washton, 1984) on patients who remained in treatment in specialized psychotherapy-alone programs for cocaine abusers. It is premature, however, to compare treatments across centers unless sample similarity has been clearly demonstrated. Difficulty contrasting and assessing studies of different pharmacological and/or psychotherapeutic cocaine abuse treatments exists not only because most are preliminary efforts and such similarity could not be demonstrated, but also because cocaine abuse treatment research is particularly vulnerable to obscuring consequences of differences in study design, and there is uncertainty as to how best to characterize subjects.

Methodological points that will require clarification and consensus before more definitive research studies to come can create a coherent body of scientifically acceptable research on treatment for cocaine abusers include:

1. Severity: Stratification of samples according to criteria of abuse severity, and creation of generally accepted indices of severity of abuse.

2. Self-selection artifacts.

3. Recovery: How long abstinence must endure before recovery occurs or whether continued use of nonstimulant substances constitutes treatment failure

4. Heterogeneity of sample: Variations in sociodemographics, psychiatric symptoms, psychosocial resources, patterns and duration of use, degree of impairment, treatment history, and so forth. Do such factors differ between treatment populations, and do they differentially affect outcome?

5. Course and neuroadaptation.

Conclusions

There is no definitive knowledge available for cocaine abuse treatment. Now that the biological aspects of such abuse are being recognized, however, new approaches are emerging. Preliminary data on pharmacological treatments are beginning to appear, and pharmacological adjuncts show potential promise for different phases of the problem and for patients with and without a psychiatric diagnosis. Currently, however, it appears no more likely that any single treatment will arise as a definitive treatment for all cocaine abusers than has occurred for opiate abusers. More likely, pharmacological approaches will become important adjuncts to psychological and life-style changing therapies. They may make it easier and more successful to treat abusers on an outpatient basis and may shorten the amount of treatment necessary.

REFERENCES

American Psychiatric Association. (1980). *Diagnostic and statistical manual of mental disorders* (3rd ed.). Washington, DC: Author.

Anker, A. L., & Crowley, T. J. (1982). Use of contingency in speciality clinics for cocaine abuse. In L. S. Harris (Ed.), *Problems of drug dependence, 1981*, NIDA Monograph No. 41 (pp. 452–459). Washington, DC: U.S. Government Printing Office.

Berggren, U., Tallstedt, G., & Ahlenius, S. (1978). The effect of lithium on amphetamine-induced locomotor stimulation. *Psychopharmacology, 59*, 41–45.

Brown, W. A., Corriveau, P., & Egert, M. H. (1978). Acute psychologica and neuroendocrine effects of dextroamphetamine and methylphenidate. *Psychopharmacology, 58*, 189–195.

Bunney, W. E., & Garland, B. L. (1983). Possible receptor effects of chronic lithium administration. *Neuropharmacology, 22*, 367–373.

Bunney, W. E., Post, R. M., Anderson, A. E., & Kopanda, R. T. (1977). A neuronal receptor sensitivity mechanism in affective illness (a review of evidence). *Human Psychopharmacology, 1*, 393–405.

Charney, D. S., Henkes, D. B., & Heninger, G. R. (1981). Receptor sensitivity and the mechanism of action of antidepressant treatment. *Archives of General Psychiatry, 38*, 1160–1180.

Cohen, S. (1981). *Cocaine Today.* New York: American Council on Drug Education, pp. 1–46.

Bronson, A. J., & Flemenbaum, A. (1978). Antagonism of cocaine highs by lithium. *American Journal of Psychiatry, 135*, 856–857.

Dackis, C. A., & Gold, M. S. (1985). Bromocriptine as treatment of cocaine abuse. *Lancet, 1*(8438), 1151–1152.

DeWit, H., Wise, R. A. (1977). Blockade of cocaine reinforcement in rats with the dopamine receptor pimozide, but not with the noradrenergic blockers phentolamine and phenoxybenzamine. *Canadian Journal of Psychology, 31*, 195–203.

Ellinwood, E. H. (1977). Amphetamine and cocaine. In M. E. Jarvik (Ed.), *Psychopharmacology in the practice of madicine* (pp. 467–476). New York: Appleton-Century-Crofts.

Flemenbaum, A. (1974). Does lithium block the effects of amphetamine? A report of three cases. *American Journal of Psychotherapy, 131*, 820–821.

Fraenkel, H. M., Van Beek-Verbeek, G., Fabriek, A., & Van Ree, J. H. (1983). Desglycinamide-arginine-vasopressin and ambulant methadone-detoxification of heroin addicts. *Alcohol and Alcoholism, 18*(4), 331–335.

Gawin, F. H., & Kleber, H. D. (1984). Cocaine abuse treatment: An open pilot trial with lithium and desipramine. *Archives of General Psychiatry, 41*, 903–910.

Gawin, F. H., & Kleber, H. D. (1985). *Cocaine use in a treatment population: Patterns and diagnostic distinctions.* NIDA Research Monograph No. 61 (pp. 182–192). Washington, DC: U.S. Government Printing Office.

Gawin, F. H., & Kleber, H. D. (1986). Abstinence symptomatology and psychiatric diagnosis in cocaine abusers. *Archives of General Psychiatry, 43*, 107–113.

Gawin, F. H., Riordan, C., & Kleber, II. D. (1985). Methylphenidate treatments of cocaine abusers without attention deficit disorder. *American Journal of Drug and Alcohol Abuse, 11*(3 & 4), 193–197.

Gold, M. S., & Byck, R. (1978). Lithium, naloxone, endorphins, and opiate receptors: Possible relevance to pathological and drug-induced manic–euphoric states in man. *The International Challenge of Drug Abuse*, NIDA Research Monograph No. 19 (pp. 192–209). DHEW Publication No. (ADM) 78-654. Washington, DC: U.S. Government Printing Office.

Gold, M. S., Pottash, A. L., Annitto, W. J., Verebey, K., & Sweeney, D. (1983). *Cocaine withdrawal: Efficacy of tyrosine.* Paper presented at the 13th annual meeting of the Society for Neuroscience, Boston, November 6–11.

Jarbe, T. (1978). Cocaine as a discriminative cue in rats: Interactions with neuroleptics and other drugs. *Psychopharmacology, 59*, 183–187.

Khantzian, E. J. (1981). Self-selection and progression in drug dependence. In H. Shaffer & M. E. Burglass (Eds.), *Classic contributions in the addictions* (pp. 154–160). New York: Brunner/Mazel.

Khantzian, E. J. (1983). An extreme case of cocaine dependence and marked improvement with methylphenidate treatment. *American Journal of Psychiatry, 140*, 784–785.

Khantzian, E. J., Gawin, F. H., Riordan, C., & Kleber, H. D. (1984). Methylphenidate treatment of cocaine dependence—a preliminary report. *Journal of Substance Abuse Issues, 1*, 107–112.

Kleber, H. D., & Gawin, F. H. (1984). Cocaine abuse: A review of current and experimental treatments. In J. Grabowski (Ed.), *Cocaine: Pharmacology, effects, and treatment of abuse*, NIDA Research Monograph No. 50 (pp. 111–129). Washington, DC: U.S. Government Printing Office.

Koide, T., & Matsushita, H. (1981). An enhanced sensitivity of muscarinic cholinergic receptors associated with dopaminergic receptor sub-sensitivity after chronic antidepressant treatment. *Life Sciences, 28*, 1139.

Kokkinidis, L., Zacharko, R. H., & Predy, P. A. (1980). Post-amphetamine depression of self-stimulation responding from the substantia nigra; reversal by tricyclic antidepressants. *Pharmacology and Biochemistry of Behavior, 13*, 379–383.

Kramer, J. C., Fischman, V. S., & Littlefield, D. C. (1967). Amphetamine abuse pattern and effects of high doses taken intravenously. *Journal of the American Medical Association, 201*, 305–309.

Mandell, A. J., & Knapp, S. (1976). Neurobiological antagonism of cocaine by lithium. In E. H. Ellinwood & M. M. Kilby (Eds.), *Cocaine and other stimulants* (pp. 187–200). New York: Plenum Press.

Naber, D., Wirz-Justice, A., Kutka, M. S., & Wehr, T. A. (1980). Dopamine receptor binding in rat striatum: Ultradian rhythm and its modification by chronic imipramine. *Psychopharmacology, 68*, 1–5.

Polchert, S. E., & Morse, R. M. (1985). Pemoline abuse (brief report). *Journal of the American Medical Association, 254*, 946–947.

Resnick, R. B., & Resnick, E. (1985). *Psychological issues in the treatment of cocaine abusers.* Paper presented at the Columbia Cocaine Symposium, Cocaine Abuse: New Treatment Approaches, New York, January 5.

Resnick, R. B., Washton, A. M., LaPlaca, R. W., & Stone-Washton, H. (1977). *Lithium carbonate as a potential treatment for compulsive cocaine use: A preliminary report.* Paper presented at the 32nd annual convention and scientific meeting of the Society of Biological Psychiatry, Toronto, April 28–May 1.

Rosecan, J. (1983). *The treatment of cocaine abuse with imipramine, L-tyrosine, and L-tryptophan.* Paper presented at the 7th World Congress of Psychiatry, Vienna, Austria, July 14–19.

Rosecan, J., & Klein, D. (1986). *Imipramine blockade of cocaine euphoria with double-blind challenge.* Paper presented at the 139th annual meeting of the American Psychiatric Association, Washington, DC.

Rounsaville, B. J., Weissman, M. M., Kleber, H., & Wilber, C. H. (1982). Heterogeneity of psychiatric diagnosis in treated opiate addicts. *Archives of General Psychiatry, 39,* 151–156.

Rowbotham, M. C., Jones, R. T., Benowit, M. L., & Jacob, P. III. (1984). Trazodone-oral cocaine interactions. *Archives of General Psychiatry, 41,* 895–899.

Siegel, R. K. (1982). Cocaine smoking. *Journal of Psychoactive Drugs, 14,* 271–359.

Simpson, D. (1974). *Depressed rates of self-stimulation following chronic amphetamine in the rat: Elevation of these depressed rates by desmethylimipramine.* Paper presented to the Eastern Psychological Association, April 19.

Spyraki, C., Fibiger, H. C., & Phillips, A. C. (1982). Cocaine-induced place preference conditioning: Lack of effects of neuroleptics and 6-hydroxydopamine lesions. *Brain Research, 253,* 195–203.

Taylor, D. L., Ho, B. T., & Fagan, J. D. (1979). Increased dopamine receptor binding in rat brain by repeated cocaine injection. *Human Psychopharmacology, 3,* 137–142.

Tennant, F. S., & Tarber, A. L. (1985). *Double-blind comparison of desipramine and placebo in withdrawal from cocaine dependence.*

Tennant, F. S., & Rawson, R. A. (1982). Cocaine and amphetamine dependence treated with desipramine. *Problems of drug dependence,* NIDA Research Monograph No. 43 (pp. 351–355). Washington, DC: U.S. Government Printing Office.

Turner, T. H., Cookson, J. C., Wass, J. A. H., Drury, P. L., Price, P. A., & Besser, G. M. (1984). Psychotic reactions during treatment of pituitary tumours with dopamine agonists. *British Medical Journal, 289,* 1101–1103.

Van Dyke, C., Ungerer, J., Jatlow, P. Barash, P., & Byck, R. (1982). Intranasal cocaine dose: Relationship of psychological effects and plasma levels. *Psychiatry in Medicine, 12*(1), 1–13.

VanKammen, D. P., & Murphy, D. L. (1975). Attenuation of the euphoriant and activating effects of d- and l-emphetamine by lithium carbonate treatment. *Psychopharmacologia, 44,* 215–224.

Wald, D., Ebstein, R. P., & Belmaker, R. H. (1978). Haloperidol and lithium blocking of the mood response to intravenous methylphenidate. *Psychopharmacologia, 57,* 83–87.

Washton, A. (1984). Data presented at the 23rd annual meeting of the American College of Neuropharmacology, San Juan, Puerto Rico, December 10.

Weiss, R. D., Mirin, S. M., & Michael, J. L. (1986). Psychopathology in chronic cocaine abusers. *American Journal of Drug and Alcohol Abuse, 12,* 17–29.

Weiss, R. D., Pope, H. G., & Mirin, S. M. (1985). Treatment of chronic cocaine abuse and attention deficit disorder, residual type, with magnesium pemoline. *Drug and Alcohol Dependence, 15,* 69–72.

Willner, P. (1984). The validity of animal models of depression. *Psychopharmacology, 83,* 1–16.

Wise, R. A. (1984). Neural mechanisms of the reinforcing action of cocaine, NIDA Research Monograph Series No. 50 (pp. 15–33). Washington, DC: U.S. Government Printing Office.

Woolverton, W. L., & Balster, R. L. (1981). Effects of antipsychotic compounds in rhesus monkeys given a choice between cocaine and food. *Drug and Alcohol Department, 8,* 69–78.

11

Treating Adolescent Cocaine Abusers

ELLEN R. MOREHOUSE

Until recently, the adolescent cocaine abuser was a rarity in most regions of the United States. But as more adolescents make cocaine their drug of choice and develop addictions, professionals working with adolescents need to be aware of some of the special issues and treatment differences involved in working with this population. This chapter will describe the use of cocaine by adolescents and offer suggestions for treating the adolescent and the family.

Extent of the Problem

In comparing cocaine use by high school seniors in 1975 with that of their counterparts in 1985, it is possible to document the increase in use. The following statistics are from a University of Michigan study of drug use among high school seniors that has been done yearly since 1975 (Johnston, Bachman, & O'Malley, 1985). Only 9% of the class of 1975 had ever used cocaine, compared to 17.3% of the class of 1985. Similarly, 5.6% of the class of 1975 had used cocaine at least once during that year, compared to 13% of the class of 1985. Whereas only 0.1% of the class of 1975 had used cocaine daily within a 30-day period, that number rose to 0.4% of the class of 1985.

The increase in cocaine use is occurring among males and females, among both college-bound and non-college-bound students, amoung students in both urban and rural areas, and in all regions of the country. Surprisingly, when compared to the three most used drugs by adolescents (alcohol, cigarettes, and marijuana), the differences in use between boys and girls and college-bound and non-college-bound students are the smallest for cocaine. Lifetime and annual cocaine use by high school seniors increased by 1.2% and 1.5%, respectively, from 1984 to 1985. Lloyd Johnson, co-author of the abovementioned study, notes, "While this year's increase is not dramatic, it breaks a pattern of stability which has held for the preceding five years." This rise reflects adolescents' attitudes toward cocaine use.

Ellen R. Morehouse, Student Assistance Services, White Plains, New York.

Although 80% of the class of 1985 acknowledged that there were harmful effects of using cocaine regularly, only 34% saw much risk in experimenting with it. The fact that fewer students in the class of 1985 than students in the class of 1984 saw much risk in cocaine experimentation (there was a decrease of 1.7%) indicates that cocaine use was becoming more acceptable to adolescents.

Although it can be documented that cocaine use has increased and is more acceptable to adolescents, one can only speculate why this has occurred. Cocaine's availability, its image, and its effects appear to be the main reasons for increased use by adolescents.

Availability

Cocaine has become more available in the United States, and this increased availability has brought a drop in price. One gram of cocaine (the approximate equivalent of 10 large or 20 small lines) ranges in price from $60 (in Florida) to $120. The introduction of "crack," rocks of cocaine free base, has made the drug even more available to adolescents because it can be purchased in a vial approximately three-quarters of an inch long that contains three rocks for $20, or in a half-inch vial containing two rocks for $10. The rocks, which are much more potent, can be smoked in a pipe or sprinkled on a marijuana cigarette and smoked. The packaging of crack makes it more attractive to adolescents for several reasons. Smoking is less frightening than snorting a powderlike substance up the nose. Smaller quantities can be purchased. The effect is more intense. Carrying a vial of ready-to-smoke rocks is more convenient. There's no fuss, no mess, and no bother.

Effects of the Drug

Cocaine produces an initial feeling of euphoria and self-confidence, two feelings greatly desired by adolescents who by nature are less confident than they would like to be. If an adolescent is also depressed or bored, as many are, the attractiveness of cocaine increases.

Cocaine's effects fit nicely with 1986 values and trends. This can be illustrated by comparing the late 1960s with the mid-1980s and comparing the effects of marijuana with those of cocaine.

In the late 1960s, being "mellow" and "laid back" were valued characteristics. Marijuana use helped adolescents achieve these feelings. In 1986, being in the "fast track" and being "a mover and a shaker" are valued characteristics; cocaine use can be helpful in producing these feelings. In the late 1960s, humility was valued; being considered "cool" and a free spirit was desirable. In 1986 self-assurance is valued; being in control, on top of things, and "hot" are desirable qualities. Just as marijuana was seen as a drug for producing effects that were highly valued in the late 1960s, cocaine is seen by many adolescents as the perfect drug for producing effects that are highly valued in 1986.

Image

Media attention to disclosures of cocaine use by the rich and famous and its former high prices have made cocaine a status drug among adolescents. Until recently, cocaine also had the image among many of a drug that could be used safely. It was seen as nonaddicting and unlikely to produce any serious negative physical or emotional consequences. Unfortunately, disclosures of cocaine use by professional athletes and top business executives reinforce these perceptions and lead adolescents to ask, "How bad can it be if he was able to play professional sports or manage a large corporation while using cocaine?"

Cocaine's image as a "classy" drug also fits nicely with the trends of 1986—a time when a classy image is desired by many adolescents and adults.

Assessment

As with any other problem, a thorough assessment is essential and determines the course of treatment (Morehouse, 1983). The assessment process begins before the adolescent is seen for treatment, when the parent, school, or other referring sources share impressions and facts about the adolescent's drug use. The goal of the assessment is to determine whether the cocaine use is causing negative consequences and how the cocaine or other drug use interferes with the adolescent's functioning. This should include knowledge of the adolescent's physical, social, emotional, family, school, legal, and financial functioning. It is also important to determine whether there is a loss of control or an inability to limit the amount used once use has started. An adolescent needs treatment if there is interference with any aspect of functioning, if use is causing negative consequences, or if there is a loss of control. If any of these three criteria is not present, it is difficult to motivate the adolescent to stop using because there have not been any negative effects.

In motivating the adolescent to stop use and begin treatment, the counselor or therapist must help the adolescent understand the probable short-term negative consequences of continued use based on the current negative consequences, as well as the probable short-term benefits of abstinence and involvement in treatment. This can be done by determining what the adolescent wants for him- or herself—a lifting of a curfew, permission to take the car, and the like—and determining what privileges and punishments the parents are prepared to give.

In motivating adolescents to begin treatment, it is also important to educate them about what treatment is. Adolescents need to know that treatment can be inpatient or outpatient; that it can include participation in Twelve Step self-help recovery groups such as Cocaine Anonymous (CA), Narcotics Anonymous (NA), and the like; that they have the right to confidentiality, with some exception; that urine testing will be required; that treatment will include education about cocaine use and chemical dependency as well as education about alternatives. Adolescents also need to know the minimum and maximum length of time treatment will be provided; the length and kind of sessions (group, individual, family); and the consequences of missed sessions, an inability to be abstinent, and a slip or relapse.

Treatment Planning

A number of factors are involved in deciding whether an adolescent needs inpatient or outpatient treatment. If the following conditions are present, the adolescent should be referred directly to inpatient treatment:

- The presence of a serious emotional problem in addition to cocaine abuse—suicidal behavior, anorexia nervosa, bulimia, psychosis, and so on.
- The presence of a serious medical condition.
- Physical addiction to another drug in addition to cocaine use.
- An unsuccessful experience in outpatient treatment.
- The absence of family members who support abstinence and treatment.
- The absence of appropriate and affordable outpatient programs.

When the foregoing conditions are not present, outpatient treatment should be suggested first, because it is less disruptive to the adolescent.

Issues in Adolescent Treatment

Regardless of whether the adolescent is seen as an inpatient or an outpatient, there are several issues that should be considered in planning the adolescent's treatment. First, it is a mistake to assume that all adolescent cocaine abusers come from dysfunctional families or that the adolescent is acting out the symptom of the family dysfunction. Some families were dysfunctional before the adolescent cocaine abuse started, whereas others become dysfunctional as a result of the abuse. Similarly, some adolescent cocaine abusers have alcohol- or drug-abusing parents whereas others do not. It is important to determine the level of chemical use and abuse by family members, since this can have a major impact on how the adolescent uses the treatment (Morehouse, 1984).

Second, most adolescents come to treatment because they are coerced by others. Therefore, their motivation to do well may have more to do with their desire to receive certain rewards and privileges and avoid punishment, rather than a true desire to get well.

Third, there is a natural tendency for the adolescent to perceive the therapist or counselor as an agent of the parent. Therefore, the therapist should expect distrust and testing. Such testing should be handled in a way that lets the adolescent know that the counselor or therapist is an *advocate* for the adolescent but refuses to be an *enabler*.

Fourth, when adolescents enter treatment, they believe no drugs equals no fun and possibly no friends. For many adolescents, this can trigger anger and depression that may be acted out in attempts to get back at the parents for causing this situation. One adolescent actually told his parents that if he couldn't continue to use drugs and drink, life "wasn't worth living." This kind of depression or anger must not be minimized. A thorough evaluation of the depression and suicide risk must occur, and the depression must be treated. In treating chemically dependent adults, it has been useful to advise them to stay away from "people, places, and things" that were associated with their drug use. Although this is also useful advice in helping adolescents recover, for some adolescents, especially those overly dependent on peers, asking them to give up their drugs *and* their friends is unacceptable; therefore, spending time with friends should not be forbidden initially. With time, the adolescent may realize that being with certain friends makes it more difficult to be drug free.

Fifth, many adolescents are fearful of inpatient or residential treatment. This fear of inpatient treatment often motivates an adolescent to work in outpatient treatment. However, helping adolescents understand what can be expected in inpatient treatment, working through their fears, explaining when inpatient treatment is indicated, and informing them of their legal rights to leave once admitted can reduce their resistance to inpatient treatment.

Sixth, in working with adolescents the treatment must be adolescent centered and focused. The counselor must be willing to advocate for the adolescent client with the parents, schools, or court systems and to expect that sometimes what is in the best interest of the adolescent may not be perceived by the parents as being in their best interest. Since parents often control an adolescent's access to treatment by providing transportation or paying fees, this conflict can result in the parents removing their child from treatment. To prevent this from occurring, the counselor needs to take the time to explain why what is being advocated is in the adolescent's best interest and ultimately in the parents' best interest as well. The following example is illustrative:

> Patti, an introverted 17-year-old cocaine abuser, found that when she was taking cocaine she became more talkative and assertive. When she began treatment and stopped using cocaine, it became apparent that she kept thoughts and feelings inside and then became depressed and angry. As she was encouraged to share her thoughts and feelings, especially with her parents, and became better able to do so, her mother began complaining to the counselor that Patti was "disrespectful." When the counselor spoke with the mother about this, it was necessary to point out to the mother how developmentally it was appropriate and important for Patti to express her thoughts and feelings, and that a difference of opinion did not mean a lack of respect. Similarly, it was important for Patti to learn to express herself in a respectful tone, to understand that it was difficult for her mother to accept that Patti was getting older, and not to be discouraged from making healthy changes by the lack of positive response from her mother.

One of the best ways to advocate for the adolescent yet provide support for the parents is to see the parents in a parents' group. This group, which should start as soon as the adolescent enters treatment, provides the parents with an opportunity to ventilate their anger, frustration, and guilt, as well as providing support as they adopt new techniques for parenting a recovering adolescent.

Seventh, each adolescent requires an individualized treatment plan that carefully considers the adolescent's developmental stages and needs. For example, all adolescents need information about their addiction and the recovery process. However, booklets and lectures appropriate for the 18-year-old may be inappropriate for the developmentally delayed 14-year-old who has less capacity for abstract thinking and therefore needs more concrete information. Similarly, a 17- or 18-year-old struggling with separation issues may resist parental involvement in the treatment, whereas a 14- or 15-year-old may request more parental involvement. Other areas where developmental stages and needs must be considered are: involvement in CA, NA, or other 12-step recovery groups; involvement in counseling groups; the use of activities in counseling sessions; and the like.

Finally, most adolescents referred for treatment for their cocaine use also use other drugs and frequently have a history of alcohol, marijuana, or other drug abuse predating their involvement with cocaine. The longer an adolescent's period of drug involvement, the greater the need for treatment to focus on habilitation instead of rehabilitation. A 16-year-old daily cocaine abuser with a 3-year history of chemical use will need a different treatment plan than a 16-year-old daily cocaine abuser with no prior chemical abuse. The first adolescent will need to develop a full range of life skills appropriate for a 16-year-old, because this adolescent's life skill development was arrested at age 13. The second adolescent may have developed the age-appropriate skills and may need to concentrate instead on refusal skills and developing specific alternatives to cocaine use.

The Beginning Phase of Treatment

In beginning the treatment with the adolescent, it is important for the counselor to reestablish what the adolescent wants for him- or herself, to reiterate a willingness to help the adolescent in getting what is wanted, and to remind the adolescent of the connection between past substance abuse and difficulty in getting what was wanted. When this occurs, the treatment is reframed as something that is helpful to the adolescent instead of something desired by parents, school, or court. This reframing helps to form an alliance between the counselor and the adolescent—an alliance that is crucial to promoting change (Unger, 1978).

It is also important for the counselor to educate the adolescent about the treatment process. Adolescents need to know what treatment is, what is expected from them, and what they can expect from the counselor and the treatment program. Specifically, they need to know that they are expected to be abstinent from all mood-altering drugs, and the reason for this; that they are encouraged or expected to attend Twelve Step recovery groups, and how frequently they must do so; that they are expected to attend all scheduled appointments and follow procedures for cancellations or make-ups; that they are required to submit to urine testing, and how often; and any other expectations. Adolescents also need to know the consequences of a slip or relapse, their right to confidentiality, and the need for their input in treatment.

It is helpful to acknowledge the adolescent's power and to make it clear to the adolescent and the family that the counselor is not a "fixer." Adolescents who are coerced into entering treatment may feel like powerless victims of others' decisions. These adolescents may act out in order to prove that they have power. Other adolescents may believe that they are powerless, which can lead to withdrawal or passivity in treatment. The adolescent, parent, and counselor must realize that it is the adolescent who has ultimate control over what goes up the nose, in the veins, or in the mouth, and it is the adolescent who makes the decision to remain abstinent or return to use. Acknowledging the adolescent's power lessens the chance that the adolescent will act out or enter into a power struggle with the therapist.

Often parents who bring adolescents to treatment expect the counselor to "fix" the adolescent. Again, it is important to empower the parents and make it clear that they are expected to assist the counselor and that the counselor cannot be the sole source of active support for the adolescent's recovery. Empowering the parents lessens the likelihood that they will sabotage the treatment and increases their involvement in the adolescent's recovery and, hence, the probability of success.

Preparing for Abstinence

Whether or not the adolescent is being treated in an outpatient or an inpatient program, he or she needs to prepare for abstinence. During the assessment the counselor determines when the adolescent was last abstinent from all mood-altering drugs, what his or her physical or emotional state was, how others (especially peers) reacted, and what triggered the return to chemical use. This information will be useful in preparing the adolescent for abstinence.

Many adolescents being treated for cocaine use have never gone more than a day or two, since they started using cocaine regularly, without using cocaine or another drug. As a result, they are not prepared for the withdrawal and the physical or psychological discomfort that may result when cocaine and other chemical use ceases.

All possible withdrawal reactions should be described, as well as measures for reducing the discomfort. Specifically, the adolescent needs to know that it might be difficult to fall asleep, that there might be an increase in dreaming, that he or she might feel bored and depressed, that there might be cocaine cravings, and so forth.

Adolescents also need to know what to say to friends when cocaine is offered, and what to do when they want to avoid cocaine-using situations, for example a party where others will be using cocaine. Specifically, adolescents need to learn how to say no and should role-play situations with the counselor in order to prepare themselves for both the pressure and the cravings to use. It is suggested that adolescents tell friends about their involvement in treatment and the regular urine testing. Explaining that a "dirty" urine might result in hospitalization or the loss of a car should keep a drug-using friend from pressuring the adolescent to use.

In preparing adolescents for abstinence, it is also helpful to have each adolescent anticipate what will be most difficult for him or her and then to prepare the adolescent to deal with the difficult situation when it arises.

Scheduling Outpatient Sessions

In an outpatient program, the adolescent should have a minimum of two contacts a week, at least one of them in a group, including at least two urine tests a week during the first 30 days. Ideally, this should be supplemented with CA, AA, or NA meetings, and at least one meeting either with the parents and adolescent alone or with the parents without the adolescent. Some adolescents will require more frequent contact because of their need for additional support or because of the counselor's need to do a more thorough assessment or establish rapport quickly. Frequent appointments demonstrate an eagerness for the counselor to get to know the adolescent and indicate to the adolescent a stance of "we are getting to know the drug-free you" and a respect for the adolescent's complex identity.

It is a mistake for counselors to be too confident that they understand adolescents. Many adolescents use slang, and definitions vary among groups. An adolescent may call something "bad," meaning it is extremely attractive and desirable. But another adolescent from the same school or community may use "bad" to mean negative and undesirable.

Second, if a counselor demonstrates too early an understanding of an adolescent, some adolescents will think that the counselor doesn't care to take the time to get to know them well, or that the counselor can be fooled by first impressions. Asking adolescents questions instead of assuming the answers conveys respect and reaffirms their power to control what is known about them. It also lessens the likelihood that they will withhold in an effort to maintain control.

Value of Groups

Adolescents should be involved in groups with other recovering adolescents as quickly as possible because group participation offers a number of advantages to the adolescent that cannot be realized in individual or family sessions. Group participation reduces feelings of isolation caused by being the only one who cannot use any drugs. Most cocaine-abusing adolescents are in a peer group with other drug-using adolescents. The adolescent who is abstinent feels he or she is the only one not using and feels isolated (Citron, 1978). Groups offer members peer support in attempting new solutions and trying out new alternatives to using substances. Role playing drug use refusal skills, discussing ways to deal with cocaine cravings, and planning alternative social experiences are just some of the early treatment tasks that can best be accomplished in group.

Group also provides an alternative socialization experience where adolescents can receive honest feedback and have an opportunity to have honest, nonexploitive relationships with peers (Berkovitz, 1972). Realizing that they have something to offer and that peers respond positively to them drug free starts to build self-confidence for adolescents who may wonder whether anyone will like them drug free.

Many adolescents distrust adults and may feel more protected if they interact with an adult in group. They also tend to perceive group participation as less associated with being ill than receiving individual counseling from an adult.

Finally, group participation gives the newly recovering adolescent practice in sharing feelings and being confronted by peers on unhealthy thinking and behavior. In this way it increases their readiness for CA, AA, or NA participation.

In addition to the benefits for the adolescent, groups also offer several advantages for the counselor. Examining how an adolescent interacts with peers helps the counselor gain a more accurate picture of the adolescent's functioning. Education about addiction and recovery can be done more effectively and efficiently in groups. Group members help the counselor confront denial, which often reappears, or confront resistance to making constructive changes.

Contacts with Parents

The parents also need frequent contact in the first 30 days. Ideally, both parents or parenting figures in the home should be seen with the adolescent at the beginning and end of the assessment. In the beginning, it is important for the parents to tell the counselor, with the adolescent present, what has occurred that makes the parents think the adolescent has a cocaine problem and needs treatment. This helps reduce the adolescent's denial and provides a good opportunity for the counselor to examine the parent–child interaction. Before the parents are asked to leave the session, confidentiality needs to be explained, as well as what will occur and what the parents can expect, for example a treatment recommendation. This procedure also ensures that the parents and the adolescent know what to expect from the initial session or sessions.

When the adolescent is seen alone, the counselor should discuss what can and should be said to the parent. When the parent(s) rejoin the adolescent, the counselor's assessment and recommendation should be discussed, in addition to the program's or counselor's expectations of the adolescent, parents, and siblings. It is crucial that the parents understand what treatment is (as described earlier) and agree to the conditions of treatment. The likelihood of involving the parents in treatment is increased if treatment is seen as beneficial to the parent as well as to the adolescent.

Initially, when the adolescent perceives the counselor as an ally or advocate, he or she is eager to have the counselor meet with the parents and "tell them." Similarly, the parents are eager to meet with the counselor because they want advice on how to handle the adolescent. Specific questions have to do with curfews and car privileges; parents' own use of alcohol; what to say to the school, relatives, or close family friends about the adolescent's involvement in treatment; how to set limits; suspicion of use; limiting contacts with drug-using peers; and other issues. As mentioned earlier, meeting with the parents in a multifamily parents' group can be most effective. Similar concerns can be shared and answered, and the parent's isolation, shame, and sense of guilt are reduced.

In addition to addressing the parents' specific questions, the counselor should use the parents' sessions to help them better understand what has happened to their adolescent and to themselves, and how they can help. For example, the counselor can encourage parents to enthusiastically acknowledge and reward their adolescent's drug-free status, to initiate parent–child activities to help reduce their adolescent's boredom and loneliness, and to rely on the results of the urine tests instead of making accusations of drug use based on suspicion. These are just three of the many actions that support an adolescent's abstinence.

Finding Alternatives

In the early phase of recovery it is necessary to reevaluate how the adolescent's cocaine use has interfered with his or her functioning. Now that the adolescent has been drug free, he or she will probably have a different perspective and therefore be better able to identify treatment needs. The following common sources of stress for newly recovering adolescent cocaine abusers should be addressed quickly in order to minimize relapse.

Social Functioning. The newly recovering adolescent cocaine abuser is caught in a social no-man's land, has no peer group, and can be very lonely. Frequently, his or her friends also abused cocaine and/or other chemicals. The recovering adolescent may not want to spend time with these friends because he or she feels uncomfortable being the only one not using, and because being with them stimulates cravings. The "friends" also may not want to spend time with the recovering adolescent because his or her abstinence may make the drug users feel self-conscious and uncomfortable.

Often the drug-free adolescents in the community are perceived as "boring," "nerds," "out of it," or "no fun." Drug-free adolescents may have been looked down on, joked about, or even taunted by the newly recovering adolescent when he or she was abusing substances. When this has happened, the newly recovering adolescent will not want to be friends with those drug-free adolescents. Similarly, the drug-free adolescents may not want to befriend the newly recovering adolescent because they did not like his or her past behavior and attitude, and don't trust him or her or want to get to know him or her now.

The need for gratifying social contact with peers should be given the highest treatment priority. Loneliness is one of the most painful feelings for adolescents and, if not dealt with, can lead to depression and relapse. Participation in adolescent recovery groups, involvement in CA or other Twelve Step programs, and involvement in other activities that promote contact with peers and focus on something other than getting high—clubs, scouting, sports, volunteer organizations, jobs—can reduce loneliness and help the adolescent establish relationships with adolescents with similar interests.

As mentioned earlier, many adolescents do not know how to socialize drug free. Therefore, treatment should examine how the adolescent feels and acts in various social situations. The following examples illustrate different kinds of social problems.

> Tom, a good-looking, bright, athletic junior with a reputation for heavy drug use, had done poorly in school and did not participate in any sports as of 9th grade because of his drug use. When he came to treatment, he admitted his friends were away at college and he really didn't have any friends to spend time with. The few acquaintances he had were people he used drugs with. In early recovery he had an easy time meeting girls and dating, but felt he didn't have any luck with girls because they always broke up with him. In early recovery Tom was cynical about peers, felt they didn't really care about him, so why should he make any effort to be nice to them. This attitude was clearly demonstrated in his tone of voice and lack of participation in group. Time was spent giving him feedback on his participation in group and examining his interaction out of group, as well as suggesting ways of improvement.

> Peter was a bright, athletic senior with an A average, who started in the varsity sport he played. He had a reputation as a "partier," "a wild man" and "a good guy." He was "best friends" with the other guys on the team, most of whom were heavy drinkers and drug users. In early recovery Peter voluntarily terminated all social contact with his friends and became very serious, somewhat withdrawn, socially isolated, and somewhat self-righteous. He began attending AA meetings daily, attended young people's AA social events, and was able to have fun with AA friends. Peter had never had a girlfriend and in recovery felt very uncomfortable with any but the most casual contact with girls, unless they were just AA friends. At first he refused to look at this issue because of the discomfort, but then he said, "AA discourages relationships before a year of sobriety is achieved." With Peter, it was necessary to involve his sponsor and point out the difference between casual dating and a serious relationship. Suggestions were made on how to begin to get to know other girls socially, not in his meetings, how to spend time together and have fun—go for an ice cream, get a pizza, go to the beach—and how to deal with sexual impulses and express affection.

Emotional Functioning. When adolescents stop using drugs, they take off an emotional blanket that shielded them from many uncomfortable emotions. In early recovery they often become flooded with these emotions and are unprepared for how to cope with them drug free. Although it is fortunate if adolescents can achieve drug-free highs, they also need help in learning how to withstand the drug-free lows. Learning how to endure hurt, disappointment, anger, frustration, boredom, nervousness, and other unpleasant emotional states without using chemicals is essential to recovery. This learning consists of first identifying the emotions and then finding a healthy outlet for their expression. The adolescent will need to try different activities to determine which outlets are effective and readily available. For example, an adolescent who finds that running is helpful for dealing with anger will need to use another outlet if there is an argument with a parent and the adolescent is made to stay in his or her bedroom for the rest of the evening. The counselor should spend time with the adolescent discussing and evaluating possible outlets so the adolescent will have a variety of ways to cope with negative emotions.

Cocaine-abusing adolescents should be told that very little can compete with the cocaine-produced euphoria. Therefore, they should expect feelings of boredom until they develop interests in other activities and can feel pleasure in participating in these activities.

Family Relationships. Many parents are surprised to find that a drug-free adolescent is still an adolescent. A drug-free adolescent can be moody, fresh, disobedient, and troublesome, and will need to rebel in ways other than using drugs in the process of the developmental task of separation. In addition, many adolescents expect that now that they are drug free, their parents will be happy, permissive, and trusting, and don't understand why they are not. Therefore, it is important for the adolescent to understand and accept that it took several weeks or months or years to destroy the trust and produce an unhappy relationship, and it will take some time to reestablish trust and rebuild the relationship. It is also important for the parent to understand and accept that although adolescents need limits, they also need increasing independence. Conjoint family sessions can be used to negotiate privileges, limits, and rewards. Ongoing parents' groups can provide a place for the parents to vent their anger, hurt, and frustration (rather than taking it out on the newly recovering adolescent) and for the parents to discuss new parenting practices with other parents going through the same situation.

Legal Issues and Indebtedness. One of the early questions that needs to be discussed with the adolescent cocaine abuser is the amount of indebtedness and to whom the money is owed. Unfortunately, an adolescent's recovery does not eliminate debts to dealers, as the following examples illustrate.

> Sam, a 16-year-old crack addict, had been drug free for 2 weeks when he ran into his former dealer at a gasoline station. When the dealer reminded Sam that he was stilled owed $800, Sam explained that he was drug free, was going to treatment, and had no way to pay him. The dealer threatened Sam with physical violence and then suggested that Sam could pay him back in car radios instead of cash. The dealer said that Sam could steal eight car radios and that would settle the debt. Sam agreed and, fearing that he would be hurt badly,

went to a mall and started breaking into cars. Sam was caught by the police and charged with the crime. Even though the dealer then "forgot" the debt because Sam was being watched by the police, Sam's parents paid over $800 in legal fees and fines. Sam was convicted and placed on probation.

Allen, an 18-year-old crack addict, owed $1,200 to his dealer. He was afraid to leave his house because he feared he'd be hurt by the dealer. In Allen's second treatment session, he agreed to tell his parents about the $1,200, and they agreed to loan him the money. Allen paid the dealer and never heard from him again.

It is common for adolescents abusing cocaine to be in debt or to have done things that result in conflicts with the law. This should be determined as quickly as possible. It is important for adolescents to understand how remaining abstinent and participating in treatment can directly improve their legal and financial situations. After releases are signed, contact should be made with the lawyer or probation officer as soon as possible to determine the situation and prepare the adolescent for all possible outcomes.

Sexual Issues. Many times adolescents, in an effort to obtain cocaine or while under the influence of cocaine, have participated in sexual behavior that they later wish had not occurred. In addition to the adolescent's own shame and embarrassment, sometimes the sexual behavior is known to many others. When this happens, the newly recovering adolescent also has to deal with a "bad reputation." It is very painful for a newly recovering adolescent to hear reminders of past sexual behavior, and it is difficult to convince acquaintances from the past that the adolescent is no longer interested in these sexual activities. Adolescents in this situation will need support and advice on how to handle these issues. For some adolescents, a change of school can make coping with this situation easier. Even if this occurs, however, the adolescent must still come to grips with the past.

Female adolescents need support in understanding that many male adolescents still perceive a double standard for sexual conduct. Male adolescents may need support in dealing with the fact that involvement in homosexual behavior while under the influence of cocaine does not necessarily mean the adolescent is homosexual. For both male and female adolescents, issues of sexual identity and current attitudes toward sexual behavior need to be addressed.

Other Issues

Relapse Prevention. Relapse prevention strategies useful with cocaine-abusing adults are also useful with adolescents, but need some modification. Adolescents have much less control over their environment than adults have. For example, an adult may be able to change jobs, but it is often impossible for an adolescent to change schools; most adults have a greater capacity to earn money than most adolescents do; most adults have greater mobility than most adolescents. Therefore, even when adolescents have identified the cues that stimulate cocaine cravings, they may have very few options on how to deal with them.

Testing. The counselor should anticipate that adolescents will test the policies and procedures of the treatment program. This can include testing their capacity to return to "limited" cocaine use, lateness, or missed appointments. It is helpful to contract with the adolescent on the consequences if this occurs. For example, an adolescent seen for outpatient treatment can contract to enter an inpatient program if there is a slip, or the parents might contract to take away car privileges. Since some level of testing behavior is common, a treatment program should incorporate methods for dealing with it.

Monitoring. The counselor treating the adolescent should have frequent contact with the school and parents to get others' perspectives on the adolescent's recovery. Although stopping all alcohol and drug use is the most essential part of recovery, it is still only a part of that process. An accurate understanding of the adolescent's functioning at school, at home, and with peers is crucial to evaluating progress in recovery.

Illness Model. Understanding and accepting the illness model of addiction has been helpful to many adults in reducing their shame and guilt and promoting participation in recovery programs. Although this is often helpful to adolescents for the same reasons, many adolescents resist this model. This resistance may come from denial, but often it is due to the adolescent's fragile ego and perception of a label of illness as a narcissistic wound.

It is well known that one difficulty in treating adolescents with chronic medical problems is that they resist taking prescribed medication or following other medical advice. The ill adolescent may feel: "If I don't take my medication, injection, or treatment, then I don't have to be reminded that I'm sick, impaired, and not perfect." Since adolescents have feelings of invulnerability and omnipotence, reminders of impairment can be intolerable. Therefore, the illness model should be explained but should not be forced on a resistant adolescent who is willing to stay drug free.

Involvement in Twelve Step Programs. Some of the advantages of involving adolescents in Twelve Step recovery programs have already been mentioned. Seeing role models who have made it; reducing their shame by sharing with others who have been there; becoming involved with empathetic adults who can provide a second-chance family; learning and working on a model for recovery; involvement with a sponsor; 24-hour-a-day, 365-day-a-year support in recovery; activities to fill the void left by abstinence from cocaine are just some of the other benefits of particiapting in Twelve Step recovery programs like AA, NA, or CA.

Although adolescents can benefit in the ways described here, they often need more preparation for their entrance into Twelve Step programs than adults do. Specifically, helping adolescents find a group that includes some other young people will make it easier for them to identify with other members and the program. Adolescents also need preparation for the format of meetings, the slogans and expressions, the friendly overtures by strangers, the spiritual aspect of meetings, the heavy smoking at many meetings, the reason that members say their name followed by "I'm an addict and/or an alcoholic," the reference to certain program materials or books, the confidentiality, and other aspects of the meeting or program that will make participation more meaningful and valuable to the adolescent. Adolescents should also be encouraged to attend different meetings until they find the one where they feel most comfortable.

Conclusion

The recovery process for adolescents can be characterized as a tough climb back. They must face the tasks of daily living without the aid of the emotional blanket provided by drugs. Many must learn new skills while feeling unsure, depressed, lonely, and bored. Gaining the trust of others, changing a reputation, dealing with legal consequences of past behavior, and trying to improve school performance can be a long and difficult process. Some adolescents and families will need support in accepting diminished or delayed goals. For example, a bright adolescent who always planned on going to a very competitive college, but did poorly during 10th and 11th grades because of extensive substance abuse, may have to accept going to a much less competitive college for a year or two, doing very well, and then transferring to the kind of college he or she always wanted to attend.

Recovery is a process with steps forward and backward for both the adolescent and the family. Building on effective treatment techniques for adult cocaine abusers while allowing for the special developmental needs of adolescents, keeping in mind that each adolescent's developmental needs are different, and building in the flexibility required to address these needs as well as the addiction should provide clinicians with the framework needed to treat cocaine-abusing adolescents effectively.

REFERENCES

Berkovitz, I. H. (Ed.). (1972). *Adolescents grow in groups.* New York: Brunner/Mazel.
Citron, P. (1978). Group work with alcoholic polydrug involved adolescents with deviant behavior syndrome. *Social Work with Groups, 1*(1), 39–52.
Fischer, J. (1978). Psychotherapy of adolescent alcohol abusers. In S. Zimberg, J. Wallace, & S. Blume (Eds.), *Practical approaches to alcoholism psychotherapy* (pp. 219–235).

New York: Plenum Press. (Available from National Council on Alcoholism, 733 Third Avenue, New York, NY 10017. Phone: (212) 986-4433.)

Johnston, L., Bachman, J., & O'Malley, P. (1985). *Monitoring the future: A continuing study of the lifestyles and values of youth.* Ann Arbor: University of Michigan Institute for Social Research.

Morehouse, E. (1983). Assessing and motivating adolescents who have drinking problems. In *Social work treatment of alcohol problems.* Treatment Series, Rutgers Center of Alcohol Studies, Publications Division (Vol. 5, pp. 119–130). New Brunswick, NJ: Lexington Press.

Morehouse, E. (1984). Working with alcohol abusing children of alcoholics. *Alcohol, Health and Research World, 8*(4), 14–19.

Unger, R. (1978). The treatment of adolescent alcoholism. *Social Casework, 59*(1), 27–37.

12

A Treatment for Cocaine-Abusing Health Care Professionals

THOMAS J. CROWLEY, SUSAN KRILL-SMITH,
CAROL ATKINSON, AND BRAD SELGESTAD

Special programs for identifying and treating drug-abusing health care professionals have arisen in recent years, coincidentally together with the national epidemic of cocaine abuse described elsewhere in this book. The Addiction Research and Treatment Service of the University of Colorado School of Medicine opened its Cocaine Clinic in 1980 (Anker & Crowley, 1982; Crowley, 1987; Helfrich, Crowley, Atkinson, & Post, 1983); this may have been the first specialized cocaine treatment program in the nation. At about the same time we opened the Halsted Clinic for drug-abusing health care professionals (Crowley, 1984, 1986). In this chapter we review the cases of those physicians, dentists, and nurses who sought evaluation or treatment in the Halsted Clinic or the Cocaine Clinic, and whose problems included cocaine abuse.

Two issues arise when we consider cocaine-abusing health care professionals. The first concerns the user: Do these cocaine abusers differ from other cocaine abusers of comparable income and education? For example, it might be hypothesized that health care professionals would have greater access to legal supplies of cocaine and other drugs, increasing the severity of their problems and their propensity to relapse. In addition, these patients' professional training with needles might influence their preferred routes of administration; intravenous (IV) drug self-administration is usually considered a more dangerous and perniciously persistent route of administration (Crowley & Rhine, 1985).

The second important issue in considering the treatment of cocaine-abusing health care professionals concerns the drug: Does the unique phar-

Thomas J. Crowley. Addiction Research and Treatment Service, Department of Psychiatry, University of Colorado School of Medicine, Denver, Colorado.

Susan Krill-Smith. Private practice, Denver, Colorado.

Carol Atkinson. Addiction Research and Treatment Service.

Brad Selgestad. Private practice, Denver, Colorado.

macology of cocaine demand a different treatment for these patients than for health care professionals who abuse other drugs? Cocaine differs from other drugs commonly abused by health care professionals in the signs and symptoms of intoxication, the course of detoxification, the irregular run–crash pattern with which the drug may be used, the irrelevance of methadone or naltrexone therapies for cocaine abuse, and cocaine's very powerful reinforcing property which tends to drive continued self-administration.

In this chapter we describe the cocaine-abusing health care professionals whom we have treated and review our evaluation and treatment approach to these patients. We include comments on the unique legal issues and the problems of confidentiality versus reporting that arise in this treatment. Finally, we discuss clinicians' problems in assessing outcome in this condition.

Description of the Sample

We discourage unwarranted generalizations from the patients we describe. Patients in drug abuse clinics in different cities differ according to the epidemiology of drug abuse patterns in those cities (e.g., DAWN, 1985) and according to each program's outreach and referral patterns. Despite that major caveat, however, a description of our patients may be useful because we find no prior descriptions of sizable groups of cocaine-abusing health care professionals.

Three of the authors work, or worked, in our Halstead Clinic or Cocaine Clinic. Each reviewed his or her case files for all patients who were health care professionals, who presented for drug abuse treatment in one of those programs, and who reported using cocaine 10 or more times. The 10-times criterion permitted us to include some patients whose major problems were with other drugs, but who also had used cocaine.

Demographics and Diagnoses. These 16 males and 10 females included 11 nurses, 10 MDs, 4 DDSs, and 1 pharmacist. None of our veterinarian patients met criteria for inclusion in this group. Of these 26 drug-abusing professionals who had used cocaine at least 10 times, only 8 had cocaine as the primary drug of abuse, qualifying for a primary DSM-III diagnosis of Cocaine Abuse (*Diagnostic and Statistical Manual of Mental Disorders*, 3rd edition; American Psychiatric Association, 1980). Eleven others had primary diagnoses of Opioid Abuse or Dependence; 6 had Mixed or Other Substance Use Disorders; and 1 had a primary diagnosis of Cannabis Abuse. We conclude that in our programs, health care professionals who abuse cocaine are very likely to abuse other drugs, in most cases to a greater extent than cocaine itself.

It is often difficult to establish clearly the co-occurrence of other psychiatric diagnoses in substance-abusing patients, because drug abuse may produce symptoms that mimic those of other syndromes. It appeared to us, however, that 4 patients met DSM-III criteria for Borderline Personality Disorder, and one of these 4 also met criteria for Anorexia Nervosa. Five other patients each were diagnosed as having one of these five DSM-III disorders: Antisocial Personality, Histrionic Personality, Major Depressive Disorder, Adjustment Disorder, and Dysthymic Disorder. The relatively infrequent presence of other psychiatric diagnoses in these patients provides further support for recent studies that find that many substance abusers have no other concurrent psychiatric problem (Woody *et al.*, 1983). And the findings further refute older views (Noyes & Kolb, 1958) that unrelievedly emphasized underlying psychopathology as principal contributor to substance abuse.

The proportion of dual-diagnosis patients is approximately the same among these health care professionals as among our general Cocaine Clinic patients, but the diagnoses vary. There are more Antisocial and Narcissistic Personality Disorders among the general Cocaine Clinic population. The low prevalence of Antisocial Personality disorder in this group of cocaine-abusing health care professionals may result from a group selection factor; people with the severe and persistent antisocial problems required for a DSM-III diagnosis of Antisocial Personality disorder probably are unable to sustain the effort and control required to complete professional training.

Discovery at Work. The drug-related performance of health care professionals may be monitored by supervisors and colleagues, licensing boards, diversion units of the Drug Enforcement Administration (DEA), and state pharmacy inspectors. Seventeen of our 26 patients entered treatment following a confrontation from one of these sources.

At the time of our evaluation, 7 patients had lost professional licenses through suspension, surrender, or revocation; 9 others were under investigation or on probation by their licensing boards. Although 10 were unknown to their licensing boards at admission, many of these had been confronted by work supervisors.

Clearly, then, drug (including cocaine) involvement represents a major risk to employment for health care professionals, and work-related monitoring propelled many of our patients into evaluation and treatment. This suggests that therapists may be called on to interact with supervisors and monitoring agencies. Indeed, at the request of 11 of these 26 patients, we made formal clinical reports to licensing boards.

Drug Source. Drug-abusing health-care professionals frequently divert pharmaceutical drugs to their own use. Rarely, for example, do physician–patients report obtaining opioid drugs from street sources. Based on admission histories we estimated how much of the cocaine used by patients described here came from pharmaceutical sources. Strikingly, only 2 patients appeared to have obtained more than 20% of their cocaine by diversion of the legal drug; the other 24 patients appeared to have obtained at least 80% of their cocaine from black market sources, and most reported *no* diversion from legal supplies. In this regard, cocaine abuse differs dramatically from abuse of other drugs by our other health care patients. Apparently, the wide availability of illegal cocaine, coupled with its relatively infrequent use in legitimate medicine and dentistry, prompts these patients to use black market cocaine.

Route of Administration. IV cocaine administration was favored by 11 of these patients, and a 12th frequently injected the drug but also smoked the free-base form. Two others mainly used the drug by free-base smoking, while 11 inhaled cocaine intranasally. Favored route of administration was unclear in the chart record of 1 patient. Frequent IV use by 46% of these patients considerably exceeds the 33% that we (Helfrich *et al.*, 1983) observed, and the 27% observed by others (Washton & Tatarsky, 1984), among cocaine-abusing patients not selected for being health care professionals. The health care professional's vocational familiarity with injection techniques may increase his or her propensity to use the IV route for cocaine administration.

Cocaine Dose. Reported doses were quite variable. Among those patients whose primary drug of abuse was cocaine, the reported dose during the patients' 2 months of maximum use ranged from 2 grams per week to 45 grams per week; the latter figure was reported by a patient who did use pharmaceutical cocaine that was not subject to cutting with adulterants and diluents. Among those for whom cocaine was not the major drug of abuse, reported doses ranged from as little as 0.25 gram per week in the 2 months of maximum use, to binge ingestion episodes of as much as 12 grams per 24 hours.

Cocaine-Related Symptoms. We and others previously have discussed signs and symptoms of cocaine abuse (Cohen, 1984; Crowley, 1987; Helfrich *et al.*, 1983; Siegel, 1984; Washton & Gold, 1984). From these cocaine-abusing health care professionals we received reports of cocaine-related vocational and financial problems, personality changes, paranoid psychosis, edgy tension, irritability, exhaustion, depression, mood swings, anxiety, marital problems, weight loss, heart palpitations, nose bleeds, shallow breathing or respiratory depression, muscular weakness, and seizures.

Other Drugs Abused. The pharmacologic sophistication of health care professionals, and the availability to them of a wide variety of drugs, may complicate the processes of history taking and urine monitoring. Our 8 patients who were primary abusers of cocaine reported that they had used one or more of the following drugs at least 10 times: alcohol, marijuana, oxycodone, amphetamines, barbiturates, benzodiazepines, methylphenidate, and various hallucinogenic drugs. Those 18 patients whose primary problem involved drugs other than cocaine, but who had used cocaine at least 10 times, also reported using one or more of the following drugs at least 10 times: meperidine, morphine, hydromorphone, pentazocine, fentanyl, heroin, methadone, various benzodiazepines, methaqualone, barbiturates, street "speed," amphetamines, marijuana, nitrous oxide, and alcohol. Some of these patients reported that in previous treatment experiences they had discovered that their urine was monitored for, say, meperidine but not pentazocine, and so they continued using the undetected drug. Clearly, treaters of these drug-wise patients must have more than minimal knowledge of abusable drugs.

Medical Problems. In our experience, health care professionals who primarily abuse opiates not infrequently report starting these drugs to treat pain or other medical complaints (Crowley, 1986). Among the present patients (who had used *cocaine* at least 10 times and who had drug abuse problems) medical complaints were less frequent. One patient had experienced serious asthma, and another had problems of arthritis, emphysema, and chronic cystitis.

Alcoholism in Relatives. Alcoholism clearly runs in families, with one's propensity to become alcoholic apparently transmitted genetically (Bohman, Sigvardsson, & Cloninger, 1981; Cloninger, Bohman, & Sigvardsson, 1981). As many as one-quarter of the sons of alcoholic fathers may, under certain reported circumstances, become alcoholic. Our cocaine-abusing patients frequently report substance abuse, usually alcoholism, among first-degree relatives. This retrospective chart review found clear statements of substance abuse, usually alcoholism, among parents or siblings in 11 of these 26 patients. Some genetically transmitted mechanism possibly may underlie a propensity to abuse *either* alcohol or cocaine, so that having alcoholic family members may increase one's risk that cocaine experimentation will lead to full-blown cocaine abuse. Recent genetic studies support this view (Cadoret *et al.*, 1986).

Procedures in Evaluation and Treatment

Value of a Defined Program

Treatment for the drug-dependent health care professional usually begins in one of several ways. Either the patient is referred into treatment by an intervention, confrontation, or ultimatum by an employer or some other significant person; or the patient is required to participate in drug–alcohol treatment by stipulation of the professional board and/or probation department; or the patient is self-referred. These patients fear breaches of confidentiality. Moreover, they often are self-reliant people who dread the dependency that they feel may be associated with treatment. A program aimed specifically at people like themselves may be easier for them to enter. Our program also has established a positive reputation with professional boards and associations, which provide confidential referrals for drug-dependent professionals. Further, we deal not only with the patient's addiction problem, but also with employers, boards, and (in some cases) the criminal justice system. We have been active in promoting rehabilitation for drug-dependent health care professionals, and our reputation for providing *confidential* treatment is extremely important.

First Contact

The patient first contacts us by telephone. We directly discuss evaluation and treatment, providing information in a nonjudgmental, supportive manner. Of utmost importance, again, is assuring confidentiality. Assurance that the therapists have knowledge of cocaine dependence and of the special issues of health care professionals is often important. Sometimes the first face-to-face contact with a patient occurs only after several such anonymous calls. An appointment for intake evaluation is scheduled as soon as possible unless there is a psychiatric or medical emergency requiring immediate attention; in the latter case, referral is made to a cooperating emergency room.

Evaluation as the First Phase of Treatment

At the initial evaluation we obtain a careful, detailed drug–alcohol history (Crowley & Rhine, 1985), as well as a psychosocial history. After obtaining simple *identifying information* (age, sex, marital status, vocation, address, and telephone number), we ask for the patient's *chief complaint*: "What brings you in to see me now?"

We then ask the patient to elaborate on the chief complaint, providing a history of the current problem or *present illness*. The patient may not couch the complaint and description of the problem in terms of drugs; one patient may state that he has a marital problem, another that she is depressed, and a third that he is unable to control his use of cocaine. We ask for details of the problem as presented by the patient. We ask about the precipitants of this current problem—what happened and who was involved. We attempt to determine the time course of the difficulties and any changes in the patient's feelings and daily functioning that occurred as the problem developed. We inquire about the patient's efforts to cope with the problem and the resources the patient has called on and found helpful. We ask what the patient hopes for regarding the outcome of the problem—his or her goal in seeking treatment.

We then obtain a detailed *drug history*; if the patient has not yet mentioned a drug problem, we simply ask why he or she has sought treatment at a drug abuse clinic. With the patient we then review the role of drugs in the problem. We specifically ask about past use of the major classes of abused drugs: stimulants (including cocaine), opioids, sedative–hypnotics, alcohol, hallucinogens, nicotine, volatile organic compounds, and gas anesthetics.

In the drug–alcohol history we ask what drugs, and how much of each, the patient has used. We ask about the temporal pattern of drug use: When was the first use? When did problems first appear from drug use? What was the time of maximum use in the patient's life? At what times has the patient tried to be abstinent, and for how long was that successful? At what times of the day or night is the patient likely to use the drug?

We further ask about routes of administration, which for cocaine may be by intranasal insufflation ("snorting"), pulmonary inhalation (free-base or crack smoking), or intravenous injection. We obtain information about the procedures that the patient uses to obtain, prepare, and administer the drugs. And we inquire about the source of the patient's drugs (avoiding information about individual names) to determine whether the patient writes prescriptions, buys on the black market, diverts office supplies, or obtains drugs by some other means.

It also is important to learn about the social setting of the drug use. We ask whether patients have used cocaine at parties, in bars, with a particular friend or a spouse, or alone. Many of these health care professionals become embarrassed or ashamed about their continued drug use; although they originally may have used the drug socially, solitary use usually evolves.

We ask what circumstances have tended to trigger drug use in the past. Loneliness, demanding work schedules, and (perhaps most important) simple drug availability frequently initiate episodes of use. Eventually, however, many patients use cocaine whenever they can, and the reinforcing property of the drug seems to be the main reason for such continued use.

We ask about the payoffs or rewards for the patient's drug use. The common answer among cocaine abusers is, "It used to feel great!" But remarkably often users go on to say that the drug has few perceptible rewards after extensive use, "but I can't stop using." Convinced that drug abuse always occurs to produce good feelings or to treat bad feelings, some clinicians discount these reports from patients of tolerance to the euphoric effect of cocaine. But in carefully constructed research situations in which rats can "report" through their behavior the subjective effects of drugs, animals repeatedly treated with cocaine also systematically report tolerance to cocaine's subjective effect (Wood, Lal, & Emmett-Oglesby, 1984). Cocaine probably can reinforce continued self-administration through systems that do not rely on positive subjective feelings.

We next question patients about the problems or costs that have resulted from their drug use. Five spheres of life commonly are affected by cocaine and other drugs: medical, legal, social–family, financial–vocational, and psychological. We previously have reported (Helfrich *et al.*, 1983) the range and prevalence of such problems among cocaine abusers. Vocational questions especially appropriate to health care professionals include cocaine-related confrontations with colleagues, partners, hospital staff members, legal authorities, supervisory committees, or licensing boards; conversely, apparent ignoring or covering up of cocaine-related problems by those same persons or agencies; diversion of cocaine or other drugs by stealing, prescription writing, or other means; careless or criminal prescribing or dispensing to others; use of cocaine before and during duty periods; and drug impairments of professional performance or judgment. We specifically inquire what it is that patients most fear losing if the drug use continues. Answers typically include health and life, spouse, and profession.

We next obtain a chronological past history of the patient's psychosocial *development*. The purpose of this information is to place in a developmental context the current problem faced by the patient, attempting to understand what led the patient to respond in his or her unique way to the current problem of drug use.

We ask where the patient was born and raised, and we ask about siblings and their ages. We then say, "Tell me about your mother" and await an answer to that open-ended question. We probe further with "What was she like with you?" We ask, "What was the best thing about your mother?" We then say, "Nobody is perfect—what would you have changed about your mother?" We then ask the same series of questions about the father, finally asking, "How did your parents get along?" These questions aim to determine the patient's experiences and feelings in early relationships, seeking patterns learned then and carried forward to influence current behavior.

Our next open-ended question is "What were you like as a kid?" We specifically inquire about friends, activities, whether the patient had been compliant or often in trouble, and about school behavior and school achievement.

The next question is "What were you like in junior high school or high school?" We again specifically probe friends, dating, clubs, activities, sports, grades, relationships with parents, legal or other troubles, and use of drugs.

We continue pursuing the chronology of the patient's life, repeatedly asking "What happened next in your life?" We specifically examine education, work, military experience, relationships with same and opposite sex, marriage and family, pleasures and strengths, drug use, health, and treatment experiences (both medical and psychological), along with a detailed description of activities and schedules for a typical recent day, from arising to retiring.

After having obtained this extensive history, we ask again about the original chief complaint: "You have told me a lot, but let me go back to the first question. Why are you here now? What are you hoping to get out of this treatment?"

On the basis of the patient's statement of the problems that propelled him or her into an evaluation, and framed in the context of the patient's past experience, we now work with the patient to reformulate a goal for treatment. We use the patient's complaints as the foundation of a treatment agreement, with attention to drug abuse woven into the fabric of that complaint. For a patient who says, "Cocaine is ruining my life," the task is relatively easy; the goal of abstinence is readily agreed on. But for a patient who describes a marital or professional problem as the major impetus for seeking treatment, we propose abstinence as a way of addressing the issue perceived by the patient as the primary problem. In this way we attempt to establish an *alliance* with the patient to jointly address the patient's troublesome life problems.

Throughout the time of this evaluation we are carefully assessing the patient's *mental status*. We observe general appearance and behavior, including grooming, body posture, facial expression, gait, and movements of the extremities and trunk. We assess the patient's speech in its rate, volume, spontaneity, grammar, vocabulary, evidence of slurring, and principal themes in the discourse. We consider the patient's affect and mood, and we specifically ask about suicidal thoughts, plans, or actions. We also assess manner of relating: is the patient, for example, shy, diffident, aggressive, forceful, seductive, remote, intellectual, desperate, relieved, hostile, compliant, suspicious, or guarded, in relation to the interviewer? If the patient shows any evidence of memory impairment or disorientation to time, person, or place, we perform a detailed mental status examination with questions addressing judgment, orientation, memory, and cognitive ability.

This detailed evaluation is not antecedent to treatment; it is a part of treatment. It shows the patient that there is an orderly process for beginning to address a problem that he or she has seen as totally disordered and out of control. It challenges denial by asking for precise details about the patient's drug use and other activities, and the consequences thereof.

In answering questions about the benefits and costs of drug use, the evaluation sets the stage for establishment of a therapeutic alliance with the patient. For the patient him- or herself has listed personal reasons for using and reasons for stopping. In those two lists both patient and therapist readily recognize the patient's ambivalence about giving up the drug. Joint recognition of this ambivalence permits an explicit statement from the outset that there is a risk of relapse back to drug use, and that treatment aims at reducing the risk of relapse.

Early in the evaluation we invite the *participation of a spouse, lover, or other family member*. There are several reasons for such participation. First, a spouse inevitably provides a fuller history, since patients often are too embarrassed about the nature and consequences of their drug use to describe it fully. Second, spouses may "enable" continued drug use. In some cases a drug-using spouse alternates between castigating the patient for excessive use, and joining in the use. In other cases the spouse, for the best of humanitarian reasons, continually attempts to cover up the patient's drug use in hopes of avoiding adverse professional and personal consequences. Thus, a spouse may have supported the patient's lies about relapses to previous therapists or hospital staff committees. It is invaluable for the therapist to know about such past enabling, and to encourage the spouse (through questioning) to reappraise whether such enabling is in the long-term interest of the patient, spouse, or others.

A third reason for including spouses is to evaluate and intervene in the family turmoil that sometimes occurs early in abstinence. A spouse, furious about past drug use, may have suppressed expressions of that anger while continued use threatened the patient's life, but such anger may burst forth destructively once abstinence begins. Indeed, family turmoil of this kind may constitute a major threat to early abstinence. Therefore, after the first joint meeting, unless we find compelling reasons to do otherwise, we prefer to include a spouse or other family member in all subsequent treatment sessions.

Patients with a history of intravenous drug use are *evaluated medically* by a physician, as are any patients who appear to be psychotic or to have an organic brain syndrome, apparent medical illness, or possible physical dependence on another drug. We employ familiar detoxification procedures (Senay, 1983) for detoxification from drugs other than cocaine, and we usually recommend hospital detoxification for cocaine abusers who also have significant physical dependence on sedative–hypnotics such as barbiturates, benzodiazepines, or alcohol.

However, our indications for hospitalization are quite limited. In addition to withdrawal from sedative–hypnotic drugs, we hospitalize for psychosis, organic mental syndromes, serious concomitant medical or psychiatric illness, and we recommend hospitalization when it seems otherwise impossible to separate the patient from the drug long enough to accomplish an outpatient evaluation.

Using these criteria, we hospitalized only 3 of these 26 patients during or following evaluation; 5 (including 1 of the 3 hospitalized by us) had been hospitalized elsewhere before referral to us for outpatient care. Thus, only 7 of the 26 patients received hospital care. (We hospitalize even fewer of the patients seen in our Cocaine Clinic who are not health care professionals, probably because those patients have less involvement with, and access to, other drugs.) We do feel that inpatient treatment can be helpful in providing a time out for some patients. In that safe environment denial of addiction can be addressed, withdrawal can occur, and the group process may lessen isolation. Psychiatric and medical workups are sometimes better managed on an inpatient basis. Clearly, however, we emphasize outpatient care. Rawson, Obert, McCann, and Mann (1986) find better outcomes among cocaine abusers treated as outpatients than among those beginning as inpatients, and Washton, Gold, and Pottash (1986) also report excellent outcomes among outpatient-treated cocaine abusers. Our experience parallels those reports.

First Weeks of Treatment

The early days of treatment are often chaotic. Frequently, patients have undergone recent confrontations with supervisors, employers, or licensing authorities. Their employment and income are threatened or actually lost. A need for alternative, nonprofessional employment may arise, an issue for which professional patients are often ill prepared. Felony charges for drug diversion are possible, although in our experience such charges are uncommon. Despite participation in treatment, spouses may be angry and disillusioned, and may provide little support. In these tumultuous times, patients are anxious, depressed, and possibly suicidal.

Despite this tumult and confusion, however, we avoid the use of adjunctive medications (such as antidepressants). Available evidence leaves us unconvinced of the efficacy of psychotropic drugs in the treatment of cocaine abuse (Crowley, 1987). We encourage patients to seek nonpharmacologic solutions to life problems. However, we do consider the use of methadone, clonidine, naltrexone, or disulfiram for those who concurrently abused opioids or alcohol with cocaine.

Contingency contracting (Crowley, 1986) may seem an especially attractive treatment technique at these times. The patient recognizes that any suspicion of relapse back to drug use would prolong and intensify problems with supervisors or licensing boards. Moreover, clear evidence of abstinence and of an intention to remain abstinent supports the patient's cause with these same agencies. Therefore, with a prior explicit agreement between patient and therapist that there remains a continuing risk of relapse, we broach with the patient the possibility of using a contingency contract to reduce that relapse risk, and also to convince others that the patient can safely resume professional practice.

We have already discussed with patients those things that they fear losing, should they resume drug use; professional licensure and practice inevitably are included in these lists. We then present a scenario: "Consider that you are severely tempted toward a relapse, and you are weighing the possible consequences. You know that if you resume drug use you risk losing your license, marriage, and health. But you also know that you have used 10,000 times before, and you probably will not lose those things for using 10,001 times; in other words, you probably can get away with just one more dose. And of course, you will tell yourself that you won't use any more after that single dose. Given those odds, the prospect is strong for a relapse (which actually is unlikely to cease after only one dose). On the other hand, if you know in advance that you are almost certain to lose your license and practice from that *first* dose, you would have a much stronger incentive to avoid that dose."

We then encourage the patient to write a letter to the licensing board, admitting a relapse to drug use and surrendering the license. We further encourage the patient to direct us in a written contract to establish a schedule for collecting frequent, random urine samples; to test them for cocaine and other drugs of abuse; and to mail the letter whenever drugs appear in the urine or the patient fails to provide a scheduled sample.

Patients often express relief that something so concrete may reduce the risk that they will relapse to drug use. They and their lawyers may use the contract to argue for continued, probationary practice; a drug abuser who abstains should be able to practice with reasonable skill and safety, and if he or she relapses while on a contract, the public is reasonably protected because the practice will terminate almost immediately. Licensing boards in our jurisdiction have looked very favorably upon these contracts, basing probationary status on them.

We have reported elsewhere on the efficacy of contingency contracts among drug-abusing health care professionals (Crowley, 1984, 1986) and among cocaine abusers generally (Anker & Crowley, 1982). It appears to us that contingency contracts probably are equally effective among health care professionals regardless of which particular drug those professionals may have abused. We usually recommend such contracts for a minimum of one year, and we often renew the contracts for several more years.

Under the contract the patient is "at risk" to produce a urine sample on any Monday, Wednesday, or Friday. Initially, we collect samples on each of those days; later, the patient phones our clinic on each of those days and receives a recorded message that informs him whether or not he is to come to the clinic on that day to produce a sample. Eventually, he may provide specimens only once or twice a month, but the frequent calls and the occasional random requirement to produce samples apparently provide continuing deterrence against relapse. Urines are analyzed for benzoylecgonine, a moderately persistent metabolite of cocaine that can be detected with a three-times-per-week schedule. If the patient also abuses less persistent drugs (such as hydromorphone), he or she is directed to call every day of the week. Of course, a trained monitor should observe directly the production of all urine samples and should take immediate physical possession of the urine.

With the contingency contract helping to sustain abstinence, we proceed with couples counseling for patients who are married or in important relationships, and with individual counseling for others. These sessions focus on avoiding early relapse, finding solutions to the real-life crises precipitated by the drug abuse and its discovery, continuing to identify circumstances that commonly triggered previous episodes of drug use, and reestablishing a rewarding marital (or other) relationship.

To avoid early relapses, we recommend that patients stay away from cocaine and those who use it or supply it. For those who have used the drug socially, we recommend that they list their cocaine-using friends, and their non-using friends, and that they arrange to spend more time with the latter and less time with the former. We suggest that they avoid those places that they have in the past associated with cocaine use, such as bars, discos, or neighborhoods where they obtained the drug.

In addition to situations of drug availability, which trigger drug craving and relapse in most drug abusers, we explore those unique situations that may encourage drug use in a particular patient. For example, one patient's depressed and alcoholic mother frequently called him from another city, demanding that he "come home" to take care of her and threatening suicide if he did not. These calls always precipitated thoughts of drug craving; this became clear to the patient when the contingency contract forced him to remain abstinent. For some other patients cocaine had become central to their sexual relationships, and sexual activity triggered fond memories of cocaine use and craving for the drug.

Alcohol intoxication appears to trigger cocaine relapses in some patients. We recommend that patients avoid all psychoactive drugs, including alcohol. This admonition is especially important for those patients whose history includes concurrent abuse of cocaine with alcohol or other drugs. We should note, however, that some of our patients have continued nonabusive ingestion of alcohol, or even marijuana, without engendering relapse to cocaine abuse.

To assist with the crises induced by the drug use and its detection, we often recommend that patients consult attorneys. These patients frequently feel both guilty and helpless when charged with professional misconduct; they believe that whatever is meted out to them must be deserved. But appropriate legal representation may soften punishments, reducing the chaos and disruption that tend to complicate rehabilitation and recovery.

At the request of patients and their attorneys, we often provide reports to patients' employers, colleagues, hospital committees, or licensing boards. In these reports we emphasize the commitment to abstinence and protection of the public embodied in the contingency contract, and patients come to see the frequent (and somewhat bothersome) urine tests as a vehicle for reestablishing professional credibility. For patients directed into treatment by employers, professional boards, or criminal justice agencies, once a release of information has been signed, therapists and patients must be clear and specific about what information regarding urine results, progress, and safety to practice is released to other agencies, together with what consequences may be faced by the patient if, for example, a urine sample contains drugs. For the therapist, information from the employer about the patient's work performance and reintegration into the work situation can be helpful for treatment.

We encourage patients to participate in both self-help and professionally led groups. Only 4 of these 26 patients elected to make regular use of Alcoholics Anonymous (AA), Narcotics Anonymous (NA), or Cocaine Anonymous (CA). Five of these patients attended with some regularity our open-ended, professionally led groups for drug-dependent health care professionals.

The marital or other primary relationships of patients often need first aid early in treatment. Spouses or lovers repeatedly have been lied to about the drug use, may feel hopeless about recovery, and may feel anger at being trapped in a painful and disappointing relationship. Once again, the contingency contract proves valuable. A spouse participating in treatment will know whether the patient is providing drug-free urines; this permits the spouse to give up distrustful vigilance and fear of further lying about drugs. Therapy sessions provide a safe venting place for the spouse's anger over financial reversals, mounting debts, months of feeling socially and sexually ignored by the patient, and other problems resulting from the prior drug use. We encourage couples to resume acting as a team in making decisions about legal steps, return to professional practice, and resuming contact with friends and colleagues lost during the period of drug use. We may discuss directly the resumption of sex, which often is suppressed by the abuse of cocaine or other drugs. Surprisingly, another issue sometimes is dealt with in these early couple's sessions: A spouse may be angry at having to give up his or her own controlled use of cocaine in order to help the patient avoid relapse.

Different, but related, issues emerge early in the treatment of those who are not married or in an important relationship. Loneliness, grief over the loss of former spouses or lovers, and ambivalence over commitment to new relationships are common themes in these patients' early days of abstinence.

Therapy's Mid-Course

As these early crises are resolved, more traditional individual or couples psychotherapy evolves. For example, the man mentioned earlier, whose mother frequently demanded his return home, had an abiding distrust of relationships with women. He perceived all women as unreasonably demanding and clutching, and the feelings were heightened when his mother did commit suicide shortly after he entered treatment. He was not in a couple relationship, and much of his individual psychotherapy focused on his real-life attempt to form trusting relationships with a series of women. Another man had begun using cocaine by isolating himself in the basement with the drug whenever he became angry at his wife. In couples treatment they discussed the rational and irrational aspects of his anger toward her, and both members of the couple seriously attempted to alter their behavior and improve their relationship.

Even during this phase, however, the risk of relapse to drug abuse continues as a central treatment focus. We repeatedly ask about thoughts of drug craving and the stimuli that trigger them. We frequently review urine results and the feelings of patients and spouses about the urine tests. We discuss the therapist's unusual role (under the contingency contract) of counselor and interpreter on the one hand, and detective and judge on the other. We discuss and jointly plan reductions in the frequency of urine tests, and we review increases in the frequency of drug cravings (which sometimes occur with less frequent urine sampling).

This is usually the longest phase of treatment, and during this prolonged period the patient has numerous opportunities to practice a drug-free life. Those circumstances that formerly stimulated drug use are now avoided or mastered in abstinence. As the duration of abstinence progresses, we continue to emphasize, however, that the patient faces a lifelong risk of relapse and must therefore develop a lifetime plan to support abstinence and avoid relapse.

We previously have reported that about half of our health care patients treated with contingency contracts experience at least brief relapses (Crowley, 1984, 1986). Of the 26 patients described here, 15 signed contingency contracts with us; 3 others had similar contingencies, since their licensing boards required frequent reports from us about urine test results and participation in treatment. Among these 18, 10 had at least brief relapses of which we are aware, either during or after the urine-monitoring period. The relapses of 2 patients were brief and had minimal adverse effects on their lives. Six of the 8 who had significant adverse effects relapsed after cessation of a brief period of urine monitoring. That experience led us to our current practice of recommending at least one year's duration of monitoring under the contingency contract.

Termination of Treatment

Our experience supports the view that substance abuse is a chronic, lifelong condition characterized by remission and relapse. It is not "cured." Therefore, the objectives of treatment are to reduce the risk of future relapses by developing a system of barriers to deter relapse, by decreasing triggering stimuli (which may lie in the external environment or in internal feelings), by successfully learning to master or avoid tasks while abstinent that the patient formerly mastered or avoided through intoxication, and by experiencing (and thus coming to value) the rewards of a drug-free life. When these objectives are met, treatment may be terminated, and most of these objectives usually are met during therapy. But the main relapse-deterring barrier during treatment is the contingency contract. Urinary detection and expected loss of license do suppress relapses, and some patients relapse quickly without that deterrent. So what can substitute for the deterring effect of urine monitoring after termination of treatment?

In couples therapy we encourage patients to educate their spouses about the risk of relapse and early signs of relapse, so that the *spouse* is prepared to detect and abort relapse. Before the termination of treatment, we recommend that patients deposit with spouses a letter addressed to the licensing board, requesting an investigation into a possible relapse. And we recommend that patients write out directions for spouses to follow if relapse is suspected: Demand a urine sample, watch its production, get it analyzed, require a competent reevaluation for possible drug problems, and (as one of our patients put it) "if I refuse to do any of these things, send the letter to the board to save my life."

Despite such efforts to build long-lasting deterrents, however, some patients do relapse when urinalyses cease. For these patients, troubled by a chronic relapsing illness, we may provide a continuing service with intermittent checkup visits and prolonged urine monitoring under contingency contracts.

Psychotherapy for Substance Abuse?

Our treatment philosophy emphasizes the importance of viewing substance abuse in the total context of patients' lives. Patients come into treatment with combinations of psychological, interpersonal, physical, economic, professional, and legal problems in addition to substance abuse, and all are addressed in treatment. Nine of the 26 patients discussed here met DSM-III criteria for diagnoses of other psychiatric illnesses in addition to substance abuse. Although psychiatric illness may not cause substance abuse, the two often interact in ways that make the treatment of dual-diagnosis patients more complex. Because of this interaction, simultaneous treatment of substance abuse and other psychological problems seems more effective than treating either alone. Relieving psychological distortions and increasing insight may enable the individual to cope more effectively with the variety of life changes necessary to overcome substance abuse. Ending substance abuse enables the patient to focus energy and attention on developing new coping strategies to deal with emotional stresses.

Problems of Outcome Research

Treatment outcome for the 26 patients described here was rated by the three clinicians on the basis of their knowledge of the clients' functioning at the end of treatment in three areas: vocation, personal relationships, and abstinence. A 5-point rating scale (4 = much better, 3 = somewhat better, 2 = unchanged, 1 = somewhat worse, 0 = much worse) was used. Nine patients were rated much better, 8 somewhat better, 3 unchanged, 2 somewhat worse, 1 much worse, and 4 unknown. Although we find these results encouraging, we acknowledge serious problems in interpreting them. In addition to the problems inherent in the use of a clinicians' post hoc rating scale, the patients had varied duration, frequency, and patterns of drug abuse; they were in different treatment situations (e.g., regulatory board involvement, contingency contracts); they were in treatment for periods ranging from 1 to 40 months; some were only evaluated and were referred elsewhere for treatment, and others chose not to complete the recommended course of treatment; and there was no way retrospectively to compare among patients the severity of other life problems (e.g., presence of psychiatric diagnosis, presence and extent of social support network). As mentioned earlier, many patients enter treatment in crisis, so spontaneous resolution of the crisis (regression toward the mean) also may have been a factor in some patients' obvious improvement.

Outcome research may be even more difficult in cocaine treatment programs than in other clinical settings. It is often difficult to hold cocaine abusers in treatment because the powerful reinforcing properties of cocaine generate very high levels of ambivalence about giving up the drug and because of the patients' cocaine-induced paranoia. Many patients enter treatment in crisis and tend to drop out after the crisis passes. We have found that presenting these patients with consent forms and explanations of random assignment to different treatments overwhelms them, so that they refuse to participate in the research or drop out of treatment. The kind of controlled research designs we would like to employ to compare types of treatment may not be possible with this population. An alternative we have considered is to use one form of treatment exclusively for a year, then change to another form of treatment the second year, and then compare outcomes for patients treated in the two years. There are a number of design problems with such a procedure, but pragmatically it might be the only approach that would work with this population.

Although we acknowledge the difficulty of doing outcome research in cocaine treatment programs, we also want to emphasize the importance of such work. Cocaine is a dangerously toxic and powerfully addictive drug. The costs in terms of both money and human suffering are enormous, yet we really don't know which treatment approach works best with which patients.

Confidentiality and Contingency Contracting among Health Care Professionals

Confidentiality is a cornerstone of the relationship between the drug-abusing patient and the clinician. Without it many fewer abusers would seek treatment, and treatment of those who did apply would be seriously hampered. Codes of ethics from the Hippocratic oath to the professional codes of the 20th century stress that treaters must not disclose what the patient has said in confidence. The protection of patients diagnosed or treated for alcohol or drug abuse is strengthened by stringent federal regulations limiting the disclosure of identity or information about anyone diagnosed or treated for alcohol or drug abuse within a treatment facility that receives aid in any form from the federal government. These regulations specify that information regarding the identity or treatment of a patient can be released only with patient consent or court order finding "good cause" after a hearing.

There are, however, several situations in which the usual right to privacy and confidentiality is abridged. Therapists' duty to warn or safeguard persons threatened with severe bodily harm or death by a patient was established in the case of *Tarasoff* v. *Regents of the University of California*. The duty to warn or protect may well be extended to unidentified persons at risk to severe harm by an impaired patient. The latter circumstance may apply in the case of an impaired health care professional, who carries responsibility for the treatment of patients. In recent years the licensing statutes of many states have defined substance abuse as unprofessional conduct. There may also arise a duty under such statutes to report a coprofessional where the therapist has knowledge of the substance abuse. A strict view of the duty to warn would suggest that most health care professionals who seek treatment for substance abuse should be reported to their respective licensing boards. This would discourage professionals from seeking treatment until forced to do so by external circumstances. The clinician on the one hand wants to protect and treat the patient, and on the other hand wants to protect the public and avoid liability if the treated health care professional is impaired by continued substance abuse.

Contingency contracts offer a possible solution to the clinician's dilemma in such cases. If the patient abstains from drug use, there is no reason to assume that the patient's patients are at risk, and hence no reason to notify the board. If the patient resumes drug use, then the contract stipulates that the board will be notified, and the consent for release of information, which is a part of the contract, gives the clinician the patient's permission to disclose information concerning the drug use.

Conclusions

Several observations stand out in this review of health care professionals who have abused cocaine and were evaluated or treated in our clinics. The first concerns the considerable involvement of these patients with other drugs. Despite extensive histories of cocaine abuse, the majority of these patients were not primary abusers of cocaine at the time that they sought treatment. Moreover, several of the relapses that occurred during or following treatment were to drugs other than cocaine. This pattern is different from the relatively pure cocaine abuse, or combination of cocaine and alcohol abuse, that characterizes most of the other patients whom we treat for cocaine abuse. Presumably, this difference relates to the extensive availability of other drugs to health care professionals.

We were surprised at the relatively low proportion of these patients who obtained their cocaine through diversion of pharmaceutical supplies. This certainly differs from the opioid abuse pattern in health care professionals, who usually obtain opioid drugs for abuse through diversion. Moreover, the proportion of patients administering cocaine by the intravenous route was unusually high in this population, a finding probably explained by the professional familiarity of these patients with IV administration techniques.

In reviewing these cases we find that our management of them was quite similar to our management of health care professionals who abused other drugs; in fact, many of these patients actually were primary abusers of other drugs (such as opioids). A major influence on our prescription of treatment to substance abusers involves the extent of potential loss from continued abuse; with these patients we use contingency contracts because the potential loss of license is so important to them and so clearly related to whether or not they abstain. But in the cases of inner-city or street people addicted to opiates (for example), we treat with methadone because the patients do not perceive themselves to be at risk for a major loss if they continue using drugs. Thus the social situation of the patients, rather than the pharmacology of the drug, is a major determinant of our treatment planning.

Although it appears to us that most patients benefited during their treatment with us, the data again force us to the conclusion that substance abuse is a chronic condition characterized by remission and relapse. With growing experience, we increasingly find ourselves recommending prolonged outpatient care with urine monitoring and some attached contingency to assist patients in sustaining prolonged abstinence. Even though relapses are not infrequent, we find (Crowley, 1986) that long-term monitoring dramatically reduces drug use by abbreviating relapses.

We also note in this review that not many of these patients used self-help groups. We have treated some patients who become very attached to such groups, with apparent benefit. The efficacy of this addition to treatment certainly deserves further research, but at present it seems warranted to recommend self-help groups more strongly for cocaine-abusing health care professionals.

Substance abuse among health care professionals is a disaster for each of these patients and for their respective professions. This may be the first report on an effort to treat a group of cocaine-abusing health care professionals. All of us working in this field, and our patients, will benefit from more clinical descriptions of these patients, of treatment programs, and of treatment outcome.

REFERENCES

American Psychiatric Association (1980). *Diagnostic and statistical manual of mental disorders* (3rd ed.). Washington, DC: Author.

Anker, A. A., & Crowley, T. J. (1982). Use of contingency contracts in specialty clinics for cocaine abuse. In *Problems of drug dependence, 1981,* NIDA Research Monograph No. 41 (pp. 452–459). Washington, DC: U.S. Government Printing Office.

Bohman, M., Sigvardsson, S., & Cloninger, R. (1981). Maternal inheritance of alcohol abuse. *Archives of General Psychiatry, 38,* 965–969.

Cadoret, R. J., Troughton, E., O'Gorman, T. W., & Heywood, E. An adoption study of genetic and environmental factors in drug abuse. *Archives of General Psychiatry, 43,* 1131–1136.

Cloninger, C. R., Bohman, M., & Sigvardsson, S. (1981). Inheritance of alcohol abuse. *Archives of General Psychiatry, 38,* 861–868.

Cohen, S. (1984). Cocaine: Acute medical and psychiatric complications. *Psychiatric Annals, 14,* 747–749.

Crowley, T. J. (1984). Contingency contracting treatment of drug-abusing physicians, nurses, and dentists In *Behavioral intervention techniques in drug abuse treatment,* NIDA Research Monograph No. 46 (pp. 68–83). Washington, DC: U.S. Government Printing Office.

Crowley, T. J. (1987). Clinical issues in cocaine abuse. In S. Fisher, A. Raskin, & E. H. Uhlenhuth (Eds.), *Cocaine: Biobehavioral aspects* (pp. 193–211). New York: Oxford University Press.

Crowley, T. J. (1986). Doctors' drug abuse reduced during contingency contracting treatment. *Alcohol and Drug Research, 6,* 299–307.

Crowley, T. J., & Rhine, M. W. (1985). The substance use disorders. In R. C. Simons & H. Pardes (Eds.), *Understanding human behavior in health and illness* (3rd ed.) (pp. 564–569). Baltimore: Williams and Wilkins.

DAWN. (1985). *National Institute on Drug Abuse Statistical Series Annual Data 1984 from the Drug Abuse Warning Network,* Series I, No. 4 (U.S. Department of Health and Human Services Publication ADM 85-1407). Washington, DC: U.S. Government Printing Office.

Helfrich, A. A., Crowley, T. J., Atkinson, C. A., & Post, R. D. (1983). A clinical profile of 136 cocaine abusers. In *Problems of drug dependence, 1982,* NIDA Research Monograph No. 43 (pp. 343–350). Washington, DC: U.S. Government Printing Office.

Noyes, A. P., & Kolb, L. C. (1958). Drug addiction. In W. B. Saunders (Ed.), *Modern clinical psychiatry* (pp. 564–574). Philadelphia: W. B. Saunders.

Rawson, R. A., Obert, J. L., McCann, M. J., & Mann, A. J. (1986). Cocaine treatment outcome: Cocaine use following inpatient, outpatient, or no treatment. In L. S. Harris (Ed.), *Problems of drug dependence, 1985,* NIDA Research Monograph No. 67 (pp. 271–277). Washington, DC: U.S. Government Printing Office.

Senay, E. C. (1983). *Substance abuse disorders in clinical practice.* Boston: Wright.

Siegel, R. K. (1984). Cocaine smoking disorders: Diagnosis and treatment. *Psychiatric Annals, 14,* 728–732.

Washton, A. M., & Gold, M. S. (1984). Chronic cocaine abuse: Evidence for adverse effects on health and functioning. *Psychiatric Annals, 14,* 733; 737–739; 743.

Washton, A. M., Gold, M. S., & Pottash, A. C. (1986). Treatment outcome in cocaine abusers. In L. S. Harris (Ed.), *Problems of drug dependence, 1985,* NIDA Research Monograph No. 67 (pp. 381–384). Washington, DC: U.S. Government Printing Office.

Washton, A. M., & Tatarsky, A. (1984). Adverse effects of cocaine abuse. In *Problems of drug dependence, 1983,* NIDA Research Monograph No. 49 (pp. 247–254). Washington, DC: U.S. Government Printing Office.

Wood, D. M., Lal, H., & Emmett-Oglesby, M. (1984). Acquisition and recovery of tolerance to the discriminative stimulus properties of cocaine. *Neuropharmacology, 23,* 1419–1423.

Woody, G. E., Luborsky, L., McLellan, A. T., O'Brien, C. P., Beck, A. T., Blaine, J., Herman, I., & Hole, A. (1983). Psychotherapy for opiate addicts: Does it help? *Archives of General Psychiatry, 40,* 639–645.

PART THREE

SPECIAL TOPICS

13

Cocaine Smoking: Nature and Extent of Coca Paste and Cocaine Free-Base Abuse

RONALD K. SIEGEL

On the evening of October 30, 1938, thousands of Americans became panic-stricken when they heard a radio broadcast that purported to describe an invasion of Martians that threatened human civilization (Cantril, Gaudet, & Hertzog, 1940). The broadcast, narrated by Orson Welles, was a fictional play based on *War of the Worlds* by H. G. Wells. The original novel was written in 1898, at a time when cocaine was a commonplace item and science fiction novels were the newest fashion in entertainment. Nearly half a century later, on January 8, 1985, the roles of science fiction and cocaine were reversed when Orson Welles narrated a television broadcast about another invasion that threatened civilization. The new invaders were cocaine and coca paste from South America. If the war was not won, according to producer Jacques Costeau (1985), "the Western world may decline."

Although the nonmedical use of cocaine had been escalating throughout the world since 1970, it was the developing practice of smoking the drug that triggered these voices of alarm. Unlike the traditional oral and intranasal methods of administering cocaine, smoking permitted extremely large concentrations of purified cocaine to be delivered rapidly to the brain (Siegel, 1984b). With a faster onset of action than produced by the more complicated injection routes of administration, cocaine smoking produced intense intoxications that often resulted in tenacious dependencies.

Definitions

Cocaine smoking is defined as the smoking of any part or product of the coca plant. These preparations include seeds, leaves, coca paste, cocaine hydrochloride or other salts, and cocaine free base. Coca paste is known by a variety of terms, including *base*, *pasta*, *pitillo*, and *basuco*. The paste is a

Ronald K. Siegel. Department of Psychiatry and Biobehavioral Sciences, School of Medicine, University of California at Los Angeles, Los Angeles, California.

crude extract of the coca leaf that is prepared by dissolving dried coca leaves in water and treating the solution with kerosene or gasoline, alkaline bases, potassium permanganate, and sulfuric acid. The resulting white or brown paste contains 40%–91% cocaine sulfate, along with companion coca alkaloids, varying quantities of the other chemicals, adulterants, and diluents (Morales-Vaca, 1984). Cocaine hydrochloride, also known as street cocaine or pharmaceutical cocaine, is the acid salt of cocaine formed with hydrochloric acid. Cocaine free base, usually prepared by simple extraction from cocaine hydrochcloride, is also known as cocaine alkaloid, cocaine base, base, or free base. While the terms associated with the use of cocaine free base were relatively unknown before 1970, they have now appeared in at least one modern dictionary (Spears, 1981). There are over 120 street expressions for cocaine free base, including crack, rock, white tornado, white cloud, and super white.

History

The smoking of coca and cocaine products is derived from a 5,000-year-old Andean practice of burning and smoking various parts of the coca plant for religious and medicinal purposes (Siegel, 1982). During the patent medicine era of the late 19th century, coca cigars and cigarettes were used in Europe and the United States for the treatment of asthma, hay fever, and opium addiction, and as a substitute for tobacco (Stewart, 1885).

In the 1970s, as the nonmedical intranasal use of cocaine hydrochloride increased dramatically, users began to experiment with smoking cocaine hydrochloride by sprinkling it on marijuana or tobacco cigarettes (Gottlieb, 1976). Since less than 1% of the cocaine survives this process, however, it was not surprising that users reported little if any intoxication. Concomitantly, users in South America began to experiment with smoking *base* (coca paste) mixed with marijuana or tobacco. Since coca paste is more concentrated than cocaine hydrochloride, and contains small amounts of the volatile cocaine alkaloid, these paste smokers were able to achieve intoxications similar to those reported with intravenous (IV) administration.

The first hospital admissions for *base* or coca paste smokers were reported in Peru in 1972, and admissions steadily increased throughout South America as a consequence of increased coca paste and cocaine production (Jeri, 1984). Indeed, the practice of smoking coca paste appears to have been transported to other countries through the illicit cocaine trafficking corridors.

In the early 1970s, traffickers in the United States learned of smoking *base*, but they confused the preparation with cocaine base or cocaine free base, which is the principal cocaine alkaloid "freed" of its hydrochloride or sulfate salt (Siegel, 1982). Medically, cocaine free base has been used in ointments, but this preparation is chemically different from all other forms of cocaine previously used nonmedically. In effect, North American users had accidentally discovered a new preparation for smoking. Unlike cocaine hydrochloride, cocaine free base cannot be easily dissolved in blood or mucous membranes; however, it is readily volatilized and can be effectively smoked. As cocaine free-base smoking spread during the next decade, it was clear that free base was a more pure and concentrated form of cocaine than even coca paste.

The phenomenon of smoking cocaine free base first appeared in California in 1974. The first hospital admission for a problem related to smoking cocaine free base was in 1975, the same year in which extraction kits and smoking accessories became commercially available. In 1978 the distribution of paraphernalia spread throughout the United States, and by 1979 cocaine free-base smoking was reported in 15 states, the Bahamas, and Puerto Rico. By 1980 use was reported throughout the United States (Siegel, 1982). Between 1980 and 1985, cocaine free-base smoking was reported in Canada, the United Kingdom, the Netherlands Antilles, Australia, and Fiji, and in some European countries such as the Netherlands (Ensing, 1985; World Health Organizations, 1984).

Since 1980 there has been an increase in the number of illicit laboratories in the United States that process coca paste ("Cocaine Labs," 1984). This has generated domestic supplies of coca paste, some of which are not refined but are smoked by individuals associated with the clandestine laboratories and trafficking (Siegel, 1985a). Concomitantly, the widespread attention given by the international press to cocaine free-base problems in the United States has familiarized South Americans with this practice. Thus, in an ironic exchange of drug patterns, coca paste smoking has now appeared in the United States (Siegel, 1985a), whereas cocaine free-base smoking has been reported in some South American countries, including Colombia and Ecuador (Ensing, 1985).

The popularity of free-base smoking in the United States has increased substantially with the recent emergence of "crack" on the illicit drug scene (Washton & Gold, 1986). Crack is not a new drug, but is does represent a new strategy in the sale and marketing of street cocaine. Crack is ready-made free-base cocaine sold in the form of tiny pellets or "rocks" which can be smoked with no further chemical processing. The significance of this shift in cocaine vending patterns stems from the fact that it makes the practice of smoking cocaine free base more readily accessible to potential users and thus increases the likelihood of exposure to cocaine smoking and its associated dangers (Washton, Gold, & Pottash, 1986).

Epidemiology

The World Health Organization (WHO) reviewed the epidemiology of cocaine smoking in 1984 and reported that the practice had reached epidemic levels in major geographical regions of North and South America (WHO, 1984). Coca paste smoking has appeared in Argentina, Bolivia, Brazil, Chile, Colombia, Ecuador, Mexico, Peru, Venezuela, and the United States. The practice is expected to appear in several other countries in which coca paste has been confiscated, including the Bahamas, Belize, Costa Rica, Panama, and Paraguay (Bureau of International Narcotics Matters, 1985). Cocaine free-base smoking has also spread from its initial appearance in the United States to Canada, the United Kingdom, Australia, Fiji, and some European countries. In all countries, use has first appeared in major urban centers and then spread to rural areas.

Coca Paste in South America

In South America, several epidemiological studies have identified coca paste smokers as primarily male, 12–45 years of age, although users as young as 8 and as old as 75 have been observed and treated in both Colombia and Bolivia (Jeri, 1984; Noya, 1984). Furthermore, the majority of coca paste smokers seeking treatment are either unemployed or from lower and middle socioeconomic groups. The incidence of hospitalization among users is high, and a significant percentage of psychiatric beds in Columbia, Peru, Bolivia, and Ecuador are used for coca paste smokers. For example, since 1984 the Antioquia Mental Hospital in Colombia has been seeing approximately 500 coca paste smokers per month (Velasquez de Pabon, 1984). Indeed, data available in 1984 indicate that approximately 30% of psychiatric patients in Peru and as many as 90% of patients in Colombia are coca paste smokers (Climent, 1984; Climent & de Aragon, 1982; Hernandez, 1984; Jeri, 1984; Noya, 1984; Velasquez de Pabon, 1984).

The number of coca paste smokers in South America has increased dramatically since the first surveys were conducted in 1979 (Jeri, 1984). In Peru, the number of coca paste smokers was estimated to be 156,000 in 1979; 1984 figures may be 90% higher (F. P. Jeri, personal communication, September 13, 1984). Taken together, approximately 20% of the Peruvian population uses coca or cocaine preparations. Several surveys in Colombia indicate that approximately 5% of university students use coca paste (Climent, 1984), the same percentage found among the general population of at least one major city. Thus, Colombia, a country that is a major location for coca paste processing laboratories and that has a population of 30 million, may have as many as 1.5 million coca paste users.

Recent international efforts have been effective in forcing the coca paste laboratories to move from Colombia, but they have relocated to Bolivia, Brazil, and the United States (Bureau of International Narcotics Matters, 1985). Bolivia, with six coca-producing areas, has been a major producer of coca (Canelas Orellana & Canelas Zannier, 1983) and now has substantial coca paste refining operations. Although careful surveys are lacking in this country, investigators have reported 20,000 coca paste smokers in one region and widespread use nationwide (Aramayo, Machicado, Velarde, & Cespedes, 1984). Approximately 3% of the Bolivian population (180,000 people) were reported to be coca paste smokers in 1982 (Morales-Vaca, 1984), with more users appearing by 1984 (Sainz, 1984). Users studied in treatment centers have included young children, young middle-class students and workers, and adult professionals (Aramayo & Sanchez, 1980; Noya, 1984).

Although other South American countries such as Brazil and Ecuador have acknowledged a growing incidence of coca paste laboratories and smoking (Bureau of International Narcotics Matters, 1985; Donoso, 1980), relatively little information is available on the nature and extent of use. Nonetheless, the increased incidence of use among 7- to 10-year-old children in those countries involved in coca paste trafficking suggests the fulfillment of a chilling prophecy made in 1964. At that time, actor Boris Karloff, the master of horror films, narrated a documentary in which a group of cocaine-addicted children in Ecuador were displayed as the promise of things to come (Starks, 1982).

Coca Paste Smoking in the United States

The spread of coca paste smoking throughout South America is important in understanding present and future trends in the United States. Since 1983 coca paste has been offered at cut-rate prices to operators in the United States for conversion to cocaine hydrochloride. The number of coca paste processing laboratories seized in the United States has risen from 6 in 1982 to 15 through June 1984, and seizures as large as 1.25 metric tons of coca paste have been reported (Select Committee on Narcotics Abuse and Control, 1985). This has generated domestic supplies of coca paste available for both use and refinement to cocaine hydrochloride.

Coca paste smoking has been reported in Florida, Arizona, and California, and a total of 45 users from these states have been studied (Siegel, 1985a). The users, 41 males and 4 females, ranged in age from 22 to 43; 27 were citizens of the United States, and the rest were aliens from South American countries. Eight users reported initial use of coca paste in South America; the others were introduced to it in the United States.

Users smoked tobacco cigarettes mixed with an estimated 250 mg of coca paste or marijuana cigarettes mixed with an estimated 100 mg of coca paste. Most users described episodes of coca paste smoking alternating with use of intranasal cocaine hydrochloride. A few users described past or current histories of smoking cocaine free base but use coca paste when cocaine free base or its associated peraphernalia were unavailable. Total daily dosages rarely exceeded 1 gram of paste for these users. Conversely, coca paste smokers in South America consume 10–25 gm daily (range, 5–90 gm) in cigarettes containing 100–500 mg.

Coca paste smokers report physical and psychological effects similar to those of cocaine free base (to be discussed). Frequently, users mentioned several characteristics of coca paste smoking that were considered more desirable than those of cocaine free base. These included low cost, convenience of use without refinement or paraphernalia, more intense intoxications, and minimal exposure to detection when smoking in public. It has been precisely these considerations that have prompted speculation (Cohen, 1985) that coca paste smoking and resultant problems could escalate throughout the United States. Indeed, despite the lower dosages consumed by users in the United States, Siegel (1985a) found that most reported adverse reactions, including respiratory problems, and that over 30% were diagnosed as having a "Cocaine Smoking Disorder" (Siegel, 1984b).

Cocaine Free-Base Use

The major areas reporting widespread patterns of cocaine free-base smoking are the Bahamas (Clarke, 1984) and the United States (Siegel, 1982). The Bahamas are located in the main cocaine trafficking corridor between South and North America, thus accounting for the widespread availability of low-cost cocaine in that country. The intranasal use of cocaine hydrochloride became popular in the mid-1970s but was replaced by the smoking of cocaine free base in 1979. By 1984, 98% of all patients seeking treatment for cocaine problems reported smoking cocaine free base as their method of use (Clarke, 1984). In 1982 patients were primarily males, 18–30 years of age, from low socioeconomic groups. In recent years, however, it has become increasingly common for both females and children as young as 9 years of age to be treated for problems associated with smoking cocaine free base.

In parts of the Bahamas and the United States, locations known as *base houses* have been found by law enforcement authorities. These houses, similar to the opium dens of the 19th century, provide users with cocaine free base, pipes, and protected areas for smoking, all for relatively lower costs than street prices. In 1984 a copy of "House Rules" was found inside one of a dozen "base houses" raided in Miami:

> Each customer has only 15 minutes to a dime hit!!! No credit—as of now . . .
> The pipe you choose is the pipe you use . . . No hounding other customers . . .

> Customers not smoking will leave . . . Smoke only in the area assigned to
> you . . . Last but not least, we all appreciate your smoking, hope that you have
> enjoyed, please return. (Stein, 1984)

On the islands of Grand Bahama, Andros, and New Providence, clandestine locations known as *base camps* provide users with abundant supplies of cocaine free base, often at no cost (Clarke, 1984).

Although there have been no precise figures on the extent of cocaine free-base smoking in the Bahamas or the United States, studies of users in the United States have suggested that perhaps 10% of cocaine users are cocaine free-base smokers (Siegel, 1984a). Since such smokers are conspicuous among cocaine users seeking clinical attention or treatment, it is not surprising that there have been several recent studies describing the specific problems of these patients. The unique patterns and problems related to the diagnosis and treatment of cocaine free-base smoking disorders are discussed in the following sections. A full discussion of the technical details and user reactions have been described elsewhere (see Anvil, 1979; Davidson, 1981; Lee, 1981; Perez-Reyes, Di Guiseppi, Ondrusek, Jeffcoat, & Cook, 1982; Raye, 1980; Siegel, 1982).

Problems of Preparing and Smoking Cocaine Free Base

Preparations

When street extraction procedures are used to prepare cocaine free base from cocaine hydrochloride, users recover 37–96% of the material, and this is assumed to be pure cocaine free base. However, many of the adulterants and diluents that are added to both coca paste and cocaine hydrochloride are not removed by these procedures and can be volatilized and inhaled in the smoking process (Siegel, 1982). These adulterants and diluents can have problematic effects when large quantities of cocaine free base are consumed.

Many preparations contain manganese carbonate (Ensing, 1985), which can cause intoxication resembling parkinsonism marked by languor, sleepiness, weakness, emotional disturbances, spastic gait, and paralysis. Lidocaine, a popular contaminant that mimics cocaine's physical appearance and benumbing taste, may also cause cocainelike seizures in the limbic system. Stimulants are often added to enhance potency; at least one of these, ephedrine, has been associated with acute sympathomimetic poisoning (Siegel, 1979). In addition, trace amounts of 2,4-D, an herbicide used in coca eradication programs, have been found in coca paste and, if present in cocaine free-base preparations, could cause eye irritations and gastrointestinal disturbances (Elsohly et al., 1984).

Although cocaine free base is commonly used for smoking, these preparations have also been used with other routes of administration. When cocaine free base is used intranasally, users do not experience a rapid reinforcing euphoria because of the relatively slow absorption of the alkaloid into the nasal mucosa (Siegel, 1985a). Nonetheless, these users, currently limited to a small number in California, report effects similar to those associated with intranasal cocaine hydrochloride. The intravenous injection of cocaine free base has been associated with a case of pulmonary edema, cardiogenic shock with severe hypotension, and signs of peripheral hypoperfusion and agitation (Purdie, 1982).

Hazards in Smoking

Cocaine free base is almost always smoked in a glass water pipe. Users place small amounts (50–120 mg) of cocaine free base on the metal screens of the pipe and apply heat from a torch (butane, propane, or alcohol), a lighter, matches, or a similar source. A low pyrolysis temperatures (approximately 200°C) fully 84% of the resultant product is intact cocaine, but only 1–5% gets through the pipe onto the mainstream of the smoke itself (although some street methods can increase the yield to 67% or higher). When cocaine free base is smoked in tobacco or marijuana cigarettes, only 6% of the pyrolysis product is intact cocaine. Consequently, users prepare and smoke considerable quantities of starting material in order to achieve desired psychoactive effects. Although the pyrolysis products have not been fully investigated, the methyl 4-(3-pyridyl) butyrate product has been found to have hypolipidemic activity, inhibiting the noradrenaline-induced free fatty acid mobilization in animals (Novak & Salemink, 1984).

Deep inhalation techniques result in rapid rises in plasma cocaine levels within minutes, and levels of 800–2,000 ng/ml have been reported. Inhalations may be repeated as often as every 5 minutes during smoking episodes or binges ranging from 30 minutes to 96 hours. Individual consumption may range from 1 gm to 30 gm per 24-hour period, although some users have reported smoking 150 gm in 72 hours. Weekly consumption for individuals in the United States who are seeking treatment has averaged 9 gm in one study and 28 gm in another. Smoking episodes may continue until supplies of cocaine are depleted or users become exhausted and fall asleep.

This method of smoking cocaine free base is extremely hazardous and carries substantial risks for both accidents and toxic reactions in all phases of use. These hazards coexist with the physical, psychiatric, and psychosocial sequelae to be discussed. Fires and explosions have been caused when the torches used in smoking ignite the flammable volatile solvents used in preparation of cocaine free base. Accidental chemical burns have occurred as a result of contact with caustic materials used in the extraction procedures, such as sodium hydroxide. The tremors, lassitude, and fatigue that follow intoxication have resulted in numerous accidental falls, bruises, lacerations from broken glassware, and chemical spills and fires. Deep inhalation of superheated smoke, sometimes coupled with rebreathing exhaled smoked from balloons, has resulted in pulmonary dysfunction, hypoxia, and other difficulties.

Indeed, the acute risks to the pulmonary system are significant. When users assist each other in forcefully blowing cocaine free-base smoke into the mouth, pneumoediastinum and pneumothorax have resulted (Shesser, Davis, & Edelstein, 1981). These conditons, detectable by X-ray films, are marked by severe chest pain, probably caused by air leaking from a ruptured alveolus or along fascial planes of the neck to the mediastinum and pericardial space (Adrouny & Magnusson, 1985). Other cocaine free-base smokers have manifested a reduction in single-breath carbon monoxide diffusing capacity, which may be a direct effect of cocaine's vasoconstrictor properties on the pulmonary vasculature (Weiss, Boldenheim, Mirin, Hales, & Mendelson, 1981).

Some pulmonary abnormalities may persist after cessation of cocaine free-base smoking. In a study of 19 cocaine free-base smokers admitted to a chemical dependency program (Itkonen, Schnoll, & Glassroth, 1984), 63% had respiratory symptoms and 58% noted dyspnea. A total of 10 patients manifested abnormal carbon monoxide diffusing capacity.

Clinical Features of Cocaine Smoking

The Intoxication

The descriptions of cocaine free-base intoxication are similar to those given for intravenous injection of cocaine hydrochloride. Immediately following inhalation there is an intense rush of euphoria. Users describe this sensation with metaphors of energy, power, and sexual orgasm. Within a few seconds, this rush is replaced by a relatively extended period of excitation and arousal, which may persist for several minutes. The rush itself appears to be little more than the subjective interpretation of a rapid change in arousal and mood state. Once that new state is reached, the euphoria is replaced by a less pleasurable excitability. After approximately 5–20 minutes, this state of arousal is rapidly replaced by a restless irritability often accompanied by dysphoria. It is this dysphoric state that appears to prompt the user to continue smoking in an effort to recapture the initial rush. Since tolerance develops rapidly to the rewarding sensations, concomitant with sensitization to irritability and dysphoria, the intoxication can capture the user in a cycle of repeating use.

Acute and Chronic Physical Effects

Cocaine free-base smokers report a highly consistent list of physical effects (Siegel, 1982). Many of these effects are simply dose-related exaggerations of symptoms common to intranasal or intravenous users; others are specifically related to the smoking method and will be discussed next.

The unique physical effects include coughing with black or bloody expectorate, dysarthria, slurred speech, sore throat, wispy voice, thirst, muscle pains in the lower back and neck, dry skin and/or lips, bleeding gums, chest pains, respiratory difficulties, dyspnea on exertion, dizziness, episodic unconsciousness, urination difficulty, visual disturbances, edema, and other skin disturbances. Complications arising from smoking cocaine free base may include syncope, myoclonic jerking and seizures, bronchitis, and pneumonia. Deaths resulting from continuous seizures, cardiac arrhythmias, respiratory paralysis, or suicide have occurred.

The local anesthetic effects of cocaine smoke in the mouth and pharyngeal structures contribute to the dry lips, wispy voice, and thirst. Since the face and head may remain in proximity to the puffs of exhaled cocaine smoke, the smoke can also irritate the eyes, cause a burning sensation, and contribute to visual disturbances such as blurred vision and mydriasis. The black sputum is related to residue from torches, tars from matches, or contaminated smoke. The bloody expectorate seen with several users is related to chronic coughing or ingestion of caustic chemicals; the sore throats reflect inhalation of superheated smoke and irritation from smoke particles. Poisoning from procaine and other local anesthetic contaminants may cause dizziness, irregular breathing, itching, erythema, excoriation, edema, and vesiculation. Bronchitis and pneumonia have been associated with ammonia contaminants.

Users often engage in binges of cocaine smoking while bending over their water pipes, and the resulting postural difficulties can contribute to the complaints of back and neck pains. After several hours of smoking in a sitting position, a sudden change to an upright posture has resulted in orthostatic hypotension coupled with dizziness and fainting.

Physical examinations may confirm the presence of many unique clinical features of cocaine smoking disorders. For example, chest X-rays and pulmonary function studies may determine that chest pains and breathing difficulties are the result of pulmonary dysfunction. Electrocardiograms are useful in diagnosing cardiac complaints. Laboratory analysis of bronchial swabs, sputum, or even samples of cocaine may be useful in detecting poisoning from contaminants. When route of administration is uncertain, radioimmunoassay of head hair may reveal high levels of cocaine in those who smoke the drug (Baumgartner, Black, Jones, & Blahd, 1982; W. A.

Baumgartner, personal communication, September 1, 1985). Finally, plasma cocaine and benzoylecgonine levels may separate smokers from intranasal users and help determine the course of detoxification.

Psychological Effects

The nature of psychological effects reported by cocaine free-base smokers differs from those associated with other routes of administration only in frequency and intensity. Accordingly, although smokers may appear to exhibit unusual features, they are usually the same psychiatric and psychosocial effects seen with other users, magnified by the intense doses and compulsive patterns of cocaine smoking. Indeed, whereas most patterns of intranasal cocaine use are limited in frequency and duration (Siegel, 1985a), cocaine free-base smokers generally follow compulsive patterns.

These compulsive patterns of use are characterized by high frequency and high intensity levels of relatively long duration, producing some degree of psychological dependency. The dependence is such that the individual user does not discontinue use without experiencing physiological discomfort or psychological disruption. The compulsive cocaine smoker usually exhibits a preoccupation with cocaine-seeking and cocaine-using behavior to the relative exclusion of other behaviors. The motivation to continue compulsive levels of use is primarily related to a need to elicit the euphoria and stimulation of cocaine in the wake of increasing tolerance and incipient withdrawal-like effects. Cocaine smokers also manifest a potentially toxic variation of compulsive use that has been called *binge* use. This pattern refers to continuous periods of repeated dosing during which users consume substantial amounts of cocaine.

Commonly reported psychological effects include paranoia, hallucinations (visual, tactile, auditory, and olfactory), craving for cocaine, asocial behavior, attention and concentration problems, irritability, hyperexcitability, violent loss of impulse control, lethargy, depression, memory problems, and a decrease in number of dreams. A wide variety of psychosocial symptoms are also reported for chronic users, including, among others, business problems, marital problems, impairment of night driving, sexual indifference, and situational impotency.

Mental status examinations and psychological assessments may confirm these effects as well as the clinical syndromes described for intravenous cocaine users: euphoria, dysphoria, and schizophreniform psychosis. Users appear to progress rapidly through four distinct stages of intoxication depending on level of cocaine dosage and chronicity of administration (Siegel, 1984b):

• *Stage 1: Euphoria.* This is marked by euphoria, affective lability, increased cognitive and motor performance, hyperalertness, anorexia, and insomnia.

• *Stage 2: Dysphoria.* This is characterized by sadness, melancholia, apathy, difficulty in attention and concentration, anorexia, and insomnia.

• *Stage 3: Paranoia.* This stage is marked by suspiciousness, paranoia, hallucinations, and insomnia.

• *Stage 4: Psychosis.* This stage is marked by anhedonia, hallucinations, stereotyped behavior, paranoid ideation, insomnia, loss of impulse control, and lack of disorientation.

An important caveat is that because of the rapid delivery of cocaine free base to the brain of smokers, this progressive psychopathology may occur within a single episode of use that may be only a few hours in duration.

Diagnosis of the Cocaine Smoking Disorder

Siegel (1982, p. 339) has suggested the following diagnostic criteria for a specific Cocaine Organic Mental Disorder termed the Cocaine Smoking Disorder:

A. Recent use of cocaine via smoking cocaine free base or coca paste.

B. At least two of the following psychological symptoms within less than 1 hour of smoking cocaine:
1. Psychomotor agitation
2. Euphoria
3. Grandiosity
4. Loquacity
5. Hypervigilance

C. At least two of the following physiological symptoms within less than 1 hour of smoking cocaine:
1. Tachycardia
2. Pupillary dilation
3. Elevated blood pressure
4. Perspiration or chills
5. Dysarthria
6. Tremors

D. Maladaptive behavioral effects (e.g., fighting, impaired judgment, interference with social or occupational functioning).

E. Not due to any other physical or mental disorder.

Although these essential features are common to other methods of cocaine intoxication, cocaine smokers often manifest an intense array of associated features. Severe intoxication often produces attentional dysfunction, confusion, rambling or incoherent speech, anxiety, and apprehension. There may be a sensitivity to light, blurring of vision, and "snow lights" seen as flashes of light in the visual periphery. Sounds are often intensified, and there may be a ringing in the ears or hearing one's name called. Tactile hallucinations may include a sensation of insects or vermin on the skin (formication). Cognitive features may include ideas of reference, paranoid ideation, a subjective sense of profound thoughts, increased sexual interest, and startle or panic reactions to minimal stimuli. Sometimes there is increased curiosity, bizarre behavior (e.g., preoccupation with repetitive tasks), concern with minutiae, intense interest in technical aspects of cocaine smoking, or ritualized behavior.

After the characteristic behavioral and physical effects have subsided, anxiety, tremulousness, irritability, and feelings of fatigue and depression may appear. This period of crashing may occur within minutes following cessation of smoking and is marked by a pronounced craving for continued cocaine smoking. Users do not appear capable of titrating dose or regulating dose regimes and will usually continue smoking until they or their supplies of the drug are exhausted.

Withdrawal

Although physical dependence on cocaine has not been firmly established, numerous studies have reported a number of withdrawal symptoms following abrupt cessation from chronic high doses of coca paste or cocaine free base smoking (Siegel, 1982; Tennant, Tarver, Johnson, & Cohen, 1984; Velasquez de Pabon, 1984). The essential clinical signs are depressed mood, fatigue, and prolonged sleep. Associated features include hyperphagia, chills, tremors, muscle pains, and involuntary motor movements. Withdrawal is usually seen within 1 or 2 days following cessation of heavy dose regimes, and symptoms may persist for 4 days or longer. During this period, craving is severe and "base dreams" involving themes of cocaine smoking are commonly reported. Since both tolerance and withdrawal-like effects have been reported, the possibility of physical dependence to cocaine smoking cannot be ruled out.

Treatment Considerations

Many cocaine smokers have reported distrust of or resistance to conventional treatment approaches. Accordingly, users often initiate their own treatment methods (Siegel, 1982). These treatment methods are classified as self-control strategies, aversion strategies, and contingency contracting (see Siegel, 1985b). They often include stimulus control strategies designed to make patients aware of the specific environmental and internal cues associated with cocaine smoking. For example, patients may attempt to reduce the strength of cues by eliminating smoking from environmental situations such as parties with peers, dealing, and associating with known users. Although self-control strategies are unreliable, if used in a supervised program they may help prepare the patient for more formal detoxification and abstinence.

In South America, the epidemic of coca paste smoking, coupled with severe disorders, has generated much pessimism concerning ultimate treatment and rehabilitation (Jeri, 1984). Traditionally, treatments for coca paste smoking disorders have used conventional psychodynamic approaches, with little effectiveness (Jeri, 1984; Silva, 1984). Clinicians have also experimented with a variety of approaches including pharmacological agents (diazepam, phenothiazines, propanolol, and antidepressants), hospitalization for detoxification, nutritional support, supportive psychotherapy, family and group therapy, work therapy, and exercise therapy (Jeri, 1984; Velasquez de Pabon, 1984). Since most programs lack adequate outpatient follow-up, however, reported results are poor, and the recidivism rate has been estimated to be as high as 83%.

Recently, treatment of coca paste smokers with behavior therapy has resulted in a reported 50% success rate in one Peruvian hospital that conducted a 4-year follow-up on patients (Navarro Cueva, 1984; Navarro Cueva, Arevalo de Navarro, & Villaneuva Merino, 1983). The techniques employed were aversive conditioning, relaxation training, assertive training, systematic desensitization, and positive reinforcement. Similar techniques have been incorporated in treatment approaches designed for cocaine freebase smokers (Siegel, 1982, 1984b, 1985b). These approaches include detoxification, support therapy, self-control strategies, behavior therapy techniques, exercise therapy, and maintenance of abstinence programs through contingency contracting.

Overview

According to Inca mythology, the sun god set a coca leaf on fire so that people would be directed to its power. The Indians adopted the custom of chewing the leaves and gave thanks by burning coca leaves and sacrificing children. Five thousand years later, comedian Richard Pryor was engulfed in a fire that focused world attention on the cause of his accident: smoking cocaine free base. Today cocaine free base has produced tenacious dependencies in hundreds of thousands of abusers, and coca paste, the newest combustible wonder from the sun god, is spreading from South to North America. Cheaper, stronger, and more destructive than even cocaine free base, coca paste can be smoked in cigarettes the Colombians call *basuca* ("bazooka") to connote its explosive nature. Users as young as 7 years old are affected, while billions of illegal dollars threaten economies and governments, and cocaine mafiosi rule as Inca kings of yore. Forced to leave Colombia for the United States, paste-refining laboratories have attracted new bazooka users in Florida, Arizona, and California.

Taken together, coca paste and cocaine free-base smoking could herald the epidemic war announced by Orson Welles in that 1985 broadcast. Reminiscent of reactions to his 1938 broadcast about an invasion from Mars, responses to cocaine smoking problems are often well intentioned yet panicked. Enforcement authorities have targeted the botanical source of the problem and, like their Inca counterparts, have started burning the leaves. In Los Angeles, fortified "rock houses" where individual doses of cocaine free base are sold by and to young children have been attacked by police battering rams (Furillo, 1984). Psychosurgery has been used on young Peruvian patients with severe intractable coca paste dependencies, although the approach is unwarranted (Llosa, 1983; Llosa & Hinojosa, 1982).

Meanwhile, users who refuse to say no or to ask for help often seem to be listening to the 1938 broadcast that Orson Welles closed by stating: "Folks, I hope we ain't alarmed you. This is just a play." Before we join the Incas in sacrificing our children and burying our dead with coca, it is time for treatment and preventative education to recognize the realities of the cocaine smoking disorders and to alert users to the dangers of playing with cocaine fires.

REFERENCES

Adrouny, A., & Magnusson, P. (1985). Pneumopericardium from cocaine inhalation. *New England Journal of Medicine, 313*(1), 48–49.

Anvil, J. M. (1979). *Freebase cocaine: The greatest thing since sex.* Philadelphia: Flash Post Express.

Aramayo, G., Machicado, E., Velarde, E., & Cespedes, J. (1984). *El consumo y los effectos de la cocaina en la sociedad Boliviana.* La Paz: Campaña Educativa sobre Estupefacientes.

Aramayo, G., & Sanchez, M. (1980). Clinical manifestations using cocaine paste. In R. Jeri (Ed.), *Cocaine 1980* (pp. 120–126). Lima: Pacific Press.

Baumgartner, W. A., Black, C. T., Jones, P. F., & Blahd, W. H. (1982). Radioimmunoassay of cocaine in hair: Concise communication. *Journal of Nuclear Medicine, 23*(9), 790–792.

Bureau of International Narcotics Matters (Department of State). (1985, February 1). *International narcotics control strategy report*, Vol. 1.

Canelas Orellana, A., & Canelas Zannier, J. C. (1983). *Bolivia: Coca cocaina.* Cochabamba: Los Amigos del Libro.

Cantril, H., Gaudet, H., & Hertzog, H. (1940). *The invasion from Mars.* Princeton: Princeton University Press.

Clarke, N. (1984). *Cocaine abuse in the Bahamas.* Paper presented at the World Health Organization Advisory Group Meeting on the Adverse Health Consequences of Cocaine and Coca Paste Smoking, Bogotá, September 10–14.

Climent, C. E. (1984). *Clinical aspects of coca-paste smoking ("basuco") in Colombia.* Paper presented at the World Health Organization Advisory Group Meeting on the Adverse Health Consequences of Cocaine and Coca Paste Smoking, Bogotá, September 10–14.

Climent, C. E., & de Aragón, L. V. (1982). Abuso de drogas en cinco colegios de Cali. *Archivo Departamento de Psiquiatría* (División de Salud, Universidad del Valle), March.

Cocaine labs on the rise. (1984). *Drug Enforcement Report, 1*(2), 4.

Cohen, S. (1985). What if cocaine were a dime a fix? *Drug Abuse and Alcoholism Newsletter, 14*(2), 1–3.

Cousteau, J. (1985). *Cousteau/Amazon: Snowstorm in the jungle* [Film]. Atlanta: WTBS.

Davidson, T. (1981). *The natural process: Base-ic instructions and baking soda recipe.* Tustin: Star Publications.

Donoso, H. (1980). Coca use in Ecuador. In R. Jeri (Ed.), *Cocaine 1980* (pp. 188–190). Lima: Pacific Press.

Elsohly, M. A., Arafat, E. S., Jones, A. B., Vincent, P. G., Engelke, B. F., Hilton, J. L., & Gentner, W. A. (1984). Study of the concentration of the herbicide (2,4-dichlorophynoxy)-acetic acid in coca leaves and paste obtained from plants treated with the herbicide. *Bulletin on Narcotics, 36*(2), 65–77.

Ensing, J. G. (1985). Bazooka: Cocaine-base and manganese carbonate. *Journal of Analytical Toxicology, 9,* 45–46.

Furillo, A. (1984, October 20). Cocaine syndicate war blamed for 25 murders. *Los Angeles Times,* pp. 1, 30.

Gottlieb, A. (1976). *The pleasures of cocaine.* Berkeley: And/Or Press.

Hernandez, G. (1984). *The epidemiology of cocaine and bazuco use in Colombia.* Paper presented at the World Health Organization Advisory Group Meeting on the Adverse Health Consequences of Cocaine and Coca Paste Smoking, Bogotá, September 10–14.

Itkonen, J., Schnoll, S., & Glassroth, J. (1984). Pulmonary dysfunction in 'freebase' cocaine users. *Archives of Internal Medicine, 144*(11), 2195–2197.

Jeri, F. R. (1984). Coca-paste smoking in some Latin American countries: A severe and unabated form of addiction. *Bulletin on Narcotics, 36*(2), 15–31.

Lee, D. (1981). *Cocaine handbook: An essential reference.* Berkeley: And/Or Press.

Llosa, T. (1983). *Follow-up study of 28 cocaine paste addicts treated by open cingulotomy.* Paper presented at the 7th World Congress of Psychiatry, Vienna, 1983.

Llosa, T., & Hinojosa, H. (1982). *Cingulectomía en la fármaco-dependencia a la pasta básica de cocaína.* Paper presented to the Peruvian Psychiatric Association, Lima, May 6.

Morales-Vaca, M. (1984). A laboratory approach to the control of cocaine in Bolivia. *Bulletin on Narcotics, 36*(2), 33–43.

Navarro Cueva, R. (1984). Adiccion a la pasta de cocaina: Tratamiento de dos casos. *Revista Latinoamericana de Psicologia, 16*(3), 435–442.

Navarro Cueva, R., Arevalo de Navarro, M. V., & Villanueva Merino, M. (1983). Terapia de la conducta en el comportamiento dependiente a drogas: Tratamiento y seguimiento de 26 casos clínicos. *Revista Peruana de Psiquiatría. Hermilio Valdizan, 1,* 29–38.

Noya, N. D. (1984). *Coca paste effects.* Paper presented to the World Health Organization Advisory Group Meeting on the Adverse Health Consequences of Cocaine and Coca Paste Smoking, Bogotá, September 10–14.

Novak, M., & Salemink, C. A. (1984). A model experiment in the study of cocaine base smoking. Isolation of methyl 4-(3-pryidyl) butyrate from cocaine pyrolysate. *Bulletin on Narcotics, 36*(2), 79–82.

Perez-Reyes, M., Di Guiseppi, S., Ondrusek, G., Jeffcoat, A. R., & Cook, C. E. (1982). Freebase cocaine smoking. *Clinical Pharmacology and Therapeutics, 32*(4), 459–465.

Purdie, F. R. (1982). Therapy for pulmonary edema following IV "freebase" cocaine use. *Annals of Emergency Medicine, 11*(4), 228–229.

Raye, D. (1980). *Pipe dreams: An inside look at free-base cocaine.* Cotati, CA: Family Publishing.

Sainz, H. F. (1984). *La herencia de la coca.* La Paz: Universo.

Select Committee on Narcotics Abuse and Control. (1985). *Annual report for the year 1984 of the Select Committee on Narcotics Abuse and Control.* House of Representatives Report 98-1199. Washington, DC: U.S. Government Printing Office.

Shesser, R., Davis, C., & Edelstein, S. (1981). Pneumomediastinum and pneumothorax after inhaling alkaloidal cocaine. *Annals of Emergency Medicine, 10*(4), 213–215.

Siegel, R. K. (1979). Cocaine substitutes. *New England Journal of Medicine, 301*(14), 817–818.

Siegel, R. K. (1982). Cocaine smoking. *Journal of Psychoactive Drugs, 14*(4), 271–359.

Siegel, R. K. (1984a). Changing patterns of cocaine use: Longitudinal observations, consequences, and treatment. In J. Grabowski (Ed.), *Cocaine: Pharmacology, effects, and treatment of abuse,* NIDA Research Monograph No. 50 (pp. 92–110). Washington, DC: U.S. Government Printing Office.

Siegel, R. K. (1984b). Cocaine smoking disorders: Diagnosis and treatment. *Psychiatric Annals, 14*(10), 728–732.

Siegel, R. K. (1985a). New patterns of cocaine use: Changing doses and routes. In N. J. Kozel & E. H. Adams (Eds.), *Cocaine use in America: Epidemiologic and clinical perspectives,* NIDA Research Monograph No. 61, (pp. 204–220). Washington, DC: U.S. Government Printing Office.

Siegel, R. K. (1985b). Treatment of cocaine abuse: Historical and contemporary perspectives. *Journal of Psychoactive Drugs, 17*(1), 1–9.

Silva, J. L. (1984). Comentarios sobre la influencia del uso de pasta de cocaina fumada en algunos cuadros clinicos. *Revista Colombiana de Psiquiatría, 13*(3), 227–242.

Spears, R. A. (1981). *Slang and euphemism.* Middle Village, NY: Jonathan David.

Starks, M. (1982). *Cocaine fiends and reefer madness.* New York: Cornwall Books.

Stein, G. (1984, June 3). Police raiders sweep "drug houses." *Miami Herald,* pp. 1c–2c.

Stewart, F. E. (1885). Coca-leaf cigars and cigarettes. *Philadelphia Medical Times and Register, 15,* 933–955.

Tennant, F. S., Tarver, A., Johnson, C., & Cohen, A. (1984). *Long term cocaine dependence: Clinical profile, plasma levels and withdrawal symptoms.* Unpublished report.

Velasquez de Pabon, E. (1984). *La basuca. Que se sabe hasta el momento.* Paper presented at the World Health Organization Advisory Group Meeting on the Adverse Health Consequences of Cocaine and Coca Paste Smoking, Bogotá, September 10–14.

Washton, A. M., & Gold, M. S. (1986). Crack. *Journal of the American Medical Association, 256*(6), 711 (letter).

Washton, A. M., Gold, M. S., & Pottash, A. C. (1986). Crack: Early report on a new drug epidemic. *Postgraduate Medicine, 80*(5), 52–58.

Weiss, R. D., Boldenheim, P. D., Mirin, S. M., Hales, C. A., & Mendelson, J. H. (1981). Pulmonary dysfunction in cocaine smokers. *American Journal of Psychiatry, 138*(8), 1110–1112.

World Health Organization. (1984). WHO Advisory Group Meeting on Adverse Health Consequences of Cocaine and Coca Paste Smoking, Bogotá, September 10–14.

14

Cocaine in the Workplace: The Ticking Time Bomb

ROBERT L. DuPONT

Cocaine is a time bomb ticking in the American workplace. Roughly one in five American workers has tried cocaine, the most compulsively reinforcing drug in widespread use. Drugs in general pose a grave threat in the workplace—to health, productivity, safety, morale, costs, and quality of work experience—for both users and non-users. In this dismal context, cocaine is uniquely dangerous.

The first step to defusing the cocaine bomb is to see it clearly. This preliminary exploration of cocaine at work has three parts. The first is a general context of the problem based on my 20 years of clinical experience. The second part, the heart of the matter, outlines nine ways in which cocaine is unique as a drug problem in the workplace. The final part describes four steps for dealing with the cocaine problem in the workplace.

The cocaine problem is part of the drug abuse epidemic that began in the early 1960s and became a national threat during the 1970s. This epidemic, though no longer limited to the United States, involves all of U.S. society and continues today. In looking at the drug epidemic from the mid-1960s to the present, three drugs are unique: alcohol, marijuana, and cocaine. These drugs have been called the gateway drugs (DuPont, 1984). Although drug use typically begins with alcohol and proceeds through marijuana to cocaine, the field of drug abuse treatment initially emphasized the "end of the line"—the heroin problem. The incidence of heroin use in the United States peaked in 1971. There are still people newly addicted to heroin, but the epidemic rise of heroin use came in the late 1960s and early 1970s. This heroin problem, including heroin use by American soldiers in Vietnam, catalyzed the federal government's involvement in drug abuse, particularly in drug abuse treatment. Of course, it was also intimately connected with the problems of inner-city life, and particularly the problems of crime, which were, and still are, important political issues. One unex-

Robert L. DuPont. Bensinger, DuPont & Associates, Inc.; Center for Behavioral Medicine, Rockville, Maryland; Department of Psychiatry, Georgetown University Medical School, Washington, DC.

plained paradox of drug epidemiology is why the heroin problem peaked so early in the overall national drug abuse epidemic.

Although heroin played an initiating role in government response to drug abuse, it was alcohol, the most commonly used intoxicant in the United States, that created the foundation for the drug epidemic itself. The lowering of the drinking age from 21 to 18 in the early 1970s contributed to the massive increase of exposure of especially vulnerable teenagers to the use of a chemical to feel good—to "get by by getting high." Unlike the more visible but much smaller heroin problem, alcohol use by youth during the 1970s was all but overlooked. After rising steadily from the time of the repeal of Prohibition in 1933, per capita alcohol consumption in the United States peaked in the 1980s. That was the good news. The bad news is that adolescent alcohol use continues at unprecedentedly high levels.

Most of us think about the drug epidemic as all but synonymous with the marijuana problem. Marijuana use rose rapidly after 1965 and appeared to peak in about 1978 in the United States. It is surprising to many Americans that the marijuana epidemic was primarily a phenomenon of the 1970s, not the 1960s. The marijuana epidemic both reflected and contributed to the rise of nontraditional values, the so-called youth culture. It was in part a middle-class dropout phenomenon, a rebellious rejection of traditional adult values.

The third step in the typical drug pattern, after alcohol and marijuana, was cocaine. Cocaine's epidemiology is different from that of heroin, alcohol, or marijuana. Cocaine use in the United States has apparently not yet peaked, in clear contrast to the use of both alcohol and marijuana. Cocaine use is unique because, unlike heroin, it is not connected exclusively with ghetto life, and, unlike marijuana, it is not particularly connected with youth, at least not primarily with teenage dropouts. All of these distinguishing characteristics of the cocaine epidemic make comparisons with other drugs perilous.

The most recent national survey data, released in October 1986 by the National Institute on Drug Abuse, showed that 22 million Americans aged 12 and older had used cocaine at least once, that 12 million had used it in the last year, and nearly 6 million had used the drug in the last month. Ninety percent of these cocaine users are between the ages of 18 and 35, and 50% are between 18 and 25. Cocaine use, though concentrated in the under-35 age group, is not limited to any geographic area, race, or social class (Kozel & Adams, 1985). In the work force today about 20 million workers have tried cocaine, and about 4 million have used it at least once within the last month. That 20 million represents about one in every five workers in the United States. Those numbers do not begin to tell the cocaine story, however, because of the unique age–gender concentration of cocaine use. If we look at males between the ages of 18 and 25, we see that about 50% of those in the work force have used cocaine; 30% of females at work, aged 18–25, have used cocaine. The numbers in the 26–34 age group are only slightly lower—about 35% for males and 25% for females. Within this 18–35 age group in the work force, an enormous number of people have experimented with cocaine. For millions of them, this experimentation has led or will lead to severe problems. Because of the powerful, seductive nature of cocaine use, every one of these 20 million workers is at risk of a serious problem with cocaine. The more they use the drug, the more they like it, and the greater the risk to them, their co-workers, their employers, their families, and their communities.

All this is by way of background about the drug epidemic, with a special focus on cocaine. This leads to a review of the drug dependence syndrome. There are two related myths that create serious handicaps in dealing with the cocaine problem. The first myth is the concept of controlled or responsible drug use. We are accustomed to this idea in relation to alcohol use. This myth has a devastating effect on our ability to understand and respond to all drug problems, particularly cocaine abuse. The second myth is that there are nonaddictive drugs. For most young people, cocaine has been labeled, by some, "nonaddictive," and this has contributed to the epidemic of cocaine use. "Responsible" cocaine use makes as much sense, on the basis of scientific understanding of cocaine's pharmacology, as "responsible" Russian roulette: If you do not pull the trigger too often, some who play the game will survive. To call cocaine nonaddictive flies in the face of modern pharmacology. One hundred percent of monkeys allowed to self-administer cocaine die of the drug's effect within 5 days. Is that a nonaddictive drug?

There are three stages of the drug dependence syndrome. The first, *experimentation*, is the most important stage. It involves going from never using the drug to trying out the drug. I call the second stage *fooling around* with—dabbling in—the drug. This is often the honeymoon stage, when users may have the confident feeling that they can control the experience, that drug use is a harmless, enjoyable part of life. The third stage is *dependence*—being *hooked*. The best way to understand this stage is to compare it to falling in love with the drug and the drug experience.

Several features of this syndrome need to be highlighted in the workplace context. All drug users *deny* both the extent and consequences of their drug use, especially to anyone who might come between them and their "lover"—the drug. Other people—employers, co-workers, family—*enable* drug use to continue. Finally, drug dependence leads to lying and *moral corruption* among all users. The user generally feels entitled to say or do whatever seems necessary in order to keep using the drug.

These three stages are all part of one *process*; they are not unrelated phenomena. The progression from one stage to the next is out of the drug user's control. The concept that it is a matter of will power for a person to manage cocaine use is devastatingly wrong. The vulnerability to dependence, to falling in love with cocaine, is a universal mammalian vulnerability. It is not restricted to those with certain qualities of character, genetics, sex, race, social class, or anything else. The vulnerability does appear to differ somewhat in degree—it is greater for some and less for others—but anyone who is willing to use cocaine frequently at intoxicating doses will eventually fall in love with it and lose control of his or her use of cocaine.

The analogy with alcohol is dangerously misleading if we try to use the disease concept, implying that there are some people who can "handle" cocaine just as some people appear to be sensible social drinkers. *No one* can handle cocaine. The idea that some people are invulnerable for genetic or other reasons is a deadly misconception.

Having looked at cocaine epidemiology and the drug dependence syndrome, our next topic is treatment of cocaine users. A remarkable thing has happened to drug abuse treatment in the last 5 years. The drug abuse treatment experience is different now than it ever was before. We have, in a sense, rehabilitated much of drug abuse treatment. This has come about in an interesting way. When I was a medical student, treatment ideas were based on two assumptions. The first was that drug problems were symptoms of some underlying primary disorder. Thus, the treatment was psychotherapy to help the patient understand that problem; once that understanding was accomplished, the drug "symptom," being secondary, would disappear. The second idea was that the clinical problem was addiction—the "man with the golden arm" phenomenon. Just get over the addiction and everything would be all right. In this view, people used drugs because they got sick when they stopped.

The logical conclusion from these two erroneous assumptions was that drug-dependent people needed psychotherapy and detoxification. If you could just get drug abusers into psychotherapy and get them drug free for a few days in a hospital, they would be fine because their problem would be eliminated. The fact that this approach did not help many people during the 40 or 50 years it was used did not discourage doctors and others from using it over and over again. In fact, this was the primary treatment model for cocaine and other drug problems until a few years ago.

The key ideas for contemporary treatment came from Minnesota, where the period of inpatient care was extended from about 7–10 days to 28 or 30 days. This time was not so much used to get the patient drug free as to plug him or her into a self-help group—Alcoholics Anonymous or Narcotics Anonymous—for a lifetime of recovery. The drug user's family was part of treatment and was plugged into Al Anon, also for life. That simple two-step process (28-day inpatient care followed by lifelong AA or NA attendance) led to a dramatic improvement in drug abuse treatment.

Cocaine was important in this process of change because cocaine revealed the foolishness of some of the old ideas. The cocaine experience showed that serious drug abusers were not addicted in the traditional sense, because they were using a "nonaddictive" drug. Yet they could not control their use of the drug. It also showed that drug users were not necessarily either dropout teenage potheads or middle-aged alcoholics.

Earlier we noted that an estimated 20 million American workers have used cocaine and that 4 million have used it within the last month. There is a common assumption that the 16 million who have not used cocaine within the last month are safe. Nothing could be further from the truth. These 16 million people are vulnerable to cocaine dependence. It is curious that in the drug field ideas that would be considered ludicrous in any other intellectual field are thought of as profound. There is the concept, for example, that there are "safe" drug users and "sick" drug users. Many experts place individuals on the drug use continuum on the basis of whether or not they have a "problem." This leads to support for the people who do not have a problem in their drug use because they are considered healthy, while others are treated as sick. These experts fail to see that the way one gets to be a "sick" cocaine user is by going through the stage of being a "healthy" cocaine user. This is like talking about speeding by saying: "You can't drive 90 miles an hour. Some people have a problem and some do not have a problem. So we will divide up the population of those who drive 90 miles an hour into the healthy speeders and the sick speeders. The sick speeders have a disease—speeding sickness—but the other speeders are okay." In this misguided line of reasoning, speeding is not the problem; it is getting into trouble with speeding that is the problem. Although this reasoning may seem ridiculous, it is the devastating delusion that has afflicted drug experts when looking at the people who use cocaine at work. It has led to enormous confusion and a reinforcement of the concept of the normality of fooling around with cocaine.

There are nine ways in which cocaine is special in the workplace:

1. First, and perhaps most obviously, is the special image of cocaine. Cocaine is chic. It is called the champagne drug or the rich man's drug. Recent epidemiologic evidence suggests that there is something (but not much) to this perception, perhaps a self-fulfilling prophecy. For example, here are some interesting figures culled from household surveys. Among those people who had less than a high school education, 5% reported ever having used cocaine; among those who had had some college, 19% had used cocaine. Of those who reported a family income of $10,000 or less, 11% had used cocaine; among those reporting a family income of $50,000 or more, 16% had used cocaine. Among laborers, 14% reported using cocaine; among managers, 27%. Thus, there is some basis for the image of cocaine as a rich

man's drug. These percentages are deceiving, however, since most cocaine users are neither rich nor poor, but simply average. Nevertheless, the unique allure of cocaine makes it attractive to people at all levels in the workplace.

2. Cocaine is a stimulant. The other drugs that have become widely used—alcohol, heroin, and marijuana—have all been depressants. The concept of alcohol as a depressant drug comes through in the way it is advertised: "Miller Time" is when you finish work. But what about the image of a stimulant drug? A stimulant drug holds out the promise of fighting fatigue and promoting work and efficiency. Of course, this is not true of cocaine or any other stimulant, but that does not discourage people from using cocaine on this basis. The idea that cocaine is a "pro-worker" drug makes cocaine use on the job itself far more likely than use of depressants like alcohol and marijuana. Only the end-stage, strung-out user of pot or booze is likely to consume the drug at work. Not so with cocaine.

3. Cocaine is a short-acting drug. This characteristic differentiates it from most of the other commonly used drugs and gives the illusion that cocaine use can be isolated and limited much more easily than marijuana or alcohol use. Cocaine promises no disabling hangover or long-term effect to interfere with work.

4. Cocaine is the only drug that shows rising incidence of first use among people in their 20s. This striking fact is not easily explained. With every other drug—cigarettes, alcohol, heroin, marijuana—there is a sharp peak of first use in the teenage years—usually the mid-teens. With cocaine, however, there is an increasing incidence as people get older, at least in their early 20s. Whether this observation means that we are in the early stages of the evolution of the cocaine epidemic, or whether it means there is something special about cocaine, the pattern is important because it means that initial use of cocaine is occurring later in many people's lives, not only in the school years but also in later years, specifically at work.

5. Cocaine use is special because of its cost. After all, one can stay stoned on pot all day, every day, for $5 or $10 a day; to really get wasted might cost as much as $20 a day. Even with today's inflated prices, pot use is cheap. You can stay totally intoxicated on alcohol, marijuana, and other drugs for relatively little money. It is cheap to destroy your life on pot or booze. There are only two exceptions among widely used drugs: heroin and cocaine. To stay high on cocaine or heroin costs hundreds of dollars a day. That economic reality does not come from the image of the drugs, but from their pharmacology. These two are short-acting drugs, not taken orally, which produce high levels of tolerance. Thus the person who is intoxicated on cocaine or heroin uses large amounts of the drug. These two habits are expensive also because of the high cost of a pharmacologically effective dose of cocaine or heroin. Finally, this is the result of relatively successful enforcement, which pushes up the price of cocaine and heroin.

Previously, when heroin was the only high-cost drug in the workplace, needing money to supply one's habit was a problem of the lowest socioeconomic group of workers. The problems of drug-related theft and other income-generating activities were limited. But the epidemic of cocaine use at work means that we have an income-demanding drug at all socioeconomic levels, including the highest levels of the organization. This puts businesses themselves at risk in a way that has never been true before. Cocaine use can lead not only to theft of typewriters or goods from the warehouse, but also to threats at the very core of the corporation. Business information and money, the lifeblood of the organization, are now at risk because of high-level employees whose moral values have been corroded by cocaine use and whose demand for money to buy cocaine is enormous. This is a new phenomenon. The potential for destructive behavior in the workplace has increased enormously. Cocaine users are in the executive suites, in the most trusted roles in business life. They can steal not only purses and word processors but corporate information highly valued by competitors and the Internal Revenue Service. This new breed of drug users can carry out corporate plundering beyond a stock clerk or maintenance worker's wildest dreams.

6. With most commonly used drugs the typical pattern of heavy use is continuous drug use. With cocaine, however, the typical pattern is binge use. Continuous use of cocaine day in and day out at a constant level, is uncommon; the typical pattern is episodic high-level use—a spree or run. That changes the nature of the problem at work and makes survey data less helpful because surveys discount episodic use. We are accustomed to thinking of the daily or regular user as the problem user, but a person can get into a lot of trouble with cocaine without ever being a daily user.

7. Cocaine uniquely causes paranoia and aggressiveness. This is important in functioning everywhere, especially at work. Cocaine users have a tendency toward violence, suspiciousness, and paranoia. This explosive disorganization of thinking is a special and dangerous result of cocaine use. At work the most common cocaine-caused problems are unreliability and theft, but hostility and aggression are also serious common problems. Even more common than aggressiveness and paranoia are the depression and fatigue that universally follow a cocaine run. For days after such a binge, cocaine users are dragged out, beat, and irritable. They often miss work and, when at work, are unable to perform normally.

8. Once a worker gets into a pattern of binge use of cocaine, it has an effect unlike that of any other drug. High-dose cocaine use takes users down suddenly—like stones falling into a pond. Many people crippled by cocaine have used other drugs off and on, sometimes at high levels, for many years. But once they start high-dose use of cocaine, they fall apart. I do not know of any other drug that does this, literally catapulting users into treatment.

They often arrive in treatment stunned by the effects of cocaine. Even if they have fooled around with cocaine for years, sudden increased access to a supply—because of a friend who is a dealer, or more money, or some other change in their life-style—can rapidly bring them down.

9. Cocaine, the stimulant, has a unique way of interacting with the use of other drugs, particularly depressants like alcohol, tranquilizers, and even heroin. In fact, many new users of heroin in the United States are being recruited to heroin through the cocaine door, for several reasons. Many of them have been introduced to intravenous (IV) drug use through IV use of cocaine. They also turn to mind-numbing depressant drugs to deal with either overstimulation or the devastating depression following cocaine use. Cocaine use also gets "normal" drug abusers over the hurdle into the "junkie" role as the compulsion to use swamps even long-standing barriers to the addict's life-style. With high-dose cocaine use, anything goes—including IV heroin, for many users.

The final section of this chapter focuses on how to deal with the problems of cocaine use at work. There can be only one basis for approaching the problems of cocaine in the workplace: zero tolerance. It is imperative for anyone dealing with any drug problem in the workplace to start by drawing the line at *any* drug use. Once one shifts to the goal of identifying drug-caused *impairment*, as opposed to drug *use*, one loses the capacity to deal effectively with the problem. Even worse is to get caught up in the goal of identifying specific job-related impairments. There are no jobs that will let one meet that standard. Only one standard will succeed: When a person comes to work, he or she must come drug free. I call this *zero tolerance* for drugs at work.

There are four steps to solving the cocaine problem in the workplace:

1. We must educate. Most people at work still do not know the facts about cocaine use as they are documented in this book. Too many people think they can use cocaine and get away with it. They think cocaine use is harmless. They do not know about the reinforcing potential; they do not know that cocaine use is out of the user's control, or about the inevitable escalation of the drug dependence syndrome. They do not know that cocaine can kill, even when used intranasally. Not knowing the basic facts about cocaine, they are misled into thinking that it is relatively harmless and easily controlled. They think of cocaine use as a benign personal decision without realizing the tremendous stake non-users, at work and elsewhere, have in that decision. We need to have clear education at the workplace about the hazards of cocaine use. We also need to undercut the current widespread tolerance for cocaine use through education. Everyone at the workplace should understand that all share the vulnerability. Drug problems are not limited to drug users. Whether or not one uses cocaine, cocaine at work is adversely affecting everyone. The issue of secondhand smoke at

the workplace provides a useful precedent in the legitimization of the interests of nonsmokers. The same process can happen with other drugs, most notably cocaine. Most workers do not use cocaine. They need to be enlisted in the battle against cocaine use.

This battle is not against cocaine users as people, but against their use of the drug. Cocaine users, along with the non-users, will benefit from reduced tolerance to cocaine use at work. This must be rooted in a thoroughgoing, honest, factual education of everyone at work about the dangers of cocaine use.

2. The second step is the most controversial. Action must be taken to say "no" to cocaine. There is only one way to achieve this goal: to implement regular urine testing to identify cocaine use. Any halfway measure is just waiting until disaster has befallen individual cocaine users, their families, and the organization. It is unfortunate that some representatives of the workers—unions and others—fight drug testing. They do so because they do not understand the drug problem and they do not understand the solution. The people who are most likely to benefit from an aggressive testing program are the workers themselves. Users and non-users need a compelling reason not to use cocaine in the first place; a person who is already using cocaine needs a reason not to continue use. Those who continue to use cocaine at work need to be caught so they can be helped.

I have worked with a great many people for whom the person who said "no" was the one who saved their lives. If we approach cocaine use as a matter of personal preference, a civil right, or a privacy matter, we are not doing any favors to anybody—the company's stockholders, its managers, non-using employees, their families, or even the drug users themselves. All we do by adopting these attitudes is enable the cocaine problem to continue. We need to have a system for saying "no" and make that system work. Of course, at work one must deal with all drug use, not just cocaine use (Dogoloff & Angarola, 1985). The prevention issues are the same. Economics, pharmacology, and fairness all require an even-handed "no drugs at work" policy.

3. We need to overcome the myths that are preventing action. We must set aside any concept of "safe" or "controlled" use of cocaine. We must overcome the barriers we have developed that keep us from effective action.

4. We need to follow up on what Alcoholics Anonymous calls Twelfth Step work by helping people who have confronted their own cocaine problem to help others. People who have used cocaine, even more than those who have used other drugs, are missionaries when they recover. They know what it means to lose control of one's life; they know how dangerous cocaine is. Many are highly motivated to recycle their knowledge and experience— to do Twelfth Step work. We should encourage them—a lot of good can come from their missionary zeal.

This chapter is not about hurting people, but about helping them. We help people by helping them understand the facts and by saying "no" to cocaine use. We hurt them by letting their cocaine problem continue.

Cocaine use in the workplace is a ticking time bomb. The 16 million people who have used cocaine but are not current users are part of the time bomb almost as much as the 4 million who actually use the drug. Every one of them is vulnerable—and so are many of the 85 million workers who have not yet used cocaine.

Have we learned enough in the last 20 years to defuse the bomb, or do we have to wait until it explodes? The dangers of cocaine at the workplace are unique, and the consequences of inaction are terrifying. The potential value in dealing with the issue concerns not only cocaine users but also all other aspects of drug use, including use of other drugs in the workplace.

The current rising tide of public concern about drug use—especially cocaine use—is the most positive development in the past 20 years of our national experience with drug abuse. If we can say "no" to drugs at work, we will not only help the 105 million working Americans, but we will also send a powerful signal to our youth: When you show up for work, you show up drug free. That deceptively simple-sounding, but profound, goal offers us our best hope of ending the drug epidemic—of seeing to it that cocaine, the current epidemic drug, is the last one.

REFERENCES

Dogoloff, L. I., & Angarola, R. T. (1985). *Urine testing in the workplace.* Rockville, MD: American Council for Drug Education.

DuPont, R. L. (1984). *Getting tough on gateway drugs: A guide for the family.* Washington, DC: American Psychiatric Press.

Kozel, N. J., & Adams, E. H. (1985). *Cocaine use in America: Epidemiological and clinical perspectives,* NIDA Research Monograph No. 61. Washington, DC: U.S. Government Printing Office.

National Institute on Drug Abuse. (1986). *Annual Household Survey.* Rockville, MD: Author.

15

Alcohol Problems in Cocaine Abusers

SHEILA B. BLUME

Drinking Patterns in Cocaine Abusers

Alcohol is the most commonly abused drug in the United States, and is usually the first such drug (other than tobacco) experienced by American youth. It is no longer unusual for boys and girls to begin drinking at 12 or 13 years of age. Despite a legal minimum purchase age of 21 years in nearly all states, more than 90% of high school seniors use alcohol. Thus it is hardly surprising that a great many cocaine abusers also have significant histories of alcohol abuse.

There are a few common patterns. Often alcohol was the first drug used, and a careful history will reveal a drinking pattern that was problematic in itself. Drinking to get high, frequent intoxication, neglect of school or other obligations, driving or performing other hazardous activities while under the influence, interpersonal problems, and vandalism and theft related to alcohol are not uncommon. Drinking is used to relieve unpleasant feelings such as anxiety, boredom, resentment, and rejection. This may occur before regular use of cocaine begins.

Once a pattern of cocaine abuse has been established, pathological drinking may continue during periods when cocaine is unavailable or when the abuser has sworn off the drug for one reason or another. In addition, a second pattern of alcohol or other sedative abuse becomes established. This pattern involves using the depressant action of alcohol as a self-medication, to counteract some of the undesired concomitants of increasing cocaine use. Tension, agitation, hyperalertness, and insomnia are all to some extent counteracted by alcohol, and thus heavy drinking becomes part of the cycle of drug use.

Alcohol, however, is far from an ideal drug for this purpose, since it is relatively short acting and is followed by its own rebound stimulation; it

Sheila B. Blume. Alcoholism and Compulsive Gambling Programs, South Oaks Hospital, Amityville, New York; Department of Psychiatry, State University of New York at Stony Brook, Stony Brook, New York.

adds its own sleep disruption to that of cocaine. Furthermore, habitual alcohol use leads to tolerance, necessitating ever-increasing doses, and the ingestion of large amounts of alcohol leads to well-known medical and psychiatric complications—gastritis, liver disease, hangovers, alcohol withdrawal shakes, and depressed mood, among others.

Finally, two important patterns represent a hazard for patients sincerely striving to recover from cocaine dependence. The first is a relapse to cocaine use precipitated by drinking. This may occur for a number of reasons. The social context of the drinking (a bar, a party) may trigger craving because of its previous association with cocaine use. In addition, the first cerebral function to be affected, even by small amounts of alcohol, is judgment. With judgment impaired, the likelihood of resisting the temptation to use cocaine is very much reduced. Rationalizations ("Just this once") and denials ("Now that I'm healthy and know all about addictions, I can handle it") become easy to believe.

The second pattern is a switching of dependencies. With cocaine no longer an option to counteract feelings of boredom, discouragement, or low self-esteem, alcohol, the legal drug ("Doesn't everybody do it?"), is used as a substitute. In this psychological setting, alcohol dependence tends to develop very rapidly.

Treatment Considerations

Whether or not there is a clear history of preexisting alcohol abuse, all patients undergoing treatment for cocaine problems must be convinced that abstinence from all dependence-producing drugs is a necessary treatment goal. Nevertheless, it remains important to evaluate past and present drinking patterns in all such patients.

Patients will often demonstrate strong denial of alcohol abuse when asked directly if they are alcoholic. They will maintain that drinking is not a problem and that they don't even like to drink. Indeed, the use of alcohol as a remedy for cocaine agitation may be an unpleasant experience for them. It is necessary, however, to explore the patient's alcohol use both during the initial evaluation and later on in individual and/or group treatment. When pathological patterns of use are identified, the therapist must point these out as evidence that the roots of alcohol dependence are already present. An even more enlightening result of the exploration of drinking patterns during group therapy will be the gradual realization by the group members that few if any of them have any concept of normal drinking. Like alcoholics in treatment, they share the fantasy that normal drinkers use alcohol to get high, to alter reality when it doesn't suit them, to solve personal problems, and to relieve negative feelings. They believe that normal drinkers do all these things and "get away with it," and this, they believe, is the only thing that distinguishes them from alcoholics. The idea of drinking without getting high is unthinkable. Exposing these fantasies also helps patients establish an abstinence goal.

The need for frequent urine testing in cocaine treatment is emphasized in this book. It is also important for a cocaine treatment program to test for alcohol use, either as part of the urine screen or with a breath alcohol testing device. Low-cost breath analyzers are now available and offer the convenience of an immediate reading.

Adjuncts to Treatment for the Dual Abusers

For the cocaine abuser with a clear history of alcohol dependence, past or present, the treatment planning process should include serious consideration of Alcoholics Anonymous (AA) and the drug disulfiram (antabuse). AA is widely available throughout the United States and worldwide. It is a valuable resource which enables the patient to identify with the speakers and other group members, and to adopt the Twelve Steps of AA as a principle for living. Being a member of the AA fellowship in no way interferes with participation in any of the other self-help movements. Most members find these groups complementary during the first year or two of abstinence and choose a primary group later in recovery.

Disulfiram is used as an aid to motivation for sobriety in alcoholic patients. It specifically blocks the action of the enzyme aldehyde dehydrogenase, which converts acetaldehyde, the first metabolic breakdown product of alcohol, to acetate. When the enzyme is blocked, acetaldehyde accumulates in the bloodstream and tissues in proportion to the amount of alcohol consumed. Therefore, the patient who drinks while taking disulfiram develops acute actealdehyde poisoning, with palpitations, swings in blood pressure, extreme flushing of the skin, nausea and vomiting, collapse, and the feeling of impending death. The patient who agrees to take disulfiram does so with full knowledge of this effect. While taking the drug, he or she knows that a drink won't make him feel better, only sick. Thus the patient is instructed to take disulfiram as part of his or her daily routine. After shaving, grooming, or putting on makeup, the patient picks up the container of tablets and asks him- or herself two questions: "Am I an alcoholic?" and "Do I want to stay sober today?" If the answer is "yes," the patient consumes the tablet, and the choice is made for the day. If the patient finds it difficult to complete this daily ritual, it is an early sign of trouble and a signal to talk things over with the therapist. Since there are medical contraindications to the use of disulfiram, and close medical supervision is needed, patients should be carefully screened. A written agreement is often used, such as that presented in Appendix 15A (Blume, 1982).

Family Alcoholism

Cocaine abusers are often the offspring of alcoholic parents and, in addition, may be living with significant others who have drinking problems. Thus participation in self-help groups such as Al-Anon (for families or friends of alcoholics) or Alateen (for teenagers living in an alcoholic family) may be helpful adjuncts to therapy. There is mounting scientific evidence that the children of alcoholic parents are at special risk throughout their lifetimes for a wide variety of physical, psychological, and social problems (Russell, Henderson, & Blume, 1985). Adults who grew up in alcoholic families, even if they no longer live with their alcoholic parent, often have unresolved issues of guilt, fears of intimacy, and unusual needs to control. Treatment for cocaine abuse in such patients is greatly facilitated if the patient can be helped to reinterpret childhood experiences through an adult understanding of the disease concept of alcoholism and the dynamics of alcoholic families (Cermak, 1986). A growing number of self-help groups for adult children of alcoholic parents have been developing nationwide over the past few years. Such groups may be of value in the long-term treatment plans for selected cocaine abusers.

A Note on the Cocaine Abuser Who Enrolls in an Alcoholism Program

Programs specializing in the treatment of alcoholism, both in- and outpatient, have reported that a rising proportion of their patients have problems with one or more drugs in addition to alcohol. It is important that these programs be alert to the patient who abuses both alcohol and cocaine, because such patients may present special problems. During the initial assessment, the patient may minimize or totally deny any cocaine history for a variety of reasons. The patient, clinging to the hope of returning to "occasional" cocaine use once his or her drinking problem is resolved, may resist facing the truth. He or she may be in treatment to avoid prosecution or to placate a loved one who is unaware of the patient's cocaine problem. Alcoholism programs should make urine drug screening an integral part of their assessment methodology and of their treatment regimen. Alcoholism patients who use cocaine surreptitiously during treatment may otherwise be misdiagnosed as hypomanic or as suffering from anxiety disorders. Urine testing not only will clarify such situations but also will deter drug use in treatment, allowing rehabilitation to proceed in a drug-free environment.

Summary

The combined abuse of cocaine and alcohol is a common therapeutic challenge. A thorough assessment of the patient's drinking history, insistence on a long-term goal of abstinence from all drugs of dependence, and a working knowledge of the effects of alcoholism on family systems are the key elements needed for the successful treatment of these patients.

Appendix 15A
Information for Those Taking Antabuse

You have requested of your physician that you be given the medication ANTA-BUSE. We feel this can be a very useful medication in many cases, but it is very important that you understand the nature of the medicine and the danger involved in its use.

Your doctor will first check to be sure that there is no physical reason why you should not have the medicine and that you are not taking any other medication which might interact in a negative way. You will be given a card which indicates that you are taking ANTABUSE. You should carry this card in your purse or wallet at all times. On the card are instructions for your care should you get sick from drinking while taking ANTABUSE.

Most people taking ANTABUSE, once they are accustomed to the medicine, feel no effect of any kind. The medicine circulates in the bloodstream and only causes trouble when alcohol is consumed. If alcohol is drunk, the ANTABUSE causes it to be converted into a poisonous substance which causes various symptoms including a drop in blood pressure, vomiting, diarrhea, flushing and collapse. This is called the ANTABUSE reaction. It may be life-threatening. The reaction may vary from mild to very severe and usually passes off after a few hours. ANTABUSE reactions have occurred as long as 14 days after the last dose of ANTABUSE, when alcohol was drunk.

People taking ANTABUSE must not only refrain from drinking alcoholic beverages, but from taking the drugs paraldehyde, Dilantin, Flagyl and Isoniazid (INAH), and any liquid medicine or food which contains alcohol. If you are unsure of the contents of a medicine, read the label on the bottle or ask your doctor. IF IN DOUBT, DO NOT TAKE WHILE ON ANTABUSE.

Like any powerful medicine, ANTABUSE will cause reactions or allergy in some of the people who take it. It is for this reason that your liver will be tested before giving you the medicine and that you are asked to stay under medical supervision as long as you are taking the medicine. Should you develop any symptoms (such as rashes, numbness, weakness or any other symptom), you should report this to your physician for evaluation of whether ANTABUSE should be stopped. Every person reacts differently, and although most people can take ANTABUSE without ill effects, as long as they are alcohol free, everyone requires supervision by a physician while taking the medicine.

Should you drink while taking ANTABUSE, ask for immediate medical aid and tell the person nearest you that you are suffering an ANTABUSE reaction. Also indicate where your card is kept. This will insure you receiving the most prompt attention possible.

Do not take EXTRA doses of ANTABUSE for any reason. If you are feeling tense, your ordinary dose is sufficient to protect you. Raising the dose will put you in danger of toxic side effects.

I have read the above information and have discussed any questions with my physician. I understand the importance of refraining from drinking alcohol while taking ANTABUSE and of remaining under medical supervision. I understand the nature of the proposed medication, attendant risks involved, and expected results, as described above, and hereby request such medication.

Signature _____

Date _____

REFERENCES

Blume, S. B. (1982). Treatment of alcoholism. In H. F. Conn (Ed.), *Current therapy 1982* (pp. 921–925). Philadelphia: Saunders.

Cermak, T. L. (1986). *Diagnosing and treating co-dependence.* Minneapolis, MN: Johnson Institute Books.

Russell, M., Henderson, C., & Blume, S. B. (1985). *Children of alcoholics: A review of the literature.* New York: Children of Alcoholics Foundation. (Available from the Children of Alcoholics Foundation, 200 Park Avenue, New York, NY 10166.)

16

Pathological Gambling in Cocaine Abusers

SHEILA B. BLUME AND HENRY R. LESIEUR

Pathological Gambling in Cocaine Abusers: Why Be Concerned?

Gambling, both legal and illegal, is a multibillion-dollar industry in the United States today. The continued trend toward legalization of gambling, in the form of state lotteries, off-track betting, and casinos, has resulted in increasing exposure of the general population to various types of wagering. For most Americans who gamble, the activity is a pleasant, if not always profitable, recreation. For a few, gambling is a profession and their source of financial support. For approximately 2–3% of the adult population, however, gambling is compulsive (Culleton & Lang, 1985; Transition Planning Associates, 1985). These individuals are pathological gamblers, victims of a serious but treatable illness.

There is reason to believe that this illness is a special problem for cocaine abusers. For example, Lesieur, Blume, and Zoppa (1986) studied 458 patients hospitalized for the treatment of alcohol and drug problems at South Oaks Hospital. None of the subjects had come into treatment because of gambling. Nine percent of the overall population were found to be pathological gamblers, and an additional 10% had some problems related to gambling but did not satisfy the diagnostic criteria of the *Diagnostic and Statistical Manual of Mental Disorders,* 3rd edition (DSM-III) (American Psychiatric Association, 1980). Of these 458 patients, 113 (25%) had a history of cocaine abuse. Among the cocaine abusers, 16 patients (14%) were pathological gamblers, and an additional 18 (16%) reported gambling-related problems.

Cocaine and gambling are often found in the same environment, and relapses into drug use may occur in gambling situations. Also, cocaine abusers may resume a pattern of gambling dependence, established in the past, after becoming abstinent from drugs.

Sheila B. Blume. Alcoholism and Compulsive Gambling Programs, South Oaks Hospital, Amityville, New York; Department of Psychiatry, State University of New York at Stony Brook, Stony Brook, New York.

Henry R. Lesieur. Department of Sociology and Anthropology, St. John's University, Jamaica, New York: Consultant, South Oaks Foundation, Amityville, New York.

Pathological Gambling: An Addiction without a Drug

Pathological gambling has much in common with other behaviors classified as addictions. The gambler's goal is to stay "in action." The action of gambling provides a feeling of intense excitement, power, and hopeful anticipation. It is the gambler's ticket of admission to fantasyland. The individual becomes dependent on that feeling and on a self-identification as a successful gambler to counteract feelings of anxiety, boredom, and resentment, and to bolster self-esteem.

Over time, compulsive gamblers find they must increase the amount and frequency of betting to feel fully in action. When they begin to lose, they desperately struggle to regain their former position by "chasing losses," or throwing "good money after bad" (Custer & Milt, 1985; Lesieur, 1984). This behavior pattern is similar in many ways to that of the cocaine abuser, who discovers a pleasurable high in the drug, becomes dependent on it, and continues to take the drug despite mounting adverse effects in a persistent attempt to reattain the initial high. Moral dilemmas, personal and social problems, and approach–avoidance conflicts characterize both pathological gambling and other addictions (Orford, 1985).

Treatment systems based on the principles of addiction treatment (Blume, 1986a) and Gamblers Anonymous (GA), a self-help group based on the principles of Alcholics Anonymous (AA) (Gamblers Anonymous, 1984) have proved effective in helping pathological gamblers recover. Several authors have commented on the coexistence of pathological gambling with other addictions, and the tendencies for switching addictions or the precipitation of relapse by behavior characteristic of another addiction (Lesieur, Blume, & Zoppa, 1986; Ramirez, McCormick, Russo, & Taber, 1983).

Characteristics of Cocaine Abusers with Problems Related to Gambling

Data from the South Oaks Hospital study quoted earlier (Lesicur, Blume, & Zoppa, 1986) were used to compare characteristics of inpatients in treatment for cocaine abuse (with or without other alcohol or drug involvement) who did report some problems related to gambling ($N = 34$), with those who did not report such problems ($N = 79$). Table 16-1 compares these groups. The groups were similar in age, occupation, religion, marital status, and the incidence of associated alcohol abuse. The problem gamblers, however, were more likely to be male (85% versus 73%) and to be the offspring of a parent they considered to be a compulsive gambler (23.5% versus 3.8%). These patients were also less likely to have attended college but more likely to have a high school diploma than were the cocaine abusers without gambling-related problems.

TABLE 16-1. Comparison of Cocaine Abuse Inpatients with and without Gambling-Related Problems

	Percentage of patients without gambling problem ($N = 79$)	Percentage of patients with gambling problem ($N = 34$)	Chi square
Sex:			
Male	73	85	1.38
Female	27	15	$p = .26$
Age:			
≤ 24	33	36	
25–34	46	45	
≥ 35	22	18	n.s.
Occupation:			
White collar	34	30	
Blue collar	44	46	n.s.
Not in labor force	19	24	
Education:			
$\leq$ High school graduate	22	12	
High school graduate	33	50	3.3
College	46	38	$p = .19$
Marital:			
Single	43	47	
Married	30	32	
Separated	11	12	n.s.
Divorced	14	9	
Widowed	1	—	
Religion:			
Catholic	65	68	
Protestant	23	24	
Jewish	6	5	n.s.
Other	3	3	
None	4	—	
Considered parent a compulsive gambler: Yes	3.8	23.5	8.4 $p < .01$
Alcohol abuse problem:			
Yes	75	71	
No	25	29	n.s.

Diagnosis of Pathological Gambling

DSM-III sets forth three diagnostic criteria for pathological gambling. There must be a chronic and progressive inability to resist the urge to gamble. In addition, the gambling must produce interference with life functioning, as manifested by problems in at least three of seven areas. These areas include family, work, and various legal and financial problems. Defaulting on debts, borrowing from illegal sources, being unable to account for claimed winnings, and needing a bailout (money from another person to pay off gambling debts) are all included as separate problem areas. Finally, the gambling must not be part of an overall antisocial personality disorder.

The proposed revision of DSM-III (DSM III-R) (American Psychiatric Association, 1985), reformulates these criteria to make them parallel to the reformulated criteria for psychoactive substance dependence. In each case there are nine criteria. Eight are very similar: frequent preoccupation with the activity, need for increasing amounts to achieve the desired effect, using (or gambling) larger amounts than intended, withdrawal symptoms when substance use ceases (or restlessness and irritability when unable to gamble), repeated efforts to cut down or stop, giving up important life activities in favor of the substance (or gambling), failing to fulfill social or job obligations because of the activity, and continuing the activity in the face of mounting problems known to be exacerbated by continuing. The ninth criterion refers to taking the substance to relieve withdrawal symptoms in the case of alcohol or drugs, and to chasing losses (repeatedly trying to win back money lost) for gambling. A minimum of three criteria are required for a diagnosis of substance dependence, and six of the nine for pathological gambling, although this may be reduced to four in the final version, based on further research (Lesieur & Blume, 1986).

In a cocaine abuser who also abuses alcohol and/or other drugs, it may be difficult to separate job, family, or financial problems due to gambling from those due to substance abuse. This is particularly true when the gambling and the substance abuse take place during the same time period. However, a careful history may reveal periods of gambling before heavy drug use, or during times when drug use is intermittent or absent. In other cases, the patient may be able to separate problems due to gambling from those consequent to dependence on substances, particularly when it comes to specific financial problems.

Prevention of Pathological Gambling in Cocaine Abusers

Optimal treatment for substance abuse always includes education of the patient and family to prevent the development of dependence on substitute drugs. Measures can also be taken to prevent pathological gambling in those who have not had previous problems. Education about gambling problems and the disease concept of pathological gambling can be helpful. Therapeutic recreation programs should prohibit gambling and discourage activities usually associated with betting, such as card games and bingo. Alternative leisure activities should be taught. Family history should be explored, and patients from families in which parents or other close relatives have experienced gambling problems should receive intensive preventive education.

Identification of Pathological Gamblers

The subject of gambling should be approached in history taking with a nonjudgmental attitude and the expectation that the patient gambles to some degree. "What are your favorite kinds of gambling?" or "Can you remember your biggest win? Your biggest loss?" are better questions than "Do you have a gambling problem?" or "How much do you gamble?" An easily administered 16-question screening instrument of tested validity and reliability, the South Oaks Gambling Screen (SOGS) is now available (Lesieur & Blume, submitted 1986).[1] A score of 5 or more out of a maximum of 20 indicates probable pathological gambling. The SOGS was based on a modification of DSM-III criteria but also correlates well with the proposed DSM-III-R revision. Additional guidance on clinical aspects of making a diagnosis of pathological gambling may be found in a recent paper by Glen (1985).

Treatment Considerations

Cocaine abusers who have a past or present history of pathological gambling should be treated for both diseases concurrently. This may be accomplished if available treatment staff have had training and experience in treating gambling problems. Recovered pathological gamblers who have been trained in counseling make excellent role models, similar to recovered alcoholics and addicts who counsel substance abusers. Gamblers Anonymous is an essential adjunct to treatment and will not interfere with other self-help group membership. Gam-Anon and Gam-A-Teen are important for family members.

Although there are many similarities between the treatment of pathological gambling and of substance abuse (Blume, 1986b), there are also important differences, so that substance abuse treatment alone should not be considered sufficient in itself. Money is a particular problem for gamblers and their families, and special techniques have been developed to plan for repaying debts and managing family finances. Involvement of spouses, parents, and significant others is particularly important in treating pathological gamblers (Gaudia, 1986; Heineman, in press). Recovered spouses of pathological gamblers who are trained in counseling make extremely beneficial members of the family treatment staff. At South Oaks, for example, such counselors have uncovered previously unrecognized gambling problems in patients through their contacts with spouses, parents, and significant others.

NOTE

1. The SOGS is available from the South Oaks Foundation, 400 Sunrise Highway, Amityville, NY 11701.

Summary

There is good reason to be concerned about pathological gambling in persons suffering from cocaine abuse. The key elements in recognition of this illness are special attention and sensitivity to the issue, organized screening for gambling problems, and a thorough gambling history. Treatment involves confronting gambling problems along with the patient's drug dependencies and aiming for abstinence from gambling with the help of Gamblers Anonymous. Involvement of the spouse and family are most important and should always be part of the overall treatment plan. With appropriate treatment, both relapse to drug use and resumption of pathological gambling can be avoided, allowing a satisfying and functional recovery.

REFERENCES

American Psychiatric Association. (1980). *Diagnostic and statistical manual of mental disorders* (3rd ed.). Washington, DC: Author.

American Psychiatric Association, Work Group to Revise DSM-III. (1985). *Draft diagnostic and statistical manual III-R.* Washington, DC: Author.

Blume, S. B. (1986a). Treatment for pathological gambling. In S. J. Levy & S. B. Blume (Eds.), *Addictions in the Jewish community* (pp. 371–379). New York: Federation of Jewish Philanthropies.

Blume, S. B. (1986b). Treatment for the addictions: Alcoholism, drug dependence and compulsive gambling in a psychiatric setting. *Journal of Substance Abuse Treatment 3*(2), 131–133.

Culleton, R., & Lang, M. (1985). *The prevalence rate of pathological gambling in the Delaware Valley in 1984.* Piscataway, NJ: Forum for Policy Research and Public Service, Rutgers University.

Custer, R., & Milt, H. (1985). *When luck runs out.* New York: Facts on File.

Gamblers Anonymous. (1984). *Sharing recovery through Gamblers Anonymous.* Los Angeles: Author.

Gaudia, R. (1986). Challenge of the compulsive gambling family. In S. J. Levy & S. B. Blume (Eds.), *Addictions in the Jewish community,* (pp. 361–368). New York: Federation of Jewish Philanthropies.

Glen, A. M. (1985). Diagnosing the pathological gambler. *Journal of Gambling Behavior, 1,* 17–22.

Heineman, M. (in press). A comparison: The treatment of wives of alcoholics with the treatment of wives of pathological gamblers. *Journal of Gambling Behavior, 3*(1).

Lesieur, H. R. (1984). *The chase.* Cambridge, MA: Schenkman.

Lesieur, H. R., Blume, S. B., & Zoppa, R. M. (1986). Alcoholism, drug abuse, and gambling. *Alcoholism: Clinical and Experimental Research, 10,* 33–38.

Lesieur, H. R., & Blume, S. B. (1986). *South Oaks Gambling Screen (the SOGS): New instrument for the identification of pathological gamblers.* Paper submitted for publication.

Orford, J. (1985). *Excessive appetites: A psychological view of addictions.* Chichester, England: John Wiley and Sons.

Ramirez, L. F., McCormick, R. A., Russo, A. M., & Taber, J. I. (1983). Patterns of substance abuse in pathological gamblers undergoing treatment. *Addictive Behaviors, 8,* 425–428.

Transition Planning Associates. (1985). *A survey of pathological gamblers in the state of Ohio.* Philadelphia: Author. (Available from Ohio Lottery Commission.)

17

Cocaine Abuse Detection by Laboratory Methods

Why should we test for cocaine use?

Cocaine has changed from an exclusive, elite drug to one many people can afford. It is widely available in high purity and at relatively low cost on the street. Even high school students and working-class adults can now afford the euphoric trip cocaine offers.

How does cocaine affect life-styles? Is there a true need to know who is using and who is not? Is it the business of the individual or of society to know? Does testing interfere with the privacy of the user? Is society placed in jeopardy by the drug-related actions of certain individuals? Who should know, why, and under what circumstances? How are the results to be used? These are just some of the questions asked by individual citizens who are employees in government, private industry, and the military.

One good reason for testing relates to the behavioral effects of cocaine. Most cocaine abusers thoroughly believe that their habit is under control and everything in their lives is "just fine." This idyllic perception could not be further from the truth; it exists only in the minds of the abusers. Outsiders and persons living around cocaine addicts know that not only are family ties broken, but business responsibilities and financial obligations are also forfeited. I often explain this dichotomy of truths (one in the mind of the addict, the other in the mind of observers) as a specific psychopharmacological effect of cocaine (Gold & Verebey, 1984). This delusion, in my opinion, is one of the most dangerous aspects of cocaine dependence.

The person who is hooked on cocaine loses a realistic attitude toward life. This becomes worse as he or she becomes more and more obsessed with the habit. Cocaine-induced delusion is combined with strong denial—complete denial of cocaine use to some relatives and co-workers, and denial that cocaine use is dangerous is expressed to those who actually see the individual use the drug. Thus, the first good reason for laboratory drug testing is to identify objectively individuals who are cocaine users.

Karl Verebey. New York State Division of Substance Abuse Services Testing and Research Laboratory, Brooklyn, New York; Department of Psychiatry, SUNY Health Science Center at Brooklyn, Brooklyn, New York.

214

Abusers may be at various stages of their dependence when identified. The earlier positive identification is made, the better the chances for successful rehabilitation. Family ties may not yet have been severed, employment not yet lost, and financial resources not yet totally exhausted. Thus, rebuilding an individual's life is facilitated by early detection. At later stages of addiction, the cocaine-driven, compulsive, irrational drive takes over all the decision-making functions of the individual.

Testing is of significant value when the cocaine user is seeking medical or psychiatric help but is hiding or denying involvement with cocaine. In this case, identification of cocaine use by testing is diagnostic. Many physical and psychiatric symptoms directly related to cocaine use are unknown to the treating physician unless he or she orders laboratory tests for the detection of drugs of abuse. Some of these cocaine-related symptoms surface in the offices of various specialists: physical symptoms at the gynecologist's or endocrinologist's office are libido, menstrual, and fertility disturbances; at the gastroenterologist's, anorexia, nausea, and vomiting; at the cardiologist's, hypertension, tachycardia, arrhythmia, and angina pectoris; and most commonly at the allergist's and ear, nose, and throat and respiratory specialist's, nasal sores, rhinitis, problems with swallowing, hoarseness, and problems of breathing. The psychiatrist sees incognito cocaine abusers for complaints of depression, mania and anxiety disorders, paranoia, and outright psychosis. With any of these symptom complaints, it behooves the physician to be suspicious and to test objectively for cocaine or other drug abuse. Thus, laboratory testing, by providing objective reports, focuses the treatment against the primary cause of the observed symptoms: cocaine abuse. In the absence of laboratory testing, the true source of the problem may remain hidden. Thus, laboratory testing by confirmation or exclusion of cocaine or other drug abuse saves time and money for the patient and increases the efficacy of treatment.

Laboratory testing is of great value as well once individuals are identified as cocaine abusers. Current strategies are intimately tied to regularly scheduled urine testing to monitor cocaine-dependent ex-addicts in treatment. Negative test results support and confirm the success of treatment, whereas positive results sound the alarm of possible relapse. Thus, objective monitoring of the patients' drug abuse by laboratory testing is a necessary component of treatment (Gold & Dackis, 1984).

Testing is often required for forensic purposes. Many health professionals such as doctors and nurses are afflicted with drug abuse problems. Often their licenses and professional certificates are in danger of suspension once their involvement with drug abuse is exposed. In many cases, rehabilitation of addicted medical professionals is tied to urine testing as a condition of probation. In fact, the addicted professionals in treatment may continue practicing as long as they submit to laboratory testing and the laboratory reports remain negative (see Chapter 12 by Crowley *et al.* for a fuller discussion of this problem.)

Drug abuse in general and cocaine abuse specifically are becoming so common that no one is above suspicion of using drugs regularly or occasionally for nonmedical reasons. Professional athletes often abuse cocaine or amphetamines. Their teams or respective national associations may prohibit psychoactive drug use, and staying drug free is often a condition that they must fulfill in order to be allowed to compete. Laboratory testing of body fluids for drugs of abuse is the objective technique used to enforce these rules.

Some cocaine users hold jobs such that they may endanger public safety and trust if they are intoxicated at work. Bankers and stockbrokers deal with their investors' money. To make rational decisions about investing their clients' money, these business professionals should not be under the influence of psychoactive drugs, especially a drug that causes delusion and impulsive risk-taking behavior. Similarly, cocaine use by other professionals may adversely affect the unsuspecting public. Cocaine addiction is not unheard of among doctors, nurses, airline pilots, bus drivers, and police officers. Feelings of omnipotence, aggressive behavior, and irrationality may be destructive to the public as well as to the drug-abusing individual.

Eradication of drug abuse from any profession can be facilitated by objective testing. Identification of drug abusers should be followed by systematic efforts of education and rehabilitation by such organizations as Employee Assistance Programs (EAP). Thus, laboratory testing is not only relevant for the detection and treatment of psychiatric and medical patients but also important in the identification of subjects whose job performance is affected by cocaine or other drug abuse. The widespread drug abuse problem in this country has influenced managers in private industry, government, and the military to start testing job applicants and, periodically, long-time members of their staff. They hope to keep the workplace free of drug abuse by virtue of testing, identification, and rehabilitation, with the expected results of increased productivity and attendance and significant reduction of accidents and theft.

What are the objections of those who oppose testing for drugs? One typical objection is fear of the potential misuse of positive laboratory reports in the workplace. Overzealous personnel managers may use positive results to destroy the future of employees instead of offering help and an opportunity for rehabilitation. In fact, such extreme policies have been adopted by the military after the discovery of large-scale drug abuse by military personnel.

Another objection is the violation of the right to privacy. Some drugs, such as marijuana and methaqualone, can be detected for many days and even weeks after a single exposure; yet the self-rated psychoactivity lasts only for a couple of hours. Even if the results of the laboratory drug tests are positive, it does not mean that the individuals were under the influence of drugs at the time of sample collection. Finally, some individuals attack the integrity and the accuracy of the tests themselves. These complaints are seldom justified, but the possibility of laboratory of administrative errors must always be kept in mind. Proper procedure and high-quality laboratory work is unfortunately not standard. One should not shop for laboratory services strictly on the basis of price, but should look for quality.

In this chapter important aspects of cocaine testing will be examined, on the basis of data available in the scientific literature. I hope to familiarize the reader with the types of tests that exist for cocaine abuse detection, what the results mean, sample collection procedures, and shopping for laboratory services, among other issues.

Cocaine Disposition

In order to understand laboratory testing related to cocaine detection, one must have a general idea about cocaine disposition in human subjects. Cocaine is administered most commonly by the intranasal route, called "snorting." Using this pathway, a dose of 10–100 mg cocaine is sniffed into the nasal sinuses. It is absorbed through the mucous membrane into the bloodstream and subsequently reaches its psychoactive site of action: the brain. Needle-loving addicts inject cocaine to get a quicker, more intense drug effect. However, free-base smoking became popular after cocaine users discovered a common pharmacological principle—that the free-base form of cocaine can reach the brain more quickly than the hydrochloride (salt) form. In fact, studies indicate that following intravenous (IV) administration and free-base smoking, bioavailability of cocaine was very similar in both time of action and blood concentrations (Perez-Reyes, Di Guiseppi, Ondrusek, Jeffcoat, & Cook, 1982). Oral administration of cocaine is not popular. It is slow in onset of action, and much of the active component breaks down before reaching the brain. Thus, the psychostimulant effects are greatly decreased when cocaine is taken orally (Wilkinson, Van Dyke, Jatlow, Barash, & Byck, 1980).

Following administration of cocaine by the intranasal, free-base or IV route, peak levels are reached in the blood in minutes, depending on the type of cocaine and the route of administration (Chow et al., 1985). The half-life of cocaine is approximately 1 hour (Wilkinson et al., 1980; Chow et al., 1985). In practical terms it means that it takes 1 hour for the body to excrete half of the drug in the blood. Cocaine's half-life value of 1 hour is very short compared to that for other drugs. Because the brief action is well known to cocaine users, frequent repeated administration, or "binging," is common, in an effort to repeat these euphoric but brief experiences. Because of the short half-life of cocaine, the time frame of cocaine abuse detection is also short, depending on the dose, frequency of use, and the sensitivity of the methods used.

Usually drugs are biotransformed in the liver to one or two major metabolites and several minor ones. The teleological reason for this process is "detoxification," that is, making compounds more water soluble for easier excretion into the urine. Most of the drug biotransformation processes occur in the liver by specific enzyme systems. Interestingly, cocaine's destructive enzyme is found in the blood as well as in the liver and some sources suggest that the major metabolite benzoylecgonine (BE) is formed spontaneously by a nonenzymatic mechanism (Ambre, Ruo, Smith, Backes, & Smith, 1982; Stewart, Inaba, Tang, & Kalow, 1977). This means that, as cocaine is transported through the blood, plasma esterases and spontaneous molecular changes constantly decrease the concentration of the active drug, cocaine, which is responsible for psychoactivity (Ambre *et al.*, 1982; Hamilton *et al.*, 1977). Also, while passing through the liver, cocaine is being biotransformed. Thus, it is understandable that, rather soon after its administration into the body, only low levels of cocaine are found in the blood or in the urine of cocaine abusers (Kogan, Verebey, DePace, Resnick, & Mulé, 1977).

The Metabolic Products of Cocaine

We need to know about cocaine's metabolites because they are the substances that can be readily identified by laboratory tests in urine samples for a much longer time than cocaine itself. Cocaine is rapidly and extensively metabolized to BE and ecgonine methyl ester (EME), as well as to many minor metabolites. The major metabolites, BE and EME, are practically inactive. In animal studies, norcocaine showed psychoactivity, but, because of its low concentration in human subjects, it probably contributes little to the pharmacological effects of cocaine. In human subjects, the urinary recovery of BE was 46% and of EME 41% of the cocaine dose (Ambre, 1985). The excretion of unchanged cocaine in urine is only about 10% of the dose, and plasma concentrations also fall rapidly after ingestion, to amounts detectable only by highly sophisticated analytical instruments. On the basis of these facts, screening for cocaine abuse is best achieved by urinalysis either for BE or EME, the two major metabolites of cocaine. A recent report indicates that EME is present in urine in large quantities during the first 12 hours after cocaine use. BE concentrations are also high, but this metabolite has a slower rate of excretion and therefore is detectable in the urine for longer than EME. Thus, most analytical methods test for BE (Ambre, Fischman, & Ruo, 1984).

Methods of Analysis, Sensitivity, and Cost

Cocaine abuse detection is most frequently performed by urinalysis for BE. Table 17-1 shows the various methods used, sensitivity limits, and ranges of cost per sample for the various chromatographic and immunologic methods. Thin-layer chromatography (TLC) screening is by far the most commonly used and inexpensive method among the chromatographic procedures. However, the TLC procedure for most drugs is not very sensitive. When using the TLC system, samples containing less than 1–2 μg/ml of BE are not detected. Thus, TLC screening misses many positive urines and is useful only for the detection of high-level cocaine abuse.

Among the immunoassays, enzyme-multiplied immunoassay (EMIT) is the most practical for mass screening. It is significantly more sensitive than TLC, no extraction of BE is required, and it is also a relatively inexpensive method. For these reasons EMIT is often used as a primary screening procedure, detecting moderate levels of cocaine abuse.

Gas–liquid chromatography (GLC) methodology is more sensitive, complicated and labor intensive than TLC and EMIT procedures. The cost is also higher. Methods developed in the 1960s and early 1970s, using flame ionization detectors, were less sensitive than the currently used capillary GLC systems combined with nitrogen detectors (Kogan et al., 1977; Wallace et al., 1976; Jatlow & Bailey, 1975). GLC methodology is mostly used for confirmation.

When confirmation of positive samples is required, this should be performed by a method for which the scientific principle differs from that of

TABLE 17-1. Benzoylecgonine Detection Methods, Sensitivity, and Cost

Chromatography	Specimen[a,b]	Sensitivity ranges[c] (ng/ml)	Cost/sample range ($)
TLC	U	1,000–2,000	2–10
GLC	U/B	10–300	20–40
HPLC	B	20–300	40–60
GC/MS	U/B	1–10	40–100
Immunologic			
EMIT	U	300–1,000	2–6
RIA	U/B	2–20	3–10

[a]U = urine.
[b]B = blood.
[c]The methods' sensitivity ranges are for all drugs, not necessarily for cocaine or benzoylecgonine.

the screening method. This means that a positive sample by an immunologic method (EMIT, radioimmunoassay [RIA]) must be confirmed by a chromatographic method (GLC, gas chromatography/mass spectometry [GC/MS]) and vice versa. This procedure is recommended to eliminate any possibility of technical errors, or of errors stemming from interfering materials or cross-reactivity. The immunologic assays are known to be less specific for a single molecule and may cross-react with molecules similar in structure to the desired substance. In the case of marijuana, the antibody interacts with many different cannabinoids present in the sample. This characteristic of immunoassays often makes them more sensitive than the chromatographic methods. On the other hand, the chromatographic assays are known to be more specific for a single molecular species, such as BE in the case of cocaine analysis. Thus, as a rule, the weaknesses are not shared by scientifically different (or alternate) methods.

The most respected analytical method is GC/MS. It is sensitive and extremely specific but is rather expensive (Graffeo, Lin, & Foltz). It is often referred to as the methodology that "fingerprints" molecules. By virtue of fragmentation pattern analysis, absolute molecular identification is possible. Since molecular bond strengths are different, when molecules are fragmented by force the breakage always occurs at weak bonds. The resulting fragments or fragmentation pattern is specific for one molecule only. Because of its high cost, GC/MS is used mostly for forensic testing. In drug screening, GC/MS identifies low-level cocaine abuse and confirms positive results obtained by other assays.

The choice of testing protocol is often tied to budgetary restrictions. In order to identify at least the moderate cocaine users by laboratory testing, EMIT or RIA should be used for screening and GLC or, ultimately, GC/MS for confirmation.

Correlation between Behavioral Effects and Concentration of Cocaine and BE

Quantitative measurement of cocaine in blood is often performed to indicate the level of intoxication of the individual or to determine the time of ingestion. Although such a correlation between concentration in blood and psychoactivity exists for alcohol, it is much weaker for cocaine and other psychoactive drugs. Nevertheless, when cocaine (C) levels are high and BE levels are low, the indication is that the cocaine was ingested recently (see Table 17-2, C/BE ratios versus time). The absolute values of concentration are greatly dependent on the dose, the route of administration, the individual metabolic rate, and the size of the subject. Thus, at best a single blood level of cocaine and BE may identify or estimate the time of use. Absolute concentrations usually do not relate to behavioral effects of cocaine; they

TABLE 17-2. Cocaine and Benzoylecgonine in Blood

Route of administration	Dose (mg)	Time of sample (hr)	C (ng/ml)	BE (ng/ml)	C/BE ratio
Chewing[a]	17–48	0.4–2.0	11–149		
Intranasal[a]	140	1.0	161		
Oral[a]	140	1.0	210		
Intravenous[a]	32	0.1	308		
Intranasal[a]	105	1.0	308		
Intranasal[a]	105	3.0	206		
Intravenous[b]	100	0.25	1,075	250	4.30
Intravenous[b]	100	1.0	500	760	0.66
Intravenous[b]	100	6.0	50	480	0.10
Intravenous[b]	100	24.0	—	125	

[a]Data from Baselt (1982).
[b]Data from Kogan, Verebey, DePace, Resnick, & Mulé (1977).

are scientific indicators rather than facts. It is true that data on expected blood levels are available at various points in time after known doses of cocaine are ingested, but the doses are seldom known in cocaine abusers, and individual differences in cocaine disposition further complicate the picture. A recent study of quantitative measurement of cocaine, BE, and EME in urine indicates that the time of cocaine ingestion may be estimated from the ratios BE/C and BE/EME (Ambre, 1985). This technique may provide the analytical toxicologist with a new technique to determine the time of cocaine ingestion from a single urine sample, in which C, BE, and EME are determined quantitatively.

Concentration of Cocaine and BE in Blood and Urine

Table 17-2 presents values of cocaine and BE in blood of subjects receiving various doses by different routes of administration. The table is presented to illustrate the ranges of blood levels observed at various times after cocaine administration. These values may be compared to the levels of method sensitivities shown in Table 17-1 for BE. For example, 24-hour BE blood level of 125 ng/ml could be detected only by the more sensitive GLC, GC/MS, and RIA procedures. TLC and EMIT are too insensitive for BE analysis in this case only 24 hours after a 100-mg IV cocaine injection.

The urine concentrations of C, BE, and EME are presented in Table 17-3. Two subjects received 96 mg of cocaine intranasally. The relatively high BE levels after 24–48 hours are misleading because the concentration was measured in a pooled urine sample between 24 and 48 hours

TABLE 17-3. Concentration of C, BE and EME in the Urine of 2 Subjects Dose 96 mg
Intranasally

Hours of collection	Subject	C	BE	EME	BZ/EME
0–8	A	1,900	45,000	36,200	1.25
	B	11,300	19,000	28,500	0.67
8–16	A	—	22,000	2,800	7.8
	B	—	19,000	18,100	1.04
16–24	A	—	15,000	1,500	10.0
	B	—	22,000	9,300	2.36
24–48	A	—	1,300	200	6.5
	B	—	3,000	100	30.0

Source: Data reproduced from the work of Ambre et al. (1984).
— = not detected.

(Ambre et al., 1984). A single urine collection at 48 hours is not expected to contain nearly as high levels of BE as the average value determination in the pooled sample. Nevertheless, the numbers are useful to compare measured concentration of BE and that of method sensitivities for BE detection in Table 17-1.

The Time Frame of Detection of Cocaine and BE

It is often asked how long cocaine can be detected after the last use. The answer depends on numerous variables: the dose, the chronicity of cocaine use, the size of the individual, and last but not least the sensitivity of the testing procedure.

Based on pharmacokinetic elimination principles, a general guide can be constructed. In Table 17-4 (A), three imaginary peak blood concentrations of C, BE, or any other substance are picked at 500, 1,000, and 10,000 ng/ml. Based on the half-life principle, the amount of substance remaining in the blood is one-half of the previous concentration following the passage of each half-life period. Therefore, in 6 half-lives, 98% of the peak concentration is eliminated from the blood. Thus, at 500-ng/ml, 1,000-ng/ml and 10,000-ng/ml peak blood levels, 8 ng/ml, 16 ng/ml, and 160 ng/ml remain in the blood, respectively. Using GC/MS and RIA at optimal sensitivities, these levels are still measurable. The samples having 500- and 1,000-ng/ml peaks rapidly approach the lower levels of sensitivity of both RIA and GC/MS (Graffeo et al., 1976; Mulé, Jukofsky, Kogan, DePace, & Verebey, 1977).

In Table 17-4 (B), the half-life values are shown for cocaine, BE, and EME. In order to have 98% elimination, each of the substances' half-life values is multiplied by 6. This gives the number of hours necessary for the

TABLE 17-4. A. The Half-Life Principle: Concentration of Chemical in Blood (ng/ml)

Peak concentration	Number of half-lives											
	1	2	3	4	5	6	7	8	9	10	11	12
500	250	125	63	31	16	8	4	2	1	.5	.2	.1
1,000	500	250	125	63	31	16	8	4	2	1	.5	.2
10,000	5,000	2,500	1,250	630	310	160	80	40	20	10	5	2

B. The Half-Life Values Related to Cocaine Disposition: Half-Life Values (hr)

	Cocaine	Benzoylecgonine	Ecgonine methylester
	1.0	7.5	3.6
98% elimination (or 6 × half-life)	6	45	21.6

completion of 98% elimination of the different substances. Cocaine, BE, and EME are 98% eliminated from the body in 6, 45, and 21.6 hours, respectively [Table 17-4 (B)]. It is clear that BE is detected for the longest time, 45 hours. The big question, however, is: What was the peak concentration? This is unknown in most cases. Looking at the example in Table 17-4, if the beginning level of BE or C was 1,000 ng/ml, after 9 half-lives the level will be 2 ng/ml—just barely measurable by RIA and GC/MS procedures. For BE, the calculations are 9×7.5 hr = 67.5 hr = 2.8 days. This means that the individual who has a peak level of BE at 1,000 ng/ml will be found positive for 2.8 days by the GC/MS and RIA methods if those methods are operated at optimal sensitivity of 1 ng/ml. The same sample will be called negative by all the other methods because they are not sensitive enough to detect 2 ng/ml, or their cutoff values for positives are higher than 2 ng/ml. Even though detection is possible at such low levels by RIA and GC/MS, it is common practice at all laboratories to raise the cutoff levels of screening and confirmation procedures significantly higher than 2 ng/ml. This is to avoid false positive results when working near the test's lower limit of sensitivity.

In reality, the rule of thumb is that by using the routine TLC for cocaine abuse screening, BE can be detected for 1–2 days, although one report claims 3–4 days (Hamilton *et al.*, 1977). EMIT at a 1,000-ng/ml cutoff value was reported to begin detecting positive levels of BE in urine within 1–4 hours of use. Peak urine levels of up to 10,000 ng/ml BE were reached in 10–12 hours, and the subjects remained positive for 18–27 hours (Van Dyke, Byck, Barash, & Jatlow, 1977). These subjects received a single intranasal dose of up to 130 mg cocaine HCl. The authors suggest that chronic users of larger doses of cocaine would be detected longer than 1 day by the EMIT (Van Dyke *et al.*, 1977). GLC with nitrogen detector and EMIT with 300-ng/ml cutoff may detect BE for 2–3 days, whereas RIA and GC/MS at optimal sensitivity may be successful for as long as 4–5 days. RIA has been reported to identify BE-positive urine samples for 6 days (Hamilton *et al.*, 1977). To identify cocaine abusers effectively, the most cost-effective and sensitive screening procedures are the RIA and the EMIT. TLC, however, which is constantly improving with increased sensitivity, due to the large volume column extraction systems, may return in the future to challenge the immunoassays for mass screening.

Choice of Body Fluid, Collection, and Specimen Handling

Which body fluid is best for the detection of cocaine abuse? If a qualitative answer—positive or negative—is desired, urinalysis is the answer. As a rule, urine has about 50–100 times more BE present in it than plasma does. This higher concentration in urine is an advantage for longer detection. If recent cocaine abuse is suspected, however, and if the aim is possibly to tie the concentration of cocaine to behavior, then the blood-level measurement of C and BE are suggested, along with quantitative urine levels of C, BE, and EME.

A word of caution is in order about the treatment of blood samples. Plasma enzymes (esterases) continue to metabolize cocaine even after the blood is taken from the subject (Stewart *et al.*, 1977). Blood samples should be collected into tubes containing sodium fluoride, which inactivates most of the enzyme activity. Because the inhibition is not 100%, plasma or serum must be separated quickly from the cells by centrifugation and stored in a freezer until analysis. Urine samples should also be refrigerated or frozen. A study indicates that within 20 hours at 37° C, as much as 80% of cocaine is decomposed in urine samples (Javaid, Dekirmenjian, Davis, & Schuster, 1978).

Another important issue concerns the circumstances of urine sample collection. Denial, which is an important component of cocaine dependence, may interfere with the legitimacy of sample collection. Cocaine addicts will do almost anything to keep their cocaine dependence a secret. This is why the collection of urine specimens must be supervised, to ensure that the person in question is the source of the sample and to guarantee the integrity of the specimen. When collection is not supervised, it is not unusual to receive someone else's urine sample or a highly diluted sample.

Samples that may lead to legal procedures require that the chain of evidence be maintained. This is important in the testing of samples where a person's rights and privileges and/or employment is at stake. With the increasing use of drug abuse testing programs in industry and government, safe procedures of proper specimen labeling and transportation are an important component of testing.

The Reliability of Testing: Interpretation of Test Results

The accuracy of test results, whether positive or negative, is often questioned. What is the likelihood of false negative or false positive results? By definition, a false negative report is a negative report on a sample that contains BE. This can occur for various reasons. One is that the sensitivity of the test used is not sufficient to detect the amount of the substance (BE) present in the sample. For economic reasons, TLC is often used for initial screening. The low TLC sensitivity of 1,000–2,000 ng/ml is not sufficient for the detection of BE in many urine samples of low-level cocaine abusers. Thus, if there is significant suspicion of cocaine use and if TLC was the method of analysis, a negative report is not absolutely reliable. Requesting a method with greater sensitivity eliminates this problem.

Other reasons for negative results on urine samples that should be positive include the dilution of the urine sample with water at the time of sample collection and/or careless laboratory procedures. To avoid these problems, sample collection must be supervised and the choice of laboratory services carefully and comparatively investigated. One should look not only for the supplementary services some laboratories offer such as computer printout and quick turnaround time but, most important, for high-quality laboratory performance. A reliable laboratory should have a good scientific reputation at the directorial, management, and technical levels. This assures that in difficult situations, decisions will be made by individuals who are considered experts on drug testing. A high-quality laboratory will also participate in quality control programs, and all of its technicians will be licensed by the appropriate health departments.

False positive results are those that report the presence of BE in urine samples that do not contain it. Such occurrences are very infrequent if a proficient, high-quality laboratory is used. As a rule, many more negative than positive samples are processed in all drug-testing laboratories. Technicians routinely repeat positive tests to ascertain that the original positive reading was correct. For samples that may have medicolegal implications, confirmation proceeds by a method having a scientifically different principle (an alternate method). Thus, positive reports are repeated at least twice, and in legal cases they are confirmed by an alternate method. This extra care with positive samples prevents laboratory-related error in reporting false positive results.

Cross-reactivity, especially with immunoassays, is always a possibility. Thus, if a cross-reacting substance is present in a sample, it would result in a false positive report. Yet, in reality, a study indicates that such threats of cross-reactivity for BE detection are minimal (Mulé et al., 1977). Alternate methods of confirmation of positive tests for BE by RIA or EMIT further eliminate false positive results caused by interfering substances.

Conclusion

Based on cocaine elimination kinetics in human subjects, the time frame for cocaine abuse detection is 2–3 days by EMIT and, at best, 5–6 days using RIA and GC/MS. In occasional cocaine users the level of BE may drop so low in 1–2 days that even the most sensitive RIA and GC/MS methods may not detect BE in the system. Therefore, the timing of sample collection is crucial. Samples should be obtained as close in time to the last cocaine use as possible. As a rule, urine has 50–100 times more BE than blood. Therefore, urinalysis for BE by a sensitive method is most promising for identification of cocaine abusers. Chronic, heavy cocaine use may be detected by urine analysis for 5–6 days by using RIA and/or GC/MC. In fact, this time frame is the longest detection reported in the literature for RIA (Hamilton *et al.*, 1977). Recommended for general screening of high-level cocaine abuse is TLC, confirmed by EMIT. This process is the cheapest but a large number of low-level cocaine abusers will be missed. Intermediate cocaine abuse is best identified by EMIT screening, with the positive samples confirmed by capillary GLC, using nitrogen detection. Low-level abuse may be best detected by RIA and GC/MS, which have the greatest sensitivity.

When forensic-level analysis is needed, GC/MS is the only procedure that provides absolute identification. Quantitative results of cocaine, BE, and EME in urine and blood may be helpful in estimating the time of ingestion. Quantitative information is obtained from GLC and GC/MS analysis of blood and/or urine samples.

Analytical methods for the detection and quantitation of cocaine and its metabolites are constantly improving. The laboratory procedures are reliable if they are performed by high-quality laboratories and if the positive results are confirmed by scientifically alternate methods.

ACKNOWLEDGMENT

The author wishes to thank Mildred Bowens for typing the manuscript.

REFERENCES

Ambre, J. (1985). The urinary excretion of cocaine and metabolites in humans: A kinetic analysis of published data. *Journal of Analytical Toxicology, 9*, 241–245.

Ambre, J., Fischman, M., & Ruo, T. I. (1984). Urinary excretion of ecgonine methyl ester, a major metabolite of cocaine in humans. *Journal of Analytical Toxicology, 8*, 23–25.

Ambre, J. J., Ruo, T. I., Smith, G. L., Backes, D., & Smith, C. M. (1982). Ecgonine methyl ester, a major metabolite of cocaine. *Journal of Analytical Toxicology, 6*, 26–29.

Baselt, R. C. (1982). *Disposition of toxic drugs and chemicals in man.* Davis, CA: Biomedical Publications.

Chow, M. J., Ambre, J. J., Ruo, T. I., Atkinson, A. J., Bowsher, D. J., & Fischman, M. W. (1985). Kinetics of cocaine distribution, elimination, and chronotropic effects. *Clinical Pharmacology and Therapeutics, 38*, 318–324.

Gold, M. S., & Dackis, C. A. (1984). New insights and treatments: Opiate withdrawal and cocaine addiction. *Clinical Therapeutics, 7*, 6–21.

Gold, M. S., & Verebey, K. (1984). The psychopharmacology of cocaine. *Psychiatric Annals, 14*, 714–723.

Graffeo, A. P., Lin, D. C. K., & Foltz, R. L. (1976). Analysis of benzoylecgonine in urine by high-performance liquid chromatography and gas chromatography–mass spectometry. *Journal of Chromatography, 126*, 717–722.

Hamilton, H. E., Wallace, J. E., Shimek, E. L., Land, P., Harris, S. C., & Christenson, J. G. (1977). Cocaine and benzoylecgonine excretion in humans. *Journal of Forensic Sciences, 22*, 697–707.

Jatlow, P. I., & Bailey, D. N. (1975). Gas chromatographic analysis for cocaine in human plasma with use of a nitrogen detector. *Clinical Chemistry, 21*, 1918–1921.

Javaid, M. I., Dekirmenjian, H., Davis, J. M., & Schuster, C. R. (1978). Determination of cocaine in human urine, plasma and red blood cells by gas–liquid chromatography. *Journal of Chromatography, 152*, 105–113.

Kogan, M. J., Verebey, K., DePace, A., Resnick, R. B., & Mulé, S. J. (1977). Quantitative determination of benzoylecgonine and cocaine in human biofluids by gas–liquid chromatography. *Analytical Chemistry*, *49*, 1965–1969.

Mulé, S. J., Jukofsky, D., Kogan, M., DePace, A., & Verebey, K. (1977). Evaluation of the radioimmunoassay for benzoylecgonine (a cocaine metabolite) in human urine. *Clinical Chemistry*, *23*, 796–801.

Perez-Reyes, M., Di Guiseppi, S., Ondrusek, G., Jeffcoat, A. R., & Cook, C. E. (1982). Free-base cocaine smoking. *Clinical Pharmacology and Therapeutics, 32*, 459–465.

Stewart, D. J., Inaba, T., Tang, B. K., & Kalow, W. (1977). Hydrolysis of cocaine in human plasma by cholinesterase. *Life Sciences*, *20*, 1557–1564.

Van Dyke, C., Byck, R., & Barash, P. G., & Jatlow, P. (1977). Urinary excretion of immunologically reactive metabolites(s) after intranasal administration of cocaine, as followed by enzyme immunoassay. *Clinical Chemistry*, *23*, 241–244.

Wallace, J. E., Hamilton, H. E., Christenson, J. G., Shimek, E. L., Land, P., & Harris, S. C. (1977). An evaluation of selected methods for determining cocaine and benzoylecgonine in urine. *Journal of Analytical Toxicology*, *1*, 20–25.

Wallace, J. E., Hamilton, H. E., King, D. E., Bason, D. J., Schwertner, H. A., & Harris, S. C. (1976). Gas–liquid chromatographic determination of cocaine and benzoylecgonine in urine. *Analytical Chemistry, 48,* 34–38.

Wilkinson, P., Van Dyke, C., Jatlow, P., Barash, P., & Byck, R. (1980). Intranasal and oral cocaine kinetics. *Clinical Pharmacology and Therapeutics*, *27*, 386–394.

18

Psychiatric and Psychodynamic Factors in Cocaine Dependence

E. J. KHANTZIAN

The powerful effects of cocaine on mood and behavior are by now well known. Early accounts dating back to Freud (1984/1884), and more recently by others (Khantzian & McKenna, 1979; Siegel, 1977), indicate that, in the short term, cocaine significantly elevates mood, energizes, empowers, and reduces appetite; its negative effects include restlessness, anxiety, excitability, irritability, impulsivity, and paranoia, as well as tactile, visual, and auditory hallucinations. It should not be surprising or unreasonable to expect that some of these effects could interact with preexisting psychopathology to make cocaine compelling, or that these same effects might cause or worsen psychopathology. It is frequently debated, and unfortunately often hotly contested, whether, in general, psychopathology causes a reliance on the effects of addictive drugs, or whether these effects cause psychopathology. There is evidence to support both possibilities, and it is likely that this will prove to be the case for cocaine as well.

In this chapter I will review the evidence suggesting that individuals are susceptible to cocaine dependence as a consequence of psychiatric disorders and other psychodynamic factors related to disturbances in affect regulation, self-esteem maintenance, self–other relations and self-care.

Considering psychiatric/diagnostic findings together with psychodynamic observations has an advantage over either approach alone. The former allows the objective identification of target symptoms and psychopathology at a point in time; the latter permits, over time, an examination and understanding of those psychological structures and functions responsible for psychological homeostasis. Failures and deficits in these structures and functions account for point-in-time symptomatic and diagnostic findings (Khantzian, 1981).

E. J. Khantzian. Department of Psychiatry, Harvard Medical School at The Cambridge Hospital, Cambridge, Massachusetts.

Recent Findings in Addicts: General

With a few important exceptions, until 25 years ago most reports on psychopathology in addicts were based on studies of confined addicts in the U.S. federal prison/hospital system, using test instruments that documented psychological traits and profiles. With the work of Chein, Gerard, Lee, and Rosenfeld (1964), however, and the subsequent expanding use of drugs in our society through the 1960s and 1970s, clinicians and investigators became increasingly involved in evaluating and treating many addicted individuals in the communities and settings in which their problems developed. The growing concerns of the "heroin epidemic" of the early 1970s resulted in an infusion of large amounts of federal funds into the treatment of narcotic addicts. Consequently, considerably more attention has been devoted to narcotic addicts than to any other group of substance-dependent individuals, and this section describing psychodynamic and psychiatric findings in general among addicts reflects this emphasis on narcotic addiction except where specified differently. I am of the opinion that the experience gained from the study and treatment of these addicts is relevant to our understanding of cocaine addicts, and we can benefit from them as we consider and treat their difficulties.

Psychodynamic Observations

A principal focus of contemporary psychoanalytic observers has been on addicts' impairments in regulating affect. Whereas early psychoanalytic formulations placed heavy emphasis on pleasurable and aggressive drives and a topographical view of the mind (i.e., conscious versus unconscious—in this case the meaning of drug/alcohol use and associated practices), more recent formulations have attempted to examine and understand better how addicts experience, modulate, and express their emotions. Kohut (1971) and Kernberg (1975) have alluded to problems of affect tolerance in addicts, implicating narcissistic and borderline personality disorders. Although there is a valid basis to consider that these personality disorders contribute to addictive disorders, others have proposed that disturbances in affect are a dimension of all severe psychopathology, and that a more precise identification of the affect disturbances in addicts is the essential determinant to be appreciated in drug dependence.

The nature of disturbance in affect management and tolerance in addicts is complex. Krystal (1982) and Krystal and Raskin (1970) have emphasized developmental impairments around affects such that addicts are unable to differentiate within themselves various feeling states (e.g., anxiety versus depression), that they somatize emotion, and that they are unable to verbalize their feelings. The term *alexithymia*, meaning "no words for feelings," originally coined by Sifneos (Sifneos, Apfel-Savitz, & Frankl, 1977) to describe psychosomatic patients, has been adopted by Krystal (1982) to highlight this problem in addicts. More recently such patients have been referred to as "dis-affected" by McDougall (1984) to underscore their problems with an absence of and dysfunction around feelings.

Beyond having confusing feelings or none at all, addicts also experience their affects as very threatening and overwhelming. Usually as a function of traumatic neglect or abuse in earlier phases of development, addicts often dread that any dose of feeling may become totally disorganizing, unmanageable, or deadly. Krystal's (1982) emphasis on problems with affect tolerance, Wurmser's (1974) observations of addicts' "defect in affect defense," and Khantzian's (1982) emphasis on narcotic addicts' major difficulties in managing violence and aggression, have in common an appreciation of addicts' inability to contain and cope with intense emotion.

In my own clinical work with addicts, I have been impressed with how uneven and deficient they have been with respect to their dependency, need satisfaction, and self-care. Although much has been written about addicts' dependent personalities—that they are "oral," weak, and clinging—it is impressive to see how much their problems arise from their defensiveness about dependency and their related inability to indulge in more ordinary human ways their needs for comfort, satisfaction, and safety. Balint (1968) has referred to such patients as suffering from a "basic fault," Kohut (1971) has referred to their "defect in . . . psychological structure"; and Krystal (1977) has proposed a deficiency in "self-soothing" capacities as part of the core vulnerabilities of addicts. These deficits are the basis for their extreme patterns of demand and entitlement which alternate with postures of self-sufficiency and disavowal. These vulnerabilities play themselves out in addicts' self-defeating and destructive attitudes and behaviors toward self and others, so that drugs become a way of removing associated distress or of permitting otherwise unobtainable needs and wants (Khantzian, 1982).

Although addicts' self-defeating and self-destructive behaviors are governed or driven to a great extent by their conflicts and impairments concerning dependency needs and other factors, I have also observed that many of the dangerous and life-threatening aspects of addictive involvement are more the result of impairments and failures in ego development that impedes the addict's self-protective and survival functions. Such capacities must be acquired in the early phases of development as a result of parental caring and protectiveness. We (Khantzian, 1978; Khantzian & Mack, 1983) have referred to these functions as "the capacity for self-care," meaning those structures and processes that serve to protect against or to anticipate harm and danger. Because addicts are impaired in this respect, they consistently fail to show worry, caution, or fear with respect to dangerous situations in general, and the dangers of drug use in particular (Khantzian, 1978, 1982).

Self-medication with addictive drugs has been implicated as a major motive for compulsive drug use. The self-medication hypothesis derives from the previously mentioned disturbances that addicts experience with respect to painful or threatening affect. The works of Chein, Gerard, Lee, and Rosenfeld (1964) and related reports by Gerard and Kornetsky (1954, 1955) were among the first to reflect this appreciation of the central role of the psychotropic effects of addictive drugs. They emphasized addicts' ego, superego, and narcissistic pathology, and pointed out that narcotics were used adaptively to cope with overwhelming anxiety in adolescence. Subsequently, on the basis of a more contemporary psychoanalytic perspective of development and ego psychology, Weider and Kaplan (1969) proposed that a "drug-of-choice" could be adopted or used as a "corrective" and a "prosthetic" to regressively avoid intense and painful affects in adolescence; and Milkman and Frosch (1973) were able to demonstrate empirically that individuals preferred or selected different drugs (i.e., amphetamines versus narcotics) on the basis of their defensive style and personality organization. Wurmser (1972, 1974) and Khantzian (1972, 1974) stressed that opiates were used progressively to counter painful affects and drives associated with shame, loneliness, rage, and aggression. In my own work I have emphasized the disorganizing and depressive influences of rage on the ego, and both Wurmser and I have proposed that the pharmacologic effects of opiates could substitute for defective or nonexistent defenses and thereby reverse painful and regressed states. In the subsequent section on diagnostic studies, we will review further how these psychotropic effects of narcotics probably interact with related documentable coexisting psychiatric disturbances and painful affects to make self-medication a compelling motive for reliance on addictive drugs.

Diagnostic and Treatment Studies

Partly on the basis of psychodynamic observations of addicts, and partly as a consequence of the development of standardized psychiatric diagnostic instruments, a number of studies have been undertaken over the past decade that document the coexistence of psychopathology in addicts. In addition to these diagnostic studies, however, a small but significant number of carefully executed studies have also appeared indicating that when target symptoms and psychopathology are identified in addicts, and are treated with the appropriate modality, the resulting symptom reduction is accompanied by a corresponding reduction in or even elimination of reliance on the addictive drug.

In several psychopharmacologic studies, target symptoms of phobia, anxiety, and depression in samples of alcohol- and/or drug-dependent individuals treated with tricyclic antidepressants responded favorably with significant improvement of subjects' addictive behavior. Quitkin, Rifkin, Kaplan, and Klein (1972) identified a small but significant proportion of alcoholics and sedative hypnotic abusers who suffer with panic disorder; they treated these subjects with imipramine, with significant symptomatic improvement and elimination of their drug–alcohol dependence. Overall, Brown, Williams, and Neill (1973) compared the efficacy of a phenothiazine, a tricyclic antidepressant, and a benzodiazepine in the treatment of anxiety–depression in a group of alcoholics. Although the patients reported a mild type of anxious depression usually responsive to benzodiazepines, the antidepressant (amitriptyline) and phenothiazine proved more effective, and the authors concluded that these alcoholics more closely resembled endogenous-type depressives in their responsiveness. Woody, O'Brien, and Rickels (1975) treated with doxepin a consecutive series of narcotic addicts who manifested an anxious depression. Both the anxiety and the depression improved, and there was a significant modification in misuse or abuse of drugs and an overall improvement in their adaptation.

A series of reports over the past decade, studying large samples of narcotic addicts in a variety of settings, using standardized diagnostic approaches, documented a high incidence of depression (30–50%), alcoholism, and personality disorder including but not limited to antisocial personality disorder (Dorus & Senay, 1980; Khantzian & Treece, 1985; Rounsaville, Weissman, Crits-Cristoph, Wilber, & Kleber, 1982; Rounsaville, Weissman, Kleber, & Wilber, 1982; Weissman, Slobetz, Prusoff, Mezritz, & Howard, 1976). In a number of these reports, the authors concluded that their findings were consistent with psychodynamic observations indicating that addicts used opiates in an attempt to self-treat unbearable feelings of dysphoria. In our own study (Khantzian & Treece, 1985) we explored the relationship between the disturbing behavior of addicts reflected in their perosnality diagnosis and the painful feeling states with which they suffer as reflected in the diagnosis of depression. In a recent report I have expanded on the self-medication hypothesis of addiction and have reviewed several other studies documenting that types and degree of psychopathology can be identified in narcotic addicts (Blatt et al., 1984; Nicholson & Treece, 1981; Treece & Nicholson, 1980; Verebey, 1982) and that, on the basis of these findings, they respond differentially to psychopharmacologic and psychotherapeutic treatments (Treece & Nicholson, 1980; Woody et al., 1983).

Cocaine Dependence

With some important exceptions, until recently there have been surprisingly few clinical descriptions or diagnostic studies of cocaine addicts. Without justification, cocaine has tended to be classified as nonaddictive, a trendy drug for the affluent and the famous (especially performing artists), and a "safe" drug with few or no dangerous side effects. As a consequence, cocaine users and addicts received little clinical or investigative attention until the 1980s, when cocaine use and the devastating consequences of its misuse spread and became evident through all sectors of our society, especially among celebrities and the rich. Notwithstanding these trends, over the past two decades a number of psychoanalytically oriented clinicians and investigators have elaborated on the psychological appeal of and predisposition toward stimulants and, more specifically, on cocaine dependence. Most recently, a few diagnostic and treatment reports have begun to appear documenting the coexistence of psychopathology in cocaine addicts, and the observation that they also may respond favorably to psychopharmacologic treatment.

In my own clinical work with cocaine addicts, I have been impressed that they share with other categories of drug/alcohol–dependent individuals some of the same vulnerabilities that generally predispose individuals to become addicted. That is, they are impaired in their capacity to recognize and regulate their emotions, they suffer with significant problems of self-esteem, they experience major difficulties in their relationships, and they can be very erratic and deficient in matters of self-care. They also suffer with coexistent psychiatric disturbances and related painful affect states. It is my impression that some of these painful affects and related behavior are especially unique to cocaine addicts and these states interact specifically with the psychotropic effects of cocaine to make them powerfully compelling.

Psychodynamic Observations

A number of psychoanalytic reports and studies have speculated on the appeal of stimulants. Weider and Kaplan (1969), in their work with adolescent drug users, observed that stimulants, including cocaine, produced increased feelings of assertiveness, self-esteem, and frustration tolerance. They proposed that the associated motoric restlessness contributed to an illusion of activity that subserved denial of passivity. Spotts and Shontz (1977), in their extensive study of 9 cocaine addicts, concluded that many of their findings were consistent with the formulations of Weider and Kaplan.

Wurmser (1974) commenting in general on stimulant abusers, emphasized that they used the effects of these drugs to eliminate feelings of boredom and emptiness by providing a sense of mastery, control, invincibility, and grandeur; he elaborated further that the drug effect served as a defense against depression and/or feelings of unworthiness and weakness. Along similar lines, Milkman and Frosch (1973) concluded that amphetamine addicts used the effects of stimulants to support an inflated sense of self-worth and a defensive style which allowed an active confrontation of their environment.

In my own work with cocaine addicts, I originally emphasized that the energizing properties of stimulants were compelling because they helped addicts to overcome fatigue and depletion states associated with depression (Khantzian, 1975). More recently (Khantzian, 1985; Khantzian & Khantzian, 1984), expanding on these observations, I further suggested that the energizing and activating property of cocaine helped chronically depressed (often subclinical and/or atypical) individuals overcome their anergia, complete tasks, and relate better to others, thus experiencing a temporary lift in their self-esteem. Along somewhat different lines, in another report (Khantzian, 1979) I indicated that certain individuals used cocaine to "*augment* a hyperactive, restless lifestyle and an exaggerated need for self-sufficiency" (p. 100, emphasis added).

Although most of these psychodynamic descriptions complement each other, no single effect of cocaine described in these reports adequately explains its appeal. It is probably some combination of cocaine's psychotropic effects on painful affect *states* (usually depression) and personality traits that interact to make the drug so seductive.

Diagnostic and Treatment Studies

As already indicated, until recently most of the clinical formulations about and descriptions of cocaine addicts were based on observations of individual cases. Only since about 1983 has there been any indication in the psychiatric literature that cocaine addicts' dependency on their drug might be related to psychopathology. Over this time two diagnostic studies using the *Diagnostic and Statistical Manual of Mental Disorders*, 3rd edition (DSM-III) (American Psychiatric Association, 1980) and several pilot studies using pharmacologic treatments have appeared that suggest that chronic cocaine dependence might be related to or a consequence of coexistent psychopathology.

Weiss and Mirin (1984) reported DSM-III diagnostic findings of 30 hospitalized cocaine-dependent individuals. Fifty-three percent of the subjects were diagnosed to be suffering with an affective disorder. Major depression was the most common diagnosis, but they also found a significant subgroup of cocaine abusers with bipolar and cyclothymic disorders who used cocaine to self-medicate their recurrent depressions as well as to enhance their hypomania during manic episodes. Significantly, in their report they also observed that 90% of the patients they studied had a DSM-III, Axis II personality diagnosis, with narcissistic and borderline personality disorders being the most frequent, and a very low frequency of antisocial personality disorder (i.e., only 1 of the 30 subjects). In their report they observed that their subjects perceived cocaine to be useful in regulating both dysphoric and elated moods. Moderate doses relieved symptoms of depression, but increasing doses were necessary to avoid postcocaine depression. The bipolar and cyclothymic patients used the cocaine to enhance their high moods in the manic phase of their illness.

Gawin and Kleber (1984) and Kleber and Gawin (1984) reported a similar rate of 50% incidence of affective disorders, DSM-III, Axis I findings, on 17 outpatient cocaine abusers. In their study, major depression, dysthymic disorder, and atypical disorder accounted for 30% of the cases, and bipolar disorder (including cyclothymic disorder) for the other 20%. Both Weiss and Mirin and Kleber and Gawin identified a small but important subgroup of patients with Attention Deficit Disorder—Residual Type (ADD) in their studies.

Gawin and Kleber (1984) conducted an open-ended clinical trial of desipramine or lithium on 16 of the 17 outpatient cocaine addicts described in the preceding paragraph. Although only 3 of the 6 cocaine addicts treated with desipramine were diagnosed as depressed, all 6 responded to the treatment with decreased craving and ultimately stopped cocaine use. The pattern of decreased craving in both groups corresponded to the usual 3–4 week response period for tricyclics in general. They also observed that the one feature all 6 patients shared in common was anhedonia, probably cocaine induced, which also lifted over the several weeks of treatment. Of the 6 patients treated with lithium, only the 3 diagnosed as cyclothymic responded to this treatment. They remained cocaine free for more than 3 months, and their cessation of cocaine use was immediate with commencement of treatment. The remaining subjects treated with lithium and those treated with psychotherapy alone continued to use cocaine. Given the small sample involved, Gawin and Kleber urge caution in overgeneralizing from their study; but their preliminary encouraging findings warrant further study and suggest that, for at least some cocaine addicts, a self-treatment motive might be involved.

Both the Weiss and Mirin (1984) and the Gawin and Kleber (1984) studies indicate that a small but significant subgroup of cocaine addicts suffer with ADD. Although only a small percentage (probably no more than 5%) of cocaine addicts suffer with ADD, the existing literature linking ADD to substance abuse and reports of treatment responsiveness to prescribed psychostimulants bears on the general issue of psychopathology in addicts, and specifically on a self-medication motive for cocaine dependence. Tarter, McBride, Buonpane, and Schneider (1977) identified a subgroup of severe alcoholics whose onset of alcoholism occurred at an earlier age and progressed very rapidly, who were diagnosed to be suffering with ADD from childhood. Wender and his associates (Wender, 1979; Wender, Reimherr, & Wood, 1981; Wood, Reimherr, Wender, & Johnson, 1976; Wood, Wender, & Reimherr, 1983), who have written extensively on ADD in adults, have underscored a strong association with alcoholism and drug abuse. In a case study reported by Turnquist, Frances, Rosenfeld, and Mobarak (1983), ADD was diagnosed in a severe, chronic 35-year-old man who had failed to respond to previous treatment interventions. Treatment with pemoline resulted in marked reduction of his restlessness, distractibility, and emotional outbursts, and resulted in a significantly improved response to alcoholism treatment and aftercare.

Three recent case reports lend further support to the observation that ADD may be an underlying motive for cocaine dependence. In 1983 I reported on an extreme case of cocaine dependence in a 33-year-old woman who showed marked improvement with methylphenidate treatment (Khantzian, 1983). Reconstruction of her childhood and adolescent history with the patient and her mother revealed symptoms consistent with ADD, and it was on this basis that she was treated with the methylphenidate. In a subsequent preliminary report (Khantzian, Gawin, Kleber, & Riordan, 1984), we reported further results and follow-up on the first case and two other cases successfully treated with methylphenidate. We concluded from these cases that cocaine addiction might be the cause or consequence of psychopathology and that in all three of the reported cases the cocaine dependence was preceded by major symptoms of ADD in childhood and adolescence. Most recently, Weiss, Pope, and Mirin (1985) reported on two additional cases of cocaine abusers also suffering with ADD, who showed marked improvement with magnesium pemolate treatment and a significant sustained reduction of cocaine abuse. These reports provide further evidence for a self-medication motive for drug dependence and a basis to suggest that some cocaine addicts treat themselves for ADD.

Comments and Conclusion

In this chapter I have reviewed evidence indicating that individuals might be predisposed to addiction as a consequence of preexistent psychopathology. I have described the general vulnerabilities and types of psychiatric disorders associated with narcotic addiction and other substance abuse; and I have tried to elaborate on the specific types of distress, dysfunction, and psychiatric disorder in cocaine addicts that seem to cause reliance on stimulants.

There is also a basis for emphasizing that a psychodynamic appreciation of how cocaine addicts experience and regulate their feelings, self-esteem, relationships, and behavior, plus an appreciation of overall personality factors, provides valuable clues to and understanding of how or why an individual might be susceptible to cocaine dependence, even in the absence of documentable psychiatric disorder.

The existing clinical descriptions and diagnostic studies have implicated several diagnostic possibilities that might predispose individuals to cocaine addiction. They include: (1) preexistent chronic depression, (2) cocaine abstinence depression, (3) hyperactive restless syndrome or attention deficit disorder, and (4) cyclothymic or bipolar illness. We need further, larger representative studies of cocaine addicts in order to substantiate these and other possibilities (Khantzian, 1985; Khantzian & Khantzian, 1984).

I have not addressed in this chapter the question of whether all cocaine addicts suffer with preexisting psychopathology, or whether anyone is susceptible to cocaine addiction. These questions are important, but informed answers will not be forthcoming until we have extensively studied and understood many more cocaine addicts and have better clarified the effects and mechanisms of action of cocaine at the neuronal and biochemical level.

REFERENCES

American Psychiatric Association. (1980). *Diagnostic and statistical manual of mental disorders* (3rd ed.). Washington, DC: Author.

Balint, M. (1968). *The basic fault.* London: Tavistock Publications.

Blatt, S. J., Berman, W., Bloom-Feshback, S., Sugarman, A., Wilber, C., & Kleber, H. (1984). Psychological assessment of psychopathology in opiate addicts. *Journal of Nervous and Mental Disease, 172,* 156–165.

Chein, I., Gerard, D. L., Lee, R. S., & Rosenfeld, E. (1964). *The road to H.* New York: Basic Books.

Dorus, W., & Senay, E. (1980). Depression, demographic dimension and drug abuse. *American Journal of Psychiatry, 137,* 699–704.

Freud, S. (1984). Uber Coca (1884). *Journal of Substance Abuse Treatment, 1,* 205–217.

Gawin, F. H., & Kleber, H. D. (1984). Cocaine abuse treatment. *Archives of General Psychiatry, 41,* 903–908.

Gerard, D. L., & Kornetsky, D. (1954). Adolescent opiate addiction: A case study. *Psychiatric Quarterly, 28,* 367–380.

Gerard, D. L., & Kornetsky, C. (1955). Adolescent opiate addiction: A study of control and addict subjects. *Psychiatric Quarterly, 29,* 457–486.

Kernberg, O. F. (1975). *Borderline conditions and pathological narcissism.* New York: J. Aronson.

Khantzian, E. J. (1972). A preliminary dynamic formulation of the psychopharmacologic action of methadone. *Proceedings of the Fourth National Methadone Conference,* San Francisco.

Khantzian, E. J. (1974). Opiate addiction: A critique or theory and some implications for treatment. *American Journal of Psychiatry, 28,* 59–70.

Khantzian, E. J. (1975). Self selection and progression in drug dependence. *Psychiatry Digest, 10,* 19–22.

Khantzian, E. J. (1978). The ego, the self and opiate addiction: Theoretical and treatment considerations. *International Review of Psychoanalysis, 5,* 189–198. Also in *Psycho-*

dynamics of drug dependence, NIDA Research Monograph No. 12, Rockville, MD, 1977, pp. 101–107.

Khantzian, E. J. (1979). Impulse problems in addiction: Cause and effect relationships. In H. Wishnie (Ed.), *Working with the impulsive person* (pp. 97–112). New York: Plenum Press.

Khantzian, E. J. (1981). Some treatment implications of the ego and self disturbances in alcoholism. In M. H. Bean & N. E. Zinberg (Eds.), *Dynamic approaches to the understanding and treatment of alcoholism* (pp. 163–188). New York: Free Press, Macmillan.

Khantzian, E. J. (1982). Psychological (structural) vulnerabilities and the specific appeal of narcotics. *Annals of the New York Academy of Science, 398,* 24–32.

Khantzian, E. J. (1983). An extreme case of cocaine dependence and marked improvement with methylphenidate treatment. *American Journal of Psychiatry, 140*(6), 784–785.

Khantzian, E. J. (1985). The self-medication hypothesis of addictive disorders. *American Journal of Psychiatry, 142,* 1259–1264.

Khantzian, E. J., Gawin, F., Kleber, H. D., & Riordan, C. E. (1984). Methylphenidate treatment of cocaine dependence—A preliminary report. *Journal of Substance Abuse Treatment, 1,* 107–112.

Khantzian, E. J., & Khantzian, N. J. (1984). Cocaine addiction: Is there a psychological predisposition? *Psychiatric Annals, 14*(10), 753–759.

Khantzian, E. J., & Mack, J. E. (1983). Self-preservation and the care of the self—Ego instincts reconsidered. *Psychoanalytic Study of the Child, 38,* 209–232.

Khantzian, E. J., & McKenna, G. J. (1979). Acute toxic and withdrawal reactions associated with drug use and abuse. *Annals of Internal Medicine, 90,* 361–372.

Khantzian, E. J., & Treece, C. (1985). DSM-III psychiatric diagnosis of narcotic addicts: Recent findings. *Archives of General Psychiatry, 42:*1067–1071.

Kleber, H. D., & Gawin, F. H. (1984). Cocaine abuse: A review of current and experimental treatments. In J. Grabowski (Ed.), *Cocaine: Pharmacology effects and treatment of abuse* (pp. 111–129). Rockville, MD: National Institute on Drug Abuse.

Kohut, H. (1971). *The analysis of the self.* New York: International Universities Press.

Krystal, H. (1977). Self-representation and the capacity for self care. *The Annual of Psychoanalysis, 6,* 209–246.

Krystal, H. (1982). Alexithymia and the effectiveness of psychoanalytic treatment. *International Journal of Psychoanalytic Psychotherapy, 9,* 353–378.

Krystal, H., & Raskin, H. A. (1970). *Drug dependence: Aspects of ego functions.* Detroit: Wayne State University Press.

McDougall, J. (1984). The "dis-affected" patient: Reflections on affect pathology. *Psychoanalytic Quarterly, 53,* 386–409.

Milkman, H., & Frosch, W. A. (1973). On the preferential abuse of heroin and amphetamine. *Journal of Nervous and Mental Diseases, 156,* 242–248.

Nicholson, B., & Treece, C. (1981). Object relations and differential treatment response to methadone maintenance. *Journal of Nervous and Mental Diseases, 169,* 424–429.

Overall, J. E., Brown, D., Williams, J. D., & Neill, L. (1973). Drug treatment of anxiety and depression in detoxified alcoholic patients. *Archives of General Psychiatry, 29,* 218–221.

Quitkin, F. M., Rifkin, A., Kaplan, J., & Klein, D. F. (1972). Phobic anxiety syndrome complicated by drug dependence and addiction. *Archives of General Psychiatry, 27,* 159.

Rounsaville, B. J., Weissman, M. M., Crits-Cristoph, K., Wilber, C., & Kleber, H. (1982). Diagnosis and symptoms of depression in opiate addicts: Course and relationship to treatment outcome. *Archives of General Psychiatry, 39,* 151–156.

Rounsaville, B. J., Weissman, M. M., Kleber, H., & Wilber, C. (1982). Heterogeneity of psychiatric diagnosis in treated opiate addicts. *Archives of General Psychiatry, 39,* 161–166.

Siegel, R. K. (1977). Cocaine: Recreational use and intoxication. In R. C. Peterson & R. C. Stillman (Eds.), *Cocaine* (pp. 119–136). Washington, DC: U.S. Government Printing Office.

Sifneos, P., Apfel-Savitz, R., & Frankl, F. (1977). The phenomenon of "alexithymia." *Psychotherapy Psychosomatics, 28,* 47–57.

Spotts, J. V., & Shontz, F. C. (1977). *The life styles of nine American cocaine users.* Washington, DC: U.S. Government Printing Office.

Tarter, R. E., McBride, H., Buonpane, N., & Schneider, D. U. (1977). Differentiation of alcoholics. *Archives of General Psychiatry, 34,* 761–776.

Treece, C., & Nicholson, B. (1980). DSM-III personality type and dose levels in methadone maintenance patients. *Journal of Nervous and Mental Diseases, 168,* 621–628.

Turnquist, K., Frances, R., Rosenfeld, W., & Mobarak, A. (1983). Pemoline in attention deficit disorder and alcoholism: a case study. *American Journal of Psychiatry, 140,* 622–624.

Vereby, K. (Ed.). (1982). *Opioids in mental illness: Theories, clinical observations, and treatment possibilities.* New York: Annals of the New York Academy of Sciences, Vol. 398.

Weider, H., & Kaplan, E. (1969). Drug use in adolescents. *Psychoanalytic Study of the Child, 24,* 399–431.

Weiss, R. D., & Mirin, S. M. (1984). Drug, host and environmental factors in the development of chronic cocaine abuse. In S. M. Mirin (Ed.) *Substance abuse and psychotherapy* (pp. 42–55). Washington, DC: American Psychiatric Association Press.

Weiss, R. D., Pope, H. G., & Mirin, S. M. (1985). Treatment of chronic cocaine abuse and attention deficit disorder, residual type with magnesium pemoline. *Drug and Alcohol Dependence, 15,* 69–72.

Weissman, M. M., Slobetz, F., Prusoff, B., Mezritz, M., & Howard, P. (1976). Clinical depression among narcotic addicts maintained on methadone in the community. *American Journal of Psychiatry, 133,* 1434–1438.

Wender, P. H. (1979). The concept of minimal brain dysfunction (MBD). In L. Bellak (Ed.), *Psychiatric aspects of minimal brain dysfunction in adults* (pp. 1–13). New York: Grune and Stratton.

Wender, P. H., Reimherr, F. W., & Wood, D. R. (1981). Attention deficit in adults. *Archives of General Psychiatry, 38,* 449–456.

Wood, D. R., Reimherr, F. W., Wender, P. H., & Johnson, G. E. (1976). Diagnosis and treatment of minimal brain dysfunction in adults. *Archives of General Psychiatry, 33,* 1453–1460.

Wood, D. R., Wender, P. H., & Reimherr, F. W. (1983). The prevalence of attention deficit disorder, residual type or minimal brain dysfunction in a population of male alcoholic patients. *American Journal of Psychiatry, 140,* 95–98.

Woody, G. E., Luborsky, L., McLellen, A. T., O'Brien, C. P., Beck, A. T., Blaine, J., Herman, I., & Hole, A. (1983). Psychotherapy for opiate addicts. *Archives of General Psychiatry, 40,* 639–648.

Woody, G. E., O'Brien, C. P., & Rickels, I. (1975). Depression and anxiety in heroin addicts: A placebo controlled study of doxepin in combination with methadone. *American Journal of Psychiatry, 132,* 447–450.

Wurmser, L. (1972). Methadone and the craving for narcotics: Observations of patients on methadone maintenance in psychotherapy. *Proceedings of the Fourth National Methadone Conference,* San Francisco.

Wurmser, L. (1974). Psychoanalytic considerations of the etiology of compulsive drug use. *Journal of the American Psychoanalytic Association, 22,* 820–843.

19

Consequences of Cocaine and Other Drug Use in Pregnancy

IRA J. CHASNOFF AND SIDNEY H. SCHNOLL

There is no question that the number of women using and abusing drugs other than opiates far exceeds the number who are addicted to narcotics (Chambers & Hart, 1977). Current data show that 63–93.5% of women use analgesics during pregnancy and that sedative drug use ranges from 22% to 28% (Doering & Stewart, 1978; Forfar & Nelson, 1973; Hill, 1973). Until recently, however, little attention had been given to pregnancies complicated by the maternal use of drugs other than heroin.

In the last five years, there has been a rapid increase in the proportion of women using and abusing nonnarcotic substances during pregnancy. Screening of all women presenting to Prentice Women's Hospital and Maternity Center for prenatal care during a 6-month period in 1982 revealed that 3% of these women had evidence of sedative–hypnotics in their urine at the time of admission to the general maternity clinic (Chasnoff, Schnoll, Burns, & Burns, 1984). In addition, as phencyclidine hydrochloride (PCP) has become one of the more frequently abused drugs in the United States (Showalter & Thorton, 1977), a number of pregnant women who were abusing PCP have presented for treatment at the Perinatal Services Component of Northwestern University's Chemical Dependence Program.

Most recently, as cocaine use has become more prevalent in the United States, there has been increasing interest in its effects on the fetus and neonate of the pregnant abuser. With an estimated 20 million Americans having tried cocaine at least once, and 5 million using it on a regular basis (Fishburne, 1980), it can be assumed that cocaine follows the same pattern of use as other substances of abuse, and that large numbers of pregnant women have used it.

Many women believe, erroneously, that the placenta acts as a barrier protecting the fetus from various toxic substances. This, however, is not so.

Ira J. Chasnoff. Departments of Pediatrics and Psychiatry, Northwestern University Medical School, Chicago, Illinois.

Sidney H. Schnoll. Departments of Medicine and Psychiatry, Medical College of Virginia, Richmond, Virginia.

Numerous reviews of drug use during pregnancy show that many drugs taken by the mother during pregnancy freely cross the placenta (Finnegan, 1976; Goldstein, Aronow, & Kalman, 1974; Hollingsworth, 1977; Mirkin, 1973; Yaffee, 1978). Drugs that act on the central nervous system are usually lipiphilic and of relatively low molecular weight, characteristics that facilitate the crossing of the substance from maternal to fetal circulation. Although the large number of variables make the exact distribution of drug between maternal and fetal circulation difficult to determine, it is reasonable to say that drugs with high abuse potential are found at significant levels in the fetus if the mother is using or abusing these drugs. This, in turn, creates the potential for problems of fetal development, which can be manifested as congenital abnormalities, fetal growth retardation, low birth weight, neonatal growth retardation, or neurobehavioral abnormalities.

In addition, one of the important effects of maternal drug use during pregnancy, especially use of drugs with high potential for abuse, is that dependence develops in the fetus as well as the mother. Thus, the fetus will experinece withdrawal when the mother is withdrawn from her drug, or at term, when the maternal drug use no longer provides the newborn with drugs. Besides the well-described withdrawal syndrome from opiates, abstinence symptoms in the newborn have been described with secobarbital (Bleyer & Marshall, 1972); phenobarbital (Blumenthal & Lindsay, 1977; Desmond, Schwanecke, Wilson, Yasanaga, & Burgdorf, 1972); diazepam (Rementeria & Bhatt, 1977); chlordiazepoxide (Athinarayanan, Pierog, Nigan, & Glass, 1976); lorazepam (de la Fuente, Rosenbaum, Morton, & Niven, 1980); and alcohol (Nicols, 1967; Schaefer, 1962). There is limited information regarding the effects of stimulants during pregnancy, with no information regarding cocaine's effects on fetal development or neonatal behavior.

It would be anticipated that cocaine crosses the placenta. Recent data from our clinic confirm this in two infants born to mothers who had used intranasal cocaine just prior to delivery. The infants excreted unchanged cocaine 12–24 hours after delivery and continued to excrete benzoylecgonine, a cocaine metabolite, for 5 days. Cocaine and its metabolites persist in the urine of the adult user for up to 27 hours after intranasal use (Barnett, Hawka, & Resnick, 1981). The persistence of benzoylecgonine in the neonates' urines for 5 days is evidence for slow metabolism of cocaine by the neonate, probably because of the immaturity or relative deficiency of plasma cholinesterases and hepatic enzymes in the newborn infant.

There are conflicting reports of cocaine's teratogenicity in animal studies (Fantel & Macphail, 1982; Mahalik, Gautieri, & Mann, 1980), and the effects of cocaine on pregnancy in the human have not been studied. A report of two cases of abruptio placentae associated with cocaine use appeared in 1983 (Acker, Sachs, Tracey, & Wise), but no further evidence for this association has been published since.

In our program at Northwestern University, 38 infants of cocaine-using pregnant women have been evaluated so far. These women, enrolled in the Perinatal Services Component, were followed throughout pregnancy and completed a course of intensive prenatal care and addiction counseling. Maternal urine samples and breathalyzer tests were obtained on a regular basis in order to screen for illicit drug and/or alcohol use. In order to evaluate the effects of cocaine specifically, the women were divided into two groups based on concurrent use or non-use of narcotics, and then compared to a group of methadone-maintained women who did not use cocaine and a group of nonaddicted pregnant women selected from the general clinic population. The four groups were similar for maternal age, race, gravidity, education, and socioeconomic class, as well as for tobacco, marijuana, and alcohol use.

Although the four groups of women were similar for gravidity, there was a significantly higher rate of spontaneous abortions among women who used cocaine during pregnancy, higher even than for those women who had used heroin (Chasnoff, Burns, Schnoll, & Burns, 1985). This increased rate of spontaneous abortions among cocaine-using women would be consistent with the pharmacologic actions of cocaine. Cocaine acts peripherally to inhibit nerve conduction and prevent norepinephrine reuptake at the nerve terminals, producing increased norepinephrine levels with subsequent vaso-constriction, tachycardia, and a concomitant acute rise in blood pressure (Ritchie & Greene, 1980). Placental vasoconstriction also occurs (Sherman & Gautieri, 1972), decreasing blood flow to the fetus. An increased rate of uterine contractions in humans has been reported with cocaine use (Weiner, 1980). This combination of factors would contribute to the high rate of spontaneous abortions among the women who used cocaine in the first trimester of pregnancy.

Third-trimester use of cocaine results in sudden onset of contractions and increased fetal activity within minutes of using cocaine. Four women in the study had onset of labor with abruptio placentae immediately following a single intravenous self-injection of cocaine. The hypertension and vasoconstriction associated with cocaine use most likely induced the abruptio placentae, a predictable outcome given the association between acute hypertension and abruptio placentae (Pritchard, Mason, Corley, & Pritchard, 1970). Among women who used cocaine at term, additional complications of labor and delivery occurred at a higher rate: precipitous delivery, fetal heart rate abnormalities, and fetal meconium passage. One infant suffered a perinatal cerebral infarction following the mother's use of 5 grams of cocaine over the 3 days prior to delivery (Chasnoff, Bussey, Savich, & Stack, 1986).

Infants were examined after delivery. Infants delivered to methadone-maintained women, whether or not they used cocaine, were of smaller birth weight, length, and head circumference; but it did not appear that intrauterine growth was specifically affected by cocaine use. This lack of intrauterine growth retardation among the infants exposed *in utero* to cocaine is consistent with reported growth patterns of other nonopiate-exposed infants (Chasnoff, Burns, Hatcher, & Burns, 1983; Chasnoff, Burns, Hatcher, & Schnoll, 1983; Chasnoff, Hatcher, & Burns, 1982). In addition, there was no significant increase in the rate of congenital malformations among infants exposed to cocaine, although one infant exposed to a heavy dose of cocaine at 5 weeks postconception did have "prune belly syndrome," with malformations of the genitourinary tract, an absence of abdominal musculature, hypospadius, and undescended testes (Chasnoff *et al.*, 1985).

Infants born to mothers using nonopiate drugs other than cocaine during pregnancy have also been studied. These infants were compared to infants born to mothers who used narcotics during pregnancy and to infants delivered to women with no history or evidence of substance abuse.

Mothers in group I ($N = 51$) conceived while on heroin. Forty-seven of these women were abusing heroin alone; the remaining 4 women abused either one or two nonnarcotic drugs in addition. Upon admission to the program, each woman was placed on a variable initial daily dose of methadone. This dosage was steadily decreased to the lowest level that would prevent craving or withdrawal in the mother. By the beginning of the third trimester, each woman was on a maintenance dose of methadone ranging from 5 to 40 mg daily (mean = 15.9, S.D. = 10.4). This dose was held at the same level for the rest of the pregnancy, and no woman was completely withdrawn during pregnancy. On daily urine screens, the women, with 3 exceptions, remained clean of narcotic and nonnarcotic drugs other than the prescribed methadone.

Mothers in group II ($N = 22$) were addicted to multiple licit or illicit nonnarcotic drugs. Each woman used two to five of the following drugs in various combinations before and during pregnancy: phenobarbital, diazepam, marijuana, alcohol, and cocaine. These women received the same regimen of prenatal care as group I, except that they did not receive methadone. Although abstinence was the objective for this group, only 5 of the women remained clean of drug use throughout the third trimester of pregnancy.

Thirteen infants were delivered to women who abused a combination of pentazocine and tripelennamine (known as Ts and blues) during pregnancy (group III). All the women in this group sporadically used other, nonnarcotic drugs, but Ts and blues were the only drugs consistently used throughout pregnancy. Although abstinence was the objective of the program, none remained clean of Ts and blues during the third trimester of pregnancy.

Group IV infants were delivered to 9 women whose primary drug of abuse throughout pregnancy was PCP. All the women had positive urine screens that demonstrated sporadic use of other nonnarcotic drugs in addition to the PCP, which was the only substance used heavily throughout the third trimester.

Three of the group II women sporadically used Ts and blues or PCP during pregnancy, but this use was very limited and did not occur in the third trimester; hence, these three women were included in group II on the basis of their primary abuse of various sedative and stimulant substances throughout pregnancy.

For neonatal assessment, infants of a group of drug-free mothers were selected in the order the women presented for prenatal care to the clinic of Prentice Women's Hospital and Maternity Center (group V, $N = 27$). These women had no history or evidence of drug or alcohol abuse, and management of prenatal care and nutrition was similar to that of the women in the four drug-abusing groups.

All groups were evaluated for maternal factors that might affect neonatal outcome: race, maternal age, education, gravidity, prenatal care, nutrition, cigarette smoking, and drug use. Analysis of variance and chi square analysis were used for statistical analysis of these parameters. All neonates were examined at birth when weight, crown-to-heel length and fronto-occipital head circumference were recorded. The Brazelton Neonatal Behavioral Assessment Scale (BNBAS) (Brazelton, 1976) was administered at 2 days of age by trained examiners who were blind to the infants' prenatal history. Results of neonatal data were analyzed using analysis of variance. For those items that reached statistical significance ($< .05$), the Fischer's least significant difference (LSD) was used to identify homogeneous subsets.

For long-term follow-up, the opiate-exposed infants (groups I and III) were combined into group A, and nonopiate-exposed infants (groups II and IV) were combined into group B. A group of control infants for long-term assessment (group C, $N = 35$) delivered to drug-free mothers enrolled in the university health maintenance organization were selected on the basis of race, maternal age, education, gravidity, and cigarette use. The Bayley Scales of Infant Development (Bayley, 1969) were administered to all infants at 3, 6, 12, and 24 months of age. The infants were examined at these same time intervals, and weight, fronto-occipital head circumference, and crown-to-heel length were recorded.

Neonatal Assessment

Demographic data (age, gravidity, education) for the women in groups I–IV were similar, as was the frequency of cigarette smoking in each of the groups. Racial distribution, however, varied between the groups. Thus, for analysis of neonatal data, race was controlled through covariate analysis when each drug-using group was compared to the group V mothers and infants.

All infants were delivered at term gestation as determined by the criteria of Ballard, Dazmaier, and Driver (1977). There was an even distribution of infants by sex in each group. Apgar scores in the five groups were similar, and no significant perinatal complications occurred in any group. Twelve infants in group I required therapy for significant withdrawal, based on clinical criteria of marked irritability, poor feeding, and/or excessive weight loss. No infants in the other drug groups required therapy for withdrawal.

Somatic Measures

Infants delivered to mothers in groups I and III had a significantly lower weight and length than did control infants. These group I and group III infants also had a significantly smaller head circumference than both the control infants and those in groups II and IV. These differences remained when race was statistically controlled. The birth weights, lengths, and head circumferences of the sedative/stimulant- and PCP-exposed infants were not significantly different from those of the control infants.

Neonatal Behavior

Significant differences in neonatal behavior were obtained in items related to interactive ability, motor maturity, and state control. Items related to visual and auditory orientation and to motor maturity differentiated the methadone-dependent group from both the control group and all other drug groups (Fischer's LSD). All four groups of drug-exposed neonates showed deficits in state control with an abnormal predominant state, an increased lability of state, and poor consolability. In addition, PCP-exposed infants (group IV) showed significantly increased lability of states and poor consolability when compared to all other drug groups (Fischer's LSD).

Infant Assessment

Two-year Follow-up. In this portion of the study, demographic data for the two drug-exposed groups of infants and the control group of infants were again similar. In addition, upon combining groups I and III (opiate-exposed infants) into group A, and groups II and IV (nonopiate-exposed infants) into group B, racial distribution was similar for the two study groups and the control group (C): 53% white, 43% black, 4% Hispanic in group A; 58% white, 39% black, 3% Hispanic in group B; 54% white, 40% black, 6% Hispanic in group C.

Somatic Growth

Infants in group A had significantly lower weight and length than the group C drug-free infants at both 3 and 6 months (*t* test). By 12 months of age, group A infants had caught up to the control infants in weight and length. Head circumference measurements for the opiate-exposed group A infants did not exhibit such catch-up growth, however, and head circumference for these infants remained significantly smaller than that of the control infants throughout the 2-year follow-up. Polydrug-exposed infants in group B exhibited normal growth patterns throughout the 2-year period for all parameters except that by 18 months head growth had slowed and mean head circumferences at 18 and 24 months were significantly smaller than those of the control infants. Growth parameters for PCP-exposed infants were almost identical to those of the polydrug-exposed infants, so that separate analysis was not performed.

Infant Development

On the Bayley Scales of Infant Development, group A infants had significantly lower Mental Developmental Index (MDI) scores than did controls at 6 and 12 months (*t* test). Group B infants had a significantly lower MDI at 6 months and Psychomotor Developmental Index (PDI) at 3 months. If PCP infants were considered separately, their scores were almost identical to those of the polydrug-exposed infants. In general, scores both for groups A and B and for the control group of infants were in the normal range but exhibited a downward trend by 24 months of age, a phenomenon not uncommon among infants from lower socioeconomic populations.

Among infants in the previously described cocaine study, by 1 month of age, two cocaine-exposed infants had died; the first at 2 weeks of age with a diagnosis of sudden infant death syndrome (SIDS) and the second infant with meningitis, which had its onset at approximately 1 week of age. No infants in the other drug groups died in the neonatal period. The occurrence of SIDS in one infant raises the question of increased risk of SIDS for infants exposed *in utero* to cocaine. Although an increased risk of SIDS has been reported for infants born to narcotic-addicted women (Chavez, Ostrea, Stryker, & Smialek, 1979), larger numbers of cocaine-exposed infants will need to be followed before the risk of SIDS for this group can be ascertained.

The extensive literature devoted to the effects of intrauterine exposure to heroin and methadone on the fetus and neonate has recently been reviewed (Householder, Hatcher, Burns, & Chasnoff, 1982), but information regarding the outcome of nonnarcotic- and cocaine-exposed neonates is sparse. In the reported studies, newborns delivered to women addicted to sedative/stimulants, cocaine, or PCP were found to demonstrate marked deficits in neonatal behavior. These three groups of infants showed significantly poorer state organization and consolability than did the drug-free controls. In addition, when internal comparisons were made, the PCP-exposed neonates were found to demonstrate more lability of state and poorer consolability than did all other groups of drug-exposed neonates. The unique neurobehavioral changes of the PCP-exposed infants during the neonatal period clearly differentiated them from the other drug-exposed newborns (Chasnoff, Burns, Hatcher, & Burns, 1983). The low threshold of stimulation and rapid changes in state are similar to behavior reported in children and adults intoxicated with PCP (Showalter & Thorton, 1977; Welch & Correa, 1980).

Sedative/stimulant- and PCP-exposed neonates did not manifest significant differences from normals in somatic growth measures at birth, orientation, or motor maturity responses. Deficits in intrauterine growth appeared mainly in narcotic-exposed infants, especially in relation to head growth. As with methadone-exposed neonates, Ts and blues–exposed neonates showed significantly lower somatic growth rates and poorer state control than did the drug-free controls, although the methadone-addicted neonates could be further differentiated by poorer visual and auditory orientation responses and poorer motor control. The similarities between the methadone-exposed and the Ts and blues–exposed neonates may be related to the mixed opiate agonist–antagonist properties of pentazocine (Chasnoff, Burns, Hatcher, & Schnoll, 1983).

There are no previous studies evaluating long-term patterns of growth and development in nonnarcotic-exposed infants, although preliminary developmental data have been examined (Chasnoff, Schnoll, Burns, & Burns, 1984). The nonnarcotic-exposed infants demonstrated normal growth patterns in weight and length throughout the 2-year follow-up period. The narcotic-exposed infants, on the other hand, demonstrated early deficits in growth at 3 and 6 months, with subsequent catch-up to normals by 12 months of age. This same early stunting of growth during the period of subacute withdrawal for the narcotic-exposed infants is similar to the early growth patterns of methadone-addicted infants reported by our group in 1982 (Chasnoff, Hatcher, & Burns, 1982). The early depression of growth could be due to the direct effect of methadone on the hypothalamic-hypophyseal axis of the newborn (Friedler & Cochin, 1972). With the slow excretion of the methadone by the newborn, plasma and tissue drug levels fall, the endocrinologic effect of the drug subsides, and growth recovers.

The mean head circumference of the opiate-addicted newborns was significantly smaller than that of controls at birth and remained so throughout the 2-year follow-up period. The inhibitory effects of heroin on fetal growth include effects on head growth (Chasnoff *et al.*, 1982; Chasnoff, Hatcher, & Burns, 1980; Naeye, Blanc, & LeBlanc, 1973). The mean head circumference of the nonnarcotic-exposed infants was normal at birth and continued so until 12 months. By 18 months of age, however, head growth had slowed, and the mean head circumference for these infants had fallen to a significantly lower level. Small head size in young infants has been reported to be predictive of poor developmental outcome (Gross, Gehler, & Eckerman, 1983) and may be another indicator of the high-risk status of all drug-exposed infants.

Two-year developmental follow-up showed that the drug-exposed infants' development, as measured on the Bayley Scales of Infant Development, was comparable to that of the drug-free infants. The isolated instances in which mean MDI or mean PDI fell to a low level are probably not clinically significant in that all scores were within the normal range as defined by the Bayley Scales (100 S.D. $\pm$ 10). Of greater concern is the fact that all three groups of infants demonstrated a downward trend in mean developmental scores by 2 years of age, a phenomenon not uncommon in infants of low socioeconomic status. From the present data, it appears that the infants' environment and subsequent lack of stimulation had a more direct influence on their 2-year development than did maternal drug use during pregnancy.

It is apparent from our experience so far with infants delivered to cocaine-using women that cocaine exerts a negative influence on pregnancy outcome as well as on neonatal neurobehavior. There is also the possibility from the data that cocaine-exposed infants are at high risk for perinatal mortality and morbidity. Only through further studies can the full impact of cocaine on pregnancy and the developing fetus be appreciated.

There are multiple problems involved in evaluating the effects of the exposure to substances of maternal abuse on the developing fetus and infant, not the least of which are the difficulties involved in following these infants over a long period of time. The chaotic and transient nature of the drug-seeking environment impairs the early intervention and intensive follow-up necessary to ensure maximum development on the part of each infant. In addition, most women from substance-abusing backgrounds lack a proper model for parenting. These factors, compounded by the early neurobehavioral deficits of the drug-exposed newborns, earmark these infants to be at high risk for developmental and school problems. Maternal and perinatal addiction programs should be aimed at not only helping the mothers to deal with their addiction but also teaching them the parenting skills necessary for proper infant stimulation and subsequent development. Future programs must develop methods to ensure adequate follow-up of all infants born to substance-abusing women.

REFERENCES

Acker, D., Sachs, B. P., Tracey, K. J., & Wise, W. E. (1983). Abruptio placentae associated with cocaine use. *American Journal of Obstetrics and Gynecology, 146,* 220–221.

Athinarayanan, P., Pierog, S. H., Nigan, S. K., & Glass, L. (1976). Chlordiazepoxide withdrawal in the neonate. *American Journal of Obstetrics and Gynecology, 124,* 212–213.

Ballard, J. L., Dazmaier, K., & Driver, M. (1977). A simplified assessment of gestational age. *Pediatric Research, 11,* 372.

Barnett, G., Hawka, R., & Resnick, R. (1981). Cocaine pharmacokinetics in humans. *Journal of Ethnopharmacology, 3,* 353.

Bayley, N. (1969). *Bayley scales of infant development.* New York: Psychological Corporation.

Bleyer, W. A., & Marshall, R. E. (1972). Barbiturate withdrawal syndrome in a passively addicted infant. *Journal of the American Medical Association, 221,* 185–186.

Blumenthal, I., & Lindsey, S. (1977). Neonatal barbiturate withdrawal. *Postgraduate Medical Journal, 53,* 157.

Brazelton, T. B. (1976). *Neonatal behavioral assessment scale.* Philadelphia: Spastics International Medical Publications.

Chambers, C. D., & Hart, L. G. (1977). Drug use patterns in pregnant women. In J. L. Rementeria (Ed.), *Drug abuse in pregnancy and neonatal effects* (pp. 73–81). St. Louis: Mosby.

Chasnoff, I. J., Burns, W. J., Hatcher, R., & Burns, K. (1983). Phencyclidine: Effects on the fetus and neonate. *Developmental Pharmacology and Therapeutics, 6,* 404–408.

Chasnoff, I. J., Burns, W. J., Hatcher, R., & Schnoll, S. H. (1983). Pentazocine and tripelennamine (T's and blues): Effects on the fetus and neonate. *Developmental Pharmacology and Therapeutics, 6,* 162–165.

Chasnoff, I. J., Burns, W. J., Schnoll, S. H., & Burns, K. A. (1985). Cocaine use in pregnancy. *New England Journal of Medicine, 313,* 666–669.

Chasnoff, I. J., Bussey, M. E., Savich, R., & Stack, C. M. (1986). Perinatal cerebral infarction and maternal cocaine use. *Journal of Pediatrics, 108,* 456–459.

Chasnoff, I. J., Hatcher, R., & Burns, W. J. (1980). Early growth patterns of methadone-addicted infants. *American Journal of Diseases of Children, 134,* 1049–1051.

Chasnoff, I. J., Hatcher, R., & Burns, W. J. (1982). Polydrug- and methadone-addicted newborns: A continuum of impairment. *Pediatrics, 70,* 210–213.

Chasnoff, I. J., Schnoll, S. H., Burns, W. J., & Burns, K. (1984). Maternal nonnarcotic substance abuse during pregnancy: Effects on infant development. *Neurobehavioral Toxicology and Teratology, 6,* 277–280.

Chavez, C. J., Ostrea, E. M., Jr., Stryker, J. C., & Smialek, Z. (1979). Sudden infant death syndrome among infants of drug-dependent mothers. *Journal of Pediatrics, 95,* 407–409.

de la Fuente, J. R., Rosenbaum, A. H., Morton, H. P., & Niven, R. G. (1980). Lorazepam-related withdrawal seizures. *Mayo Clinic Proceedings, 55,* 190.

Desmond, M. M., Schwanecke, R. P., Wilson, G. S., Yasanaga, S., & Burgdorf, I. (1972). Maternal barbiturate utilization and neonatal withdrawal symptomatology. *Journal of Pediatrics, 80,* 190–197.

Doering, P. L., & Stewart, R. B. (1978). The extent and character of drug consumption during pregnancy. *Journal of the American Medical Association, 239,* 843–846.

Fantel, A. G., & Macphail, B. J. (1982). The teratogenicity of cocaine. *Teratology, 26,* 17–19.

Finnegan, L. (1976). Clinical effects of pharmacologic agents on pregnancy, the fetus and the neonate. *Annals of the New York Academy of Sciences, 281,* 74.

Fishburne, P. M. (1980). *National survey on drug abuse: Main findings 1979.* Rockville, MD: National Institute on Drug Abuse.

Forfar, J. O., & Nelson, M. N. (1973). Epidemiology of drugs taken by pregnant women: Drugs that may affect the fetus adversely. *Clinical Pharmacology and Therapeutics, 14*, 632–642.

Friedler, G., & Cochin, J. (1972). Growth retardation in offspring of female rats treated with morphine prior to conception. *Science, 175*, 654–656.

Goldstein, A., Aronow, L., & Kalman, S. M. (1974). Absorption, distribution and elimination of drugs. In *Principles of drug action: The basis of pharmacology* (pp. 198–210). New York: Wiley.

Gross, S. J., Oehler, J. M., & Eckerman, C. O. (1983). Head growth and developmental outcome in very low-birth-weight infants. *Pediatrics, 71*, 70–75.

Hill, R. M. (1973). Drugs ingested by pregnant women. *Clinical Pharmacology and Therapeutics, 14*, 654–659.

Hollingsworth, M. (1977). Drugs and pregnancy. *Clinical Obstetrics and Gynecology, 4*, 503.

Householder, J., Hatcher, R., Burns, W. J., & Chasnoff, I. J. (1982). Infants born to narcotic-addicted mothers. *Psychological Bulletin, 92*, 453–468.

Mahalik, M. P., Gautieri, R. F., & Mann, D. E. (1980). Teratogenic potential of cocaine hydrochloride in CF-1 mice. *Journal of Pharmaceutical Sciences, 69*, 703–706.

Mirkin, B. L. (1973). Maternal and fetal distribution of drugs in pregnancy. *Clinical Pharmacology and Therapeutics, 14*, 643–653.

Naeye, R. L., Blanc, W. A., & LeBlanc, W. (1973). Heroin and the fetus. *Pediatric Research, 7*, 321.

Nicols, M. M. (1967). Acute alcohol withdrawal in a newborn. *American Journal of Diseases of Children, 113*, 714–715.

Pritchard, J. A., Mason, R., Corley, M., & Pritchard, S. (1970). Genesis of severe placental abruption. *American Journal of Obstetrics and Gynecology, 108*, 22–27.

Rementeria, J. L., & Bhatt, K. (1977). Withdrawal symptoms in neonates from intrauterine exposure to diazepam. *Journal of Pediatrics, 90*, 123–126.

Ritchie, J. M., & Greene, N. M. (1980). Local anesthesia. In A. G. Goodman, L. S. Goodman, & A. Gilman (Eds.), *The pharmacologic basis of therapeutics* (pp. 300–320). New York: Macmillan.

Schaefer, O. (1962). Alcohol withdrawal syndrome in a newborn infant of a Yukon Indian mother. *Canadian Medical Association Journal, 87*, 1333–1334.

Sherman, W. T., & Gautieri, R. F. (1972). Effect of certain drugs on perfused human placenta X: Norepinephrine release by bradykinin. *Journal of Pharmaceutical Sciences, 61*, 878–883.

Showalter, C. V., & Thorton, W. E. (1977). Clinical pharmacology of phencyclidine toxicity. *American Journal of Psychiatry, 134*, 1234–1238.

Weiner, N. (1980). Norepinephrine, epinephrine, and the sympathomimetic amines. In A. G. goodman, L. S. Goodman, & A. Gilman (Eds.), *The pharmacologic basis of therapeutics* (pp. 138–175). New York: Macmillan.

Welch, M. J., & Correa, G. A. (1980). PCP intoxication in young children and infants. *Clinical Pediatrics, 19*, 510–514.

Yaffee, S. J. (1978). Drug use during pregnancy. *Drug Therapy*, June, 137–146.

Index

A

Absorption, cocaine, 62–63
  inhaled or smoked, 64–65
  nasal and oral administration, 63–
    64
  parenteral administration, 64
Abstinence
  initial, 109–111
  preparing for, in adolescent
    treatment program, 142
  violation effect (AVE), 112–113
Actions, mechanisms of cocaine's, 59–
    60
  neurochemical substrates, 60
  pharmacokinetics, 61
Acute cocaine reactions, emergency
    treatment of, 87–88, 93
  adverse effects, 88–90
  medical, 90–92
  psychological, 92–93
Acute tolerance, 123
Addictions, tendency to multiple, 26
Addictive personality, 100
Administration, routes of cocaine, 56–
    58, 89–90, 155, 217
  See also Free-base use; IV use;
    Smoking, cocaine; Snorting
Adolescents, cocaine use among, 16,
    17–18, 135, 150
  assessment of, 137–138
  extent of problem, 135–136
    availability, 136
    effects, 136–137
    image, 137
  treatment of
    beginning phase of, 141–142

contacts with parents, 144–145
emotional functioning, 146–147
family relationships, 147
illness model, 149
involvement in Twelve Step
  programs, 149–150
issues in, 138–141
legal issues and indebtedness, 147–
  148
monitoring, 149
planning, 138
preparing for abstinence, 142
relapse prevention, 148–149
scheduling outpatient sessions,
  142–143
sexual issues, 148
social functioning, 145–146
testing behavior, 149
value of groups, 143–144
Adverse effects, 88
  dose effects, 88–89
  routes of administration, 89–90
  user susceptibility, 89
Affluence, 4
AIDS, 28, 49, 50, 91
Al-Anon, 195, 205
Alateen, 205
Alcohol, 112
  abstinence from cocaine and, 102,
    108, 109
  and cocaine relapse, 164
  combined use of cocaine and, 26,
    67–68
  as foundation for drug epidemic,
    192, 193
  problems in cocaine abusers, 17,
    202–207

Alcoholics Anonymous (AA), 81, 102, 115, 165, 195, 200
  adolescent involvement in, 142, 144, 146, 149
  for alcohol problems in cocaine abusers, 204
  and Gamblers Anonymous, 209
Alcoholism, 156, 205
Alexithymia, 231
Allergic reactions, 91
Amantadine, 82
American Medical Association (AMA), 24
American Psychiatric Association, 73, 75, 119, 153, 208, 211, 235
Amitryptilene, 126, 233
Amphetamines, 3, 24, 26, 49, 81
  dependence on, 118
  differences between cocaine and, 66
  IV injection of, 50
  use of, by athletes, 216
Anesthetic, cocaine used as, 23, 24, 55, 59–60, 63
Anhedonia, 126
Antabuse (disulfiram), 103, 204, 206–207
Antidepressants, tricyclic (TCAs), 124–128, 233
Anxiety, 14, 92, 116
Apomorphine, 81–82
Arrhythmias, 25
Attention deficit disorder (ADD), 30, 100, 116, 119, 120, 236–237
  and magnesium pemoline, 123–124
Automobile accidents, cocaine-related, 14, 17
Availability, 4, 7, 136
AVE (abstinence violation effect), 112–113

Benzodiazepine, 233
Benzoylecgonine (BE), 61–62, 218, 219, 225, 226
  concentration of cocaine and, in blood and urine, 221–222
  correlation between behavioral effects and concentration of cocaine and, 220–221
  time frame of detection of cocaine and, 222–224
Binge use, 185, 198
Bipolar disorder, 30, 100, 116, 119, 120
Blood
  and urine, concentration of cocaine and BE in, 221–222
  vs. urine for detection of cocaine abuse, 224–225
Blood vessel constriction, 27
Body packer syndrome, 44–45, 89–90
Brain changes, chemical, 30
Brain function, cocaine effects on, 58–59
Brain mechanisms, in cocaine dependency, 73, 82–83
  brain pleasure systems, cocaine, and dopamine, 76–77
  catecholamine depletion hypothesis, 79–80
  cocaine dependency, 74–76
  effects of cocaine on specific neurotransmitters, 77–79
  hormonal changes, 80–81
  neuropharmacology of cocaine, 73–74
  pharmacological treatments, 81–82
Brazelton Neonatal Behavioral Assessment Scale (BNBAS), 245
Bromocriptine, 81–82, 99, 116, 124
Bureau of International Narcotics Matters, 179

B

Bahamas, free-base use in, 180–181
Barbiturates, 26
Bayley Scales of Infant Development, 245, 247, 249

C

Caffeine, 55
  combined use of cocaine and, 67–68

Cardiovascular deaths, due to cocaine, 45–47, 67–68
Cardiovascular reactions, 91
Catecholamine depletion hypothesis, of cocaine dependency and withdrawal, 79–80
Central nervous system (CNS), 58, 59
Chemistry, cocaine, 56
Cocaine Anonymous (CA), 81, 102, 113, 114, 115, 165
  for treatment of adolescent cocaine abusers, 138, 140, 142, 144, 145, 149
"Cocaine bugs," 30, 93
Cocaine Clinic, 152, 153, 161
Coca leaves, 3, 67, 175–176
  chewing of, 55, 63
  harvesting of, 4
  herbal teas made from, 90
Coca paste smoking, medical and biological consequences of, 28–29, 176, 180
  See also Smoking, cocaine
Coffee, 55
  combined use of cocaine and, 67–68
Confidentiality and contingency contracting, among health care professionals, 169–170
Consolidation, after recovery from cocaine abuse, 113
Contingency contracts, 162–163, 164, 165, 167
  confidentiality and, among health care professionals, 169–170
Control, testing, after initial abstinence, 112
Convulsions, 48, 59
Crack, 20, 43, 136, 177
  flooding of marketplace with, 4
  medical and biological consequences of, 28
"Crash," cocaine, 13, 76, 79
Cravings, 73, 76
  pharmacological treatments for, 81–82, 92
  treatment of urges and, 110–111
Cyclothymic disorder, 30, 100, 119, 120

D

Dade County, Florida, cocaine overdose deaths in, 35–36, 37
Death(s), cocaine-induced
  from body packing, 44–45
  cardiovascular, due to cocaine, 45–47
  delayed, 24–25
  historical perspective on, 33–34
  infectious complications leading to, 49–50
  profile of, 50
  from recreational use, 35–38
  from smoking cocaine, 43
  from snorting, 42
  sudden, 23–24, 25
    cocaine psychosis and, 47–49
    medical complications and, from IV cocaine abuse, 38–41
  from use of cocaine during sexual activity, 42–43
Decadence, societal, 6
Delirium, cocaine-induced excited, 47, 48
Denial, 225
  resistance and, 109–110
Dental care, neglect of, by cocaine abusers, 26
Dependency, cocaine, 67, 74–76
  catecholamine depletion hypothesis of, 79–80
  hormonal changes in, 80–81
  pharmacological treatments in, 81–82
Depression, 100, 119, 120–121
  misuse of cocaine as cure for, 3, 6
  resulting from use of cocaine, 14, 30, 82, 116
Desipramine, 82, 99, 120, 126–127, 236
Diagnostic and Statistical Manual of Mental Disorders (DSM-III), 5, 99, 119, 124, 208, 235–236
  and cocaine-abusing health care professionals, 153, 154, 167
  and cocaine dependence, 73, 118
  and cyclothymic disorder, 120
  and pathological gambling, 210–211, 212

Discharge planning, in inpatient treatment, 104–105
Disposition, cocaine, 217–218
Disulfiram, *see* Antabuse
Dopamine (DA), 8, 30, 73, 74, 126, 130
  agonists, stimulants and, 123–124
  brain pleasure systems, cocaine and, 76–77
  effects of cocaine on, 77–78
Dose effects, 88–89
Doxepin, 233
Drug Abuse Warning Network (DAWN), 35, 87, 153
Drug Enforcement Administration (DEA), 36, 154
Drug(s)
  cocaine's interactions with other, 26, 67–68
  complete abstinence from other, as treatment goal, 108
  dependence syndrome, 194–195
Dysphoria, cocaine, 29, 47, 92, 186

E

Ecgonine methyl ester (EME), 61–62, 218, 221, 222–224
Electroencephalographic (EEG) activity, 58–59
Elixirs, oral, 57, 63
Emergency treatment, 87–88, 93
  acute medical reactions, 90–92
  acute psychological reactions, 92–93
  adverse effects, 88–90
  cocaine preparations, 88
Emotional functioning, adolescent, 146–147
Employee Assistance Programs (EAP), 216
Enzyme-multiplied immunoassay (EMIT), 219, 220, 221, 224, 226
Ephedrine, 181
Epinephrine, 24
Euphoria, cocaine, 29, 73, 130, 186
  See also Intoxication
Euphoric recall, 111–112

Evaluation, in inpatient treatment, 98–101
External factors, in outbreak of cocainism, 4–5

F

Family involvement, in treatment, 115–116
Fatigue, chronic, 14
Free-base use, 107, 177, 217
  compared with snorting and IV use, 14–15, 21
  deaths from, 43
  increase in, 20
  medical and biological consequences of, 28
  See also Smoking, cocaine

G

Gam-Anon, 212
Gam-A-Teen, 212
Gamblers Anonymous (GA), 209, 212, 213
Gambling, pathological, in cocaine abusers, 208–209, 212–213
  characteristics of, 209, 210
  diagnosis of, 210–211
  identification of, 212
  prevention of, 211
  treatment of, 212
Gas chromatography/mass spectometry (GC/MS), 220, 221, 222–224
Gas-liquid chromatography (GLC), 219, 220, 221, 224
Groups, treatment
  anonymous, 101–102
  cocaine recovery, 114–115
  communication skills, 103
  hospital exercise, 103
  medication, 103
  peer support, 102

self-help, 115, 171
therapy, 102–103
value of, for adolescents, 143–144

H

Hallucinosis, cocaine, 29
Halsted Clinic, 152, 153
Harrison Act (1914), 3
Headaches, 14
Health care professionals, cocaine-
    abusing, 152–153, 170–171, 215–
    216
  confidentiality and contingency
    contracting among, 169–170
  description of sample, 153–156
  problems of outcome research, 168–
    169
  procedures in evaluation and
    treatment
    evaluation as first phase of
      treatment, 157–162
    first contact, 157
    first weeks of treatment, 162–165
    psychotherapy, 167–168
    termination of treatment, 166–167
    therapy's mid-course, 165–166
    value of defined program, 156–157
Heart attacks, 25
  and cardiovascular deaths due to
    cocaine, 45–47
Hedonism, 6
Hematologic reactions, 91
Hepatitis, 28
Heroin
  addicts, intravenous (IV), 10
  cocaine combined with, 26
  cocaine compared with, 24–25, 75
  epidemic, 192–193, 230
  use of, during pregnancy, 241, 244,
    247, 248–249
Hormonal changes, in cocaine
    dependency
  prolactin, 80
  thyroid function, 80–81
Hotline, 76

first cocaine, 10–11
surveys, 11–19, 20
HTLV-III virus, 28
Hypertension, 25
  and cardiovascular deaths due to
    cocaine, 45–47
Hyperthermia, 38, 47, 90
Hypomania, 92

I

Ignorance, about cocaine, 5, 7
Illness model, 149
Image, cocaine's, 137, 196–197
Imipramine, 82, 99, 126, 127–128, 129,
    233
Infectious complications, of cocaine
    abuse, 27, 49–50
Inhaled cocaine, absorption rate from,
    64–65
Inpatient treatment, 96–98, 105
  discharge planning, 104–105
  evaluation, 98–101
  rehabilitation, 101–104
Insomnia, chronic, 14
Internal factors, in outbreak of
    cocainism, 5–6
Internal Revenue Service, 198
Intoxication, cocaine, 92, 183
  See also Euphoria
Intracranial electrical self-stimulation
    (ICSS), 124–126
Intranasal cocaine use. See Snorting.
Intravenous cocaine use. See IV use.
Intrinsic drug factors, in outbreak of
    cocainism, 6–7
Irritability, 14
IV use, 57, 58, 107, 152, 217
  absorption rate from, 64
  compared with snorting and free-
    base use, 14–15, 21
  infectious complications from, 49–50
  medical and biological consequences
    of, 27–28
  medical complications and sudden
    death from, 38–41

K

Kindling, 38, 59, 66

L

Laboratory testing, cocaine abuse
        detection by, 214–217, 226–227
    choice of body fluid, collection, and
        specimen handling, 224–225
    cocaine disposition, 217–218
    concentration of cocaine and BE in
        blood and urine, 221–222
    correlation between behavioral
        effects and concentration of
        cocaine and BE, 220–221
    interpretation of test results, 225–226
    metabolic products of cocaine, 218
    methods of analysis, sensitivity, and
        cost, 219–220
    reliability of testing, 225–226
    time frame of detection of cocaine
        and BE, 222–224
Legalization, 7
Librium, 26
Lidocaine, 181
Life-style change, 113
Lithium, 81, 120, 121–122, 236
Lower income groups, cocaine use
        among, 16

M

Magnesium pemoline, 123–124
Manganese carbonate, 181
Marijuana, 96, 112, 164
    abstinence from cocaine and, 102,
        108, 109
    combined use of cocaine and, 67–68
    context of, in drug pattern, 192, 193
    effects of cocaine vs., 136–137
Media encouragement, 4–5
Medical and biological consequences,
        23, 31
    chemical brain changes, 30

chronic problems, 26
cocaine-induced sudden death, 23–24
cocaine use
    free-base, 28
    intranasal, 27
    intravenous, 27–28
coca paste smokers, 28–29
delayed deaths, 24–25
medical complications
    chronic, 26
    nonfatal acute, 25
psychiatric complications, 29–30
self-medicating with cocaine, 30
tanking up, 25
Medical and Surgical Reporter, 23
Metabolism, cocaine, 61–62, 218
Methamphetamine, 24, 129
Methaqualone, 34
Methylphenidate (MPH), 120, 123,
        124, 237
Michigan, University of, study of
        adolescent drug use by, 135
Minority groups, cocaine use among,
        16
Monoamine oxidase inhibitors
        (MAOIs), 128, 129
Morphine, 35
    addiction, misuse of cocaine as cure
        for, 3
Mydriasis, 47
Mythology, prevailing cocaine, 5, 194,
        200

N

Naltrexone, 103
Narcotics Anonymous (NA), 81, 115,
        165, 195
    adolescent involvement in, 138, 140,
        142, 144, 149
Nasal infections, 14
Nasal reactions, 90
Nasal septal perforation, 27
National Commission on Marijuana
        and Drug Abuse, 19–20

National Institute on Drug Abuse
    (NIDA), 55, 87, 193
Nausea, 14
Needles, dirty, 27, 28
Neurochemical substrates, 60
Neuroleptics, 81, 130
Neurological reactions, 91
Neuropharmacology of cocaine, 73–74
Neurotransmitter(s)
    effect of cocaine on, 77–79
    precursors, 129–130
Nicotine, 55, 56, 65
    combined use of cocaine and, 68
Norcocaine, 62, 218
Norepinephrine (NE), 74, 76
    effects of cocaine on, 78–79
Northwestern University, Chemical
        Dependence Program of, 241,
        243

O

Oral ingestion, 57, 58
    absorption rate from, 63–64
Outbreak, cocaine, 3, 8–9
    discussion of, 7–8
    external factors in, 4–5
    internal factors in, 5–6
    intrinsic drug factors in, 6–7
    supply factors in, 3–4
Outpatient treatment, 106–107
    cocaine recovery groups in, 114–115
    contraindications for, 107
    family involvement in, 115–116
    goals of, 108
    pharmacologic, 116
    phases of, 109
        consolidation, 113
        initial abstinence, 109–111
        relapse prevention and life-style
            change, 111–113
    psychiatric issues in, 116
    scheduling sessions for adolescents
        in, 142–143
    self-help groups in, 115

success rates in, 117
urine testing in, 108–109

P

Panic disorder, 30, 233
Paranoia, 14
    cocaine-induced, 47, 186
Parenteral administration, 64
Patent medicines, cocaine-containing, 3
Peer pressure, 4, 7
Pemoline, 120, 237
    magnesium, 123–124
Pharmacokinetics, 61
Pharmacological treatments, 81–82,
        116, 118–119, 131–132
    comparison of, to psychotherapeutic
        interventions, 131
    lithium carbonate, 121–122
    miscellaneous agents, 130–131
    monoamine oxidase inhibitors
        (MAOIs), 128, 129
    neurotransmitter precursors, 129–130
    self-medicating with cocaine, 119–
        121
    stimulants and dopamine agonists,
        123–124, 125
    tricyclic antidepressants (TCAs),
        124–128
Pharmacologic imperative, 6–7
Phencyclidine (PCP), 35, 48, 49, 241
    consequences of use of, during
        pregnancy, 244–245, 246, 247,
        248
Phenelzine, 128
Phenothiazine, 233
Predisposition, 5–6
Pregnancy, use of cocaine and other
        drugs during, 50, 91–92, 241–
        245
    infant assessment, 246
        infant development, 247–249
        somatic growth, 247
    neonatal assessment, 245–246
        neonatal behavior, 246
        somatic measures, 246

Preparations, cocaine, 88
Price of cocaine, decrease in, 4, 17, 136
Prohibition, 193
Prolactin (PRL), 30
   changes in, due to cocaine
      dependency, 80
Psychiatric and psychodynamic factors,
      in cocaine dependence, 229,
      237–238
   cocaine dependence, 234
      diagnostic and treatment studies,
         235–237
      psychodynamic observations, 234–
         235
      recent findings in addicts in general,
         230
      diagnostic and treatment studies,
         232–233
      psychodynamic observations, 230–
         232
Psychiatric complications, cocaine-
      induced, 29–30
Psychiatric issues, in outpatient
      treatment, 116
Psychodynamic factors. *See* Psychiatric
      and psychodynamic factors.
Psychopathology, cocaine-exacerbated,
      30
Psychopharmacology, cocaine
   absorption, 62–65
   chemistry, 56
   cocaine effects on brain function,
      58–59
   dependence, 67
   historical notes, 55–56
   interactions with other drugs, 67–68
   mechanisms of action, 59–61
   metabolism, 61–62
   routes of administration, 56–58
   tolerance, 65–67
Psychosis, cocaine, 29–30, 92–93, 186
   and sudden death, 47–49
Psychotherapy
   comparison of pharmacological
      treatments to, 131
   for substance abuse, 167–168

Pulmonary reactions, 90
Pure Food and Drug Act (1906), 3

Q

Quaaludes, 26, 34
Quechua Indians, 67

R

Radioimmunoassay (RIA), 220, 221,
      222–224, 226
Recovery groups, cocaine, 114–115
Rehabilitation, in inpatient treatment,
      101–104
Relapse prevention, 111–113
   for adolescents, 148–149
Resistance and denial, 109–110
Reverse tolerance, 38, 48
Rorschach test, 100

S

Schizophrenia, 30, 66–67
Seizures, 14, 25, 35, 42
Select Committee on Narcotics Abuse
      and Control, 179
Self-help groups, 115, 171
Self-medicating, 232, 233
   with cocaine, 30, 119–121
Serotonin, effects of cocaine on, 79
Sexual activity, death from use of
      cocaine during, 42–43
Sexual functioning, disrupted, 14
Sexual issues, support and advice for
      adolescents on handling, 148
Sinus infections, 14
Smoking, cocaine, 57, 58, 175–177
   absorption rate from, 64–65
   acute and chronic physical effects of,
      184–185
   crack, emergence of, 177
   deaths from, 43

definitions of, 175–176
disorder, diagnosis of, 186–187
epidemiology of, 178
    coca paste in South America, 178–179
    coca paste in United States, 179–180
    free base use, 180–181
hazards of free base, 182–183
history of, 176–177
intoxication from, 183
medical and biological consequences of, 28–29
overview of, 188–189
psychological effects of, 185–186
treatment considerations for, 187–188
withdrawal from, 187
Smuggling cocaine, and body packer syndrome, 44–45, 89–90
Snorting, 5, 13, 57–58, 217
    absorption rate from, 63–64
    compared with free-base and IV use, 14–15, 21
    death from, 42
    medical and biological consequences of, 27
    outpatient treatment of, 107
"Snow lights," 93
Snuffing, 57
Social functioning, adolescent, 145–146
Sociopathy, 6
South America, 90
    coca paste smoking in, 28–29, 178–179, 188
    supply channels from, 3–4
Speedball, 26
Stereotyped behavior, 92
Stimulants, and dopamine agonists, 123–124
Strategy Council on Drug Abuse, 19–20
Street cocaine, 38, 122
    risk factors in, 26, 35
Stress, life, 6
Strokes, 25

Sublingual use, 57
Success rates, in outpatient treatment, 117
Sudden infant death syndrome (SIDS), 247
Suicides, cocaine-induced, 14, 34, 50
Supersensitivity, 126
Supply factors, in outbreak of cocainism, 3–4
Survey(s), hotline, 11–12, 20
    comparison of national, 15–19
    national (1983), 12–15
Susceptibility, 5–6
    user, 89

T

Tanking up, 25
Tarasoff v. *Regents of the University of California*, 169
Teas, coca leaf herbal, 90
Thematic Apperception Test (TAT), 100
Thin-layer chromatography (TLC), 219, 221, 224, 225
Thyroid function, changes in, due to cocaine dependency, 80–81
Thyroid-stimulating hormone (TSH), 30, 81
Thyrotropin-releasing hormone (TRH), 30, 80–81
Thyroxine (T4), 81
Tobacco, 55, 65
    combined use of cocaine and, 67–68
Tolerance
    acute, 123
    cocaine, 65–67, 75, 76, 118
    reverse, 38, 48
    zero, 199
Treatment(s), for cocaine abuse
    of adolescents, 138–150
    of alcohol problems in cocaine abusers, 203–204, 206–207
    of cocaine smoking, 187–188
    emergency, 87–93

Treatment(s), for cocaine abuse
        (*continued*)
    of health care professionals, 156–168
    improvements in, 195–196
    inpatient, 96–105
    outpatient, 106–117
    of pathological gamblers, 212
    pharmacological, 118–132
    in workplace, 199–201
Tricyclic antidepressants (TCAs), 124–
        128, 233
Tryptophan, 127, 129
Tuberculosis, misuse of cocaine as cure
        for chronic, 3
Twelve Step programs, 115, 200, 204
    involving adolescents in, 138, 140,
        141, 145, 149–150
Tyrosine, 127, 129

                            U

United States
    coca paste smoking in, 179–180
    free-base use in, 180–181
Urine
    vs. blood for detection of cocaine
        abuse, 224–225
    concentration of cocaine and BE in
        blood and, 221–222
    testing, 98, 103, 108–109, 200, 204,
        205

                            V

Valium, 26
Vomiting, 14

                            W

Warning signs and setups, of potential
        relapse, 112
Withdrawal, cocaine, 75, 106, 118, 187
    catecholamine depletion hypothesis
        of, 79–80
    characteristics of, 76
Women, cocaine use among, 15–16
Workplace, cocaine use in, 17, 19, 192,
        216
    general context of problem of, 192–
        196
    steps for dealing with, 199–201
    unique qualities of, 196–199
World Health Organization (WHO),
        177, 178

                            Z

Zero tolerance, 199